Exploratory Social Network Analysis with Pajek

This is the first textbook on social network analysis integrating theory, applications, and professional software for performing network analysis (Pajek). Step by step, the book introduces the main structural concepts and their applications in social research with exercises to test the understanding. In each chapter, each theoretical section is followed by an application section explaining how to perform the network analyses with Pajek software. Pajek software and data sets for all examples are freely available, so the reader can learn network analysis by doing it. In addition, each chapter offers case studies for practicing network analysis. In the end, the reader has the knowledge, skills, and tools to apply social network analysis in all social sciences, ranging from anthropology and sociology to business administration and history.

Wouter de Nooy specializes in social network analysis and applications of network analysis to the fields of literature, the visual arts, music, and arts policy. His international publications have appeared in *Poetics* and *Social Networks*. He is Lecturer in methodology and sociology of the arts, Department of History and Arts Studies, Erasmus University, Rotterdam.

Andrej Mrvar is assistant Professor of Social Science Informatics at the University of Ljubljana, Slovenia. He has won several awards for graph drawings at competitions between 1995 and 2000. He has edited *Metodoloski zvezki* since 2000.

Vladimir Batagelj is Professor of Discrete and Computational Mathematics at the University of Ljubljana, Slovenia and is a member of the editorial boards of *Informatica* and *Journal of Social Structure*. He has authored several articles in *Communications of ACM*, *Psychometrika*, *Journal of Classification*, *Social Networks*, *Discrete Mathematics*, *Algorithmica*, *Journal of Mathematical Sociology*, *Quality and Quantity*, *Informatica*, *Lecture Notes in Computer Science*, *Studies in Classification*, *Data Analysis*, and *Knowledge Organization*.

Structural Analysis in the Social Sciences

Mark Granovetter, editor

The series *Structural Analysis in the Social Sciences* presents approaches that explain social behavior and institutions by reference to relations among such concrete entities as persons and organizations. This contrasts with at least four other popular strategies: (a) reductionist attempts to explain by a focus on individuals alone; (b) explanations stressing the casual primacy of such abstract concepts as ideas, values, mental harmonies, and cognitive maps (thus, "structuralism" on the Continent should be distinguished from structural analysis in the present sense); (c) technological and material determination; (d) explanation using "variables" as the main analytic concepts (as in the "structural equation" models that dominated much of the sociology of the 1970s), where structure is that connecting variables rather that actual social entities.

The social network approach is an important example of the strategy of structural analysis; the series also draws on social science theory and research that is not framed explicitly in network terms, but stresses the importance of relations rather than the atomization of reduction or the determination of ideas, technology, or material conditions. Though the structural perspective has become extremely popular and influential in all the social sciences, it does not have a coherent identity, and no series yet pulls together such work under a single rubric. By bringing the achievements of structurally oriented scholars to a wider public, the *Structural Analysis* series hopes to encourage the use of this very fruitful approach.

Mark Granovetter

Other Books in the Series

1. Mark S. Mizruchi and Michael Schwartz, eds., *Intercorporate Relations: The Structural Analysis of Business*
2. Barry Wellman and S. D. Berkowitz, eds., *Social Structures: A Network Approach*
3. Ronald L. Brieger, ed., *Social Mobility and Social Structure*
4. David Knoke, *Political Networks: The Structural Perspective*
5. John L. Campbell, J. Rogers Hollingsworth, and Leon N. Lindberg, eds., *Governance of the American Economy*
6. Kyriakos Kontopoulos, *The Logics of Social Structure*
7. Philippa Pattison, *Algebraic Models for Social Structure*
8. Stanley Wasserman and Katherine Faust, *Social Network Analysis: Methods and Applications*
9. Gary Herrigel, *Industrial Constructions: The Sources of German Industrial Power*
10. Philippe Bourgois, *In Search of Respect: Selling Crack in El Barrio*
11. Per Hage and Frank Harary, *Island Networks: Communication, Kinship, and Classification Structures in Oceana*
12. Thomas Schweizer and Douglas R. White, eds., *Kinship, Networks and Exchange*
13. Noah E. Friedkin, *A Structural Theory of Social Influence*
14. David Wank, *Commodifying Communism: Business, Trust, and Politics in a Chinese City*
15. Rebecca Adams and Graham Allan, *Placing Friendship in Context*
16. Robert L. Nelson and William P. Bridges, *Legalizing Gender Inequality: Courts, Markets and Unequal Pay for Women in America*
17. Robert Freeland, *The Struggle for Control of the Modern Corporation: Organizational Change at General Motors, 1924–1970*
18. Yi-min Lin, *Between Politics and Markets: Firms, Competition, and Institutional Change in Post-Mao China*
19. Nan Lin, *Social Capital: A Theory of Social Structure and Action*
20. Christopher Ansell, *Schism and Solidarity in Social Movements: The Politics of Labor in the French Third Republic*
21. Thomas Gold, Doug Guthrie, and David Wank, eds., *Social Connections in China: Institutions, Culture, and the Changing Nature of Guanxi*
22. Roberto Franzosi, *From Words to Numbers*
23. Sean O'Riain, *Politics of High Tech Growth*
24. James Lincoln and Michael Gerlach, *Japan's Network Economy*
25. Patrick Doreian, Vladimir Batagelj, and Anuška Ferligoj, *Generalized Blockmodeling*
26. Eiko Ikegami, *Bonds of Civility: Aesthetic Networks and Political Origins of Japanese Culture*
27. Wouter de Nooy, Andrej Mrvar, and Vladimir Batagelj, *Exploratory Social Network Analysis with Pajek*

Exploratory Social Network Analysis with Pajek

WOUTER DE NOOY
Erasmus University Rotterdam

ANDREJ MRVAR
University of Ljubljana

VLADIMIR BATAGELJ
University of Ljubljana

CAMBRIDGE
UNIVERSITY PRESS

CAMBRIDGE UNIVERSITY PRESS
Cambridge, New York, Melbourne, Madrid, Cape Town, Singapore, São Paulo

Cambridge University Press
40 West 20th Street, New York, NY 10011-4211, USA

www.cambridge.org
Information on this title: www.cambridge.org/9780521841733

First published 2005

Printed in the United States of America

A catalog record for this book is available from the British Library.

Library of Congress Cataloging in Publication Data
Nooy, Wouter de, 1962–

   Exploratory social network analysis with Pajek / Wouter de Nooy, Andrej Mrvar,
Vladimir Batagelj.
      p.   cm. – (Structural analysis in the social sciences)
   Includes bibliographical references and index.
   ISBN 0-521-84173-9 – ISBN 0-521-60262-9 (pbk.)
   1. Social networks – Mathematical models.   2. Social networks – Computer
simulation   3. Pajek (Electronic resource)   I. Mrvar, Andrej.
II. Batagelj, Vladimir, 1948–   III. Title.   IV. Series.
   HM741.N475   2004
   300'.285 – dc22   2004041846

ISBN-13   978-0-521-84173-3 hardback
ISBN-10   0-521-84173-9 hardback

ISBN-13   978-0-521-60262-4 paperback
ISBN-10   0-521-60262-9 paperback

To Anuška,
who makes things happen

Contents

Illustrations

Tables

Preface

In the social sciences, social network analysis has become a powerful methodological tool alongside statistics. Network concepts have been defined, tested, and applied in research traditions throughout the social sciences, ranging from anthropology and sociology to business administration and history.

This book is the first textbook on social network analysis integrating theory, applications, and professional software for performing network analysis. It introduces structural concepts and their applications in social research with exercises to improve skills, questions to test the understanding, and case studies to practice network analysis. In the end, the reader has the knowledge, skills, and tools to apply social network analysis.

We stress learning by doing: readers acquire a feel for network concepts by applying network analysis. To this end, we make ample use of professional computer software for network analysis and visualization: Pajek. This software, operating under Windows 95 and later, and all example data sets are provided on a Web site (http://vlado.fmf.uni-lj.si/pub/networks/book/) dedicated to this book. All the commands that are needed to produce the graphical and numerical results presented in this book are extensively discussed and illustrated. Step by step, the reader can perform the analyses presented in the book.

Note, however, that the graphical display on a computer screen will never exactly match the printed figures in this book. After all, a book is not a computer screen. Furthermore, newer versions of the software will appear, with features that may differ from the descriptions presented in this book. We strongly advise using the version of Pajek software supplied on the book's Web site (http://vlado.fmf.uni-lj.si/pub/networks/book/) while studying this book and then updating to a newer version of Pajek afterwards, which can be downloaded from http://vlado.fmf.uni-lj.si/pub/networks/pajek/default.htm.

Overview

This book contains five sections. The first section (Part I) presents the basic concepts of social network analysis. The next three sections present the three major research topics in social network analysis: cohesion

(Part II), brokerage (Part III), and ranking (Part IV). We claim that all major applications of social network analysis in the social sciences relate to one or more of these three topics. The final section discusses an advanced technique (viz., blockmodeling), which integrates the three research topics (Part V).

The first section, titled Fundamentals, introduces the concept of a network, which is obviously the basic object of network analysis, and the concepts of a partition and a vector, which contain additional information on the network or store the results of analyses. In addition, this section helps the reader get started with Pajek software.

Part II on cohesion consists of three chapters, each of which presents measures of cohesion in a particular type of network: ordinary networks (Chapter 3), signed networks (Chapter 4), and valued networks (Chapter 5). Networks may contain different types of relations. The ordinary network just shows whether there is a tie between people, organizations, or countries. In contrast, signed networks are primarily used for storing relations that are either positive or negative such as affective relations: liking and disliking. Valued networks take into account the strength of ties, for example, the total value of the trade from one country to another or the number of directors shared by two companies.

Part III on brokerage focuses on social relations as channels of exchange. Certain positions within the network are heavily involved in the exchange and flow of information, goods, or services, whereas others are not. This is connected to the concepts of centrality and centralization (Chapter 6) or brokers and bridges (Chapter 7). Chapter 8 discusses an important application of these ideas, namely the analysis of diffusion processes.

The direction of ties (e.g., who initiates the tie) is not very important in the section on brokerage, but it is central to ranking, presented in Part IV. Social ranking, it is assumed, is connected to asymmetric relations. In the case of positive relations, such as friendship nominations or advice seeking, people who receive many choices and reciprocate few choices are deemed as enjoying more prestige (Chapter 9). Patterns of asymmetric choices may reveal the stratification of a group or society into a hierarchy of layers (Chapter 10). Chapter 11 presents a particular type of asymmetry, namely the asymmetry in social relations caused by time: genealogical descent and citation.

The final section, Part V, on roles, concentrates on rather dense and small networks. This type of network can be visualized and stored efficiently by means of matrices. Blockmodeling is a suitable technique for analyzing cohesion, brokerage, and ranking in dense, small networks. It focuses on positions and social roles (Chapter 12).

The book is intended for researchers and managers who want to apply social network analysis and for courses on social network analysis in all social sciences as well as other disciplines using social methodology (e.g., history and business administration). Regardless of the context in which the book is used, Chapters 1, 2, and 3 must be studied to understand the topics of subsequent chapters and the logic of Pajek. Chapters 4 and 5 may be skipped if the researcher or student is not interested in networks

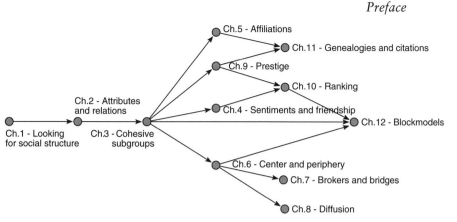

Figure 1. Dependencies between the chapters.

with signed or valued relations, but we strongly advise including them to be familiar with these types of networks. In Parts III (Brokerage) and IV (Ranking), the first two chapters present basic concepts and the third chapter focuses on particular applications.

Figure 1 shows the dependencies among the chapters of this book. To study a particular chapter, all preceding chapters in this flow chart must have been studied before. Chapter 10, for instance, requires understanding of Chapters 1 through 4 and 9. Within the chapters, there are not sections that can be skipped.

In an undergraduate course, Part I and II should be included. A choice can be made between Part III and Part IV or, alternatively, just the first chapter from each section may be selected. Part V on social roles and blockmodeling is quite advanced and more appropriate for a postgraduate course. For managerial purposes, Part III is probably more interesting than Part IV.

Justification

This book offers an introduction to social network analysis, which implies that it covers a limited set of topics and techniques, which we feel a beginner must master to be able to find his or her way in the field of social network analysis. We have made many decisions about what to include and what to exclude and we want to justify our choices now.

As reflected in the title of this book, we restrict ourselves to exploratory social network analysis. The testing of hypotheses by means of statistical models or Monte Carlo simulations falls outside the scope of this book. In social network analysis, hypothesis testing is important but complicated; it deserves a book on its own. Aiming our book at people who are new to social network analysis, our first priority is to have them explore the structure of social networks to give them a feel for the concepts and applications of network analysis. Exploration involves visualization and manipulation of concrete networks, whereas hypothesis testing boils down to numbers representing abstract parameters and probabilities. In our view, exploration yields the intuitive understanding of networks and basic network concepts that are a prerequisite for well-considered hypothesis testing.

From the vast array of network analytic techniques and indices we discuss only a few. We have no intention of presenting a survey of all structural techniques and indices because we fear that the readers will not be able to see the forest for the trees. We focus on as few techniques and indices as are needed to present and measure the underlying concept. With respect to the concept of cohesion, for instance, many structural indices have been proposed for identifying cohesive groups: n-cliques, n-clans, n-clubs, m-cores, k-cores, k-plexes, lambda sets, and so on. We discuss only components, k-cores, 3-cliques, and m-slices (m-cores) because they suffice to explain the basic parameters involved: density, connectivity, and strength of relations within cohesive subgroups.

Our choice is influenced by the software that we use because we have decided to restrict our discussion to indices and techniques that are incorporated in this software. Pajek software is designed to handle very large networks (up to millions of vertices). Therefore, this software package concentrates on efficient routines, which are capable of dealing with large networks. Some analytical techniques and structural indices are known to be inefficient (e.g., the detection of n-cliques), and for others no efficient algorithm has yet been found or implemented. This limits our options: we present only the detection of small cliques (of size 3) and we cannot extensively discuss an important concept such as k-connectivity. In summary, this book is neither a complete catalogue of network analytic concepts and techniques nor an exhaustive manual to all commands of Pajek. It offers just enough concepts, techniques, and skills to understand and perform all major types of social network analysis.

In contrast to some other handbooks on social network analysis, we minimize mathematical notation and present all definitions verbatim. There are no mathematical formulae in the book. We assume that many students and researchers are interested in the application of social network analysis rather than in its mathematical properties. As a consequence, and this may be very surprising to seasoned network analysts, we do not introduce the matrix as a data format and display format for social networks until the end of the book.

Finally, there is a remark on the terminology used in the book. Social network analysis derives its basic concepts from mathematical graph theory. Unfortunately, different "vocabularies" exist within graph theory, using different concepts to refer to the same phenomena. Traditionally, social network analysts have used the terminology employed by Frank Harary, for example, in his book *Graph Theory* (Reading, Addison-Wesley, 1969). We choose, however, to follow the terminology that prevails in current textbooks on graph theory, for example, R. J. Wilson's *Introduction to Graph Theory* (Edinburgh, Oliver and Boyd, 1972; published later by Wiley, New York). Thus, we hope to narrow the terminological gap between social network analysis and graph theory. As a result, we speak of a vertex instead of a node or a point and some of our definitions and concepts differ from those proposed by Frank Harary.

Acknowledgments

The text of this book has benefited from the comments and suggestions from our students at the University of Ljubljana and the Erasmus University Rotterdam, who were the first to use it. In addition, Michael Frishkopf and his students of musicology at the University of Alberta gave us helpful comments. Mark Granovetter, who welcomed this book to his series, and his colleague Sean Farley Everton have carefully read and commented on the chapters. In many ways, they have helped us make the book more coherent and understandable to the reader. We are also very grateful to an anonymous reviewer, who carefully scrutinized the book and made many valuable suggestions for improvements. Ed Parsons (Cambridge University Press) and Nancy Hulan (TechBooks) helped us through the production process. Finally, we thank the participants of the workshops we conducted at the XXIInd and XXIIIrd Sunbelt International Conference on Social Network Analysis in New Orleans and Cancun for their encouraging reactions to our manuscript.

Most data sets that are used in this book have been created from sociograms or listings printed in scientific articles and books. Notwithstanding our conviction that reported scientific results should be used and distributed freely, we have tried to trace the authors of these articles and books and ask for their approval. We are grateful to have obtained explicit permission for using and distributing the data sets from them. Authors or their representatives whom we have not reached are invited to contact us.

Part I

Fundamentals

Social network analysis focuses on ties among, for example, people, groups of people, organizations, and countries. These ties combine to form networks, which we will learn to analyze. The first part of the book introduces the concept of a social network. We discuss several types of networks and the ways in which we can analyze them numerically and visually with the computer software program Pajek, which is used throughout this book. After studying Chapters 1 and 2, you should understand the concept of a social network and you should be able to create, manipulate, and visualize a social network with the software presented in this book.

1

Looking for Social Structure

1.1   Introduction

The social sciences focus on structure: the structure of human groups, communities, organizations, markets, society, or the world system. In this book, we conceptualize social structure as a network of social ties. Social network analysts assume that interpersonal ties matter, as do ties among organizations or countries, because they transmit behavior, attitudes, information, or goods. Social network analysis offers the methodology to analyze social relations; it tells us how to conceptualize social networks and how to analyze them.

In this book, we present the most important methods of exploring social networks, emphasizing visual exploration. Network visualization has been an important tool for researchers from the very beginning of social network analysis. This chapter introduces the basic elements of a social network and shows how to construct and draw a social network.

1.2   Sociometry and Sociogram

The basis of social network visualization was laid by researchers who called themselves sociometrists. Their leader, J. L. Moreno, founded a social science called *sociometry*, which studies interpersonal relations. Society, they argued, is not an aggregate of individuals and their characteristics, as statisticians assume, but a structure of interpersonal ties. Therefore, the individual is not the basic social unit. The social atom consists of an individual and his or her social, economic, or cultural ties. Social atoms are linked into groups, and, ultimately, society consists of interrelated groups.

From their point of view, it is understandable that sociometrists studied the structure of small groups rather than the structure of society at large. In particular, they investigated social choices within a small group. They asked people questions such as, "Whom would you choose as a friend [colleague, advisor, etc.]?" This type of data has since been known as *sociometric choice*. In sociometry, social choices are considered the most important expression of social relations.

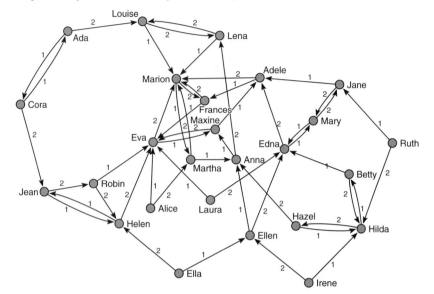

Figure 2. Sociogram of dining-table partners.

Figure 2 presents an example of sociometric research. It depicts the choices of twenty-six girls living in one "cottage" (dormitory) at a New York state training school. The girls were asked to choose the girls they liked best as their dining-table partners. First and second choices are selected only. (Here and elsewhere, a reference on the source of the data can be found under Further Reading, which is at the end of each chapter.)

Figure 2 is an example of a sociogram, which is a graphical representation of group structure. The sociogram is among the most important instruments originated in sociometry, and it is the basis for the visualization of social networks. You have most likely already "read" and understood the figure without needing the following explanation, which illustrates its visual appeal and conceptual clarity. In this sociogram, each girl in the dormitory is represented by a circle. For the sake of identification, the girls' names are written next to the circles. Each arc (arrow) represents a choice. The girl who chooses a peer as a dining-table companion sends an arc toward her. Irene (in the bottom right of the figure), for instance, chose Hilda as her favorite dining-table partner and Ellen as her second choice, as indicated by the numbers labeling each arrow.

A sociogram depicts the structure of ties within a group. This example shows not only which girls are popular, as indicated by the number of choices they receive, but also whether the choices come from popular or unpopular girls. For example, Hilda receives four choices from Irene, Ruth, Hazel, and Betty, and she reciprocates the last two choices. But none of these four girls is chosen by any of the other girls. Therefore, Hilda is located at the margin of the sociogram, whereas Frances, who is chosen only twice, is more central because she is chosen by "popular" girls such as Adele and Marion. A simple count of choices does not reveal this, whereas a sociogram does.

The sociogram has proved to be an important analytical tool that helped to reveal several structural features of social groups. In this book, we make ample use of it.

1.3 Exploratory Social Network Analysis

Sociometry is not the only tradition in the social sciences that focuses on social ties. Without going into historical detail (see Further Reading for references on the history of social network analysis), we may note that scientists from several social sciences have applied network analysis to different kinds of social relations and social units. Anthropologists study kinship relations, friendship, and gift giving among people rather than sociometric choice; social psychologists focus on affections; political scientists study power relations among people, organizations, or nations; economists investigate trade and organizational ties among firms. In this book, the word *actor* refers to a person, organization, or nation that is involved in a social relation. We may say that social network analysis studies the social ties among actors.

The *main goal* of social network analysis is detecting and interpreting patterns of social ties among actors.

This book deals with exploratory social network analysis only. This means that we have no specific hypotheses about the structure of a network beforehand that we can test. For example, a hypothesis on the dining-table partners network could predict a particular rate of mutual choices (e.g., one of five choices will be reciprocated). This hypothesis must be grounded in social theory and prior research experience. The hypothesis can be tested provided that an adequate statistical model is available.

We use no hypothesis testing here, because we cannot assume prior research experience in an introductory course book and because the statistical models involved are complicated. Therefore, we adopt an exploratory approach, which assumes that the structure or pattern of ties in a social network is meaningful to the members of the network and, hence, to the researcher. Instead of testing prespecified structural hypotheses, we explore social networks for meaningful patterns.

For similar reasons, we pay no attention to the estimation of network features from samples. In network analysis, estimation techniques are even more complicated than estimation in statistics, because the structure of a random sample seldom matches the structure of the overall network. It is easy to demonstrate this. For example, select five girls from the dining-table partners network at random and focus on the choices among them. You will find fewer choices per person than the two choices in the overall network for the simple reason that choices to girls outside the sample are neglected. Even in this simple respect, a sample is not representative of a network.

We analyze entire networks rather than samples. However, what is the entire network? Sociometry assumes that society consists of interrelated groups, so a network encompasses society at large. Research on the so-called Small World problem suggested that ties of acquaintanceship connect us to almost every human being on the earth in six or seven steps, (i.e., with five or six intermediaries), so our network eventually covers the entire world population, which is clearly too large a network to be studied. Therefore, we must use an artificial criterion to delimit the network we are studying. For example, we may study the girls of one dormitory only. We do not know their preferences for table partners in other dormitories. Perhaps Hilda is the only vegetarian in a group of carnivores and she prefers to eat with girls of other dormitories. If so, including choices between members of different dormitories will alter Hilda's position in the network tremendously.

Because boundary specification may seriously affect the structure of a network, it is important to consider it carefully. Use substantive arguments to support your decision of whom to include in the network and whom to exclude.

Exploratory social network analysis consists of four parts: the definition of a network, network manipulation, determination of structural features, and visual inspection. In the following subsections we present an overview of these techniques. This overview serves to introduce basic concepts in network analysis and to help you get started with the software used in this book.

1.3.1   Network Definition

To analyze a network, we must first have one. What is a network? Here, and elsewhere, we use a branch of mathematics called *graph theory* to define concepts. Most characteristics of networks that we introduce in this book originate from graph theory. Although this is not a course in graph theory, you should study the definitions carefully to understand what you are doing when you apply network analysis. Throughout this book, we present definitions in text boxes to highlight them.

> A *graph* is a set of vertices and a set of lines between pairs of vertices.

What is a graph? A graph represents the structure of a network; all it needs for this is a set of vertices (which are also called points or nodes) and a set of lines where each line connects two vertices.

A *vertex* (singular of vertices) is the smallest unit in a network. In social network analysis, it represents an actor (e.g., a girl in a dormitory, an organization, or a country). A vertex is usually identified by a number.

A *line* is a tie between two vertices in a network. In social network analysis it can be any social relation. A line is defined by its two endpoints, which are the two vertices that are *incident* with the line.

A *loop* is a special kind of line, namely, a line that connects a vertex to itself. In the dining-table partners network, loops do not occur because girls are not allowed to choose themselves as a dinner-table partner. However, loops are meaningful in some kinds of networks.

A line is directed or undirected. A directed line is called an *arc*, whereas an undirected line is an *edge*. Sociometric choice is best represented by arcs, because one girl chooses another and choices need not be reciprocated (e.g., Ella and Ellen in Figure 2).

A *directed graph* or *digraph* contains one or more arcs. A social relation that is undirected (e.g., is family of) is represented by an edge because both individuals are equally involved in the relation. An *undirected graph* contains no arcs: all of its lines are edges.

Formally, an arc is an ordered pair of vertices in which the first vertex is the *sender* (the *tail* of the arc) and the second the *receiver* of the tie (the *head* of the arc). An arc points *from* a sender *to* a receiver. In contrast, an edge, which has no direction, is represented by an unordered pair. It does not matter which vertex is first or second in the pair. We should note, however, that an edge is usually equivalent to a *bidirectional arc*: if Ella and Ellen are sisters (undirected), we may say that Ella is the sister of Ellen and Ellen is the sister of Ella (directed). It is important to note this, as we will see in later chapters.

The dining-table partners network has no *multiple lines* because no girl was allowed to nominate the same girl as first and second choice. Without this restriction, which was imposed by the researcher, multiple arcs could have occurred, and they actually do occur in other social networks.

In a graph, multiple lines are allowed, but when we say that a graph is *simple*, we indicate that it has no multiple lines. In addition, a simple undirected graph contains no loops, whereas loops are allowed in a simple directed graph. It is important to remember this.

A *simple undirected graph* contains neither multiple edges nor loops.

A *simple directed graph* contains no multiple arcs.

Now that we have discussed the concept of a graph at some length, it is very easy to define a network. A network consists of a graph and additional information on the vertices or lines of the graph. We should note that the additional information is irrelevant to the structure of the network because the structure depends on the pattern of ties.

A *network* consists of a graph and additional information on the vertices or the lines of the graph.

In the dining-table partners network, the names of the girls represent additional information on the vertices that turns the graph into a network. Because of this information, we can see which vertex identifies Ella in the sociogram. The numbers printed near the arcs and edges offer additional information on the links between the girls: a 1 indicates a first choice and a 2 represents a second choice. They are called *line values*, and they usually indicate the strength of a relation.

The dining-table partners network is clearly a network and not a graph. It is a directed simple network because it contains arcs (directed) but not multiple arcs (simple). In addition, we know that it contains no loops. Several analytical techniques we discuss assume that loops and multiple lines are absent from a network. However, we do not always spell out these properties of the network but rather indicate whether it is simple. Take care!

Application

In this book, we learn social network analysis by doing it. We use the computer program Pajek – Slovenian for spider – to analyze and draw social networks. The Web site dedicated to this book (http://vlado.fmf.uni-lj.si/pub/networks/book/) contains the software. We advise you to download and install Pajek on your computer (see Appendix 1 for more details) and all example data sets from this Web site. Store the software and data sets on the hard disk of your computer following the guidelines provided on the Web site. When you have done so, carry out the commands that we discuss under "Application" in each chapter. This will familiarize you with the structural concepts and with Pajek. By following the instructions under "Application" step by step, you will be able to produce the figures and results presented in the theoretical sections unless stated differently. Sometimes, the visualizations on your computer screen will be slightly different from the figures in the book. If the general patterns match, however, you know that you are on the right track.

Network data file   Some concepts from graph theory are the building blocks or *data objects* of Pajek. Of course, a network is the most important data object in Pajek, so let us describe it first. In Pajek, a network is defined in accordance with graph theory: a list of vertices and lists of arcs and edges, where each arc or edge has a value. Take a look at the partial listing of the data file for the dining-table partners network (Figure 3, note that part of the vertices and arcs are replaced by [...]). Open the file `Dining-table_partners.net`, which you have downloaded from the Web site, in a word processor program to see the entire data file.

```
*Vertices   26
    1 "Ada"            0.1646 0.1077 0.5000
    2 "Cora"           0.0481 0.3446 0.5000
    3 "Louise"         0.3472 0.0759 0.5000
    4 "Jean"           0.1063 0.6284 0.5000
  [...]
   25 "Laura"          0.5101 0.6557 0.5000
   26 "Irene"          0.7478 0.9241 0.5000
*Arcs
    1    3    2
    1    2    1
    2    1    1
    2    4    2
    3    9    1
    3   11    2
  [...]
   25   15    1
   25   17    2
   26   13    1
   26   24    2
*Edges
```

Figure 3. Partial listing of a network data file for Pajek.

First, the data file specifies the number of vertices. Then, each vertex is identified on a separate line by a serial number, a textual label [enclosed in quotation marks (" ")] and three real numbers between 0 and 1, which indicate the position of the vertex in three-dimensional space if the network is drawn. We pay more attention to these coordinates in Chapter 2. For now, it suffices to know that the first number specifies the horizontal position of a vertex (0 is at the left of the screen and 1 at the right) and the second number gives the vertical position of a vertex (0 is the top of the screen and 1 is the bottom). The text label is crucial for identification of vertices, the more so because serial numbers of vertices may change during the analysis.

The list of vertices is followed by a list of arcs. Each line identifies an arc by the serial number of the sending vertex, followed by the number of the receiving vertex and the value of the arc. Just as in graph theory, Pajek defines a line as a pair of vertices. In Figure 3, the first arc represents Ada's choice (vertex 1) of Louise (vertex 3) as a dining-table partner. Louise is Ada's second choice; Cora is her first choice, which is indicated by the second arc. A list of edges is similar to a list of arcs with the exception that the order of the two vertices that identify an edge is disregarded in computations. In this data file, no edges are listed.

It is interesting to note that we can distinguish between the structural data or graph and the additional information on vertices and lines in the network data file. The graph is fully defined by the list of vertex numbers and the list of pairs of vertices, which defines its arcs and edges. This part of the data, which is printed in regular typeface in Figure 3, represents the structure of the network. The vertex labels, coordinates, and line values (in italics) specify the additional properties of vertices and lines that make these data a network. Although this information is extremely useful, it is not required: Pajek will use vertex numbers as default labels and set line values to 1 if they are not specified in the data file. In addition, Pajek can use several other data formats (e.g., the matrix format), which we do not discuss here. They are briefly described in Appendix 1.

It is possible to generate ready-to-use network files from spreadsheets and databases by exporting the relevant data in plain text format. For medium or large networks, processing the data as a relational database helps data cleaning and coding. See Appendix 1 for details.

We explain how to create a new network in Section 1.4. Let us first look at the network of the dining-table partners. First, start Pajek by double-clicking the file `Pajek.exe` on your hard disk. The computer will display the Main screen of Pajek (Figure 4). From this screen, you can open the dining-table partners network with the *Read* command in the *File* menu or by clicking the button with an icon of a folder under the word *Network*. In both cases, the usual Windows file dialog box appears in which you can search and select the file `Dining-table_partners.net` on your hard disk, provided that you have downloaded the example data sets from the book's Web site.

File>Network> Read

When Pajek reads a network, it displays its name in the Network drop-down menu. This menu is a list of the networks that are accessible to Pajek. You can open a drop-down menu by left-clicking on the button with the triangle at the right. The network that you select in the list is shown when

Network drop-down menu

Figure 4. Pajek Main screen.

the list is closed (e.g., the network `Dining-table_partners.net` in Figure 2). Notice that the number of vertices in the network is displayed in parentheses next to the name. The selected network is the **active network**, meaning that any operation you perform on a network will use this particular network. For example, if you use the *Draw* menu now, Pajek draws the dining-partners network for you.

The Main screen displays five more drop-down menus beneath the Network drop-down menu. Each of these menus represents a data object in Pajek: partitions, permutations, clusters, hierarchies, and vectors. Later chapters will familiarize you with these data objects. Note that each object can be opened, saved, or edited from the *File* menu or by using the three icons to the left of a drop-down menu (see Section 1.4).

1.3.2   Manipulation

In social network analysis, it is often useful to modify a network. For instance, large networks are too big to be drawn, so we extract a meaningful part of the network that we inspect first. Visualizations work much better for small (some dozens of vertices) to medium-sized (some hundreds of vertices) networks than for large networks with thousands of vertices. When social networks contain different kinds of relations, we may focus on one relation only; for instance, we may want to study first choices only in the dining-table partners network. Finally, some analytical procedures demand that complex networks with loops or multiple lines are reduced to simple graphs first.

Application
Network manipulation is a very powerful tool in social network analysis. In this book, we encounter several techniques for modifying a network or selecting a subnetwork. Network manipulation always results in a new network. In general, many commands in Pajek produce new networks or other data objects, which are stored in the drop-down menus, rather than graphical or tabular output.

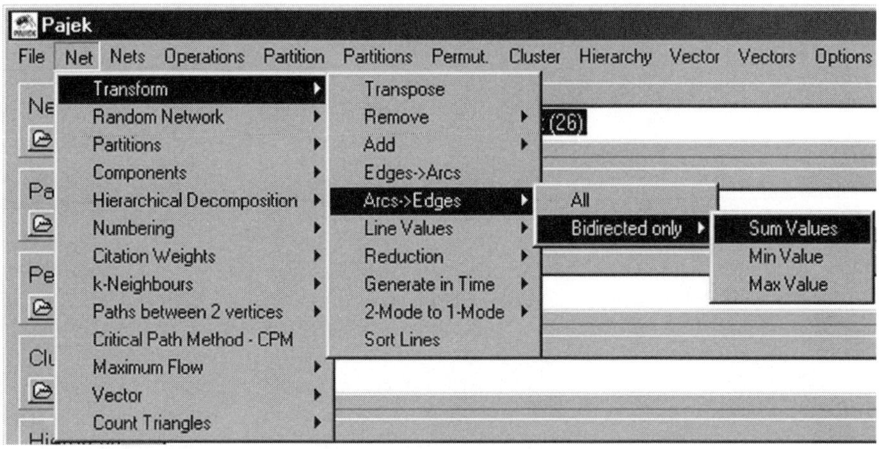

Figure 5. Menu structure in Pajek.

The commands for manipulating networks are accessible from menus in the Main screen. The Main screen menus have a clear logic. Manipulations that involve one type of data object are listed under a menu with the object's name; for example, the *Net menu* contains all commands that operate on one network and the *Nets* menu lists operations on two networks. Manipulations that need different kinds of objects are listed in the *Operations* menu. When you try to locate a command in Pajek, just consider which data objects you want to use.

Menu structure

The following example highlights the use of menus in Pajek and their notation in this book. Suppose we want to change reciprocated choices in the dining-table partners network into edges. Because this operation concerns one network and no other data objects, we must look for it in the *Net* menu. If we left-click on the word *Net* in the upper left of the Main screen, a drop-down menu is displayed. Position the cursor on the word *Transform* in the drop-down menu and a new submenu is opened with a command to change arcs into edges (*Arcs→Edges*). Finally, we reach the command allowing us to change bidirectional arcs into edges and to assign a new line value to the new edge that will replace them (see Figure 5). We choose to sum the values of the arcs, knowing that two reciprocal first choices will yield an edge value of two, a first choice answered by a second choice will produce an edge value of three, and a line value of four will result from a reciprocal second choice.

Net>Transform>
Arcs→Edges>
Bidirected
only>Sum
Values

In this book, we abbreviate this sequence of commands as follows:

[Main]Net>Transform>Arcs→Edges>Bidirected only>Sum Values

The screen or window that contains the menu is presented between square brackets and a transition to a submenu is indicated by the > symbol. The screen name is specified only if the context is ambiguous. The abbreviated command is also displayed in the margin (see above) for the purpose of quick reference.

When the command to change arcs into edges is executed, an information box appears asking whether a new network must be made

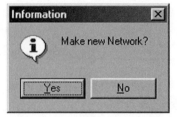

Figure 6. An information box in Pajek.

(Figure 6). If the answer is yes, which we advise, a new network named Bidirected Arcs to Edges (SUM) of N1 (26) is added to the Network drop-down menu with a serial number of 2. The original network is not changed. Conversely, answering no to the question in the information box causes Pajek to change the original network.

Exercise I

Net>Transform>
Remove>lines
with value>
higher than

Remove all second choices from the original network of dining-table partners with the command summarized in the left margin. Which number do you enter in the dialog box headed "Remove lines with high values" and why is this command part of the *Net* menu? (The answers to the exercises are listed in Section 1.9.)

1.3.3 Calculation

In social network analysis, many structural features have been quantified (e.g., an index that measures the centrality of a vertex). Some measures pertain to the entire network, whereas others summarize the structural position of a subnetwork or a single vertex. Calculation outputs a single number in the case of a network characteristic and a series of numbers in the case of subnetworks and vertices.

Exploring network structure by calculation is much more concise and precise than visual inspection. However, structural indices are sometimes abstract and difficult to interpret. Therefore, we use both visual inspection of a network and calculation of structural indices to analyze network structure.

Application

Report screen

File>Show
Report Window

In Pajek, results of calculations and other kinds of feedback to the user are automatically reported in a separate window that we call the Report screen. If you closed the Report screen or if it is hidden behind other screens, you can show it again with the *Show Report Window* command in the *File* menu of Pajek's Main screen.

The Report screen displays numeric results that summarize structural features as a single number, a frequency distribution, or a cross-tabulation. Calculations that assign a value to each vertex are not reported in this screen. They are stored as data objects in Pajek, notably as partitions and vectors (see Chapter 2). The Report screen displays text but no network

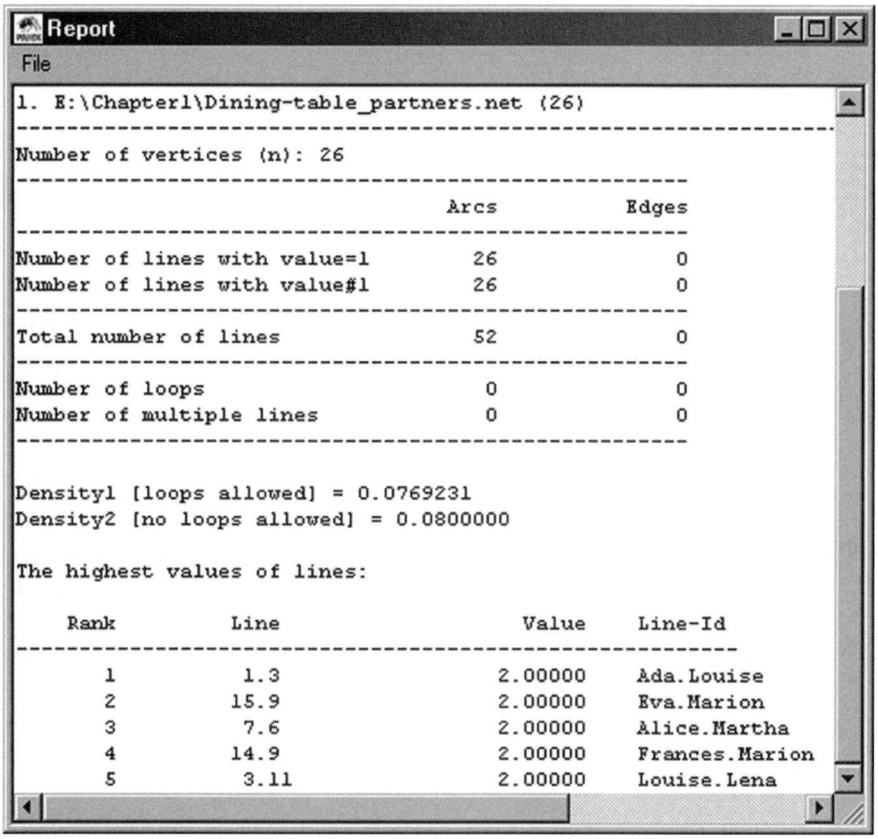

```
┌────────────────────────────────────────────────────────────┐
│ ▓ Report                                          _ □ ✕     │
├────────────────────────────────────────────────────────────┤
│ File                                                        │
├────────────────────────────────────────────────────────────┤
│ 1. E:\Chapter1\Dining-table_partners.net (26)        ▲     │
│ ------------------------------------------------------      │
│ Number of vertices (n): 26                                 │
│ --------------------------------------------------          │
│                              Arcs          Edges           │
│ --------------------------------------------------          │
│ Number of lines with value=1    26            0            │
│ Number of lines with value#1    26            0            │
│ --------------------------------------------------          │
│ Total number of lines           52            0            │
│ --------------------------------------------------          │
│ Number of loops                  0            0            │
│ Number of multiple lines         0            0            │
│ --------------------------------------------------          │
│                                                            │
│ Density1 [loops allowed] = 0.0769231                       │
│ Density2 [no loops allowed] = 0.0800000                    │
│                                                            │
│ The highest values of lines:                               │
│                                                            │
│    Rank        Line              Value      Line-Id        │
│ -------------------------------------------------------     │
│       1         1.3            2.00000    Ada.Louise        │
│       2        15.9            2.00000    Eva.Marion        │
│       3         7.6            2.00000    Alice.Martha      │
│       4        14.9            2.00000    Frances.Marion    │
│       5         3.11           2.00000    Louise.Lena   ▼   │
│ ◄ ┃                                                    ► ║  │
└────────────────────────────────────────────────────────────┘
```

Figure 7. Report screen in Pajek.

drawings. The contents of the Report screen can be saved as a text file from its *File* menu.

The Report screen depicted in Figure 7 shows the number of vertices, edges, and arcs in the original dining-table partners network. This is general information on the network that is provided by the command *Info>Network>General* (as you know now, this means the *General* command within the *Network* submenu of the *Info* menu). In addition to the number of vertices, edges, and arcs, the screen shows the number of multiple lines and loops and two indices of network density that are explained in Chapter 3. Also, this command displays the number of lines requested in the dialog box depicted in Figure 8.

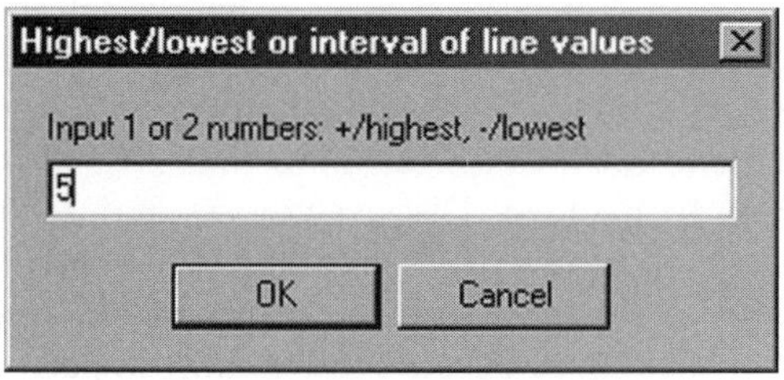

Info>Network> General

```
┌──────────────────────────────────────────────────┐
│ Highest/lowest or interval of line values    ✕   │
├──────────────────────────────────────────────────┤
│ Input 1 or 2 numbers: +/highest, -/lowest        │
│ ┌──────────────────────────────────────────────┐ │
│ │ 5│                                           │ │
│ └──────────────────────────────────────────────┘ │
│                                                  │
│        ┌────────────┐    ┌────────────┐          │
│        │    OK      │    │   Cancel   │          │
│        └────────────┘    └────────────┘          │
└──────────────────────────────────────────────────┘
```

Figure 8. Dialog box of *Info>Network>General* command.

In this example, we typed a 5 in the dialog box, so the report screen shows the five lines with the highest line values that are second choices in the dining-table partners network. In the Report screen, each line is described by its rank according to its line value, a pair of vertex numbers, the line value, and a pair of vertex labels. Hence, the first line in Figure 7 represents the arc from Ada (vertex 1) to Louise (vertex 3), which is Ada's second choice.

Exercise II

Can you see the number of first choices from the listing in Figure 7 and does this number surprise you? Which number should you enter in the dialog box depicted in Figure 8 to get a list of all arcs representing first choices?

1.3.4   Visualization

The human eye is trained in pattern recognition. Therefore, network visualizations help to trace and present patterns of ties. In Section 1.2, we presented the sociogram as the first systematic visualization of a social network. It was the sociometrists' main tool to explore and understand the structure of ties in human groups. In books on graph theory, visualizations are used to illustrate concepts and proofs. Visualizations facilitate an intuitive understanding of network concepts, so we use them frequently.

Our eyes are easily fooled, however. A network can be drawn in many ways, and each drawing stresses different structural features. Therefore, the analyst should rely on systematic rather than ad hoc principles for network drawing. In general, we should use automatic procedures, which generate an optimal *layout of the network*, when we want to explore network structure. Subsequently, we may edit the automatically generated layout manually if we want to present it.

Some basic principles of network drawing should be observed. The most important principle states that the distance between vertices should express the strength or number of their ties as closely as possible. In a map, the distance between cities matches their geographical distance. In psychological charts, spatial proximity of objects usually expresses perceived similarity. Because social network analysis focuses on relations, a drawing should position vertices according to their ties: vertices that are connected should be drawn closer together than vertices that are not related. A good drawing minimizes the variation in the length of lines. In the case of lines with unequal values, line length should be proportional to line value.

The legibility of a drawing poses additional demands, which are known as *graph drawing esthetics*. Vertices or lines should not be drawn too closely together and small angles between lines that are incident with the same vertex should be avoided. Distinct vertices and distinct lines should not merge into one lump. Vertices should not be drawn on top of a line that does not connect this vertex to another vertex. The number of crossing lines should be minimized because the eye tends to see crossings as vertices.

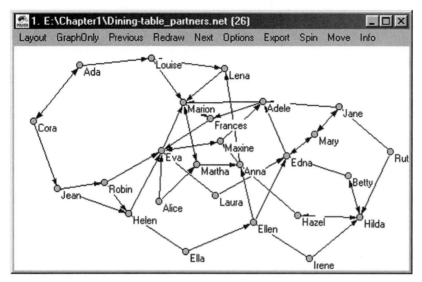

Figure 9. Draw screen in Pajek.

Application

Pajek offers many ways to draw a network. It has a separate window for drawing, which is accessed from the *Draw>Draw* menu in the Main screen. The Draw screen has an elaborate menu of choices (see Figure 9), some of which are presented in later chapters. Use the index of Pajek commands in this book to find them. We discuss the most important commands now to help you draw your first network.

It is very important to note the following. Figure 9 is a screen shot of the Draw screen in Pajek. This figure does not necessarily exactly match the Draw screen that you see on your computer. First, the size of the computers' Draw screens may be different. Second, on your computer screen the vertices are most probably red instead of gray. In this book, colors are replaced by grays; we discuss this matter in greater detail in Chapter 2.

Next, compare Figure 9 to Figure 2. Although the two figures display the same network, there are differences. Reciprocal arcs, for example, are drawn as straight arcs with two heads in Figure 9, whereas they are two arcs in Figure 2. Figure 2 is exported to a format (Encapsulated PostScript) that is optimal for publication in a book. It also allows manual editing (e.g., moving the vertex labels a little bit so as not to obscure arcs or headings of arcs). In Section 1.3.4.3 and Appendix 2, you can learn more about this format and how to edit it. The Draw screen of Pajek as shown in Figure 9, however, is meant for efficient drawing and redrawing of networks, so it is less detailed.

Keep in mind that the level of detail in the book is greater than that on the screen. This does not mean that the layout of the network in the Draw screen is wrong and that you followed the wrong procedure or applied the wrong commands.

Finally, Figure 2 displays line values, whereas Figure 9 does not. Do not worry about such differences unless the text is explicitly discussing this aspect. There are many options for changing features of the layout

Draw screen

[Draw]
Options>Lines>
Mark Lines>
with Values

in the Draw screen, which may be turned on or off. The line values, for instance, can be displayed by selecting the option *with Values* in the *Mark Lines* submenu of the *Lines* command in the *Options* menu of the Draw screen. Activate this option now – pressing *Ctrl-v* will have the same effect (see Appendix 3) – and you will see the line values on your computer screen. Line values will now be shown until you turn this option off. Note the difference between a command and an option in Pajek: a command is executed once, whereas an option remains effective until it is turned off.

1.3.4.1   Automatic Drawing

Automated procedures for finding an optimal layout are a better way to obtain a basic layout than manual drawing, because the resulting picture depends less on the preconceptions and misconceptions of the investigator. In addition, automated drawing is much faster and quite spectacular because the drawing evolves before your eyes.

Layout>Energy menu

In Pajek, several commands for automatic layout are implemented. Two commands are accessible from the *Layout>Energy* menu and we refer to them as energy commands. Both commands move vertices to locations that minimize the variation in line length. Imagine that the lines are springs pulling vertices together, though never too close. The energy commands "pull" vertices to better positions until they are in a state of equilibrium. Therefore, these procedures are known as *spring embedders*.

Layout>Energy> Starting positions: random, circular, Given xy, Given z

The relocation technique used in both automatic layout commands has some limitations. First, the results depend on the starting positions of vertices. Different starting positions may yield different results. Most results will be quite similar, but results can differ markedly. The *Starting positions* submenu on the *Layout>Energy* menu gives you control over the starting positions. You can choose random and circular starting positions, or you can use the present positions of vertices as their starting positions: option *Given xy*, where x and y refer to the (horizontal and vertical) coordinates of vertices in the plane of the Draw screen. The fourth option (*Given z*) refers to the third dimension, which we present in Chapter 5.

The second limitation of the relocation technique is that it stops if improvement is relatively small or if the user so requests in a dialog box (Figure 10). This means that automatic layout generation outputs a drawing that is very good but not perfect. Manual improvements can be made. However, make small adjustments only to reduce the risk of discovering a pattern that you introduced to the drawing yourself. To improve a

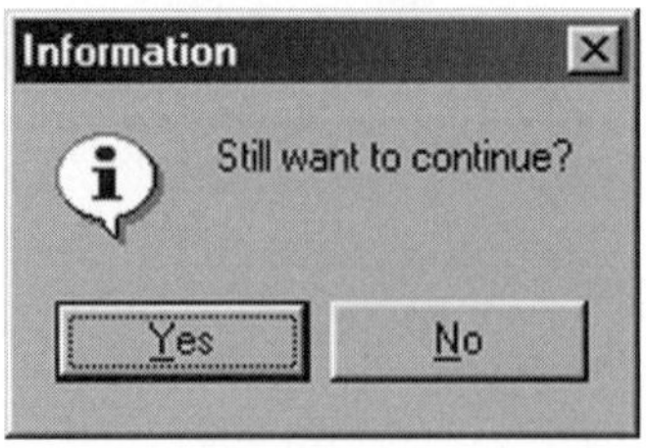

Figure 10. Continue dialog box.

drawing it is usually worth the effort to repeat an energy command a couple of times with given starting positions.

Because of these limitations, take the following advice to heart: *never rely on one run of an energy command*. Experiment with both commands and manual adjustment until you obtain the same layout repeatedly.

The first energy command is named Kamada–Kawai after its authors. This command produces regularly spaced results, especially for connected networks that are not very large. The dining-table partners network as available from the book's Web site was energized in this way. Kamada–Kawai seems to produce more stable results than the other energy command (Fruchterman Reingold) but it is much slower and it should not be applied to networks containing more than five hundred vertices. With Kamada–Kawai, commands *Fix first and last* and *Fix one in the middle* enable you to fix vertices that should not be relocated. The first command fixes the two vertices with the lowest and highest serial numbers. This is very useful if these vertices represent the sender and target in an information network. The second command allows you to specify one vertex that must be placed in the middle of the drawing.

Layout>Energy> Kamada– Kawai>Free, Fix first and last, Fix one in the middle

The second energy command, which is called Fruchterman Reingold, is faster and works with larger networks. This command separates unconnected parts of the network nicely, whereas Kamada–Kawai draws them on top of one another. It can generate two- and three-dimensional layouts, as indicated by commands *2D* and *3D* in the submenu. We discuss three-dimensional visualizations in Chapter 5.

Layout>Energy> Fruchterman Reingold> 2D, 3D

The third command in the submenu, which is labeled *Factor*, allows the user to specify the optimal distance between vertices in a drawing energized with Fruchterman Reingold. This command displays a dialog box asking for a positive number. A low number yields small distances between vertices, so many vertices are placed in the center of the plane. A high number pushes vertices out of the center toward positions on a circle. An optimal distance of 1 is a good starting point. Try a smaller distance if the center of the drawing is quite empty, but try a higher distance if the center is too crowded.

Layout>Energy> Fruchterman Reingold>Factor

Each energy command has strong and weak points. We advise starting with Fruchterman Reingold and using several optimal distances until a stable result appears. The drawing can then be improved using Kamada–Kawai with the actual location of vertices as starting positions. Finally, improve the drawing by manual editing, which we discuss under Section 1.3.4.2.

Exercise III

Manipulate the *Factor* option of the *Fruchterman Reingold* energy command to obtain a sociogram of the dining-table partners network with a clear distinction between vertices in the center and vertices in the margin or periphery. Do you think your drawing is better than the original? Justify your answer.

1.3.4.2   Manual Drawing

Pajek supports manual drawing of a network. Use the mouse to drag individual vertices from one position to another. Place the cursor on a

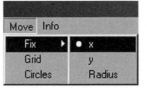

Figure 11. A selected option in the Draw screen.

vertex, hold down the left mouse button, and move the mouse to drag a vertex. Notice that the lines that are incident with the vertex also move. You can drop the vertex anywhere you want, unless you constrain the movement of vertices with the options in the *Move* menu.

Move>Fix, Grid, Circles   The *Move* menu in the Draw screen has (at least) three options: *Fix*, *Grid*, and *Circles*. The *Fix* option allows you to restrict the movement of a vertex. It cannot be moved either horizontally or vertically if you select *x* or *y*, respectively, in the drop-down menu. Select *Radius* to restrict the movement of a vertex to a circle. The options *Grid* and *Circles* allow you to specify a limited number of positions to which a vertex can be moved. In the case of small networks, this generates esthetically pleasing results. In Pajek, when you select an option, it is marked by a dot (Figure 11).

Redraw   You can zoom in on the drawing by pressing the right mouse button and dragging a rectangle over the area that you want to enlarge. Within the enlargement, you can zoom in again. To return to the entire network, you must select the *Redraw* command on the Draw screen menu. It is not possible to zoom out in steps. The *GraphOnly* menu is similar to the *Redraw* menu, except that *GraphOnly* removes all labels as well as the heads of the arcs (press *Ctrl-l* to redisplay them). It shows vertices and lines only. This option speeds up automatic layout of a network, which is particularly helpful for drawing large networks. The *Previous* and *Next* commands on the menu allow you to display the network before or after the current network in the *Network* drop-down menu, so you need not return to the Main screen first to select another network. Note, however, that this is true only if the option *Network* is selected in the *Previous/Next>Apply to* submenu of the *Options* menu.

Previous

Next
GraphOnly

Options menu: Transform, Layout, Mark Vertices Using   The *Options* menu offers a variety of choices for changing the appearance of a network in the Draw screen and for setting options to commands in other Draw screen menus (Figure 12). Many drawing options are self-explanatory. Options for changing the shape of the network are listed in the *Transform* and *Layout* submenu, whereas options for the size, color, and labeling of vertices and lines are found in several other submenus. Figure 12 shows the *Options>Mark Vertices Using* submenu and its options for changing the type of vertex label displayed. Note the keyboard shortcuts in this submenu: pressing the *Ctrl* key along with the *l*, *n*, or *d* key has the same effect as selecting the accompanying item in the submenu.

[Draw]Info> Closest Vertices   To improve your drawing, Pajek can evaluate a series of esthetic properties, such as closest vertices that are not linked or the number of crossing lines. This allows you to find the worst aspects of a drawing and to improve them manually. The *Info* menu in the Draw screen allows you to

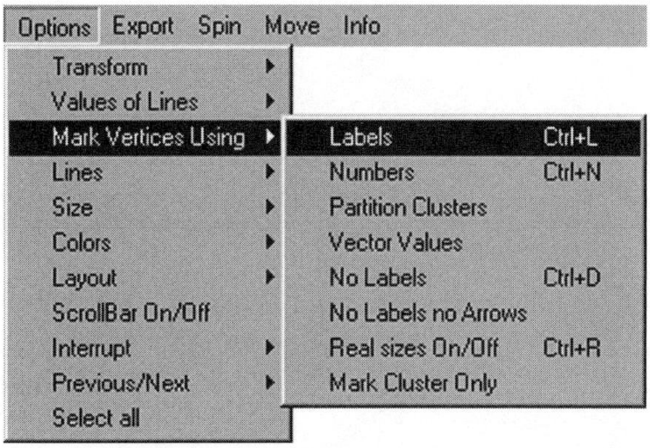

Figure 12. *Options* menu of the Draw screen.

select one or all esthetic properties. If you select one of these commands (e.g., *Closest Vertices*), Pajek identifies the vertices that perform worst on this feature: they are identified by a color (other than light blue) in the drawing and they are listed in the Report screen [e.g., vertices 10 (Maxine) and 14 (Frances) are closest]. In the Draw screen, they are now colored yellow. Because they are not directly linked, it may be wise to move them apart a little.

When you select all esthetic properties, each property will be associated with a color (see Figure 13 for esthetic information on the dining-table partners network as supplied on the book's Web site). Sometimes, vertices violate several esthetic indices, so they ought to be marked by several colors. Because this is not possible, some colors may not show up in the drawing. There are no rules of thumb for optimal scores on the esthetic properties. The *Info* command helps to identify the vertices that perform worst, but it is up to you to see whether you can improve their placement.

[Draw]Info>All Properties

Exercise IV
Open the original dining-table partners network and improve it according to the esthetic criterion for minimizing crossing lines. Which vertex can you move to reduce the number of crossing lines?

1.3.4.3 Saving a Drawing
To present pictures of networks to an audience, we have to save our visualizations. This subsection sketches the ways in which network drawings can be exported from Pajek.

```
-------------
 Layout Info
-------------
Yellow: The closest vertices: 10 and 14. Distance: 0.07267
LimeGreen: The smallest angle: 2.1.2. Angle: 0.00000
Red: The shortest line: 9.14. Length: 0.08530
Blue: The longest line: 11.20. Length: 0.29546
Pink: Number of crossings: 13
White: Closest vertex to line: 6 to 15.25. Distance: 0.03463
```

Figure 13. Textual output from *[Draw]Info>All Properties*.

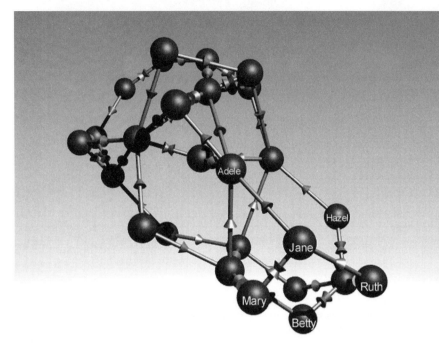

Figure 14. A 3-D rendering of the dining-table partners network.

[Main]File>
Network>Save

If a researcher wants to save a layout for future use, the easiest thing to do is to save the network itself. Remember that a network consists of lists of vertices, arcs, and edges. The list of vertices specifies a serial number, a label, and coordinates in the plane for each vertex. Relocation of a vertex in the Draw screen changes its coordinates and the latest coordinates are written to the network file on execution of the *Save* command. When the network is reopened in Pajek, the researcher obtains the layout he or she saved, that is, the general pattern because the size and colors of vertices and lines are usually not specified in the network data file.

Export menu

Pajek offers several ways to save the drawing as a picture for presentation to an audience. They are listed in the *Export* menu of the Draw screen. Three commands produce two-dimensional output (EPS/PS, SVG, and Bitmap) and another three commands yield three-dimensional output (VRML, MDL MOLfile, and Kinemages). Although three-dimensional representations can be quite spectacular (Figure 14: a ray-traced image from a VRML model exported by Pajek), we do not discuss them in this chapter but rather in Chapter 5. Here we briefly outline the commands for two-dimensional output (see Appendix 2 for more details).

Export>Bitmap

The *Bitmap* export command produces an image of the Draw screen: each screen pixel is represented by a point in a raster, which is called a bitmap. You get exactly what you see; even the size of the picture matches the size of the Draw screen (e.g., see Figure 9). Every word processor and presentation program operating under Windows can load and display bitmaps. Bitmaps, however, are cumbersome to edit, they are "bumpy," and they lose their sharpness if they are enlarged or reduced.

Vector graphics produce more pleasing results than bitmaps. In a vec-   *Export>EPS/PS,*
tor graphic, the shape and position of each circle representing a vertex   *SVG,Options*
and each line, arc, loop, or label are specified. Because each element in the
drawing is defined separately, a picture can be enlarged or reduced without
loss of quality and its layout can be manipulated easily. Pajek can export
vector graphics in two formats, which are closely related: PostScript (command *EPS/PS*) and Scalable Vector Graphics (command *SVG*). PostScript
(PS) and Encapsulated PostScript (EPS) are meant for printing, whereas
the Scalable Vector Graphics format was developed for the Web. The user
can modify the layout of both PostScript and Scalable Vector Graphics
drawings in the *Export>Options* submenu, which is covered in detail in
Appendix 2.

In this book, we use vector graphics because of their high quality. For
example, the sociogram shown in Figure 2 was exported from Pajek as
Encapsulated PostScript. However, PostScript and Scalable Vector Graphics are formats that are not universally supported by Windows software.
For example, most printers cannot print Encapsulated PostScript directly.
Appropriate software (e.g., CorelDraw) is necessary to edit vertices, labels, and lines or to convert a vector graphic to a format that your word
processor can handle (e.g., Windows MetaFile). To display Scalable Vector Graphics on a Web page, download a plug-in from the Web site of
Adobe Systems Incorporated (see Appendix 2 for details).

1.4   Assembling a Social Network

To perform network analysis, social relations must be measured and
coded. In this section, we briefly discuss data collection techniques for
social network analysis and explain how to convert data to a network file
for Pajek.

There are several ways to collect data on social relations. Traditionally,
sociometrists focus on the structure of social choice within a group. They
gather data by asking each member of a group to indicate his or her
favorites (or opponents) with respect to an activity that is important to
the group. For example, they ask pupils in a class to name the children
they prefer to sit next to. In a questionnaire, respondents may write down
the names of the children they choose or check their names on a list. These
methods are called *free recall* and *roster*, respectively. The latter method
reduces the risk that respondents may overlook people.

Sometimes, the respondent is asked to nominate a fixed number of favorites. In sociometry, it was very popular to restrict the number of choices
to three. For example, in the dining-table partners network each girl was
asked to make three choices. This restriction is motivated by the empirical
discovery that the more choices that are allowed the more they concentrate on people who are already highly chosen. When asked for their best
friends, most people mention four or fewer people. If they have to mention more people, they usually nominate people they think they should like
because they are liked by many others. However, restricting the number
of choices reduces the reliability of the data: choices are less stable over

time and correlate less well than other measurement techniques such as unrestricted choices, ranking (rank all other group members with respect to their attractiveness), or paired comparison (list all possible pairs of group members and choose a preferred person in each pair). A researcher who fixes the number of choices available to respondents eliminates the difference between a respondent who entertains many friendships and a loner.

Fixed and free choice, ranking, and paired comparison are techniques that elicit data on social relations through questioning. However, there are several data collection techniques that register social relations rather than elicit them. For example, the amount of interaction between pupils in a class may be observed by a researcher; respondents may be asked to register their contacts in a diary; membership lists and files that log contacts in electronic networks may be coded; family relations or transactions can be retrieved from archives and databases. The rapid growth of electronic data storage offers new opportunities to gather data on large social networks.

Indirect data are usually better than reported data, which rely on the often inaccurate recollections of respondents. However, it is not always easy to identify people and organizations unambiguously in data collected indirectly: is a Mr. Jones on the board of one organization the same Mr. Jones who is CEO of another firm? It goes without saying that network analysis demands correct identification of vertices in the network.

Application

When you have collected your data, it is time to create a network that can be analyzed with Pajek. In Section 1.3.1, we discussed the structure of a Pajek network file. This is a simple text file that can be typed out in any word processor that exports plain text. Do not forget to attribute serial numbers to the vertices ranging from 1 to the number of vertices. Save the network from the word processor as plain, unformatted text (DOS text, ASCII) and use the extension .net in the file name. If your data are stored as a relational database, the database software may be able to produce the Pajek network file; see Appendix 1 for an example.

Net>Random Network> Total No. of Arcs

It is also possible to produce the network file in Pajek. First, make a new random network with the command *Net>Random Network>Total No. of Arcs*. In the first dialog box, type in the number of vertices you want. In the second dialog box, request zero arcs to obtain a network without lines. The command creates a new network and adds it to the *Network* drop-down menu in the Main screen. When you draw it (*Draw>Draw*), you will see that the vertices are nicely arranged in a circle or ellipse (Figure 15).

File>Network> Edit

Editing Network screen

As a second step, add lines to the network, which may be done in the Main screen or in the Draw screen. In the Main screen, both the *Edit* button at the side of the *Network* drop-down menu (a picture of a writing hand) and the command *File>Network>Edit* open a dialog box that allows you to select a vertex by serial number or by label. Next, the Editing Network screen is shown for the selected vertex (Figure 16). In the Draw screen, you can open the Editing Network screen by right-clicking a vertex.

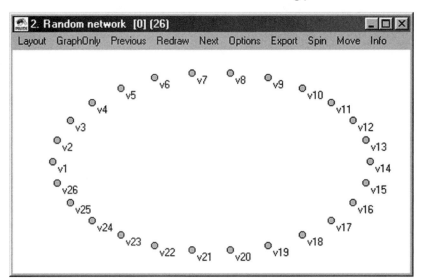

Figure 15. Random network without lines.

Double-clicking the word *Newline* in the Editing Network screen opens a dialog box allowing the user to add a line to or from the selected vertex. To add an edge, type the number of another vertex. Type the number of the vertex preceded by a + sign to add an arc *to* the selected vertex and use a − sign to add an arc *from* the selected vertex. Each new edge and arc is displayed as a line in the Editing Network screen. For example, Figure 16 displays an arc from vertex 4 to vertex 1, an arc from vertex 1 to 3, and an edge (indicated by a dash between vertex numbers) between vertices 1 and 2. Also, you can delete a line in the Editing Network screen: just double-click the line you want to delete.

[Editing Network] Newline

By default, all lines have unit line value as indicated by the expression val = 1.000 in the Editing Network screen. Line values can be changed in this screen by selecting the line (left-click) and right-clicking it. A dialog box appears that accepts any number (positive, zero, or negative) as input.

As a final step, save the network. Networks in Pajek are not automatically saved. Because network analysis usually yields many new networks, most of which are just intermediate steps, Pajek does not prompt the user to save networks. Save the new network as soon as you finish editing it.

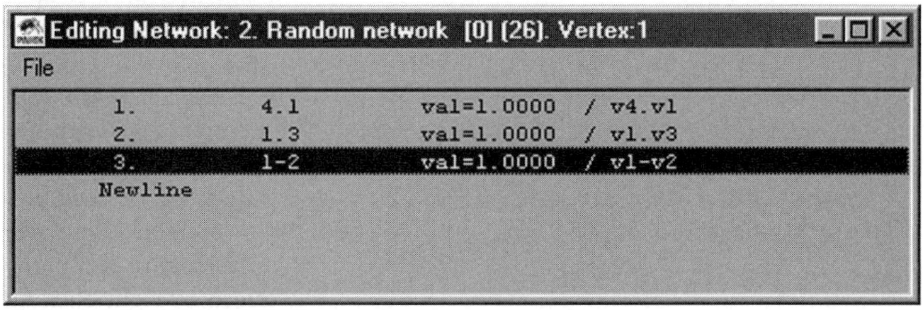

File>Network> Save

```
Editing Network: 2. Random network [0] [26]. Vertex:1      _ □ ×
File
        1.          4.1         val=1.0000   / v4.v1
        2.          1.3         val=1.0000   / v1.v3
        3.          1-2         val=1.0000   / v1-v2
     Newline
```

Figure 16. Edit Network screen.

Use *Save* from the submenu *File>Network* or use the save button (the picture of a diskette) at the side of the Network drop-down menu. We recommend that you save a network in Pajek Arcs/Edges format for easy manual editing and for a maximum choice of layout options (see Appendix 2). Give the file a meaningful name and the extension .net.

Exercise V
Create some random networks with as many vertices and arcs as the dining-table partners network (without multiple lines). Energize them and inspect the number of crossing lines. Which systematic differences occur between the random networks and the original dining-table partners network?

1.5   Summary

This chapter introduced social network analysis and emphasized its theoretical interest in social relations between people or organizations and its roots in mathematical graph theory. A network is defined as a set of vertices and a set of lines between vertices with additional information on the vertices or lines. This flexible definition permits a wide variety of empirical phenomena, ranging from the structure of molecules to the structure of the universe, to be modeled as networks. In social network analysis, we concentrate on relations between people or social entities that represent groups of people (e.g., affective relations between people, trade relations between organizations, or power relations between nations).

This simple definition of a network covers all types of networks encountered in this book: directed and undirected networks and networks with and without loops or multiple lines. Most social networks are simple undirected or directed networks, which contain no multiple lines, and loops usually do not occur. As a result of transformations, however, networks may acquire multiple lines and loops. The results of analytic procedures may depend on the kind of network we are analyzing, so it is important to know what kind of network it is.

The mathematical roots of network analysis permit powerful and well-defined manipulations, calculations, and visualizations of social networks. Exploratory social network analysis as we present it here makes ample use of these three techniques. In exploring a social network, we first visualize it to get an impression of its structure. The sociogram, which originates from sociometry, is our main visualization technique.

We are convinced that doing social network analysis is a good way to learn about it. Therefore, the program Pajek for network analysis is an integral part of the course. We urge you to practice the commands demonstrated rather than just read about them. The data related to each example in the book are available from the book's Web site (http://vlado.fmf.uni-lj.si/pub/networks/book/). This chapter introduced the menu structure of Pajek and some basic commands for visualizing networks. You are now ready to start analyzing social networks.

1.6   Questions

1. A sociogram is
   a. an index of sociability.
   b. a graphic representation of group structure.
   c. the structure of sociometric choices.
   d. a set of vertices connected by edges or arcs.
2. Which of the following definitions is correct?
   a. A graph is a set of vertices and a set of lines.
   b. A graph is a set of vertices and a set of edges.
   c. A graph is a network.
   d. A graph is a set of vertices and a set of pairs of vertices.
3. Have a look at the following networks and choose the correct statement.

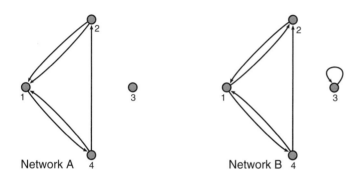

a. Neither A nor B is a simple directed graph.
   b. A is not a simple directed graph but B is.
   c. A and B are simple directed graphs.
   d. A and B are networks but not graphs.
4. Social network analysis is exploratory if
   a. the researcher has no specific ideas on the structure of the network beforehand.
   b. it deals with social settings that are unexplored by social scientists.
   c. the network is studied outside a laboratory.
   d. it does not try to predict network structure from a sample.
5. Which of the following statements is correct?
   a. A line can be incident with a line.
   b. A line can be incident with a vertex.
   c. An edge can be incident with a line.
   d. A vertex can be incident with a vertex.
6. Open the dining-table partners network and remove all second choices (see Exercise I in Section 1.3.2).
   a. What in your opinion is the most striking result if you draw the new network?
   b. Which energy command do you recommend to optimize this drawing? Explain your choice.

1.7   Assignment

Your first social network analysis: investigate the friendship network within your class as it is or as you perceive it. Choose the right kind of network to conceptualize friendship ties (directed, undirected, valued, with multiple lines and loops?), collect the data (design a questionnaire or state the friendships you observe), make a Pajek network file, and then draw and interpret it. If you use perceived friendship ties, it is worthwhile to compare your network to networks made by other students. Where do they differ?

1.8   Further Reading

- The example of the girls' school dormitory is taken from J. L. Moreno, *The Sociometry Reader* (Glencoe, Ill.: The Free Press, 1960, p. 35).
- A brief history of social network analysis can be found in J. Scott, *Social Network Analysis: A Handbook* [London, Sage (2nd ed. 2000), 1991, Chapter 2].
- Stanley Milgram originated research on the Small World problem; for example, see S. Milgram, "Interdisciplinary thinking and the small world problem." In: M. Sherif & C. W. Sherif (Eds.), *Interdisciplinary Relationships in the Social Sciences* (Chicago, Aldine, 1969, pp. 103–20).
- For the problem of boundary specification and sampling see S. Wasserman & K. Faust, *Social Network Analysis: Methods and Applications* (Cambridge, Cambridge University Press, 1994, Section 2.2, pp. 30–5). Information on data collection can be found in Section 2.4 (pp. 43–59). This impressive monograph is a good starting point for further reading on any topic in social network analysis.

1.9   Answers

Answers to the Exercises

I. Because first choices have line values of 1 and second choices have line values of 2, you must type 1 in the dialog box that appears on activation of the command *Net>Transform>Remove>lines with value>higher than*. This command is part of the *Net* menu because it operates on a single network only.

II. In Figure 7, the line starting with "Number of lines with value = 1" shows the number of lines with line value one: 26 arcs. Because the line value of 1 represents a first choice here, the number of first choices is 26. This should not come as a surprise because each of the 26 girls was supposed to inidicate one first choice among her peers. To get a list of all first choices in the dining-table partners network, we should have entered -26 or the range 27 to 52 (type the two numbers seperated by a space), which contains the arcs on ranks 27 up to and including 52, in the dialog box.

III. Setting *Factor* to 2 or higher will yield a drawing with a lot of vertices placed on a circle and few vertices in the middle, notably Anna, Eva, or Edna. This drawing is not an improvement; the selection of central vertices is arbitrary. Repeat the energy command several times (with random starting positions) and you will find different persons in the center.

IV. Select the command *No. of Crossings* in the *Info* menu of the Draw screen. The vertices in the center are now colored pink: their lines cross. The Report screen shows the number of crossing lines to be 13. The easiest improvement is to drag Alice to a position above the arc from Laura to Eva. Now Alice's arcs cross no others and the number of crossing lines is reduced to 12. However, it is even better to drag Alice and Martha to the left of the arc from Francis to Eva, because Martha and Marion are connected by mutual choice, which counts twice at every crossing. If you do this, it is better to drag Maxine below the arc from Martha to Anna, because Eva and Maxine are doubly connected. Another improvement is made if Adele is placed to the left of the arc from Anna to Lena. We reach a minimum of seven crossing arcs. Can you do better?

V. The random networks seem to be "messier" than the original dining-table partners network. This is clearly reflected by the fact that the number of crossing lines in the energized drawing is much higher: approximately forty crossing lines compared to thirteen in the dining-table partners network. There are several possible reasons. First, in the dining-table partners network, each girl makes two choices, whereas the number of arcs emanating from a vertex in the random network differs: you may find isolates next to vertices sending four or more arcs. The vertices sending many arcs are likely to "clutter" the view. Another reason pertains to the ratio of mutual choices. In the actual selection of dining-table partners, there is a fair chance that girls will nominate each other. In the sociogram, this is represented by a bidirectional arc, which needs no more space than a single arc.

Answers to the Questions in Section 1.6

1. Answer b is correct because a sociogram is a specific way of drawing the structure of ties within a human group.

2. A graph is defined as a set of vertices and a set of lines between pairs of vertices (see Section 1.3.1), so answer d is correct: lines can be defined as pairs of vertices. Answer a does not specify that the lines must have the graph's vertices as their endpoints, so this answer is not correct. Answer b has the same fault and it restricts the definition to undirected graphs, which is not correct according to our definitions. Answer c ignores the difference between a graph and a network.

3. Answer b is correct. A simple directed graph contains at least one arc (so it is directed) and no multiple lines; it may contain loops. Therefore, network B is a simple directed graph but network A is not because of its multiple lines. Answer d is wrong because there is no

additional information on the vertices and arcs, such as vertex labels or line values.

4. Answers a and d are correct.
5. Answer b is correct.
6. See also the answer to Exercise I.
   a. The network is no longer connected. Some girls and pairs of girls are disconnected (e.g., Cora, and Ada and Jean and Helen).
   b. We prefer Fruchterman Reingold because Kamada–Kawai sometimes draws disconnected parts on top of one another.

2

Attributes and Relations

2.1   Introduction

In Chapter 1, we argued that social network analysis focuses on social relations. A network is a set of vertices and lines. Both vertices and lines have characteristics that we may want to include in our analysis (e.g., the gender of people and the strength of their ties). As noted in Chapter 1, properties of relations are represented by line values in the network (e.g., first and second choices among girls in the dormitory). Now, we add characteristics of the vertices to the analysis. How can we use information on the actors to make sense of the social network?

In this chapter, we present techniques that combine relational network data and nonrelational attributes, such as psychological, social, economical, and geographical characteristics of the vertices in the network. The attributes enhance our interpretation of network structure and they enable us to study subsections of the network. In addition, we briefly discuss how to use the network position of vertices in statistical analysis; social network analysis and statistics are two complementary sets of techniques. After having studied this chapter, you will understand the basic data used in network analysis and you will be able to combine relational and non-relational data.

2.2   Example: The World System

Social network analysis can be applied to large-scale phenomena. In 1974, Immanuel Wallerstein introduced the concept of a capitalist world system, which came into existence in the sixteenth century. This system is characterized by a world economy that is stratified into a core, a semiperiphery, and a periphery. Countries owe their wealth or poverty to their position in the world economy. The core, Wallerstein argues, exists because it succeeds in exploiting the periphery and, to a lesser extent, the semiperiphery. The semiperiphery profits from being an intermediary between the core and the periphery.

The world system is based on a global division of labor. Countries in the core specialize in capital-intensive and high-tech production, whereas peripheral countries apply themselves to low-valued, labor-intensive

29

products or unprocessed, raw materials. Core countries import raw and less-processed products from the periphery and turn them into expensive high-tech products that are exported to countries in the core, semiperiphery, and periphery. In consequence, there is much trade among core countries, but little trade between countries in the periphery. The core dominates the world trade in a double sense: core countries are more often involved in trade ties than peripheral countries and the value of exports from core countries exceeds the value of imports because their products have higher added value. This is why core countries do very well economically.

Which countries belong to the core, semiperiphery, or periphery? In political economy, several attempts have been made to answer this question, some of which are based on social network analysis. The network analysts analyzed the structure of the trade relation and classified countries according to the pattern of their trade ties; for instance, the nations that trade with almost all other countries are classified as core countries. World trade statistics, which are widely available, offer the data required for this analysis.

In this chapter, we use statistics on world trade in 1994. We included all countries with entries in the paper version of the *Commodity Trade Statistics* published by the United Nations, but we had to add data on some countries for 1993 (Austria, Seychelles, Bangladesh, Croatia, and Barbados) or 1995 (South Africa and Ecuador) because they were not available for 1994. Countries that are not sovereign are excluded because additional economic data are not available: For example, the Faeroe Islands and Greenland or Macau, which belong to Portugal and Denmark respectively. In the end, the network contains eighty countries and most missing countries are located in central Africa and the Middle East or belong to the former USSR.

The arcs in our network represent imports into one country from another. We restrict ourselves to one class of commodities rather than total imports and we picked miscellaneous manufactures of metal, which represents high-technology products or heavy manufacture. We use the absolute value of imports (in 1,000 U.S.$) but we did not register imports with values less than 1 percent of the country's total imports on this commodity. The network data are stored in the file Imports_manufactures.net.

In addition, we use several attributes of the countries in our analysis, namely their continent (Continent.clu), their structural world system position in 1994 (World_system.clu), their world system position in 1980 according to a previous analysis by Smith and White (World_system_1980.clu; see the reference in Section 2.10), and their gross domestic product per capita in U.S. dollars in 1995 (GDP_1995.vec). Note that in this chapter, we do not determine the world system position of the countries, we use results from an advanced structural technique called blockmodeling, which is presented in Chapter 12. The three world system positions in 1994 – core, semiperiphery, and periphery – are defined such that the core countries trade a lot of manufactures of metal among themselves and they export a lot to the countries in the semiperiphery, whereas the countries in the semiperiphery and periphery do not export a substantial amount of these manufactures.

2.3   Partitions

A partition of a network is a classification or clustering of the network's vertices. Each vertex is assigned to exactly one class or cluster (we use these words as synonyms); for example, one country is assigned to the core and another to the semiperiphery. A partition may contain a special class that collects the vertices we cannot classify because data are missing. Usually, the classes are identified by integers; for instance, a core country receives code 1 in the partition, and a country in the semiperiphery gets a 2. In this format, a partition is simply a list of nonnegative integers, one for each vertex in the network.

> A *partition* of a network is a classification or clustering of the vertices in the network such that each vertex is assigned to exactly one class or cluster.

In network analysis, partitions store discrete characteristics of vertices. A property is *discrete* if it consists of a limited number of classes; for instance, we may code the continents of countries by digits such that African countries consitute class 1, Asian countries constitute class 2, and so on. Six classes will suffice. A classification contains a limited number of classes and most classes contain several vertices because we want the classes to represent groups of actors rather than single actors or nothing at all. Partitions, therefore, are very useful for making selections from a network to reduce its size and complexity. We discuss this in Section 2.4.

In some cases, the order of class numbers in a partition is arbitrary for instance, in the partition of nations according to continents: there is no compelling reason why African countries should have a lower class code than Asian countries. In other instances, however, the order is meaningful. For instance, it would be foolish to assign the semiperiphery to class 1, the core to class 2, and the periphery to class 3, because this would not correctly reflect the obvious ranking of the three classes. Finally, the class codes may represent "real" numbers, for instance, the number of lines incident with a vertex: all vertices in class 1 are incident with one line, vertices in class 2 are incident with two lines, and so on, so make sure that you attach the right meaning to class numbers!

Partitions may specify a *structural property* such as world system position, which is a result of network analysis or a characteristic measured independently of the network (e.g., the continent where a nation is located). We call the latter *attributes* of vertices.

Figure 17 displays the trade in manufactures of metal and their position in the world system in 1994. In line with the spatial connotations of the concepts of core, semiperiphery, and periphery, the core countries are placed in the center (black vertices), the semiperiphery constitutes the middle ring (gray vertices), and the peripheral countries (white vertices) are located on the outer ring. The intense trade ties among the countries in the core and between the core and semiperiphery are apparent, just like the relative absence of trade in manufactures of metal among countries in the periphery. We should, however, note that the impression of clear

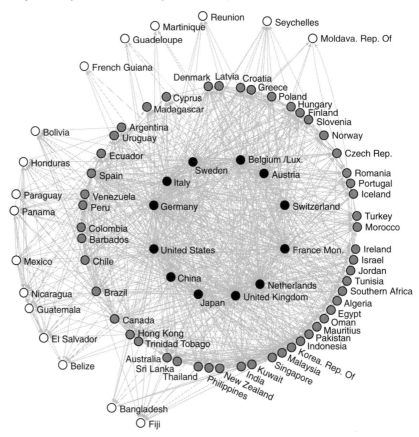

Figure 17. World trade of manufactures of metal and world system position.

boundaries between the three classes has deliberately been created by the researcher: this layout shows the world system positions rather than proves them.

Application

File>Partition> Read

File>Partition> Save

Partition drop-down menu

In Pajek, partitions are a data object on their own, so they are accessible from a drop list once they are read (*File>Partition>Read*). Partitions are saved in files with the extension .clu (*File>Partition>Save*) and these files are just lists of nonnegative integers preceded by a line which specifies the number of vertices. The first integer represents a property of the first vertex (e.g., world system position), the second integer belongs to the vertex with serial number 2, and so on. You should change neither the sequence of vertices in a network nor the sequence of entries in a partition because this will destroy the compatibility of the partition and the network: vertices are then no longer associated with the corresponding classes.

File>Pajek Project File

Although partitions can be stored separately, we can also save them with the network to which they belong. Pajek has a special data format – the project file – that may contain all networks, partitions, and other

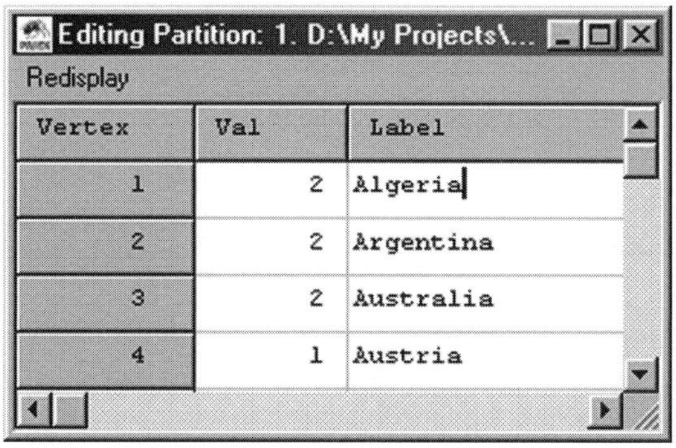

Figure 18. Edit screen with partition according to world system position.

data objects that belong together. You may, for example, read the world trade network and associated partitions and vectors from the project file World_trade.paj with the command *File>Pajek Project File>Read*. With the *Save* command from the same submenu, you can create your own project file, which contains all data (networks, partitions, and so on) at the time you save the project. We advise to open the project file World_trade.paj now.

If you edit it, it is easy to see that a partition consists of a series of integers. Choose the command *Edit* in the *File>Partition* submenu or simply click on the edit button at the left of the Partition drop-down menu (with the writing hand) to open the Edit screen (see Figure 18). The Edit screen contains three columns, which display the vertex number (*Vertex*), the class code (*Val*), and the vertex label (*Label*). The first vertex in the world trade network represents Algeria, which belongs to class 2 (semiperiphery), and the fourth vertex is Austria, part of the core (class 1). You may click on the class code to change it manually but you can also change the labels of vertices in the network. Note that the labels are displayed only if the associated network is selected in the Network drop-down menu.

Editing Partition Screen

File>Partition> Edit

The command *Partition* in the *Info* menu produces a frequency table of the classes in the active partition, which offers a quick way to inspect a partition. On execution, this command displays two dialog boxes. In the first box, which is similar to the dialog box associated with the *Info>Network>General* command (see Section 1.3.3), the user may request a listing of vertices with the highest or lowest class numbers. Type a positive integer to list vertices with the highest class numbers and type a negative integer to list vertices with the lowest class numbers. The second dialog box allows for suppressing classes in the table which occur seldom; for instance, type 5 in this dialog box to exclude classes with four vertices or less from the frequency tabulation.

Info>Partition

The *Info>Partition* command presents a table that lists the number of vertices in each class of the partition. In Table 1, we can see that twelve countries belong to the first class, which is 15 percent of all countries. The number 12 is the *frequency* (abbreviated to *Freq* in the table) with which class 1 occurs among the vertices. Pajek does not "know" that this

Table 1. *Tabular Output of the Command* Info>Partition

Class	Freq	Freq%	CumFreq	CumFreq%	Representative
1	12	15.0000	12	15.0000	Austria
2	51	63.7500	63	78.7500	Algeria
3	17	21.2500	80	100.0000	Bangladesh
SUM	80	100.0000			

class refers to the core. It can only help the interpretation of the meaning of the class by showing a representative of the class, that is, the label of a vertex that belongs to this class. Together, the core and semiperiphery contain sixty-three of the eighty countries (column CumFreq), which is 78.75 percent (CumFreq%).

Draw>
Draw
-Partition

Because partitions contain discrete classes, the class to which a vertex belongs can be represented by the color of the vertex. Each class is associated with a color (e.g., vertices in class 1 are yellow). It is easy to obtain a colored sociogram. First, make sure the right network and partition are selected in the drop-down menus of the Main screen, for example, the manufactures of metal network (`Imports_manufactures.net`) in the Network drop-down menu and the world position partition (`World_system.clu`) in the Partition drop-down menu. Next, execute the command *Draw-Partition* from the *Draw* menu (or press *Ctrl-p*). If the selected network and partition are compatible, that is, if the number of entries in the partition is equal to the number of vertices in the network, Pajek draws the network with vertex color determined by the partition.

Layout>Energy>
Kamada–
Kawai>Free

Move>Circles

In Figure 17, the circular layout was created in the following way. First, the layout was energized with the Kamada–Kawai energy command. This brought most core countries to the center and most peripheral countries to the margin of the sociogram. Then, manual movements of vertices was restricted to three circles and eighty positions on each of them with the *Circles* command in the *Move* menu. Finally, the countries were manually dragged toward the nearest position on the appropriate circle.

Then, what you get is a sociogram such as in Figure 17 in color. On your screen, the core countries are yellow, the countries in the semiperiphery are green, and the peripheral countries are red. Because this book is printed in black and white, we cannot reproduce the colors here but we stored all the color illustrations in a document (`illustrations.pdf`) on the Web site dedicated to this book (http://vlado.fmf.uni-lj.si/pub/networks/book/) so you can check the colors that you are expected to see on your screen.

Options>
Colors>
Partition
Colors

For black-and-white printing, a limited number of grays can replace color. Pajek offers a command to switch between colors and grays in the *Colors* submenu of the *Options* menu in the Draw screen: the command *Partition Colors*. On selection of this command, Pajek displays a dialog box such as that in Figure 19. It contains forty colored squares and the partition's class numbers with which they are associated. For class numbers above 39, Pajek cycles through the first forty colors again: the vertex color of class 40 is equal to the color of class zero, and so on. Press the button labeled "Default GreyScale 1" to change the first five colors (classes

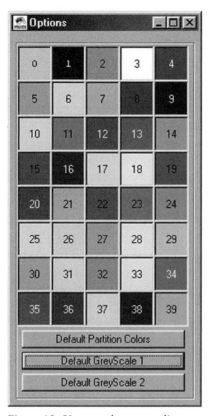

Figure 19. Vertex colors according to a partition in Pajek.

zero to four) into grays (this color scheme is represented in Figure 19) or the button "Default GreyScale 2" to change the first eleven colors into grays. The button "Default Partition Colors" resets the original colors. Unless stated differently, we use partition color scheme "GreyScale 1" in the sociograms printed in this book.

In addition, you can change the color of a particular class by means of the Partition Colors dialog box. If you want to change the color associated with a particular class, click on the square with the desired color and type the number of the class you want this color to be associated with in the dialog box that appears and Pajek will swap the colors. Press the button labeled "Default Partition Colors" if you want to restore the original colors of classes.

When colors or grays do not suffice, you may display the class numbers of the vertices in the vertex labels of a sociogram. Select the option *Partition Clusters* in the *Options>Mark Vertices Using* submenu in the Draw screen. Until you turn this option off, vertex labels in the Draw screen will begin with their class number between brackets, provided, of course, that a network and a matching partition are being drawn.

Options>Mark Vertices Using>Partition Clusters

In Pajek, you can create a new partition that can be edited manually. In the *Partition* menu, the command *Create Null Partition* makes a new partition for the selected network. All vertices are placed in class zero. With the edit command, which was discussed previously (*File>Partition>Edit*),

Partition>Create Null Partition

Draw>Draw-
SelectAll

you can assign vertices to other classes: just change their class numbers in the list. You can obtain the same result with the command *Draw-SelectAll* from the *Draw* menu in the Main screen (shortcut: *Ctrl-a*). This command creates a new partition and displays it in the Draw screen.

Change the class
number of
vertices

In the Draw screen, you can raise the class number of a vertex by 1 in the following way: click on the vertex with the middle mouse button – if available – or with the left mouse button while holding down the *Shift* key on the keyboard. If the cursor is not on a vertex, all class numbers are raised. Clicking a vertex while the *Alt* key is pressed subtracts 1 from the class number and clicking between vertices with the *Alt* key pressed lowers the class numbers of all vertices provided that they are larger than zero, which is the minimum value. In this way, you can easily create a partition that groups a small number of vertices.

Layout>Energy>
Kamada–
Kawai>Fix
selected vertices

In a sociogram with colored classes, it is very easy to move all vertices that belong to one class. Position the cursor *near* but not *on* a vertex, press the left mouse button and drag: all vertices in the class will move simultaneously. This is a very useful technique. In addition, the Kamada–Kawai energy procedure has a special command for energizing networks with class colors; you can restrict the automatic relocation to the vertices in class 0 with the *Fix selected vertices* command. If the partition does not contain vertices in class zero, Pajek issues a warning and it does not change the layout of the network.

menu Partition

menu Partitions

There are several ways to manipulate partitions, make a new partition or combine two partitions. We encounter most of these techniques in later chapters. Suffice it to say here that the commands that involve one partition are located in the *Partition* menu, whereas commands operating on two partitions can be found in the *Partitions* menu of the Main screen.

Exercise I

Open the original manufactures of metal trade network and energize the positions of the core countries only. What changes? Hint: create a new partition in which the core countries belong to class zero and the other countries to class one or higher and energize it with the *Fix selected vertices* command.

2.4   Reduction of a Network

Partitions divide the vertices of a network into a number of mutually exclusive subsets. In other words, a partition splits a network into parts. Therefore, we can use partitions to reduce a network in three ways: extract one part (local view), shrink each class of vertices into one new vertex (global view), or select one part and shrink neighboring classes to focus on the internal structure and overall position of this class (contextual view). We now discuss the three types of reduction.

2.4.1   Local View

The easiest way to reduce a network is to select one class of vertices. Of course, a mere selection of vertices is not very interesting; we must also select all lines between them – and their loops eventually – if we want to inspect the structure of ties in this part of the network. This operation is called subnetwork extraction and its result is called an *induced subnetwork* that offers a *local view*.

> To *extract* a subnetwork from a network, select a subset of its vertices and all lines that are only incident with the selected vertices.

If we want to examine the trade in manufactures of metal within South America, we can extract the subnetwork of South American countries, which is depicted in Figure 20. From the energized drawing, it is clear that Brazil occupies a central position, whereas French Guiana, Martinique, and Guadeloupe are isolated. Apparently, these islands trade with countries in other parts of the world. Finally, geography appears to be important within the continent, because neighboring countries are close in the network.

Application

To extract a subnetwork, we need a network and a partition that defines the sets (classes) of vertices that we want to extract. Therefore, the extraction commands are located in the *Operations* menu. In this section, we use the manufactures of metal trade network (Imports_manufactures.net) and the continents partition (Continent.clu).

To obtain a local view of the South American trade network, use the command *Partition* from the *Operations>Extract from Network* submenu. Because South America is the sixth class in the partition, select class 6 in the two dialog boxes that appear. Pajek produces a new network, which contains fifteen countries. Energize it to obtain a drawing similar to Figure 20.

Operations> Extract from Network> Partition

It is very important to note that the original partitions do not fit the induced subnetwork because the subnetwork contains fewer vertices than

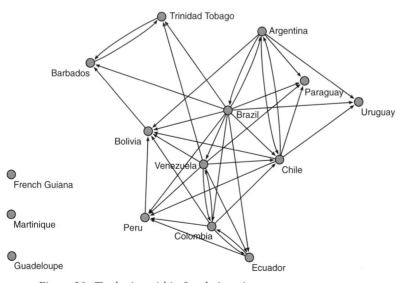

Figure 20. Trade ties within South America.

Pajek								
File	Net	Nets	Operations	Partition	**Partitions**	Permut.	Cluster	Hierarchy	Vect

Network
1. Imports_manufa

Partition
3. World_system.c

Permutation

First Partition: 3. World_system.clu (80)
Second Partition

Extract Second from First
Add Partitions
Fuse Partitions
Expand   ▶
Intersection
Make Random Network
Info   ▶

Figure 21. The *Partitions* menu.

the original vertices. This is a pity, because we may want to know, for instance, the world system position of the countries in the South American trade network. However, we can extract a new partition that matches the induced subnetwork in a few steps.

Partitions>First Partition

Second Partition

Extract Second from First

First, we must select the original partition that we want to translate to the induced subnetwork as the first partition in the *Partitions* menu. Make sure that the world system partition is selected in the Partition drop-down menu. Then, select command *First* in the *Partitions* menu. Nothing seems to happen but open the *Partitions* menu again and you will see the name of the world system partition in it (Figure 21). Second, select the partition that you used to extract the network – in our case the continents partition – as the second partition in the *Partitions* menu. You need this partition to identify the subset of vertices that must be extracted from the world positions partition. Finally, execute the command *Extract Second from*

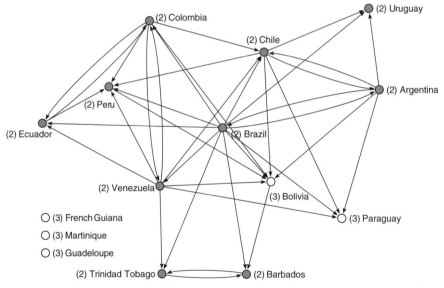

Figure 22. World system positions in South America: (2) semiperiphery and (3) periphery.

First from this menu. Dialog boxes will ask for the class numbers to be extracted and if you type 6 twice, Pajek produces a new partition for the fifteen South American countries. Figure 22 shows the South American trade network drawn with this partition.

2.4.2   Global View

Instead of zooming in on a particular region of the network, we may also zoom out to obtain a global view. Now, we are no longer interested in each individual vertex but we want to study relations between classes, for instance, continents. Which continents have strong trade ties? In this example, a global view of the network covers the whole world but we should note that a global view may also pertain to ties between groups in a local setting.

To *shrink* a network, replace a subset of its vertices by one new vertex that is incident to all lines that were incident with the vertices of the subset in the original network.

In network analysis, we obtain a *global view* by shrinking all vertices of a class to one new vertex. In our example, we shrink all countries within a continent to a new vertex that represents the entire continent (see Figure 23). Lines incident with shrunken vertices are replaced, for instance, all imports by South American countries from European countries are replaced by one new arc pointing from Europe to South America. Its line value is equal to the sum of all original line values. In the network of trade ties, line values indicate the value of imports expressed in

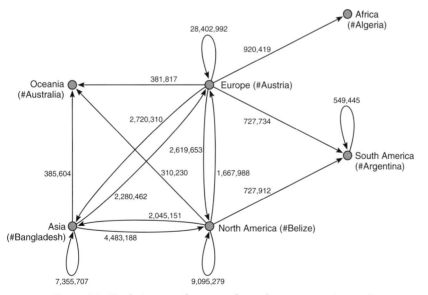

Figure 23. Trade in manufactures of metal among continents (imports in thousands of U.S.$).

thousands of U.S. dollars (U.S.$), so values of lines in the shrunken network represent the value of total imports of metal manufactures. Lines between shrunken vertices within one class, (e.g., trade in manufactures of metal within South America), are replaced by a loop.

Figure 23 shows the world trade network that is shrunk according to continents. To obtain a clear picture, we deleted arcs (total imports) with summed values below three hundred million U.S. dollars. We can see that South American countries import manufactures of metal with a total value of 729 million U.S. dollars from Europe but they do not export a substantial amount to Europe, so there is an asymmetrical trade tie between South America and Europe. The countries in Oceania and Africa are also importing rather than exporting. Trade within South America (549 million U.S.$) is much higher than in Oceania and Africa but internal trade is at its highest in Europe.

Application

Operations> *The command Partition in the Operations>Shrink Network submenu*
Shrink shrinks classes of vertices in a network according to the active partition,
Network> in this case, the continents partition. A dialog box asks for the minimum
Partition number of connections between clusters. This is the minimum number of lines that must exist between shrunken vertices to obtain a new line in the shrunken network. We recommend choosing 1 (the default value). In a second dialog box, you may choose a class of vertices that must not be shrunk to give them a contextual view. Shrink all classes to obtain a global view, so type any class number that is not present in your partition or accept the default value (zero). Finally, Pajek shrinks all classes except the selected class and adds the shrunken network to the Network drop-down menu.

File>Partition> Pajek's *Shrink Network* command also creates a new partition – called
Edit shrinking – along with the new network identifying the classes in the partition that was used to shrink the original network. However, Pajek does not know the meaning of these classes, so it cannot assign meaningful new labels to shrunken classes. It chooses the label of the first vertex of a class that is shrunk and adds a pound sign (#) to obtain a label for the shrunken class. For example, Argentina happens to be the first South American country in the network, so the vertex that represents this continent carries the label "#Argentina" in the shrunken network. We added the names of continents to Figure 23 manually by editing the shrunken partition ("Shrinking") with the *File>Partition>Edit* command (see Section 2.3).

Net>Transform> In Figure 23, we removed lines with summed values below three hun-
Remove>lines dred million U.S. dollars to obtain a clear picture. Lines with low values
with value> can be removed automatically with the command *Remove>lines with*
lower than *value>lower than* in the *Net>Transform* submenu. We entered 300000 as the threshold for this operation, because import values are measured in thousands of U.S. dollars.

In a shrunken network, a class of vertices is replaced by one new vertex; in our example, the Latin American countries are substituted by a new vertex representing this continent. Properties of the original vertices, such

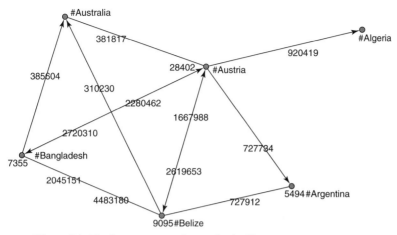

Figure 24. Trade among continents in the Draw screen.

as their world system position, are lost: it is impossible to assign the entire continent to a particular world system position. Therefore, it is impossible to use the data from a partition that was not used to shrink the network.

Note that the way a network is shrunk depends on the option selected in the *Options>Blockmodel – Shrink* submenu. By default, option 0 is selected, which means that the number of links in the original network is used to decide whether a new line is added to the shrunken network. This option causes Pajek to display the dialog box mentioned above. We advise not to select another option from this submenu until you understand blockmodeling, which is presented in Chapter 12.

[Main]
Options>
Blockmodel –
Shrink

Loops, which signify the trade within a continent in this example, cannot be drawn in the Draw screen. If the option *Options>Lines>Mark Lines>with Values* (shortcut *Ctrl-v*) has been selected, the line values are shown in the Draw screen (see Figure 24), including the values of loops, which are printed very close to the vertices. The value of a loop can be examined more closely if you right click a vertex in the Draw screen. Among the lines, which are then listed in the Editing Network dialog box, you can find the loop, for instance, the line from #Argentina to #Argentina. Its line value is 549445, which means that the total value of trade in manufactures of metal among South American countries amounted to 549,445,000 U.S. dollars.

[Draw]
Options>Lines>
Mark Lines>
with Values

2.4.3 Contextual View

A global view shows the position of South America in the world system and a local view clarifies the central position of Brazil within the South American trade network. But how do countries in this regional network relate to the rest of the world? From which continents do the isolated islands import their manufactures of metal? If you want to focus on one class of vertices (e.g., countries on one continent) and take into consideration aggregated ties to the "outside world," you need a contextual view.

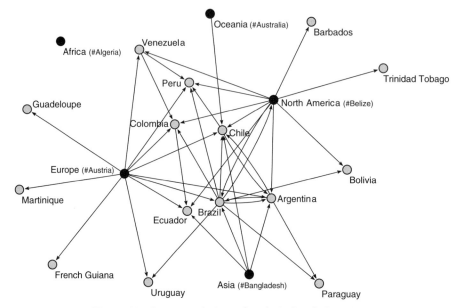

Figure 25. Contextual view of trade in South America.

In a *contextual view*, all classes are shrunk except the one in which you are particularly interested. In Figure 25, all countries are shrunk to continents (black vertices) except the South American countries (gray vertices). We removed ties between continents because we already know them from Figure 23 and we discarded trade in manufactures of metal with summed values under ten million U.S. dollars to obtain an intelligible drawing. This sociogram shows the South American countries in the context of world trade. Clearly, Africa and Oceania are not important trading partners to South American countries. The larger countries on the continent import from Europe and North America, but smaller countries are connected to either North America (Barbados, Trinidad and Tobago, Bolivia) or Europe (Uruguay, Guadeloupe, Martinique, and French Guiana). Former colonial ties surely play a part here.

There are many ways to extract or shrink a network and extraction and shrinking can even be combined. Subnetwork extraction and shrinking are important techniques to dissect a network and to obtain partial views of a network when its structure is too complicated to understand at a first glance.

Application

Operations>
Shrink
Network>
Partition

Net>Transform>
Remove>lines
with value>
lower than

A contextual view is obtained by partially shrinking the network, so we can use the *Shrink Network* command. In the dialog box asking for the class that should not be shrunk, type the appropriate class number, namely class 6 for South America. Lines with summed values below ten million U.S. dollars can be removed automatically with the command *Remove>lines with value>lower than* in the *Net>Transform* submenu as discussed.

Lines between continents can be deleted automatically provided that you have a partition that identifies the continents in the shrunken network. You may create this partition manually with the commands described under *Application* in Section 2.3: create a null partition and assign the five shrunken continents to class 1. Now, you can execute the command *Operations>Transform>Remove Lines>Inside Clusters* to remove the lines between vertices in the continents class (class 1, enter 1 twice in the dialog box).

Operations> Transform> Remove Lines>Inside Clusters

Exercise II
Create a global view of the trade relation (manufactures of metal) between the core, semiperiphery, and the periphery. Explain the structural differences between the world system positions from this network.

2.5   Vectors and Coordinates

Partitions store discrete properties of vertices and vectors store continuous properties. In principle, a continuous property may take any value within a defined range; for instance, the surface of a country may take any value between zero square kilometers (or miles) and the total surface of the Earth. When two countries have different sizes, it is always possible to imagine a country that is smaller than one and bigger than the other.

In practice, of course, we do not care about differences in sizes of countries smaller than a square kilometer, but the principle is important: continuous properties are not meant to group vertices into classes, so they cannot be used to reduce a network by extraction or shrinking. Continuous properties express a particular and often unique value of a vertex, for instance, the wealth of a country indicated by its gross domestic product per capita. In practice, no two countries have exactly the same GDP per capita because it is equal to the quotient of the economic production of a country and the size of its population, both of which are usually figures that characterize no other country. Most quotients yield results with decimals, so a vector is not a list of integers but a list of real numbers.

A *vector* assigns a numerical value to each vertex in a network.

In our discussion of partitions, we have distinguished between structural indices and attributes. This distinction applies to continuous properties or vectors as well. In later chapters, we encounter several examples of vectors that represent structural features of vertices, for instance, their centrality (Chapter 6). GDP per capita of a country is an example of a continuous attribute that is measured independently of the network and added to the graph as additional data: it is a continuous attribute.

A special continuous property of a vertex is its location in a sociogram. Location is expressed by coordinates, real numbers that correspond with positions on one or more axes. For example, the two-dimensional Draw screen has two axes, a horizontal x axis and a vertical y axis. Both axes

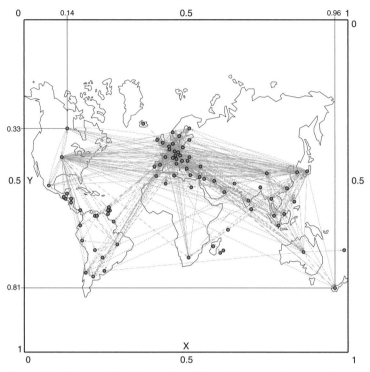

Figure 26. Geographical view of world trade in manufactures of metal, ca. 1994.

range from zero to 1 (see Figure 26). The position of a vertex in the Draw screen is determined by two coordinates (e.g., Canada is located at 0.14 on the *x* axis and 0.33 on the *y* axis).

Because coordinates are real numbers, they can be stored as vectors: one representing the location of vertices on the *x* axis and the other locations on the *y* axis. In Figure 26, we did something special: we made sure that locations in the Draw screen matched geographical locations on a map of the world projected behind the network (see Appendix 2 for details on how to produce this image). Now, vectors express geographical coordinates and we can see geographical patterns in a social network.

Application

File > Vector

Info > Vector

In Pajek, vectors have a drop-down menu of their own. A vector (e.g., the vector GDP_1995.vec containing GDP per capita in 1995) can be opened, edited, and saved like a network or a partition. Basic information can be gathered from the output of the *Info > Vector* command. When you execute this command, you can ask for a list of highest or lowest vector values. In a second dialog box, you can specify the number or boundaries of the classes of values that will be reported in the frequency distribution (Figure 27). Note that vector values are supposed to be continuous, so each value probably occurs only once. As a consequence, it is not informative to list each separate value as an entry in the frequencies table; values must be joined into classes. You may either list selected values that must be

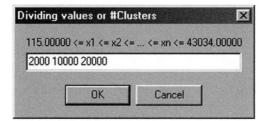

Figure 27. *Info > Vector* dialog box.

used as class boundaries (as in Figure 27) or specify the number of classes preceded by the pound (#) sign.

In the Report screen, the *Info > Vector* command outputs some statistics on the vector values; for instance, it tells us that GDP per capita ranges from 115 to 43,034 U.S. dollars, with an average of 10,249.9 U.S. dollars and standard deviation 10,834.7. Then it prints the requested frequencies table, which is shown in Table 2. The first entry of this table contains the twenty-two countries with GDP per capita ranging from the lowest value up to and including 2,000 U.S. dollars. The second entry contains the twenty-seven countries with GDP per capita over 2,000 U.S. dollars up to and including 10,000 U.S. dollars, and so on. In the first column, the round bracket means "from" and the square bracket means "up to and including."

As we discussed before, partitions and vectors have different applications: partitions serve to select subsets of vertices from a network, whereas vectors specify numerical properties that can be used in calculations. Sometimes, however, you may want to change partitions into vectors or vice versa. It is very easy to convert a partition to a vector: just use the *Make Vector* command in the *Partition* menu. Note, however, that conversion may be meaningful only if classes in a partition express a quantity – if they are numbers that can meaningfully be added, subtracted, and so on. *Partition > Make Vector*

The translation of a vector into a partition is more complicated because you have to change real numbers into integers, which can be done in several ways in the *Vector > Make Partition* submenu. Truncation is the easiest way, which means that you drop the decimals from the real numbers in the vector to obtain integers that can be stored in a partition. A GDP per capita of 115 U.S. dollars up to but not including 116 U.S. dollars is changed to class 115 in a new partition. In the command name, *Abs* stands for absolute, which means that negative vector values are *Vector > Make Partition > by Truncating (Abs)*

Table 2. *Distribution of GNP per Capita in Classes*

Vector Values			Freq	Freq%	CumFreq	CumFreq%
(	...	2000]	22	27.5000	22	27.5000
(	2000...	10000]	27	33.7500	49	61.2500
(	10000...	20000]	15	18.7500	64	80.0000
(	20000...	43043]	16	20.0000	80	100.0000
TOTAL			80	100.0000		

transformed into positive class numbers because partitions cannot hold negative integers.

Vector>Make Partition>by Intervals>First Threshold and Step

Another way to convert a vector into a partition is to recode vector values into classes of fixed width; for instance, recode GDP per capita into classes of 10,000 U.S. dollars. Use the command *by Intervals>First Threshold and Step* in the *Vector>Make Partition* submenu and specify the upper bound of the lowest class as the first threshold (e.g., 10000 for a class including a minimum value up to and including 10,000) and class width as the step (e.g., fill in 10000 again). Note that Pajek does not accept a comma separating thousands from hundreds.

Vector>Make Partition>by Intervals> Selected Thresholds

In the case of GDP per capita, a conversion of values to classes with fixed width is not very useful. GDP per capita is unevenly distributed, so many countries are lumped together in the lowest classes, whereas higher classes contain few countries. In this example, it is better to create classes of unequal width, namely narrow classes for low values and wider classes for higher values, with the command *Selected Thresholds* in the *Make Partitions by Intervals* submenu. In the dialog box, specify the boundaries between classes (e.g., 2000, 10000, and 20000). Just type the numbers separated by spaces and do not use $<=$ as specified in the top of the dialog box. The $<=$ sign means that all classes include the upper boundary.

Draw> Draw-Vector

Draw> Draw-Partition-Vector

[Draw] Options>Size> of Vertices

In a sociogram, vector values are represented by the size of vertices if you use *Draw-Vector* or *Draw-Partition-Vector* from the *Draw* menu. The area of a vertex is proportional to its vector value. Note that GDP per capita ranges from 115 to 43,034 U.S. dollars, but in the Draw screen vertices usually have sizes between 2 to 4. If you draw a network with vector sizes ranging from 115 to 43034, vertices are so large that they do not fit in the screen. Pajek may issue a warning that it changes the size of the vertices. If vertices are still too large, you can adjust the vector values to get reasonable sizes in a drawing. The *Options>Size>of Vertices* command of the Draw screen offers the simplest way to achieve this. In the dialog box issued by this command, enter 0 to activate the *AutoSize* utility of Pajek, which computes optimal vertex sizes automatically.

In Figure 28, countries with higher GDP per capita have larger vertices, according to their vector values. We can see that the wealthiest countries are part of the core and strong semiperiphery, but note that geographical location is also important; Scandinavian countries have similar (high) GDP per capita, whether they belong to the core (Sweden) or to the semiperiphery (Norway, Denmark, Finland).

Representation of vector values by size of vertices is not useful for negative numbers, because negative size is meaningless. Pajek ignores negative signs of vector values when it computes the size of a vertex in a drawing. Vertices with large negative value are drawn as big as vertices with large positive value, which is quite misleading. Always check whether negative vector values exist with the *Info>Vector* command.

Options>Mark Vertices Using>Vector Values

Vector values may also be displayed as vertex labels in the Draw screen: select the option *Vector Values* in the *Options>Mark Vertices Using* submenu. In most networks, the result is visually not very attractive but it is a good way to check the exact vector values of vertices in a drawing.

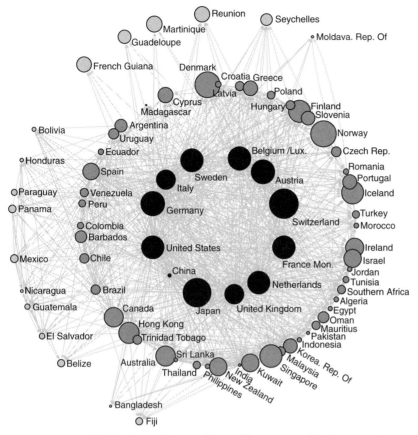

Figure 28. Trade, position in the world system, and GDP per capita.

In Section 2.4.1, we learned how to select a part of a network (e.g., the trade in manufactures of metal among countries of one continent) and how to reduce a partition to fit the extracted network. In a similar way, we can adjust vectors to induced subnetworks. Recall that we need a partition to extract a network; a partition of countries according to their continent is needed for extracting countries of one continent from the network. We can use the same partition for extracting the vector values, for instance, GDP per capita, of the selected countries. First, make sure that the partition which was used to reduce the network is selected in the Partition drop-down menu. Next, execute the command *Extract Subvector* in the *Vector* menu. Just like the command for extracting a partition, the *Extract Subvector* command asks the user to choose a class of vertices or range of classes which must be extracted: enter 6 to select South American countries. Finally, Pajek adds the reduced vector to the Vector drop-down menu.

Vector > Extract Subvector

To obtain a global or contextual view, we shrink networks (see Sections 2.4.2 and 2.4.3). Recall that a class of vertices is replaced by one new vertex in a shrunken network; we replaced all countries belonging to the same continent by a vertex representing the continent. To use vector values associated with the original network (e.g., GDP per capita of a

Vector > Shrink Vector

country) we must also shrink the vector. The command *Shrink Vector* in the *Vector* menu accomplishes this provided that you have selected the relevant vector and the partition that you want to use for the shrinking, namely `Continent.clu`. The command allows you to choose among taking the sum, mean, minimum, maximum, or median of the vertices in a class that will be shrunk. In the example of GDP per capita, it makes sense to calculate the mean or median GDP per capita on a continent.

As noted, coordinates of vertices can be thought of as vectors. In Chapter 1, we have learned that coordinates of vertices are saved in the network data file, so we do not need vectors to store the location of vertices. However, vectors of coordinates are useful if, for instance, you want to use coordinates from one network in another network with the same vertices, for instance, you have a network of trade in another product and you want to use the geographical coordinates from the manufactures of metal trade network.

Net>Vector>Get Coordinate

You can save the present coordinates of the vertices as vectors with the *Get Coordinate* command in the *Net>Vector* submenu. You must create a vector of coordinates for each axis separately. The *Put Coordinate* command in the *Operations>Vector* submenu loads coordinates from vectors: one vector for each axis. In our example, geographical location of countries can be read from two vectors: `x_coordinates.vec` and `y_coordinates.vec`. Note that the save and load commands are listed in different menus. For saving coordinates, you need only a network, but for loading coordinates from a vector you need a vector to load from and a network to add coordinates to. Therefore, the load command is situated in the *Operations* menu.

Operations> Vector>Put Coordinate

Options> Transform>Fit Area

When you load coordinates from a file that was not created by Pajek, the Draw screen may be blank. This happens if the coordinates are not in the range between zero and 1. In this case, use the *Options>Transform>Fit Area* command in the Draw screen and Pajek will fit the sociogram to the size of the screen.

Exercise III
Shrink all countries to continents except the North American countries in the network of trade in metal manufactures. Remove the lines between the continents and trade ties with values under five million U.S. dollars (recall that line values reflect trade in thousands of U.S.$). Draw the energized network with vertex sizes reflecting (mean) GDP per capita. Describe the structure that you see.

2.6   Network Analysis and Statistics

In this chapter, we use attributes of vertices in social network analysis; for instance, we compare GDP per capita of countries to their visual positions in the trade network. We find that countries in the core of the world trade system have higher GDP per capita than countries in the periphery. Thus, social network analysis handles relational data as well as attributes of vertices.

Attributes like GDP per capita are usually analyzed with statistical techniques. GDP per capita is compared, for instance, to population growth and level of education to find out which properties of countries are associated. GDP per capita is found to be higher in countries with a lower population growth and a higher level of education. Statistics offers a wide range of techniques to describe attributes and investigate the association between attributes, but it cannot handle relational data directly. If we are able to express structural properties of vertices as attributes or properties of actors, however, they can be included in statistical analysis.

The position of countries in the world system that we use here was calculated from the world trade network. It is stored in a partition, which can be used in statistical analysis. Continuous structural indices, such as vertex centrality (Chapter 6), can be stored as vectors. Partitions and vectors that store structural properties of vertices are the bridge between network analysis and statistics.

In this book, some examples of statistical analysis are given but are restricted to basic statistical techniques that are incorporated in Pajek. After all, this is not a course in statistics. Nevertheless, the link between statistics and social network analysis should be well understood, because the two techniques make up a powerful combination.

Application

One of the basic statistical techniques implemented in Pajek is the cross-tabulation of two partitions and some measures of association between the classifications represented by two partitions. Let us look at the world trade example. Our partition of positions in the world trade network was derived from the trade in manufactures of metal around 1994. In addition, we have at our disposal a classification of countries according to their position in the world system in 1980 that was proposed by Smith and White (World_system_1980.clu). To analyze the transition of countries between world system positions from 1980 to 1994, we can use simple statistical techniques.

First, we must select the two partitions that we want to compare. In Section 2.3, we learned how to do this. Select the partition with world system positions in 1980 (World_system_1980.clu) in the Partition drop-down menu and execute the command *First Partition* from the *Partitions* menu. Next, select the world system positions partition in 1994 (World_system.clu) and execute the command *Second Partition* in the same menu. When you open the *Partitions* menu now, you will see the names of the selected partitions in the menu. To obtain a cross-tabulation and measures of association, the selected partitions must refer to the same network: the same number of vertices in the same order. It is meaningless to compare partitions that do not refer to exactly the same vertices.

Partitions>First Partition, Second Partition

Second, select the *Info>Cramer's V, Rajski* command from the *Partitions* menu. Pajek will show a cross-tabulation and some measures of association in the Report screen. Table 3 contains the results of the *Info* command. In the cross-tabulation, the rows contain the four classes according to world system position in 1980: core countries in class 1, strong

Partitions>Info> Cramer's V, Rajski

Exploratory Network Analysis with Pajek

Table 3. *Output of the* Info *Command*

Cramer's V, Rajski
Rows: 1. World_system_1980.clu (80)
Columns: 3. World_system.clu (80)

	1	2	3	Total
1	10	1	0	11
2	1	16	0	17
3	0	15	0	15
4	0	4	5	9
TOTAL	11	36	5	52

Warning: 28 vertices with missing values excluded from cross tabulation!
Warning: 8 cells (66.67%) have expected frequencies less than 5!
The minimum expected cell frequency is 0.87!
Chi-Square: 66.2597
Cramer's V: 0. 7982
Rajski(C1↔C2): 0.3422
Rajski(C1→C2): 0.6827
Rajski(C1←C2): 0.4069

semiperiphery in class 2, weak semiperiphery in class 3, and periphery in class 4. The columns contain the three world system positions in 1994: core countries in class 1, semiperiphery in class 2, and periphery in class 3. Countries with an unknown world system position are automatically omitted by Pajek; their number is reported below the table. As a result, the first column represents eleven of the twelve countries in the core of the trade system in 1994. We do not know the world system position of China in 1980, so it is placed in class 9999998 in the `World_system_1980.clu` partition. Note that rows and columns are swapped when the first and second partition are exchanged in the *Partitions* menu.

From this table, we may conclude that the composition of the core has hardly changed between 1980 and 1994 (see the row and column of the cross-tabulation labeled "1"). The countries in the strong and weak semiperiphery in 1980 constitute the major part of the semiperiphery in 1994 (column 2), and four countries were promoted from the periphery in 1980 to the semiperiphery in 1994 (row 4, column 2).

Statistical indices of association tell us how strong the association is. Indices range from 0 to 1 and as a rule of thumb we may say that values between 0 and .05 mean that there is no association, values between .05 and .25 indicate a weak association, values from .25 to .60 indicate a moderate association, and values over .60 indicate a strong association.

In Pajek, two types of association indices are computed: Cramer's V and Rajski's information index. Cramer's V measures the statistical dependence between two classifications. It is not very reliable if the cross-tabulation contains many cells that are (nearly) empty, so Pajek issues a warning if this is the case. Rajski's indices measure the degree to which the information in one classification is preserved in the other classification. It has three variants: a symmetrical version, represented by (C1↔C2) in the output of Pajek, and two asymmetrical versions, which indicate the extent to which the first classification can be predicted by the second (C1←C2) or the second classification can be predicted by the first (C1→C2).

In our example, Cramer's V is not very reliable because many cells have low expected frequencies. Rajski's information indices suggest that world system position in 1994 can be predicted quite well from the positions in 1980: Rajski C1→C2 is .68. The two world system positions are strongly associated.

Exercise IV

Determine the statistical association between the position of countries in the world system of trade in metal manufactures in 1994 and their GDP per capita in 1995. Hint: translate the GDP per capita vector into a partition with four classes: 0 to two thousand U.S. dollars, two to ten thousand U.S. dollars, ten to twenty thousand U.S. dollars, and twenty thousand and higher U.S. dollars.

2.7 Summary

In this chapter, we used properties of vertices to find and interpret patterns of ties in a network. These properties are stored in partitions or vectors. Both partitions and vectors are lists of numbers, one number for each vertex in a network, but numbers in partitions refer to discrete classes, whereas vector values express continuous properties of vertices. Classes in partitions are represented by integers (e.g., countries on the African continent have code 1) and negative class numbers are not allowed. Vectors contain real numbers, which can be negative.

Social networks are often large and complicated. To understand network structure, it helps to study reductions of the network first. Partitions can be used to reduce a network in two ways: by extraction and by shrinking. Extraction is the selection of a subset of vertices from a network as well as the lines among these vertices. You can now concentrate on the structure of a part of the network, which is called a local view. In contrast, shrinking a network means that you lump together sets of vertices and lines incident with these vertices (e.g., you replace all African countries by one vertex representing the African continent). This yields a global view of the network if all classes are shrunk and a contextual view if one class of vertices is not shrunk. In all cases, classes of a partition define the subsets of vertices that are extracted or shrunk.

Properties of social actors that are not based on their structural position in a network are called attributes. They are added to a network to enhance the analysis and interpretation of its structure. Partitions and vectors, however, can also contain structural indices of vertices, which result from network analysis (e.g., the world system position of countries that is inferred from the trade network). These properties may be included in statistical analysis, so partitions and vectors are the nexus between social network analysis and statistics. In Chapter 3 techniques to compute structural properties of vertices in a network are discussed.

2.8   Questions

1. Which of the following statements is correct?
   a. Each property of a vertex or a line is an attribute.
   b. Each property of a vertex is an attribute.
   c. Each nonrelational property of a vertex is an attribute.
   d. Each nonrelational property of a line is an attribute.
2. There are two lists of numbers. Numbers in list A range from -1 to 1 and list B contains numbers between 1 and 10. Which statements can be correct?
   a. A and B are partitions.
   b. A is a partition and B is a vector.
   c. A is a vector and B is a partition.
   d. A and B are vectors.
3. Suppose that the average population growth rate between 1990 and 1995 is available for the countries in the trade network, coded as 0 = negative growth, 1 = 0 to 1.0 percent, 2 = 1.0 to 3.0 percent, and 3 = 3.0 percent and over. Would you use a partition or a vector for these data?
   a. A partition because we cannot add or subtract the codes meaningfully.
   b. A partition because percentages are recoded to integers.
   c. A vector because negative population growth is possible.
   d. A vector because percentages are "real" numbers.
4. What happens to the sociogram of a network if the order of numbers in the accompanying partition is changed?
   a. Nothing changes in the sociogram.
   b. Pajek does not draw the partition any longer.
   c. Pajek uses other colors to draw the vertices.
   d. Vertices are drawn in the wrong color.
5. Which of the following statements is correct about the networks below?

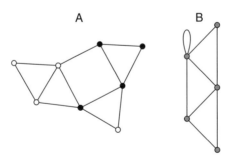

   a. A is extracted from B.
   b. B is extracted from A.
   c. A is shrunk from B.
   d. B is shrunk from A.

6. Which of the following statements is correct about the networks of Question 5?
   a. B is a contextual view of A.
   b. A is a global view of B.
   c. B is a local view of A.
   d. A is a local view of B.

2.9   Assignment

Analyze the manufactures of metal trade network of Asian countries (local view) and their position with regard to other continents (contextual view). Does the structure of trade ties match the world system positions of countries, their prosperity (indicated by GDP per capita), and their geographical locations? Try to apply the theory of the world system, which was outlined in Section 2.2.

2.10   Further Reading

- In *The Modern World System: Capitalist Agriculture and the Origins of the European World-Economy in the Sixteenth Century* (New York: Academic Press, 1974), Immanuel Wallerstein introduced the concept of a world system. The *Capitalist World-Economy* (Cambridge/Paris: Cambridge University Press & Editions de la Maison des Sciences de l'Homme, 1979) is a collection of essays that introduces the theory of a world economy. Bornschier and Trezzini ("Social stratification and mobility in the world system – Different approaches and recent research." In: *International Sociology* 12 (1997), 429–55) offer a summary of research traditions which use the concept of a world system or world economy.
- See Snyder and Kick ("Structural position in the world system and economic growth 1955–70." In: *American Journal of Sociology* 84 (1979), 1096–126) for the first (published) application of social network analysis to world systems theory and see Smith and White ("Structure and dynamics of the global economy – network analysis of international-trade 1965–1980." In: *Social Forces* 70 (1002), 857–93) for the research design followed here.
- Our data on imports are taken from the Statistical Papers. Commodity Trade Statistics [Series D Vol. XLIV, No. 1–34 (1994)] published by the United Nations and we gathered additional economic and demographic data from the Statistical Yearbook of the United Nations (Ed. 43, IVATION Datasystems Inc.). Imports of miscellaneous manufactures of metal are listed as SITC code 69 in the commodity trade statistics.

2.11   Answers

Answers to the Exercises

I. If you want to fix the locations of the countries of the semiperiphery and periphery in the Draw screen, you must create a partition in which the core countries belong to class zero and the other countries to another class. The easiest way to achieve this is to create and draw a new empty partition with the *Draw>Draw-Select All* command in the Main screen. The Draw screen opens and shows the world trade network with all vertices in class zero (light blue). Pressing down the *Shift* key, click somewhere between the vertices to raise all class numbers to one. Then, zoom in on the core countries, dragging your mouse around them while pressing the right mouse button. After you have zoomed in on the core countries, lower their class number back to zero by clicking between the vertices while pressing the *Alt* key. Press Redraw in the Draw screen and you will see that the core countries are the only ones that belong to class zero in the partition. Now you have the right partition and you can select the *Energy>Kamada–Kawai>Fix selected vertices* command to optimize the location of the core countries with respect to the other countries. You will probably see that Japan is pulled toward the Latin American countries, Canada, and the Philippines, whereas Austria moves in the direction of the Eastern European countries (Czech Republic, etc.).

II. Make sure that the partition with world system positions is active in the Partition drop-down menu and select the original trade network in the Network drop-down menu. Shrink the network with the *Operations>Shrink Network>Partition* command. The energized shrunken network may look like the sociogram depicted below (Figure 29), although the loops are not visible in the Draw screen.

The shrunken network shows several characteristics of the world system. First, the values associated with the loops reveal that trade between countries within one position of the world system decreases

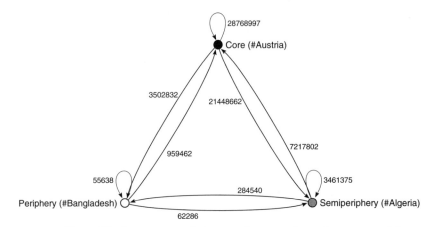

Figure 29. Aggregate trade in manufactures of metal among world system positions.

from core to periphery: from twenty-eight billion U.S. dollars within the core to fifty-five million within the periphery. Second, values of arcs between world system positions show asymmetries in world trade. Core countries export goods at a much higher value to the semiperiphery than vice versa and the semiperiphery exports more to the periphery than the other way around. The values of arcs indicate that the larger the difference in world system position, the larger the difference between exports and imports.

III. In the partition according to continents, `Continent.clu`, the North American countries constitute class 4. Shrink the network according to this partition, entering 4 in the dialog box asking for the class that must not be shrunk. Now you have the contextual view of the North American countries, from which you can remove the lines among the shrunken continents (see Section 2.4.3) and the lines with values less than 5000 (command *Net>Transfrom>Remove>lines with value>lower than*). Make sure that you select the original partition according to continents again in the Partition drop list before you apply the *Vector>Shrink Vector>Mean* command to the GDP per capita vector. Finally, draw the shrunken network with vector values (command *Draw>Draw-Vector* in the Main screen) and energize it. The result should be similar to the sociogram depicted here (Figure 30). The United States occupies a central place in the trade of metal manufactures among the North American countries. South America and to a lesser extent Europe play an important part in the trade ties of the smaller countries on the North American continent.

IV. You can extract a partition from the GDP vector with the *Make Partition>by Intervals>Selected Thresholds* command (see Section 2.5). Select the world system positions partition as the first partition in the *Partitions* menu and the GDP partition as the second. The *Info>Cramer's V, Rajski* command produces the table depicted below (Table 4). The table shows that the core countries have higher

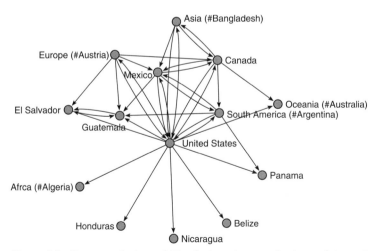

Figure 30. Contextual view of North American trade ties and (mean) GDP per capita.

Table 4. *Cross-Tabulation of World System Positions (Rows) and GDP per Capita (Columns)*

3. World_system.clu (80) / 4. From Vector 3 [2000 10000 20000] (80)					
	1	2	3	4	Total
1	1	0	2	9	12
2	13	21	10	7	51
3	8	6	3	0	17
TOTAL	22	27	15	16	80

Warning: 7 cells (58.33%) have expected frequencies less than 5!
The minimum expected cell frequency is 2.25!
Chi-Square: 31.5510
Cramer's V: 0.4441
Rajski(C1↔C2): 0.0962
Rajski(C1→C2): 0.1460
Rajski(C1←C2): 0.2200

GDP per capita (classes 3 or 4) than countries in the semiperiphery and periphery, which are found in the lower GDP classes. The association between world system position and GDP per capita, however, is weak according to Rajski's indices. The low GDP per capita of China, which is one of the core countries, is partly responsible for the moderate association.

Answers to the Questions in Section 2.8

1. Statement c is correct. Attributes (e.g., the continent of a country) are properties of vertices (viz., countries) and not lines, therefore statements a and d are incorrect. Recall that properties of lines are called line values. Properties that express the structural position of a vertex in a network (e.g., centrality) are distinguished from social, economic, psychological, and other characteristics that do not measure network position. We restrict the concept of an *attribute* to the latter, nonrelational, kind of property.

2. Statements c and d can be correct. List A contains negative numbers, so it must be a vector. List B contains positive numbers, so it is either a partition (if it contains integers) or a vector.

3. Statement a is the right choice. Aggregation of the percentages into four classes of unequal width implies that we cannot make meaningful calculations on the class numbers; for instance, add and divide class numbers of two countries. We cannot say that two countries have average population growth of 2.5. Classes of equal width, such as rounding to the nearest integer, would yield "real" numbers, which may safely be used in calculations. But this is not the case here (statement b). The properties of the original percentages no longer matter after they have been aggregated in classes, so statements c and d are incorrect.

4. Answer d is correct. Changing the order of numbers in a partition does not change the total number of entries or the class numbers. The number of entries of a partition must match the number of vertices in the network, otherwise Pajek does not draw the partition. Answer b is incorrect. Class numbers determine the colors used. Because they do

not change, the same colors are used (answer c is incorrect). The order of entries in a partition determines which class is assigned to which vertex: the class number in the first entry of a partition is assigned to the first vertex in the network, and so on. Changing the order of entries in a partition changes the links between vertices and entries with class numbers, so at least some vertices will be drawn in other colors (answer d).

5. Statement d is correct. Network B contains fewer vertices than network A, so B is extracted or shrunk from A and not the other way around (statements a and c). B is shrunk from A (statement d), because we find a loop in B but no loops in A and because there is no subset of five vertices in network A that are connected like B: three triangles which share a line with at least one other triangle. In fact, the white vertices in network A are shrunk to one new vertex, namely the vertex with the loop in network B.

6. Answer a is correct. B is shrunk from A, but not all vertices are shrunk: the black vertices are not shrunk (see answer to Question 5). A partially shrunken network offers a contextual view.

Part II

Cohesion

Solidarity, shared norms, identity, collective behavior, and social cohesion are considered to emerge from social relations. Therefore, the first concern of social network analysis is to investigate who is related and who is not. Why are some people or organizations related, whereas others are not? The general hypothesis here states that people who match on social characteristics will interact more often and people who interact regularly will foster a common attitude or identity.

In this part of the book, which covers Chapters 3 through 5, we discuss several measures of cohesion. You will learn to detect cohesive subgroups within several types of social networks.

3

Cohesive Subgroups

3.1   Introduction

Social networks usually contain dense pockets of people who "stick to-gether." We call them cohesive subgroups and we hypothesize that the people involved are joined by more than interaction. Social interaction is the basis for solidarity, shared norms, identity, and collective behavior, so people who interact intensively are likely to consider themselves a social group. Perceived similarity, for instance, membership of a social group, is expected to promote interaction. We expect similar people to interact a lot, at least more often than with dissimilar people. This phenomenon is called *homophily*: birds of a feather flock together.

In this chapter, we present a number of techniques to detect cohesive subgroups in social networks, all of which are based on the ways in which vertices are interconnected. These techniques are a means to an end rather than an end in themselves. The ultimate goal is to test whether structurally delineated subgroups differ with respect to other social characteristics, for instance, norms, behavior, or identity. Does the homophily principle work? May we conclude that a cohesive subgroup represents an emergent or established social group?

3.2   Example

In 1948, American sociologists executed a large field study in the Turrialba region, which is a rural area in Costa Rica (Latin America). They were interested in the impact of formal and informal social systems on social change. Among other things, they investigated visiting relations between families living in *haciendas* (farms) in a neighborhood called Attiro. The network of visiting ties (`Attiro.net`, drawn in Figure 31) is a simple directed graph: each arc represents "frequent visits" from one family to another. The exact number of visits was not recorded. Line values classify the visiting relation as ordinary (value 1), visits among kin (value 2), and visits among ritual kin (i.e., between godparent and godchild), but we do not use them in this chapter. Loops do not occur because they are meaningless.

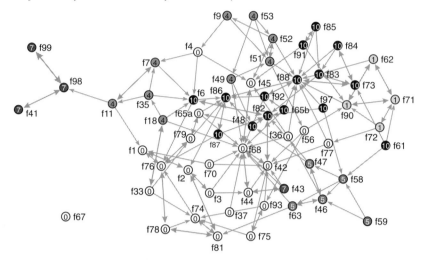

Figure 31. Visiting ties in Attiro.

We compare cohesive subgroups in this network with an ethnographic classification of the families into six family–friendship groupings that were made by the researchers on substantive criteria (Attiro_grouping.clu; we adjusted the class numbers to get optimal grays with the *Options>Colors>Partition Colors>Default Greyscale 2* option). In rural areas where there is little opportunity to move up and down the social ladder social groups are usually based on family relations. All relevant data are collected in the project file Attiro.paj. Open this file now and draw the network with its partition to obtain a sociogram like Figure 31 (*Draw>Draw-Partition* command). You may want to use real colors instead of grays for easy recognition of the family–friendship groupings.

Which cohesive subgroups can we find in the Attiro network and do they match the family–friendship groupings? Figure 31 offers a visual impression of the kin visits network and the family–friendship groupings, which are identified by the colors and numbers within the vertices (in the Draw screen, class numbers are displayed in parentheses next to the vertices). As is shown, the network is tightly knit with family–friendship groupings 0 and 10 dominating the center. Most families that belong to one grouping are connected by visiting ties, so they are rather close in the network. Exceptions occur, however; notably family f43 (bottom right), which is separated from the other vertices in the seventh family–friendship grouping (left). In subsequent sections, we set out this first impression in detail.

3.3   Density and Degree

Intuitively, cohesion means that a social network contains many ties. More ties between people yield a tighter structure, which is, presumably, more cohesive. In network analysis, the density of a network captures this idea.

It is the percentage of all possible lines that are present in a network. Maximum density is found in a complete simple network, that is, a simple network in which all pairs of vertices are linked by an edge or by two arcs, one in each direction. If loops are allowed, all vertices have loops in a complete network.

> *Density* is the number of lines in a simple network, expressed as a proportion of the maximum possible number of lines.
>
> A *complete network* is a network with maximum density.

In this definition of density, multiple lines and line values are disregarded. Intuitively, multiple lines between vertices and higher line values indicate more cohesive ties. Although density measures have been proposed that account for multiplicity and line values, we prefer not to present them. We count distinct lines only, which means that we treat a multiple line as one line and multiple loops as one loop. We discuss other measures that capture the contribution of multiple lines and line values to cohesion in Chapter 5.

In the kin visiting relation network, density is 0.045, which means that only 4.5 percent of all possible arcs are present. It is very common to find density scores as low as this one in social networks of this size. Density is inversely related to network size: the larger the social network, the lower the density because the number of possible lines increases rapidly with the number of vertices, whereas the number of ties which each person can maintain is limited. In a visiting relation network, there is a practical limit to the number of families you can visit. Therefore, including more families in the network will reduce network density.

This is a problem if you want to interpret or compare network density. Density in the visiting network in San Juan Sur, which is another neighborhood in the Turrialba region, is 0.036. This is slightly lower than in Attiro but the difference may be due to a larger number of families in San Juan Sur (seventy-five families). Therefore, we can not draw a conclusion from this comparison.

> The *degree* of a vertex is the number of lines incident with it.

Network density is not very useful because it depends on the size of the network. It is better to look at the number of ties in which each vertex is involved. This is called the degree of a vertex. Vertices with high degree are more likely to be found in dense sections of the network. In Figure 31, family f88 (a member of family–friendship grouping number 10) is connected to thirteen families by fifteen visiting ties (note that the double-sided arcs between f88 and f73, f92 indicate that these families are linked by mutual visits), so its degree is 15. The lines incident with this family contribute substantively to the density of the network near this family.

A higher degree of vertices yields a denser network, because vertices entertain more ties. Therefore, we can use the *average degree* of all vertices to measure the structural cohesion of a network. This is a better measure of overall cohesion than density because it does not depend on network size, so average degree can be compared between networks of different sizes.

> Two vertices are *adjacent* if they are connected by a line.
>
> The *indegree* of a vertex is the number of arcs it receives.
>
> The *outdegree* is the number of arcs it sends.

In a simple undirected network, the degree of a vertex is equal to the number of vertices that are adjacent to this vertex: its *neighbors*. Each line that is incident with the vertex connects it to another vertex because multiple lines and loops, which contribute to the degree of a vertex without connecting it to new neighbors, do not occur. In a directed network, however, there is a complication because we must distinguish between the number of arcs received by a vertex (its indegree) and the number of arcs sent (its outdegree). Note that the sum of the indegree and the outdegree of a vertex does not necessarily equal the number of its neighbors, for instance, family f88 is involved in fifteen visiting ties but it has thirteen adjacent families because families f73 and f92 are counted twice (Figure 31).

In this section, we restrict ourselves to degree in undirected networks. When we encounter a directed network, we symmetrize it, which means that we turn unilateral and bidirectional arcs into edges. A discussion of indegree in directed occurs in Chapter 9, which presents the concept of prestige.

> To *symmetrize* a directed network is to replace unilateral and bidirectional arcs by edges.

Application

[Main] Info>
Network>
General

Let us analyze the network of visiting ties in Attiro (`Attiro.net`), which contains neither multiple lines nor loops. In Pajek, the density of a network can be obtained by means of the *Network* submenu of the *Info* menu in the Main screen. Choose the command *General* to display basic information on the selected network, such as the number of vertices and lines as well as its density. When executed, this command displays a dialog box asking the user to specify the number of lines to be displayed. When you are only interested in network density, request zero lines. Pajek computes two density indices in the Report screen. The first index allows for loops and the second does not. Because loops are meaningless in a visiting relation network – people do not visit themselves – the second index is valid. Density in the directed network is 0.045.

Net>Transform>
Arcs→Edges>
All

File>Network>
Save

In undirected simple networks, the degree of a vertex is equal to its number of neighbors. This is the easiest interpretation of degree, so we concentrate on undirected simple networks in this section. The kin visiting network, however, is directed, so we must symmetrize it first. Use the *Arcs->Edges>All* command in the *Net>Transform* submenu to replace all arcs by edges. Pajek will ask whether you want to make a new network and we advise you to do so because you may want to use the directed network later. Next, Pajek asks whether you want to remove multiple lines. To obtain a simple undirected network, that is, a network without multiple lines and loops, you should choose option 1 (sum the line values of lines that will be joined into a new line), 2 (count the number of lines that are joined), 3 (preserve the minimum value of joined lines), or 4 (take their maximum line value) in this dialog box. It does not matter which of these four options you choose because in this chapter we pay no attention to line values. Now, the network is symmetrized and it is simple because multiple lines are removed and there were no loops in the original network. You may want to save it (*File>Network>Save*) for future use under a new name (e.g., Attiro_symmetrized.net).

Degree is a discrete attribute of a vertex (it is always an integer), so it is stored as a partition. We obtain the degree partition with a command from the *Net>Partitions>Degree* submenu: *Input*, *Output*, or *All*. *Input* counts all incoming lines (indegree), *Output* counts all outgoing lines (outdegree), and *All* counts both. Note that an edge, which has no direction, is considered to be incoming as well as outgoing, so each edge is counted once by all three degree commands. In an undirected network, therefore, it makes no difference whether you select *Input*, *Output*, or *All*. In addition, these commands create a vector with the normalized degree of vertices, that is, their degree divided by the number of potential neighbors in the network.

Net>Partitions> Degree

The command *Info>Partition* displays the partition as a frequency table (see Table 5). Class numbers represent degree scores, so we can see that the degree of vertices varies markedly from zero to fourteen neighbors in the symmetrized network. Clearly, family f68 is connected to most families by visiting ties. One family, family f67, is isolated in the network: it is linked to no other families by regular visits.

Info>Partition

The average degree of all vertices can be calculated from the degree distribution. In this example, the class numbers in the degree partition

Partition>Make Vector

Table 5. *Frequency Distribution of Degree in the Symmetrized Network of Visits*

Class	Freq	Freq%	CumFreq	CumFreq%	Representative
0	1	1.6667	1	1.6667	f67
1	3	5.0000	4	6.6667	f37
2	1	1.6667	5	8.3333	f59
3	19	31.6667	24	40.0000	f3
4	20	33.3333	44	73.3333	f1
5	4	6.6667	48	80.0000	f45
6	6	10.0000	54	90.0000	f51
7	2	2.3333	56	93.3333	f6
8	1	1.6667	57	95.0000	f86
9	1	1.6667	58	96.6667	f42
13	1	1.6667	59	98.3333	f88
14	1	1.6667	60	100.0000	f68
SUM	60	100.0000			

represent integers, namely the number of neighbors of a vertex, but this is not true for all partitions. As a consequence, no average class number is calculated and presented by the *Info>Partition* command. To obtain the average degree, we have to convert the degree partition to a vector and calculate summary statistics on the vector. In Chapter 2, you learned how to do this: use *Partition>Make Vector* to create a vector from the degree partition and use the *Info>Vector* command to obtain the average, which is 4.27. Families in Attiro regularly visit more than four families on average.

Exercise I
Open the visiting relation network in San Juan Sur (`SanJuanSur.net`), symmetrize it, and determine the average degree. Is this network more cohesive than the Attiro network in this respect?

3.4   Components

Vertices with a degree of one or higher are connected to at least one neighbor, so they are not isolated. However, this does not mean that they are necessarily connected into one lump. Sometimes, the network is cut up in pieces. Isolated sections of the network may be regarded as cohesive subgroups because the vertices within a section are connected, whereas vertices in different sections are not. The network of visits in Attiro is not entirely connected (see Figure 31). In this section, we identify the connected parts of a network, which are called components, but we must introduce some auxiliary graph theoretic concepts first.

Let us have a look at a simple example (Figure 32). Intuitively, it is clear that some vertices are connected to other vertices, whereas others are not; for instance, vertex v2 is adjacent to no other vertex, but the other four vertices have one or more neighbors. If we consider the arcs to be roads, we can walk from vertex v5 to v3 and, not considering the direction of the arcs, we can proceed from vertex v3 to v1. We say that there is a semiwalk from vertex v5 to vertex v1. From vertex v2, however, we can walk nowhere.

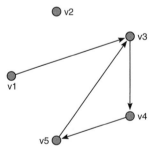

Figure 32. A simple unconnected directed network.

A *semiwalk* from vertex *u* to vertex *v* is a sequence of lines such that the end vertex of one line is the starting vertex of the next line and the sequence starts at vertex *u* and ends at vertex *v*.

A *walk* is a semiwalk with the additional condition that none of its lines are an arc of which the end vertex is the arc's tail.

Imagine that the arcs represent one-way streets, so we take into account the direction of the arcs. Now, we can drive from vertex v5 to vertex v3 but we cannot arrive at vertex v1. In graph theory, we say that there is a walk from vertex v5 to v3 but there is not a walk from vertex v5 to v1. In a walk, you have to follow the direction of the arcs.

Walks and semiwalks are important concepts but we need another, related concept to define whether a network is connected. We should note that there are many – in fact, infinitely many – walks from vertex v5 to v3 in our example; for instance, v5→v3→v4→v5→v3 is also a walk and we may repeat the circular route v5→v3→v4→v5 as many times as we like. Clearly, we do not need these repetitions to establish whether vertices are connected, so we use the more restricted concepts of paths and semipaths, which demand that each vertex on the walk or semiwalk occurs only once, although the starting vertex may be the same as the end vertex. In the example, the walk v5→v3 is a path but the walk v5→v3→v4→v5→v3 is not because vertices v5 and v3 occur twice. A path is more efficient than a walk, one might say, because it does not pass through one junction more than once.

A *semipath* is a semiwalk in which no vertex in between the first and last vertex of the semiwalk occurs more than once.

A *path* is a walk in which no vertex in between the first and last vertex of the walk occurs more than once.

Now we can easily define the requirements a network must meet to be connected. A network is weakly connected – often we just say connected – if all vertices are connected by a semipath. In a (weakly) connected network, we can "walk" from each vertex to all other vertices if we neglect the direction of the arcs, provided that there are any. The example of Figure 32 is not connected because vertex v2 is isolated: it is not included in any semipath to the other vertices.

In directed networks, there is a second type of connectedness: a network is strongly connected if each pair of vertices is connected by a path. In a strongly connected network, you can travel from each vertex to any other vertex obeying the direction of the arcs. Strong connectedness is more restricted than weak connectedness: each strongly connected network is also weakly connected but a weakly connected network is not necessarily strongly connected. Our example is not weakly connected, so it cannot be strongly connected.

> A network is (weakly) *connected* if each pair of vertices is connected by a semipath.
>
> A network is *strongly connected* if each pair of vertices is connected by a path.

Although the network of our example is not connected as a whole, we can identify parts that are connected; for instance, vertices v1, v3, v4, and v5 are connected. In comparison with the isolated vertex v2, these vertices are relatively tightly connected, so we may say that they are a cohesive group. If the relation represents communication channels, all vertices except vertex v2 may exchange information. Vertices v1, v3, v4, and v5 constitute a (weak) component because they are connected by semipaths and there is no other vertex in the network which is also connected to them by a semipath.

Formally, we say that a (weak) component is a maximal (weakly) connected subnetwork. Remember that a subnetwork consists of a subset of the vertices of the network and all lines between these vertices. The word *maximal* means that no other vertex can be added to the subnetwork without destroying its defining characteristic, in this case connectedness. If we would add the only remaining vertex – v2 – the subnetwork is no longer connected. In contrast, if we would omit any of the vertices v1, v3, v4, or v5, the subnetwork is not a component because it is not maximal: it does not comprise all connected vertices.

Likewise, we can define a strong component, which is a maximal strongly connected subnetwork. The example network contains three strong components. The largest strong component is composed of vertices v3, v4, and v5, which are connected by paths in both directions. In addition, there are two strong components consisting of one vertex each, namely vertex v1 and v2. Vertex v2 is isolated and there are only paths from vertex v1 but no paths to this vertex, so it is not strongly connected to any other vertex. It is asymmetrically linked to the larger strong component. In general, the ties among strong components are either asymmetrical or absent. In Chapter 10, we elaborate on this feature.

> A (weak) *component* is a maximal (weakly) connected subnetwork.
>
> A *strong component* is a maximal strongly connected subnetwork.

In an undirected network, lines have no direction, so each semiwalk is also a walk and each semipath is also a path. As a consequence, there is only one type of connectedness, which is equivalent to weak connectedness in directed networks, and one type of component. In an undirected network, components are isolated from one another, there are no lines between vertices of different components. This is similar to weak components in directed networks.

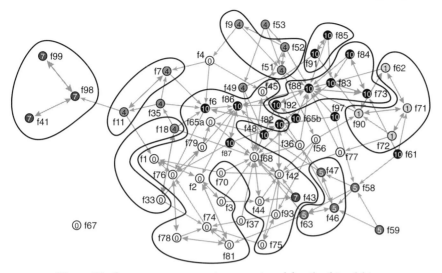

Figure 33. Strong components (contours) and family–friendship groupings (vertex colors and numbers) in the network of Attiro.

In a directed network, should you look for strong or weak components? The choice depends on substantive and practical considerations. Substantive reasons pertain to the importance you attach to the direction of a relation: does it matter to social processes whether actor A turns to actor B, actor B turns to actor A, or both? If the flow of communication is being investigated, it probably does not matter who initiates a contact. If family f98 visits both families f11 and f99 (Figure 33, left), it may inform family f11 about family f99 and the other way around. Families f11 and f99 may share information although there is no path between them. In this case, direction of the relation is quite unimportant and weak components are preferred.

If substantive arguments are indecisive, the number and size of components may be used to choose between strong and weak components. Recall that strong components are more strict than weak components, which means that strong components usually are smaller than weak components. It is a good strategy to detect weak components first. If a network is dominated by one large weak component (e.g., the network in Attiro), we advise to use strong components to break down the weak component in a next step.

Figure 33 shows the strong components in the visiting relation network. Each strong component of more than one vertex is manually delineated by a contour. Each vertex outside the contours is a strong component on its own (e.g., families f67 and f59). The original classification according to family–friendship groupings is represented by vertex colors and by the numbers inside the vertices. We see that the large weak component is split up in several small strong components, some of which approximate family–friendship groupings, for instance, family–friendship groupings one (at the right) and seven (at the left).

Components can be split up further into denser parts by considering the number of distinct, that is, noncrossing, paths or semipaths that connect the vertices. Within a weak component, one semipath between each pair of vertices suffices but there must be at least two different semipaths in a *bi-component*. The concept of a bi-component is discussed in Chapter 7. This can be generalized to *k-connected components*: maximal subnetworks in which each pair of vertices is connected by at least *k* distinct semipaths or paths. A weak component, for instance, is a 1-connected component and a bi-component is a 2-connected component.

Application

Net>
Components>
Strong

Draw>
Draw-Partition

With Pajek, it is easy to find components in the visiting relation network (Attiro.net). The *Net* menu has a submenu to find three types of components: strong, weak, and bi-components. We discuss bi-components in Chapter 7. When you execute commands *Strong* or *Weak*, a dialog box appears asking for the minimum size of components. Sometimes, very small components are not interesting, for instance, isolated vertices, which are counted as separate components if minimum component size is set to 1 vertex. Raise this number to exclude them. The command creates a partition in which each class represents a component. Draw the network with the strong components partition (*Draw>Draw-Partition*) to see the clusters enclosed in contours in Figure 33. Draw it with the original family–friendship groupings partition to obtain the clusters represented by vertex color in Figure 33. Figure 33 combines these two layouts.

Net>
Components>
Weak

In undirected networks, it makes no difference whether you select strong or weak components because the commands yield identical results. Furthermore, weak components in a directed network are equal to components in the symmetrized network. Therefore, it is not necessary to symmetrize a directed network when you want to know its components: just compute weak components in the directed network.

3.5   Cores

The distribution of degree reveals local concentrations of ties around individual vertices but it does not tell us whether vertices with a high degree are clustered or scattered all over the network. In this section, we use degree to identify clusters of vertices that are tightly connected because each vertex has a particular minimum degree within the cluster. We pay no attention to the degree of one vertex but to the degree of all vertices within a cluster. These clusters are called *k-cores* and *k* indicates the minimum degree of each vertex within the core; for instance, a 2-core contains all vertices that are connected by degree two or more to other vertices within the core. A *k*-core identifies relatively dense subnetworks, so they help to find cohesive subgroups. As is shown, however, a *k*-core is not necessarily a cohesive subgroup itself!

> A *k-core* is a maximal subnetwork in which each vertex has at least degree *k* within the subnetwork.

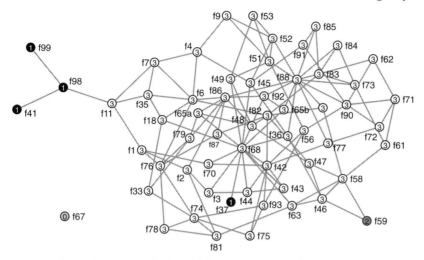

Figure 34. *k*-cores in the visiting network at Attiro.

The definition of a *k*-core is more complicated than you might think. It is easiest to explain if we apply it to a simple undirected network and, as a rule, we apply it only to this type of network. In a simple undirected network, the degree of a vertex is equal to the number of its neighbors, as discussed in Section 3.3, so a *k*-core contains the vertices that have at least *k* neighbors within the core. A 2-core, then, consists of all vertices that are connected to at least two other vertices within the core. In the definition, the word *maximal* means that we are interested in the largest set of vertices that satisfy the required property, in this case a minimum number of *k* neighbors within the core.

The undirected visiting relation network, which we obtained by symmetrizing the directed network, contains a large 3-core (white vertices in Figure 34). In the 3-core, each family is connected to at least three other families. In addition, there is a 2-core (dark gray), a 1-core (black), and a 0-core (light gray). Do the *k*-cores in the kin visits network represent cohesive subgroups? For the 3-core, this seems to be true because it is clearly a dense pocket within the network. The 2-core and the 0-core, however, consist of one vertex (families f59 and f67) and the 1-core is situated at two different places in the network (at the left and at the bottom). It is silly to regard them as cohesive subgroups.

The meaning of the lower *k*-cores can be illustrated by the simple example in Figure 35. This little network is connected, so all ten vertices

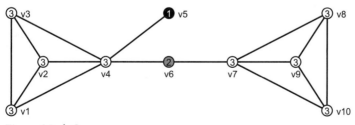

Figure 35. *k*-Cores.

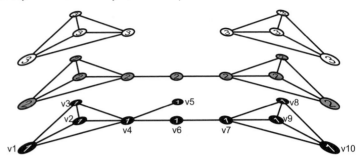

Figure 36. Stacking or nesting of *k*-cores.

are linked to at least one other vertex. As a result, all vertices belong to the 1-core, which is drawn in black at the bottom of Figure 36. One vertex, v5, has only one neighbor, so it is not part of the 2-core (gray, in the middle of Figure 36). Vertex v6 has a degree of 2, so it does not belong to the 3-core (white, in the top of Figure 36). A vertex belongs to the highest *k*-core, so the resulting sociogram looks like Figure 35: the different levels are stacked one on top of the other. We say that *k*-cores are *nested*: a vertex in a 3-core is also part of a 2-core, but not all members of a 2-core belong to a 3-core.

The example illustrates another feature of *k*-cores, namely that a *k*-core does not have to be connected. As a result of nesting, different cohesive subgroups within a *k*-core are usually connected by vertices that belong to lower cores. In Figure 36, vertex v6, which is part of the 2-core, connects the two segments of the 3-core. If we eliminate the vertices belonging to cores below the 3-core, we obtain a network consisting of two components, which identify the cohesive subgroups within the 3-core.

This is exactly how *k*-cores help to detect cohesive subgroups: remove the lowest *k*-cores from the network until the network breaks up into relatively dense components. Then, each component is considered to be a cohesive subgroup because they have at least *k* neighbors within the component. In (very) large networks, this is an effective way of finding cohesive subgroups. In the Attiro visiting relation network, however, this strategy does not work because there are no unconnected *k*-cores. Elimination of the lower *k*-cores does not split the network into separate components.

Application

Net>Partitions>
Core>Input,
Output, All

In Pajek, *k*-cores are detected with the *Core* command in the *Net> Partitions* submenu. The *Input*, *Output*, and *All* commands operate exactly in the same way as in the *Net>Partitions>Degree* submenu, distinguishing among input cores, output cores, and cores that ignore the direction of lines. We advise using the *All* command and applying it only to simple undirected networks. The command yields a partition that assigns each vertex to the highest *k*-core in which it appears. Vertex colors and the numbers inside the vertices display the *k*-core partition in Figure 34. In this example, the *k*-cores do not match the ethnographic clustering into family–friendship groupings.

*Operations>
Extract from
Network>
Partition*

*Net>
Components>
Strong*

With the *k*-core partition, you can easily delete low *k*-cores from the network to distill the densest sections in the network. Select the *k*-core partition in the Partition drop list and execute the *Operations>Extract from Network>Partition* command. Select the lowest and highest *k*-cores that you want to extract from the network, in this case the third *k*-core. Subsequently, use the *Net>Components>Strong* command to check whether the selected *k*-core levels are split into two or more components.

Exercise II
Determine the *k*-cores in the network `ExerciseII.net` and extract the 4-core from this network.

3.6   Cliques and Complete Subnetworks

In the visiting relation network, most vertices belong to one large 3-core. If we want to split this large 3-core into subgroups, we need a stricter definition of a cohesive subgroup. In this section, we present the strictest structural form of a cohesive subgroup, which is called a clique: a set of vertices in which each vertex is directly connected to all other vertices. In other words, a clique is a subnetwork with maximum density.

A *clique* is a maximal complete subnetwork containing three vertices or more.

The size of a clique is the number of vertices in it. Maximal complete subnetworks of size 1 and 2 exist, but they are not very interesting because they are single vertices and edges or bidirectional arcs, respectively. Therefore, cliques must contain a minimum of three vertices.

Unfortunately, it is very difficult to identify cliques in large networks: the computational method is very time-consuming and even medium-sized networks may contain an enormous number of cliques. In this book, therefore, we restrict ourselves to the analysis of small complete subnetworks, which may or may not be cliques. We concentrate on complete *triads*, that is, complete subnetworks consisting of three vertices, but the argument is easily extended to complete subnetworks of size four or more.

Figure 37 shows the complete undirected and directed triad as well as an example of a network that contains several complete triads. Note that the complete triad with vertices v1, v5, and v6 is a clique because we cannot add another vertex from the network to this subnetwork such that it is still complete. This subnetwork is maximal with respect to completeness. In contrast, triad v2, v4, v5 is not a clique because we can add vertex v3 and the subnetwork is still complete. Vertices v2 to v5 constitute a clique of size 4, which, by the way, is made up of four complete triads.

Figure 37 shows a very important feature of cliques and complete subnetworks, namely that they can overlap. The complete triad v1, v5, v6 overlaps with the complete triad v2, v4, v5 because they share vertex v5. As a consequence, it is impossible to assign all vertices unambiguously

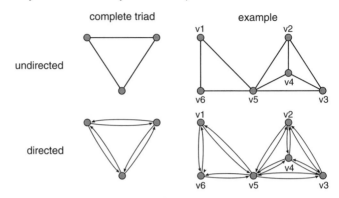

Figure 37. The complete triad and an example.

to one clique or complete subnetwork. We cannot equate each clique or complete subnetwork with a cohesive subgroup and this is a serious complication if we want to classify vertices into cohesive subgroups.

In social network analysis, structures of *overlapping cliques*, which are thought to represent social circles rather than individual cliques, are regarded as cohesive subgroups. Cliques or complete triads are the densest sections or "bones" of a network, so the structure of overlapping cliques are considered its "skeleton." Sometimes, additional conditions are imposed on the overlap of cliques (e.g., a minimum number or percentage of vertices that two cliques must share) but we do not use them here.

Application

Net>Transform> Arcs →Edges> All

Because clique detection is particularly useful for dense networks, we now analyze the symmetrized (undirected) network of visiting ties in Attiro, which has higher density (0.072) than the directed network (0.045). Symmetrize the network with the *Net>Transform>Arcs→Edges>All* command and avoid multiple lines by selecting option 1, 2, 3, or 4 in the "Remove multiple lines?" dialog box. This network is too dense to spot complete triads and structures of overlapping triads visually. Even the best energized drawing contains many crossing edges, which makes it difficult to see complete triads; there are probably many.

Nets>First Network, Second Network

The first step, then, is to detect all complete triads within the network. In other words, we have to find all occurrences of one particular network or fragment – in our case, a complete triad – in another network, namely the original network. The command is situated in the *Nets* menu, which contains all operations on two networks, and it requires that the fragment and the original network are identified as the *First Network* and *Second Network*, respectively, in this menu. The project file Attiro.paj contains the network triad_undir.net, which is a single complete undirected triad. Select this network as the first network in the *Nets* menu and select the symmetrized visiting ties network as the second network: select the network in the drop list and click the *Nets>First Network* or *Nets>Second Network* command. Now, the names of these networks are shown in the *Nets* menu.

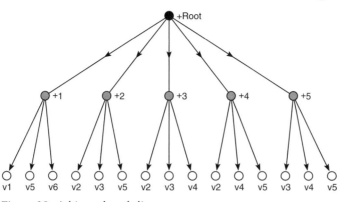

Figure 38. A hierarchy of cliques.

Next, we can find all complete triads in the network by executing the *Find* command of the *Fragment (1 in 2)* submenu. Executing this command, Pajek reports the number of fragments it has found and it creates one or more new data objects, depending on the options selected in the *Options* submenu of the *Fragment* command. We recommend to have the option *Extract subnetwork* checked only. This produces a network labeled "Subnetwork induced by Sub fragments." It is called *induced* because Pajek selects vertices and lines within the fragments (complete triads) only. This network contains the overlapping cliques that we are looking for and we discuss it at the end of this section. In addition, Pajek creates a hierarchy and a partition. The partition counts the number of fragments to which each vertex belongs and the hierarchy lists all fragments: complete triads in our example.

Nets>Fragment (1 in 2)>Find

Nets>Fragment (1 in 2)>Options

A *hierarchy* is a data object that we have not yet encountered. It is designed to classify vertices if a vertex may belong to several classes. In the visiting relation network, for instance, a family may belong to several complete triads. A hierarchy is a list of groups and each group may consist of groups or vertices. Ultimately, vertices are the units which are grouped. Figure 38 shows the hierarchy for the example of overlapping complete triads of Figure 37. There are five complete triads; each of them is represented by a gray vertex in Figure 38. Each complete triad consists of three vertices (white in Figure 38). Note that most vertices appear more than once because the triads overlap. At the top of the hierarchy, one node (black) connects all groups; it is called the root of the hierarchy.

A hierarchy is stored as a data object in the Hierarchy drop-down menu. You can browse a hierarchy in an Edit screen, which is opened with the *Edit* command in the *File>Hierarchy* submenu or by the Edit button to the left of the Hierarchy drop list. On opening, the Edit screen displays the root only. Click on the plus sign preceding the root to display the (first level of) groups in the hierarchy.

Hierarchy drop-down menu

File>Hierarchy> Edit

Figure 39 shows part of the 36 complete triads in the visiting relation network of Attiro. Select a group with your left mouse button and click with the right mouse button to display its vertices in a separate window. If the original network is selected in the Network drop-down menu, vertex

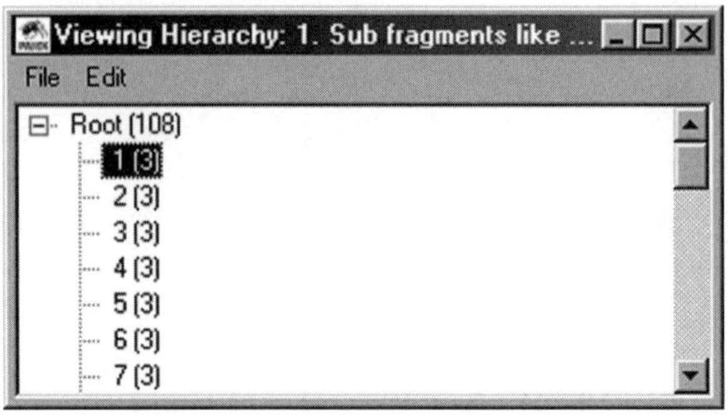

Figure 39. Viewing a hierarchy in an Edit screen.

labels are displayed next to their numbers in this window. In this way, you can see which vertices belong to a complete triad.

Info>Partition   Now let us turn to the induced network and the partition created by the *Nets>Fragment (1 in 2)>Find* command. The partition, labeled "Sub fragments," shows the number of triads that include a particular vertex. Using the *Info>Partition* command in the Main screen, you can see that two vertices belong to no less than seven complete triads, whereas thirteen vertices are not included in any of the complete triads. The latter vertices are not part of the structure of overlapping cliques, so they are eliminated from the induced network (labeled "Subnetwork induced by Sub fragments"), which contains the remaining forty-seven vertices of the Attiro network.

Partitions>   With this partition, we can make the original partition according to
Extract Second   family–friendship groupings (in `Attiro_grouping.clu`) match the
from First   new induced network. Select the original partition as the first partition in the *Partitions* menu and select the fragments partition as the second partition in this menu. Then execute the *Partitions>Extract Second from First* command and specify one as the lowest class number and seven (or higher) as the highest class number to be extracted. Pajek creates a new partition holding the family–friendship groupings of the forty-seven vertices in the induced network of overlapping complete triads. Draw this network and partition, and energize it with Kamada–Kawai to obtain a sociogram such as Figure 40 (use *Default GreyScale 2* in the *[Draw] Options>Colors>Partition Colors* dialog screen to get the grays).

The induced subnetwork is displayed in Figure 40. It has three components of overlapping complete triads, so we say that we have found three social circles under the criterion of complete triads that share at least one member. Family–friendship grouping 1 is a separate social circle but the other family–friendship groupings are interconnected although they are clearly clustered within the largest component. Family–friendship grouping 10 occupies a pivotal position in this structure, connecting groupings zero, 5, and part of family–friendship grouping 4.

In a directed network, you may follow the same procedure but you have to use a complete directed triad as a fragment (e.g., `triad_dir.net`). In general, you will find fewer cliques in the directed network than undirected cliques in the symmetrized network. In the directed Attiro network, for

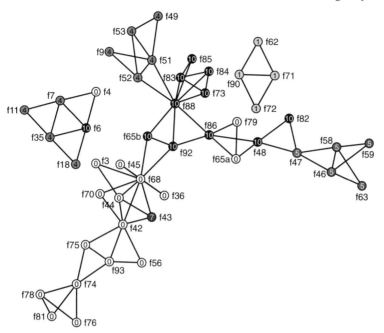

Figure 40. Complete triads and family–friendship groupings (colors and numbers inside vertices).

instance, there is just one complete directed triad, containing families f62, f71, and f90, so we cannot speak of overlapping cliques in the directed network.

3.7 Summary

In this chapter, social cohesion was linked to the structural concepts of density and connectedness. Density refers to the number of links between vertices. A network is strongly connected if it contains paths between all of its vertices and it is weakly connected when all of its vertices are connected by semipaths. Connected networks and networks with high average degree are thought to be more cohesive. This also applies to sections of a network (subnetworks). We expect local concentrations of ties in a social network to identify cohesive social groups.

There are several techniques to detect cohesive subgroups based on density and connectedness, three of which are presented in this chapter: components, k-cores, and cliques or complete subnetworks. All three techniques assume relatively dense patterns of connections within subgroups, but they differ in the minimal density required, which varies from at least one connection (weak components) to all possible connections (cliques). Two more techniques based on a similar principle (m-slices and bicomponents) are presented in later chapters. There are many more formal concepts for cohesive subgroups but all of them are based on the notions of density and connectedness.

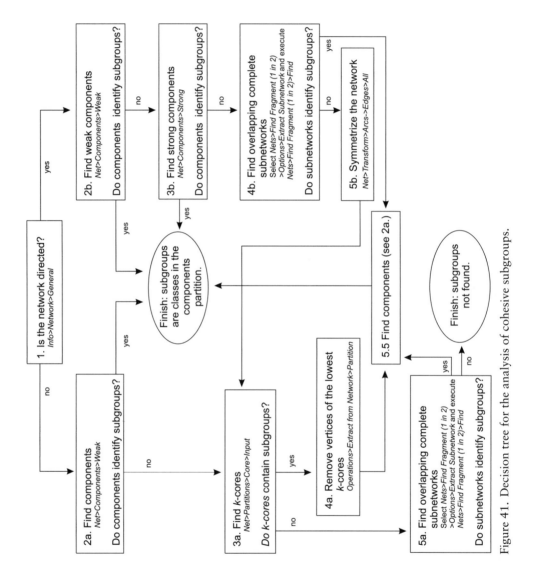

Figure 41. Decision tree for the analysis of cohesive subgroups.

Components identify cohesive subgroups in a straightforward manner: each vertex belongs to exactly one component. The link between cohesive subgroups and k-cores or cliques is more complicated. k-Cores are nested, which means that higher k-cores are always contained in lower k-cores, so a vertex may belong to several k-cores simultaneously. In addition, k-cores are not necessarily connected: the vertices within one k-core can be spread over several components. To identify cohesive subgroups, the researcher has to eliminate vertices of low k-cores until the network breaks up into relatively dense components. Cliques or complete subnetworks, such as complete triads, may overlap, that is, share one or more vertices, so a component of overlapping cliques is regarded as a cohesive subgroup rather than each clique on its own.

Because the techniques to detect cohesive subgroups are based on the same principle, substantive arguments to prefer one technique over another are usually not available. The choice of a technique depends primarily on the density of the network. In a dense network, the structure of overlapping cliques reveals the cohesive skeleton best, whereas components and k-cores unravel loosely knit networks better. In exploratory research, we recommend looking for components first and then applying k-cores and searching for complete triads to subdivide large k-cores if necessary (see the decision tree in Figure 41).

Another choice pertains to the treatment of directed relations. In general, symmetrizing directed relations yields higher density, thus more or larger cohesive subgroups. For k-cores, we recommend to use simple undirected or symmetrized networks to make sure that k equals the number of neighbors to which each vertex is connected in a core. In a directed network, components may be weak or strong. Strong components and complete directed triads are based on reciprocal ties, whereas weak subgroups consider unilateral ties as well.

In this chapter, we use the word *subgroup*, but a cohesive subgroup is not necessarily a social group. We need to check this by comparing the structural subgroups with respect to the social characteristics, behavior, and opinions of their members. Sometimes, our prior knowledge about the entities in the network enables us to make sense of the cohesive subgroups we detect. Otherwise, we must systematically compare the partition which identifies cohesive subgroups with partitions representing social attributes of the vertices.

3.8 Questions

1. Inspect the networks that are depicted below. If we symmetrize the directed networks, which ones become identical to the undirected network?

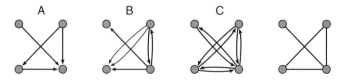

   a. A, B, and C
   b. A and B only
   c. A and C only
   d. A only
2. Which of the following statements is correct?
   a. Density is the degree sum of all vertices in a simple undirected network.
   b. Density is the degree sum of all vertices divided by the number of vertices in a simple undirected network.
   c. Density is the number of arcs divided by the number of pairs of vertices in a simple directed graph.
   d. Density is the number of edges divided by the number of pairs of vertices in a simple undirected graph.
3. Which of the following statements about the network below are correct?

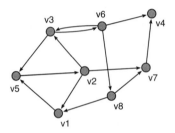

   a. v6 and v4 are not connected by a semipath.
   b. v1 and v4 are not connected by a path.
   c. There is no path from v7 to v3.
   d. There is no path from v1 to v8.
4. How many strong components does the network of Question 3 contain?
   a. No strong components
   b. 1 strong component
   c. 2 strong components
   d. 3 strong components
5. Which of the following statements is correct?
   a. A subnetwork is maximal if it cannot be enlarged without loosing its structural characteristic.
   b. A subnetwork is not maximal if it does not cover the whole network.
   c. A subnetwork is maximal if it is connected.
   d. A subnetwork is maximal if it is complete.
6. Which of the following statements is correct for simple undirected networks?
   a. In a 1-core, each vertex has exactly one neighbor.
   b. A component containing 2 or more vertices is always a 1-core.
   c. Each 1-core is a clique.
   d. Each 3-core is a clique.

7. Count the number of 3-cores in the network below. Vertex colors indicate the level of k (white: $k = 1$; light gray: $k = 2$; dark gray: $k = 3$; black: $k = 4$).

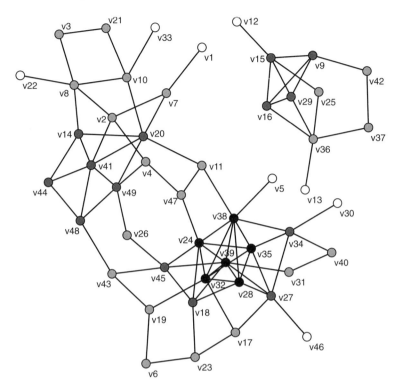

a. One 3-core
b. Two 3-cores
c. Three 3-cores
d. Four 3-cores

3.9   Assignment

The researchers assigned the families of another village in the Turrialba region, San Juan Sur, to family–friendship groupings on the basis of their answers to the question: in case of a death in the family, whom would you notify first? Their choices are stored in the file SanJuanSur_deathmessage.net. In this file, the coordinates of families correspond with the locations of families in the original sociogram drawn by the researchers. The partition SanJuanSur_deathmessage.clu contains the family–friendship groupings for this network.

We would like to reconstruct the way the families were assigned to family–friendship groupings. Find out which type of cohesive subgroups match the family–friendship groupings best and use the indices of statistical association presented in Chapter 2, Section 2.6, to assess how well they match. Do you think that the researchers used additional information to assign families to family–friendship groupings?

3.10   Further Reading

- The example is taken from Charles P. Loomis, Julio O. Morales, Roy A. Clifford, & Olen E. Leonard, *Turrialba: Social Systems and the Introduction of Change* (Glencoe (Ill.): The Free Press, 1953). We will also use these data in Chapter 9 on prestige.
- Chapter 6 in John Scott, *Social Network Analysis: A Handbook* [London: Sage (2nd ed. 2000), 1991] offers an overview with some additional types of connected subnetworks. Chapter 7 in Stanley Wasserman and Katherine Faust, *Social Network Analysis: Methods and Applications* (Cambridge: Cambridge University Press, 1994) is even more detailed.

3.11   Answers

Answers to the Exercises

I. In the symmetrized network of San Juan Sur without multiple lines, vertex degree ranges from 1 to 12 and the average degree is 4.13 (change the degree partition into a vector and inspect the vector with the *Info>Vector* command).

II. Open the network `ExerciseII.net` and determine the k-core partition with one of the *Net>Partition>Core* commands. Inspecting the core partition with the *Info>Partition* command, you will see that 13 vertices belong to the 4-core, 33 (13 + 20) to the 3-core, 47 (33 + 14) vertices to the 2-core, and all 49 vertices (47 + 2) to the 1-core. You can extract the 4-core from the network with the *Operations>Extract from Network>Partition* command (just extract class 4). The extracted 4-core is not connected, as shown in the figure below; it consists of two parts.

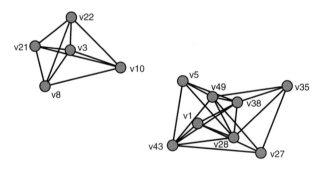

Answers to the Questions in Section 3.8

1. Answer c is correct. Symmetrizing a network means that unilateral and bidirectional arcs are replaced by an edge. Multiple arcs (e.g., from the

top-right vertex to the bottom-left vertex in network B) are replaced by multiple edges. Therefore, the undirected network is not a symmetrized version of network B.

2. Answer d is correct. Density is defined as the number of lines in a network, expressed as a proportion of the maximum possible number of lines. In a simple undirected network, a pair of vertices can be connected by one edge because multiple lines do not occur. In addition, loops do not occur. Therefore, the number of pairs of vertices equals the maximum possible number of lines and answer d is correct. Recall that an edge is defined as an unordered pair of vertices and an arc as an ordered pair. In a simple directed network, each pair of vertices may be connected by two arcs, so the maximum possible number of lines is twice the number of pairs. Morever, a simple directed network may also contain loops. Thus, answer c is incorrect. Answers a and b refer to the sum of degrees and average degree, which are other kinds of indices.

3. Answer c is correct because the only path which originates in v7 leads to v4, where it stops because v4 sends no arcs. Answer a is incorrect because there are several semipaths between v6 and v4 (e.g., v6→v3←v2→v7→v4) and each path (v6→v4) is also a semipath. Answer b is incorrect because there is a path from v1 to v4 (e.g., v1→v5→v2→v7→v4). Answer d is incorrect because there is a path from v1 to v8 as follows: v1→v5→v2→v3→v6→v8.

4. Answer d is correct. Vertex v4 is a strong component on its own because it has no path to any other vertex. Vertex v7 is the start of one path, which ends at v4. Because there is no path in the opposite direction, v7 is not a member of a larger strong component. The third strong component consists of the remaining six vertices, which are connected by paths in both ways.

5. Statement a is correct; for example, a component is a maximal connected subnetwork because no vertex can be added in such a way that the subnetwork is still connected. Connectedness in itself is not enough for a subnetwork to be maximal (statement c), nor is completeness (statement d). A maximal subnetwork does not need to include all vertices in the network (statement b is incorrect).

6. Answer b is correct for every simple undirected network. In a component, of size 2 or more, vertices must be linked to at least one other vertex for the component to be connected, so each component is at least a 1-core. A star network is a 1-core because all vertices except the central vertex has just one neighbor. Nevertheless, the central vertex has more than one neighbor, so answer a is incorrect. *k*-cores are not necessarily cliques, so answers c and d are not correct.

7. Answer a is correct. A *k*-core is not necessarily connected, so all unconnected parts of the 3-core still belong to one 3-core.

4

Sentiments and Friendship

4.1 Introduction

In the preceding chapter, we discussed several techniques for finding cohesive subgroups within a social network. People who belong together tend to interact more frequently than people who do not. In the current chapter, we extend this idea to affective relations that are either positive or negative, for instance, friendship versus hostility, liking versus disliking. We expect positive ties to occur within subgroups and negative ties between subgroups.

Hypotheses about patterns of affective relations stem from social psychology and they are widely known as balance theory. First, we introduce this theory and discuss how it was incorporated in network analysis. Then, we apply it to affective relations, that is, social relations that are subjective and mental rather than tangible.

4.2 Balance Theory

Social psychology is interested in group processes and their impact on individual behavior and perceptions. In the 1940s, Fritz Heider formulated a principle that has become the core of balance theory, namely that a person feels uncomfortable when he or she disagrees with his or her friend on a topic. Figure 42 illustrates this situation: P is a person, O is another person (the Other), and X represents a topic or object. P likes O, which is indicated by a positive line between P and O, but they disagree on topic X because P is in favor of it (positive line), whereas O is opposed to it (negative line). Note the convention of drawing negative ties as dashed lines, which is also adopted in Pajek.

Heider predicted that P would become stressed and feel an urge to change the imbalance of the situation, either by adjusting his opinion on X, by changing his affections for O, or by convincing himself or herself that O is not really opposed to X. Research in small groups corroborated the hypothesis that people feel stressed in a situation of imbalance.

A social psychologist (Dorwin Cartwright) and a mathematician (Frank Harary) translated Heider's ideas into network analysis. They defined a special kind of network to represent structures of affective ties, namely

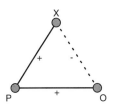

Figure 42. A Person–Other–Object (X) triple.

a signed graph. In a signed graph, a positive or negative sign is attached to each line indicating whether the associated tie (e.g., an affection) is positive or negative.

A *signed graph* is a graph in which each line carries either a positive or a negative sign.

In a signed graph, Heider's Person–Other–Object triple is represented by a cycle, that is, a path in which the first and last vertex coincide. All balanced cycles contain an even number of negative lines or no negative lines at all; for instance, there is one negative line in the cycle of Figure 42, which is an uneven number, so this triple is not balanced. P, and possibly O, will feel stressed in this situation.

However, affective relations do not need to be symmetrical. My feelings for you may differ from your feelings toward me. Affections are projected from a person to something or someone else. Therefore, it is usually better to represent affect ties by arcs rather than edges. It is easy to generalize balance theory to signed directed graphs: ignore the direction of arcs and count the number of negative arcs in each semicycle (a closed semipath). In Figure 43, the sequence of arcs from P to X, on to O, and back to P constitute a semipath and a semicycle but not a path and a cycle, because not all arcs point toward the next vertex within this sequence. The semicycle is unbalanced because it contains an uneven number of negative arcs.

A *cycle* is a closed path.

A *semicycle* is a closed semipath.

A (semi-)cycle is *balanced* if it does not contain an uneven number of negative arcs.

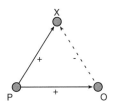

Figure 43. P-O-X triple as a signed digraph.

Fritz Heider was concerned with the feelings and perceptions of one person. Therefore, Figure 43 contains affections from person P to the other (O) and to the object or topic X. Even O's tie to X is measured from the perspective of P: it is P's idea about what O thinks of X, which does not necessarily correspond to O's real opinion. In social psychology, this phenomenon is called *attribution*. Of course, O may have positive or negative affect for P as well, and if X is a human being (or an animal) rather than a topic, X may also express affections for P and O.

Network analysts are interested in the feelings of all members of a group toward each other. This has led to the notion of *structural balance*, which expects balance in the overall pattern of affect ties within a human group rather than in one person's affections and attributions.

Cartwright and Harary formulated exact conditions for a signed graph to be balanced. They noted that a balanced signed graph can be partitioned into two clusters such that all positive arcs are contained within the clusters and all negative arcs are located between clusters. You might say that a balanced network is extremely polarized because it consists of two factions and actors only have positive ties with members of their own faction, whereas they have negative ties with members of the other faction. Clusters group people who like each other but who dislike members of the other cluster. It is easy to check this in Figure 44, which uses gray and black to identify the clusters.

In addition, they proved that a signed graph is balanced if all of its semicycles are balanced. Find one unbalanced semicycle and you know that the network is unbalanced.

A signed graph is *balanced* if all of its (semi-)cycles are balanced.

A signed graph is *balanced* if it can be partitioned into two clusters such that all positive ties are contained within the clusters and all negative ties are situated between the clusters.

But why would human groups consist of two clusters or factions instead of three or more? In Figure 44, for instance, vertices v7, v9, and v12 could very well be a cluster on their own. To allow for three or more clusters,

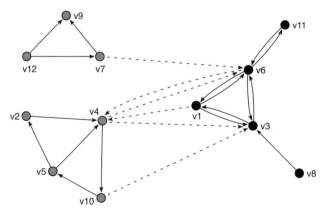

Figure 44. A balanced network.

balance was generalized to *clusterability*. A signed network is clusterable if there is a partition satisfying the criterion that positive lines connect vertices within a cluster and negative lines are incident with vertices in different clusters, no matter the number of clusters. The network analyst Davis proved that a network is clusterable if it contains no semicycles with exactly one negative arc. Clearly, balance is a special case of clusterability because all balanced semicycles are clusterable.

A cycle or semicycle is *clusterable* if it does not contain exactly one negative arc.

A signed graph is *clusterable* if it can be partitioned into clusters such that all positive ties are contained within clusters and all negative ties are situated between clusters.

In the course of time, balance theory has been generalized to models that incorporate hierarchy. We present these models in Chapter 10. Some of them apply to unsigned networks but we analyze signed relations only in the current chapter. To find subgroups in unsigned networks, we advise using the techniques for tracing cohesive subgroups, which is presented in Chapter 3.

4.3   Example

In this chapter, we use a case that has been reanalyzed by network analysts many times, namely the ethnographic study of community structure in a New England monastery by Samuel F. Sampson. The study describes several social relations among a group of men (novices) who were preparing to join a monastic order. We use the affect relations among the novices, which were collected by asking them to indicate whom they liked most and whom they liked least. The novices were asked for a first, second, and third choice on both questions.

The social relations were measured for several moments in time. The file Sampson.net contains the affect relations at five different moments. The first choice of the most liked peer is coded with line value 3, the second choice with line value 2, and the third choice with line value 1. Least liked choices are coded with negative line values as follows: −3 for the most disliked colleague, −2 for the second choice, and −1 for the third choice. In the present section, however, we focus on the affective ties between the novices at the fourth moment in time (T4), which was one week before four of them were expelled from the monastery. For the sake of illustration, we use their first choices only, which are recoded to 1 for *most liked* and −1 for *least liked*. The data are available in the file Sampson_T4.net. The Pajek project file Sampson.paj contains all networks and partitions.

Some novices had attended the minor seminary of "Cloisterville" before they came to the monastery; they are identified as class 1 in the partition Sampson_cloisterville_T4.clu. Based on his observations and analyses, Sampson divided the novices into four groups, which are represented by classes in the partition `Sampson_factions_T4.clu`: Young Turks (class 1), Loyal Opposition (class 2), Outcasts (class 3), and an interstitial group (class 4). The Loyal Opposition consists of the novices who entered the monastery first. The Young Turks arrived later, in a period of change. They questioned practices in the monastery, which the members of the Loyal Opposition defended. Some novices did not take sides in this debate, so they are labeled "interstitial." The Outcasts are novices who were not accepted into the group.

4.4   Detecting Structural Balance and Clusterability

Social networks are seldom perfectly balanced or clusterable. In some applications, researchers want to know whether a social network is more balanced or clusterable than we may expect by chance. If so, they conclude that the actors in the network adjust their ties to balance. In exploratory social network analysis, however, we are primarily interested in detecting balanced clusters, which represent cohesive subgroups within the network.

There are several ways to detect clusters in a signed network such that positive lines are within clusters and negative lines between clusters. Sometimes, clusters can be found by visual exploration. If we draw positive lines, which indicate attraction, as short as possible and negative lines, which signal repulsion, as long as possible, clusters of positive ties are clearly visible in a sociogram. In Figure 45, which is drawn in this manner (as is explained under "Application"), we can see three clusters in the network of novices. Because there are three clusters, the network is clusterable rather than balanced.

Because the network is highly clusterable and not very dense, we can visually check that all positive arcs are situated within clusters and almost

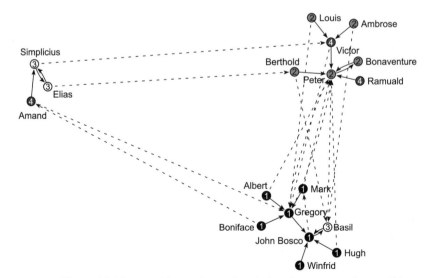

Figure 45. First positive and negative choices between novices at *T*4.

all negative arcs are directed from one cluster to another. The only negative arc within a cluster points from John Bosco to Mark at the bottom of the sociogram. Note that the triple John Bosco, Mark, and Gregory contains exactly one negative arc, so it is unclusterable and it will yield problems in any clustering we may attempt.

In Figure 45, vertex colors and class numbers indicate the factions that Sampson delineated: Young Turks (black, class 1), Loyal Opposition (light gray, class 2), Outcasts (white, class 3), and the interstitial group (dark gray, class 4). The social cleavage between the Young Turks (black) and the Loyal Opposition (light gray) is evident, but the Outcasts are not clustered perfectly. Ramuald and Victor are clustered with the Loyal Opposition and they probably felt somewhat related to them because they all (except Louis) came from Cloisterville.

If sociograms are not as orderly as Figure 45, we must use computational techniques to find the clustering that fits balance or clusterability best. In exploratory network analysis, a good strategy is to try many clusterings and select the one containing the lowest number of forbidden lines: positive lines between clusters or negative lines within a cluster. The number of forbidden lines is an error score that measures the degree of balance or clusterability in a network: more errors mean less balance or clusterability.

In Figure 45, there is just one forbidden line if we partition the novices into three clusters, namely the negative arc from John Bosco to Mark in the bottom right cluster. It is up to the researcher to decide whether the degree of balance or clusterability is acceptable. Criteria cannot be specified without the use of estimation techniques, which fall outside the scope of this book, because the acceptability of an error score depends on the size and density of a network. The error score allows us to pick the best fitting clustering, but it does not say whether it is good enough.

The approach of rearranging vertices into clusters over and over again and selecting the best solution, is an *optimization technique* that has three features that are worth noting. First, an optimization technique may find several solutions or partitions that fit equally well. It is up to the researcher to select one or present them all.

Second, it is possible that this technique does not find the best fitting clustering, although this is expected to happen only in exceptional cases. Nevertheless, there is no guarantee that there is not a better solution, unless, of course, you find a clustering which fits perfectly. We advise repeating the procedure many times and inspecting the results visually to see whether you can find a better solution.

Third, starting options may yield different results; for instance, the procedure finds another solution if it is told to look for two clusters instead of three or four. It is usually possible to estimate the approximate number of clusters from an energized sociogram, but it is hard to tell the exact number of clusters that will yield the lowest error score. Therefore, it is important to repeat the optimization technique with different numbers of clusters.

In addition, the user may attribute different weights or penalties to forbidden positive and negative arcs. For instance, researchers have noted that negative arcs within a cluster are tolerated less than positive arcs between clusters, so we can raise the penalty on negative arcs within clusters. In the network of affect relations between novices depicted in Figure 45, this would mean that John Bosco's negative feelings for Mark are more important than Gregory's positive affection for John Bosco. Hence, the optimization technique will split the bottom cluster between John Bosco and Gregory. Different weights may produce different results.

Application

[Draw]
Options> Values
of Lines>
Similarities

A sociogram that minimizes the length of positive lines and maximizes the length of negative lines can be made in two steps. First, select the option *Similarities* in the *Options> Values of Lines* submenu of the Draw screen. This option tells the energy procedures that line values indicate similarity or attraction: the higher a line value, the closer two vertices should be drawn. Negative line values mean that vertices are dissimilar and must be drawn far apart. In Pajek, signs of lines are represented by the sign of the line values (e.g., 1 and -1) so positive arcs are short and negative arcs are long in an energized drawing. Note that this option remains effective until another option is selected. Second, apply an energy procedure to the sociogram. Figure 45 was created with the Kamada–Kawai energy command.

The command *Balance*, which searches an optimal clustering in a signed network, is located in the *Operations* menu because it requires two different data objects: a network and a partition. The network contains the vertices and ties that must be clustered and the partition specifies the number of clusters and the initial clustering that the computer tries to improve.

Partition> Create
Random
Partition

If you have no partition with a meaningful initial clustering, you can easily make a random partition with the *Create Random Partition* command in the *Partition* menu. This command issues two dialog boxes. The first box asks for the number of vertices or *dimension* of the partition. By default, Pajek shows the number of vertices in the network that is currently active, which is the right number because you want the partition to fit this network. In the second dialog box, you enter the number of clusters you want to detect in the network. In this example, you may want to obtain three clusters.

Operations>
Balance

The *Balance* command asks how many times it must try to find an optimal clustering. In each repetition, it starts with a new random partition. If a starting partition fits quite well, the optimization technique will not find better solutions because all changes will increase the error score initially. This could happen, for instance, with a starting clustering based on visual inspection of the energized sociogram. With several random starting partitions, the procedure is unlikely to miss a good clustering that differs greatly from your expectations, although this is not guaranteed. In a small network, one hundred repetitions is a reasonable first choice but you are advised to try many more repetitions if the computer needs little time for one hundred repetitions.

Next, you have to specify the error weight of a forbidden negative arc, that is, a negative arc within a positive cluster. This weight is called α and

```
---------------------------------------------------------------------------
Partitioning Signed Graphs
---------------------------------------------------------------------------
 Working...
Number of clusters: 3, alpha: 0.500
-------  Starting partition -------
Errors:        5.50          Lines
-----------------------------------
               -1.00 :        6.3
               -1.00 :       14.4
                1.00 :        1.3
                1.00 :        3.1
                1.00 :        6.4
                1.00 :        7.2
                1.00 :        8.4
                1.00 :        9.8
                1.00 :       10.4
                1.00 :       14.1
                1.00 :       15.2
-----------------------------------
-------      Improvements    -------
        1:        1.50
        2:        0.50
-------  Final partition  1-------
Errors:        0.50          Lines
-----------------------------------
                1.00 :        7.2
-----------------------------------
-------  Final partition  2-------
Errors:        0.50          Lines
-----------------------------------
               -1.00 :        1.7
-----------------------------------
-------  Final partition  3-------
Errors:        0.50          Lines
-----------------------------------
                1.00 :        2.1
-----------------------------------
 3 solutions with 0.50 errors found.
Time spent:  0:00
```

Figure 46. Output listing of a *Balance* command.

it is .5 by default. The error weight for an erroneous positive arc is equal to $1 - \alpha$, so negative and positive arcs are treated equally by default. If you want to penalize a forbidden negative arc more than an erroneous positive arc, raise α in the dialog box, for instance, to .75. In consequence, a forbidden positive arc is weighted by .25, which is a third of the weight attached to an out-of-place negative arc.

Figure 46 shows the results for the novices network. We used a random partition containing three classes as the starting partition and it was instructed to weigh positive and negative errors equally ($\alpha = .5$). First, the listing displays the error score and the erroneous arcs in the initial clustering. There are many errors, which are identified by their line value (1 or − 1) and their vertex numbers in the listing of lines. Using a random starting partition of your own, you will probably find a different list of errors. You should, however, find final solutions that match the ones displayed here, so let us concentrate on them.

With sufficient repetitions, the *Balance* command finds three solutions with exactly one "forbidden" arc. In the first clustering, a positive arc wrongly connects vertices 7 (Mark) and 2 (Gregory), which are apparently members of different clusters. In the second clustering, a negative arc from vertex 1 (John Bosco) to vertex 7 (Mark) is a problem because

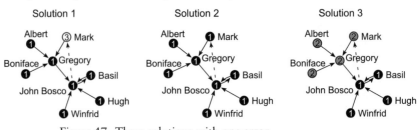

Figure 47. Three solutions with one error.

it is situated within a cluster. In the third clustering, the positive arc from vertex 2 (Gregory) to vertex 1 (John Bosco) causes problems. As expected, the unclusterable triple John Bosco-Mark-Gregory causes these problems. Nevertheless, the clustering is nearly perfect, so we may conclude that the network is clusterable. To know whether it is balanced as well, we must repeat the procedure with a starting partition containing two clusters.

All optimal solutions are saved as partitions in the *Partitions* dropdown menu. Drawing the network with these partitions, we can see that clusters at the left and at the top are correctly identified. The cluster at the bottom is split in three ways (Figure 47): Mark is added to the cluster of Simplicius, Elias, and Amand (solution 1); he is part of an undivided cluster including Gregory and John Bosco (solution 2); or he is grouped with Albert, Boniface, and Gregory, who are separated from John Bosco, Basil, Hugh, and Winfrid (solution 3). The first and last solution are most likely if negative arcs within a cluster are considered slightly more problematic than positive arcs between clusters. For instance, try *Balance* with α set to .6.

Let us conclude this section with a warning. The *Balance* command triggers a procedure that is very time-consuming, so it should not be applied to networks with more than a hundred vertices unless you do not need your computer for some hours or days. In Pajek, commands that should be applied only to small networks are marked by an asterisk in the menu.

Exercise I
Use Sampson's classification according to factions (Sampson_factions_T4.clu) to find four optimal clusters in the network of first choices at time four (Sampson_T4.net). Weigh positive and negative errors equally. Do the optimal clustering(s) match Sampson's classification?

4.5   Development in Time

Balance theory expects a tendency toward balance. In the course of time, affect relations within a human group are hypothesized to become more balanced or clusterable. This raises the question of how to analyze the evolution of social networks. In this section, we discuss the simplest way to analyze longitudinal networks, namely by comparing network structure at different points in time.

Sampson measured affect relations at the monastery at five moments. At the time of the first measurement (*T*1), the group consisted mainly of novices who soon left the monastery to study elsewhere. The second measurement (*T*2) concerns the period just after the arrival of a number of newcomers. The third measurement (*T*3) shows affective ties around the time when one of the newcomers (Brother Gregory) organized a meeting to discuss the situation in the monastery. This meeting fueled a process of polarization, which led to the expulsion of four novices (among them Brother Gregory) one week after the fourth measurement (*T*4). The expulsion triggered the voluntary departure of many novices in the next few weeks. At the time of the fifth measurement (*T*5), no more than seven of the eighteen novices were still living in the monastery, so this network is difficult to compare to the previous networks. We analyze the networks at *T*2, *T*3, and *T*4 only.

Application
Pajek has special facilities for longitudinal networks. Figure 48 shows part of the network file Sampson.net. By now, the structure of the

```
*Vertices     25
          1  "Leo"           0.1000   0.5000   0.5000 [1-1]
          2  "Arsenius"      0.1126   0.4005   0.5000
          3  "Bruno"         0.1495   0.3073   0.5000
          4  "Thomas"        0.2084   0.2262   0.5000
          5  "Bartholomew"   0.2857   0.1623   0.5000
          6  "John Bosco"    0.3764   0.1196   0.5000 [2-4]
          7  "Gregory"       0.4749   0.1008   0.5000
          8  "Basil"         0.5750   0.1071   0.5000
          9  "Martin"        0.6703   0.1381   0.5000 [1-1]
         10  "Peter"         0.7550   0.1918   0.5000 [1-5]
         11  "Bonaventure"   0.8236   0.2649   0.5000 [1-*]
         12  "Berthold"      0.8719   0.3528   0.5000
         13  "Mark"          0.8968   0.4499   0.5000 [1-4]
         14  "Brocard"       0.8968   0.5501   0.5000 [1-1]
         15  "Victor"        0.8719   0.6472   0.5000 [1-4]
         16  "Ambrose"       0.8236   0.7351   0.5000 [1-*]
         17  "Ramuald"       0.7550   0.8082   0.5000 [2-5]
         18  "Louis"         0.6703   0.8619   0.5000 [2-*]
         19  "Winfrid"       0.5750   0.8929   0.5000 [2-5]
         20  "Amand"         0.4749   0.8992   0.5000 [2-4]
         21  "Hugh"          0.3764   0.8804   0.5000
         22  "Boniface"      0.2857   0.8377   0.5000
         23  "Albert"        0.2084   0.7738   0.5000
         24  "Elias"         0.1495   0.6927   0.5000
         25  "Simplicius"    0.1126   0.5995   0.5000
*Arcs
          6        7       2  [3]
          6        7      -2  [4]
          6        8       2  [2]
          6        8       3  [4]
          6       10      -2  [3]
          6       11       1  [3]
          6       11       3  [2]
          6       12      -2  [2]
          6       13      -1  [2]
          6       13      -3  [4]
          6       15       3  [3]
          6       17      -1  [4]
          6       17      -3  [2,3]
```

Figure 48. Partial listing of Sampson.net.

lists of vertices and arcs are familiar, so the focus is on the time indicators in square brackets that are added to each vertex and arc. For instance, Brother John Bosco was at the monastery from $T2$ up to and including $T4$. He left before $T5$. This is also true for Brothers Gregory and Basil; Pajek assumes that a time indicator remains valid until it encounters a new one (e.g., with Brother Martin, who left the monastery after $T1$). Bonaventure arrived at the monastery before the first measurement and he stayed after the last measurement. The asterisk (*) indicates infinity.

At $T3$, the arc from vertex 6 (John Bosco) to vertex 7 (Gregory) has a value of 2, indicating a positive second choice. At $T4$, however, it has turned into a second negative choice (line value -2). In Figure 48, the last line indicates that John Bosco chooses Ramuald (vertex 17) as the person he likes least (line value -3) at $T2$ and $T3$. Note that time is always represented by positive integers and a line value must be specified before the time indication in the arcs and edges lists.

Net>Transform> Generate in Time

The time notation can be used to split the longitudinal network into separate networks for different moments or periods. The submenu *Net>Transform>Generate in Time* offers the user several commands for generating a series of cross-sectional networks. First, you can choose to obtain a network for each period requested (option *All*) or to produce a network only if it differs from the previous one (option *Only Different*). The latter command is useful if a network does not change much over time. Whichever command you choose, you will have to specify the first and last time point you want to analyze as well as the time interval (step) between successive networks. In our example, we start at $T2$ (enter 2) and stop at $T4$ (enter 4), and we want a network for each moment in between, so we choose step value 1. Step values must be positive integers. For example, with a step value of 2, starting at the first moment in time, the command would create a network for the first, third, and fifth moments, and so on.

Note that serial numbers of vertices change in generated networks when vertices disappear from the network (as at $T5$) or when new vertices are added, because numbers of vertices must always range from 1 to the number of vertices in Pajek. As a result, a partition accompanying the original longitudinal network may not match the generated cross-sectional networks. Therefore, the *Generate in Time* command automatically creates new partitions for each generated network from the active partition, provided that it matches the original longitudinal network.

Previous

Next

Options> Previous/Next> Apply to

Options> Previous/Next> Optimize Layouts

After generating networks for separate moments, you can easily switch from one moment to another with the commands *Previous* and *Next*, provided that the option *Network* is selected in the *Options> Previous/Next>Apply to* submenu in the Draw screen. If one of the energy options in the *Options>Previous/Next>Optimize Layouts* submenu has been selected, Pajek automatically energizes the network when you step to the next or previous network. It is sensible to inspect all generated networks to check whether the results are as intended. Errors in time indicators may have serious consequences; for instance, if Brother John Bosco is not present at $T3$ – by mistake, the indicator reads [2,4] instead of [2–4] – all arcs to and from him are deleted from the network at $T3$.

Table 6. *Error Score with all Choices at Different Moments (α = .5)*

	Time Points		
Number of Clusters	*T*2	*T*3	*T*4
2 (balance)	21.5	16.0	12.5
3	17.5	11.0	10.5
4	19.0	13.5	12.5
5	20.5	16.0	15.0

Having generated networks for *T*2, *T*3, and *T*4, we can analyze the degree of balance or clusterability with the *Operations>Balance* command in each period. Table 6 shows the error scores associated with the optimal clustering for several numbers of clusters and different time points. Some optimal solutions are hard to find; you may need thousands of repetitions in some cases. Note that the network now consists of all three positive and negative choices at *T*2, *T*3, and *T*4. First choices count three times (line values are 3 and −3 for the first positive and negative choice respectively), second choices count double (values 2 or −2), and third choices count once (1 or −1). The error score is computed from these line values, which explains why it is quite large compared to error scores in the previous section: a forbidden first choice contributes .5 (*α*) times 3 instead of .5 times 1 to the error score.

Table 6 helps us to draw a conclusion on the evolution of balance and clusterability in the network of novices. Each clustering fits better in the course of time and the partition with three clusters fits best at any moment, so we may conclude that there is a tendency toward clusterability rather than balance. This is probably due to a process of polarization, which ends when several novices leave the monastery. Instead of a continuing trend toward balance or clusterability, human groups probably experience limited periods of polarization, which are reflected in increasingly balanced or clusterable patterns of affective ties.

Exercise II
Check whether the networks of first positive and negative choices display a tendency toward balance or clusterability from the second to the fourth moment in time. Hint: use the command *Net>Transform>Remove>lines with value>within interval* to remove the lines with values from −2 to 2 from the longitudinal network (Sampson.net) before you split it into separate networks for different moments.

Net>Transform>Remove>lines with value>within interval

4.6 Summary

In this chapter, we discuss cohesive subgroups in signed networks, that is, in networks with positive and negative ties. If relations represent affections, people who like each other tend to huddle together, whereas negative sentiments exist predominantly between groups. This principle stems from balance theory and has been generalized to groups with three or more clusters (clusterability). Balance and clusterability occur in times of polarization between opposing factions.

We may determine whether affective ties are patterned according to balance theory by searching for a partition or clustering that satisfies the principle that positive lines are found within clusters and negative lines between clusters. If a signed network can be partitioned into two clusters according to this principle, the network is balanced. A partition with three or more clusters is a clusterable network.

The weighted number of lines that do not conform to the balance theoretic principle, namely negative lines within a cluster and positive lines between clusters, indicates the degree of balance or clusterability in a network. This is called the error score of the best fitting clustering. For one network, we compare error scores for different numbers of clusters to find the optimal clustering. If the error score is acceptable, the clusters represent cohesive groups. In addition, we may compare error scores of a network at different moments to check whether group structure displays a tendency toward balance that is predicted by balance theory.

4.7   Questions

1. Which of the following statements is correct?
   a. A signed graph is balanced if it is clusterable into two clusters.
   b. A signed graph is balanced if it is not clusterable.
   c. A signed graph is balanced if its vertices can be partitioned into two groups.
   d. A signed graph cannot be balanced because it is undirected.
2. Have a look at the following two networks and check which of the following statements is correct.

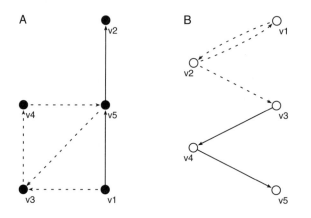

   a. A and B are balanced.
   b. A is balanced and B is clusterable.
   c. A is clusterable and B is balanced.
   d. Neither A nor B is balanced.

3. How many cycles and semicycles does network A of Question 2 contain?
   a. No cycles and two semicycles
   b. One cycle and one semicycle
   c. One cycle and two semicycles
   d. Two cycles and one semicycle
4. Which of the following statements about the sequence of lines v2-v3-v4-v5 in network B (Question 2) is correct?
   a. It is neither a semiwalk nor a semipath.
   b. It is a semiwalk and a semipath.
   c. It is a walk and a semipath.
   d. It is a walk and a path.
5. An analysis of 58 alliance (a line value of 1) and 58 antagonistic (a line value of -1) ties among 16 tribes in New Guinea yields error scores reported in the table below ($\alpha = .5$). Which conclusion do you support? Please, state your reasons.

	Number of Clusters			
	2	3	4	5
Error score	7.0	2.0	4.0	6.0

   a. The tribal network is balanced.
   b. The tribal network is clusterable.
   c. The tribal network is neither balanced nor clusterable.
   d. It is impossible to draw a conclusion from these results.
6. In the best fitting clustering presented in Question 5, how many arcs violate the balance theoretic principle?
   a. Two arcs
   b. Four arcs
   c. Six arcs
   d. Seven arcs

4.8   Assignment

In 1943, Leslie D. Zeleny administered a sociometric test to forty-eight cadet pilots at an U.S. Army Air Forces flying school. Cadets were trained to fly a two-seated aircraft, taking turns in flying and aerial observing. Cadets were assigned at random to instruction groups ranging in size from five to seven, so they had little or no control over who their flying partners would be. The sociometric test was used to improve the composition of instruction groups. Zeleny asked each cadet to name the members of his flight group with whom he would like to fly as well as those with whom he would not like to fly. The data are available in the project file `Flying_teams.paj`, which contains a network (`Flying_teams.net`) and the original (alphabetical) instruction groups (`Flying_teams.clu`).

Which instruction groups would you advise to reduce the risk of cadets flying with partners they do not want? Try to find groups of five to ten cadets.

4.9   Further Reading

- The example was taken from S. F. Sampson, *A Novitiate in a Period of Change: An Experimental and Case Study of Social Relationships* (Ph.D. thesis Cornell University, 1968). An analysis of the data using the method presented in this chapter can be found in P. Doreian and A. Mrvar, "A partitioning approach to structural balance" (in *Social Networks*, 18 (1996), 149–68).
- The New Guinea data were reported in K. Read, "Culture of the central highlands, New Guinea," in *Southwestern Journal of Anthropology* [10 (1954), 1–43] and reanalyzed in P. Hage and F. Harary, *Structural Models in Anthropology* (Cambridge/New York: Cambridge University Press, 1983). The data are also distributed with UCINET network analysis software.
- The flying teams data are taken from J. L. Moreno (et al.), *The Sociometry Reader*. Glencoe, Ill.: The Free Press, 1960, 534–47.
- For an overview of balance theory in social network analysis, consult Chapter 6 in S. Wasserman and K. Faust, *Social Network Analysis: Methods and Applications* (Cambridge: Cambridge University Press, 1994).
- Fritz Heider introduced the notion of balance in his article "Attitudes and Cognitive Organization," which appeared in the *Journal of Psychology* [21 (1946), 107–12]. A more detailed account can be found in his book *The Psychology of Interpersonal Relations* (New York: Wiley, 1958). F. Harary, R. Z. Norman, and D. Cartwright, *Structural Models: An Introduction to the Theory of Directed Graphs* (New York: Wiley, 1965) formalized the concept of balance. The lucidity of this book makes it a pleasure to read. Clusterability was defined by J. A. Davis in the article "Clustering and structural balance in graphs." In: *Human Relations* 20 (1967), 181–7. *Discrete Mathematical Models* by F. S. Roberts (New York: Prentice Hall, 1976) is a good book to further your understanding of several mathematical models including balance.

4.10   Answers

Answers to the Exercises

I. With a sufficient number of repetitions, the Balance command finds two optimal partitions with one mistake each (.5 error score). In one partition, Mark (vertex 7) is considered a cluster on his own, so his choice of Gregory (vertex 2) as his most liked colleague is erroneously situated between two classes instead of within a class (Figure 49, left).

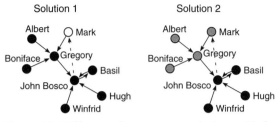

Figure 49. Differences between two solutions with four classes.

In the other partition, Mark, Albert, Gregory, and Boniface are separated from John Bosco, Basil, Hugh, and Winfrid (Figure 49, right). Now, the positive arc from Gregory (vertex 2) to John Bosco (vertex 1) is troublesome. The first solution matches Sampson's classification into factions better because he assigned Gregory, Albert, Boniface, John Bosco, Hugh, and Winfrid to the Young Turks (class 1 in Figure 45). In both partitions, however, the interstitial group (Amand, Victor, and Ramuald; class 4) is divided over the Loyal Opposition (class 2) and the Outcasts (class 3).

II. Remove the lines with values from −2 to 2 from the longitudinal network (Sampson.net) with the command *Net>Transform> Remove>lines with value>within interval* (enter −2 as the lower limit and 2 as the upper limit) and then split it with *Net>Transform> Generate in Time>All.* For the networks at time two to four, find the optimal balanced partitions with the *Operations>Balance* command as described in Section 4.5. If you use many repetitions, you should find the results summarized in Table 7. We already obtained some results for time four in Section 4.4 but now the error scores are three times as high because the line values are 3 and −3 instead of 1 and −1. The error scores tend to diminish in the course of time and they are lowest with three or four classes: this indicates a tendency toward clusterability rather than balance.

Answers to the Questions in Section 4.7

1. Answer a is correct. Balance is a special case of clusterability, because a network is balanced if it can be partitioned into two clusters in such a way that all positive lines are within clusters and all negative lines are between clusters.

Table 7. *Error Score with First Choices Only (α = .5)*

Number of Clusters	Time Points		
	T2	*T3*	*T4*
2 (balance)	7.5	4.5	3.0
3	4.5	3.0	1.5
4	4.5	3.0	1.5
5	4.5	3.0	3.0
6	6.0	4.5	4.5

2. Answer c is correct. Semicycles v1-v3-v4-v5 and v3-v4-v5 contain three negative arcs, so network A is not balanced. Cycle v1-v3-v5 has two negative arcs. There is no (semi-)cycle with exactly one negative arc, so network A is clusterable. Network B contains just one (semi-)cycle, namely v1-v2, which contains two negative arcs. Hence, network B is balanced. Network A can be partitioned into according to the principle of positive arcs within clusters and negative arcs between clusters: v1, v2, and v5 are a cluster and v3 and v4 are separate clusters. Likewise, network B can be divided into two clusters: v2 versus the rest.

3. Answer c is correct, see the answer to Question 2.

4. Answer d is correct. The sequence of lines is a walk because the lines are adjacent and they point in the same direction: the head of one arc is the tail of the next arc. This walk is a path because all vertices are distinct, meaning that no vertex occurs more than once in the walk.

5. Answer b is the most likely conclusion. Clearly, a partition with three clusters fits better than a partition with two clusters. Therefore, the network is clusterable rather than balanced. Strictly speaking, however, even an error score of 2.0 is too high and you should conclude that the network is neither balanced nor clusterable (answer c).

6. Answer b is correct. Alpha is .5, which means that every "forbidden" arc – positive or negative – contributes .5 to the error score. Because the absolute line values are 1, four arcs in the wrong places yield a total error score of 2.0, which is the minimal error score in the table.

5

Affiliations

5.1 Introduction

Membership of an organization or participation in an event is a source of social ties. In organizations and events, people gather because they have similar tasks or interests and they are likely to interact. Members of a sports club, for instance, share a preference for a particular sport and play with or against one another. Directors and commissioners on the boards of a corporation are collectively responsible for its financial success and meet regularly to discuss business matters. Inspired by the sociology of Georg Simmel, groups of people that gather around one or more organizations and events are called *social circles*.

In previous chapters, we studied direct ties among people, such as the choice of friends, or among other social entities, for instance, trade relations between countries. Note that we studied relations among actors of one kind: relations between people or between organizations, but not between people and organizations. Now, we focus on the latter type, which is called an affiliation. Data on affiliations can be obtained relatively easily and they are very popular in data mining.

Affiliations are often institutional or "structural," that is, forced by circumstances. They are less personal and result from private choices to a lesser degree than sentiments and friendship. Of course, membership in a sports team depends much more on a person's preferences than detention in a particular prison ward, but even the composition of sports teams depends on circumstances and on decisions made by coaches and sports club authorities. Affiliations express institutional arrangements and because institutions shape the structure of society, networks of affiliations tell us a lot about society. People are often affiliated with several organizations and events at the same time, so they belong to a number of social circles, or, in other words, they are the intersection of many social circles. Society may be seen as a fabric of intersecting social circles.

Although membership lists do not tell us exactly which people interact, communicate, and like each other, we may assume that there is a fair chance that they will. Moreover, joint membership in an organization often entails similarities in other social domains. If, for example, people have chosen to become members in (or have been admitted to) a particular golf club, they may well have similar professions, interests, and social

101

status. Different types of affiliations do not overlap in a random manner: social circles usually contain people who are clustered by affiliations to more than one type of organization. From the number or intensity of shared events, we may infer the degree of similarity of people. However, this argument can be reversed: organizations or events that share more members are also more close socially. A country club with many members from the local business elite can be said to be part of the business sphere.

In this chapter, we present a technique for analyzing networks of affiliations that focuses on line values. In addition, we discuss three-dimensional displays of social networks.

5.2   Example

In political science, economy, and sociology, much attention has been paid to the composition of the boards of large corporations. Who are the directors of the largest companies and, in particular, who sits on the boards of several companies? If a person is a member of the board of directors in two companies, he or she (although women are seldom found in these positions) is a multiple director, who creates an interlocking directorate or interlock between firms.

The network of interlocking directorates tells us something about the organization of a business sector. It is assumed that interlocking directorates are channels of communication between firms. In one board, a multiple director can use the information acquired in another board. Information may or may not be used to exercise power, depending on the role played by the director. If directors are elected because of their social prestige within a community, they serve the public relations of a firm, but they do not influence its policy: they fulfill a symbolic role. However, multiple directors who have executive power may coordinate decisions in several companies, thus controlling large sections of an economy. Then, interlocking directorates are power lines.

In this chapter, we use a historical example: the corporate interlocks in Scotland in the beginning of the twentieth century (1904–5). In the nineteenth century, the industrial revolution brought Scotland railways and industrialization, especially heavy industry and the textile industry. The amount of capital needed for these large-scale undertakings exceeded the means of private families, so joint stock companies were established that could raise the required capital. Joint stock companies are owned by the shareholders, who are represented by a board of directors. This opens up the possibility of interlocking directorates. By the end of the nineteenth century, joint stock companies had become the predominant form of business enterprise at the expense of private family businesses. However, families still exercised control through ownership and directorships.

The data are taken from the book *The Anatomy of Scottish Capital* by John Scott and Michael Hughes. It lists the (136) multiple directors of the 108 largest joint stock companies in Scotland in 1904–5: 64 nonfinancial firms, 8 banks, 14 insurance companies, and 22 investment and property companies (`Scotland.net`). The companies are classified according to industry type (see `Industrial_categories.clu`): 1 – oil & mining, 2 – railway, 3 – engineering & steel, 4 – electricity & chemicals, 5 – domestic products, 6 – banks, 7 – insurance, and 8 – investment. In addition, there is a vector specifying the total capital or deposits of the firms in 1,000 pounds sterling (`Capital.vec`). The data files are collected in the project file `Scotland.paj`.

Exercise I
Open the project file `Scotland.paj` and draw the network of firms and directors with the affiliation partition. What do the classes in the affiliation partition mean?

5.3   Two-Mode and One-Mode Networks

By definition, affiliation networks consist of at least two sets of vertices such that affiliations connect vertices from different sets only. There are usually two sets, which are called *actors* and *events*, for example, directors (actors) and boards of corporations (events). Affiliations connect directors to boards, not directors to directors or boards to boards, at least not directly. Figure 50 shows a fragment of the interlocking directorates network in Scotland: a set of directors (gray in the figure, possibly green on your computer screen) and firms (black or yellow). Note that lines always connect a gray and a black vertex (e.g., director J. S. Tait to the Union Bank of Scotland). This type of network is called a *two-mode network* or a *bipartite network*, which is structurally different from the one-mode networks, which we have analyzed thus far because all vertices can be related in a *one-mode network*.

> In a *one-mode network*, each vertex can be related to each other vertex.
>
> In a *two-mode network*, vertices are divided into two sets and vertices can only be related to vertices in the other set.

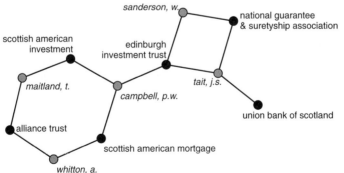

Figure 50. A fragment of the Scottish directorates network.

We can describe the two-mode network of Scottish directorships in the usual manner by its number of vertices (108 firms and 136 multiple directors – see the affiliation partition) and lines (358 affiliations or board seats), the number of components (16 isolated firms without multiple directors, three small components containing 2 firms, and one large component), and its degree distribution. Recall that the degree of a vertex is equal to the number of its neighbors if the network does not contain multiple lines and loops. Because this is the case in the directorships network, the degree of a firm specifies the number of its multiple directors. This is known as the *size of an event*. The degree of a director equals the number of boards he sits on, which is called the *rate of participation* of an actor. Have a look at Figure 50 and determine the size of events and participation rates of its vertices.

In our description of a two-mode network, we must distinguish between actors and events, because simple measures such as degree have different meanings for actors and events. There are more complications: some structural indices must be computed in a different way for two-mode networks. Consider, for example, the concept of completeness, which we defined as the maximum possible number of lines in a network (see Chapter 3). In a one-mode network, this number is much higher than in a two-mode network because each vertex can be related to all other vertices in a one-mode network but it can only be related to part of the vertices in a two-mode network. As a consequence, the density of a two-mode network, which is the actual number of lines divided by the maximum possible number of lines, must be computed differently for one-mode and two-mode networks.

Techniques for analyzing one-mode networks cannot always be applied to two-mode networks without modification or change of meaning. Special techniques for two-mode networks are very complicated and fall outside the scope of this book. So, what can we do? The solution commonly used, which we will follow, is to change the two-mode network into a one-mode network, which can be analyzed with standard techniques.

We can create two one-mode networks from a two-mode network: a network of interlocking events and a network of actors that are members of the same organization or attend common events. Figure 51 shows the one-mode network of firms (events) that is derived from the network in Figure 50. It is constructed in the following way. Whenever two firms share a director in the two-mode network, there is a line between them in the one-mode network. For instance, J. S. Tait creates a line between the Union Bank of Scotland and The Edinburgh Investment Trust because he sits on the boards of both companies. Because he is also on the board of the National Guarantee and Suretyship Association, he is responsible for lines between three firms. Each line can be labeled by his name. In addition, he creates a loop for each of these firms. The number of loops incident with a vertex shows the number of its neighbors in the two-mode network. In our example, it shows the number of multiple directors on the board of a firm: the size of the event. In short, the actors in the two-mode network become the lines and loops in the one-mode network of events.

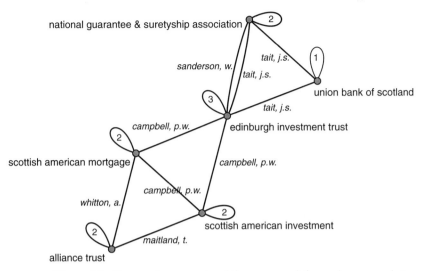

Figure 51. One-mode network of firms created from the network in Figure 50.

From Figure 51, it is clear that firms can be connected by multiple lines, namely in the case that two firms share more than one director. The derived network, therefore, usually is not a simple network. Because it may also contain loops, you must take care when you interpret the degree of a vertex in a network derived from a two-mode network.

Multiple lines can be replaced by a single line to obtain a *valued network* with a line value indicating the original number of lines between two vertices. Such a line value is called a *line multiplicity*. Figure 52 shows the valued network of directors (comembership) that can be derived from the example in Figure 50. Now, the events of the two-mode network are represented by lines and loops in the one-mode network of actors. J. S. Tait meets W. Sanderson in board meetings of two companies. We are confident that you can trace the firms that are responsible for the lines in this network.

Although we stated that one-mode networks derived from two-mode networks can be analyzed with standard techniques, there is a risk of

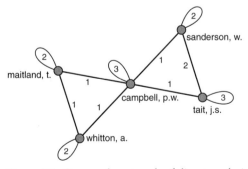

Figure 52. One-mode network of directors derived from Figure 50.

interpreting the results erroneously. A direct tie in a derived one-mode network is easy to interpret: it indicates that two boards have common directors or that two directors meet at one or more boards. Absence of a direct tie implies that two boards do not share a director (e.g., Alliance Trust and Edinburgh Investment Trust in Figure 51) or that two directors do not meet in a board, for instance, A. Whitton and J. S. Tait in Figure 52.

The interpretation of subgroups consisting of three or more vertices is more complicated in derived one-mode networks. Figure 51 contains three cliques of size three. Two cliques are due to directorships of one person, namely P. W. Campbell and J. S. Tait, but one clique is not: the clique of size three with Scottish American Mortgage, Alliance Trust, and Scottish American Investment exists thanks to the memberships of three directors (Campbell, Whitton, and Maitland). In a valued network, this difference is not visible because the multiple lines labeled by names of directors are replaced by single lines with multiplicity values. When interpreting a derived valued network, restrict your conclusions about the number of shared persons (or events) to pairs of vertices. For threesomes and larger sets of vertices you can conclude only that they share one or more actors or events, but you do not know the actual number.

Application

Pajek has special facilities for two-mode networks. We advise to use the data format for two-mode data, which is an ordinary list of vertices and list of edges with the special feature that the list of vertices is sorted: the first part contains all vertices that belong to one subset and the remainder lists the vertices of the other subset. In our example (Scotland.net), vertices numbered 1 to 108 are firms and 109 to 224 are multiple directors. The first line of the data file specifies the total number of vertices and the number of vertices in the first subset (e.g., *Vertices 244 108). When Pajek opens a data file in this format, it automatically creates a partition that distinguishes between the first subset of vertices (class 1) and the second (class 2). This partition is labeled "Affiliation partition" in the Partition drop-down menu.

Net>Transform> 2-Mode to 1-Mode >Rows, Columns

You need the affiliation partition to derive a one-mode network from the two-mode network. The submenu *Net>Transform>2-Mode to 1-Mode* contains commands for translating two-mode into one-mode networks. You can create a one-mode network on each of the two subsets of vertices. By convention, vertices of the first subset are called rows, whereas columns refers to the second subset. These terms are derived from matrix notation, which we present in Chapter 12. The subsets are defined by the affiliation partition. In our example, the first subset contains the firms, so the *Rows* command in the *2-Mode to 1-Mode* submenu will create a network of firms, provided that the two-mode network and affiliation partition are selected in the drop lists of the Main screen. The *Columns* command creates a network of directors.

Net>Transform> 2-Mode to 1-Mode> Include Loops, Multiple lines

Check the *Include Loops* option before you derive a one-mode network if you want to know the number of affiliations per vertex in the new network. Depending on the subset you choose for induction, loops specify

Table 8. *Line Multiplicity in the One-Mode Network of Firms*

Line Values	Frequency	Freq%	CumFreq	CumFreq%
(...1.0000]	231	83.6957	231	83.6957
(1.0000...2.0000]	28	10.1449	259	93.8406
(2.0000...3.0000]	7	2.5362	266	96.3768
(3.0000...4.0000]	3	1.0870	269	97.4638
(4.0000...5.0000]	1	0.3623	270	97.8261
(5.0000...6.0000]	0	0.0000	270	97.8261
(6.0000...7.0000]	0	0.0000	270	97.8261
(7.0000...8.0000]	6	2.1739	276	100.0000
TOTAL	276	100.0000		

the participation rate of actors or the size of events. When the option *Multiple lines* is checked, the derived network will contain one line for each shared actor or event with labels of the events or actors that create the lines. If this option is not checked, a valued network without multiple lines is created with line values expressing line multiplicity. Usually, you do not want loops or multiple lines in the one-mode network, so we do not check these options now.

There is an easy way to display the distribution of line values in Pajek; for example, line multiplicity in a derived one-mode network can be displayed by executing the command *Line Values* from the *Info>Network* submenu. In a dialog box, you may either specify custom class boundaries or you may choose a number of classes of equal width. To obtain classes of equal width, type a number preceded by a pound (#) sign in the dialog box. Usually, the number suggested by the dialog box serves the purpose.

Info>Network> Line Values

Table 8 lists the multiplicity of the lines in the one-mode network of Scottish firms. The first class contains 231 lines with values up to and including 1. Because there are no lines with a multiplicity of less than 1, this class contains all lines with multiplicity one: the single lines. The next class contains lines with values higher than 1, up to and including lines with a value of 2. We assume that you will understand that all 28 lines in this class have a multiplicity of 2. They refer to pairs of firms interlocked by two directors.

You can use the affiliation partition, which distinguishes between the two modes (actors and events), to select the vertices of one mode from a partition or vector associated with the two-mode network. The standard techniques for extracting one or more classes from one partition or vector according to another, which was presented in Chapter 2, can be used to this end.

Imagine, for example, that we want to know the degree of the firms in the two-mode network, which is equal to the number of their multiple directors (the size of the events). We compute the degree in the usual manner with the *Degree>Input* command in the *Net>Partitions* submenu. The partition created by this command does not distinguish between the firms and the directors, so we must extract the firms from it. We select the degree partition as the first partition in the *Partitions* menu to extract the firms

Net>Partitions> Degree>Input

Partitions> Extract Second from First

from it. Next, we select the affiliation partition as the second partition in the *Partitions* menu because it identifies the firms within the network. Finally, we extract class 1 (the firms) of the affiliation partition from the degree partition with the *Partitions>Second from First* command. Now, we can make a frequency distribution (*Info>Partition*) of the degree of the firms. In the same way, we can translate partitions belonging to a two-mode network to a one-mode network derived from it.

Exercise II

Derive the one-mode network of firms without loops and multiple lines from the two-mode network in Scotland.paj. Energize and adjust the network manually until you obtain a structure such as the one depicted in Figure 53. Pay no attention to the contours, which were added manually in special drawing software (see Appendix 2), or to the colors of the vertices.

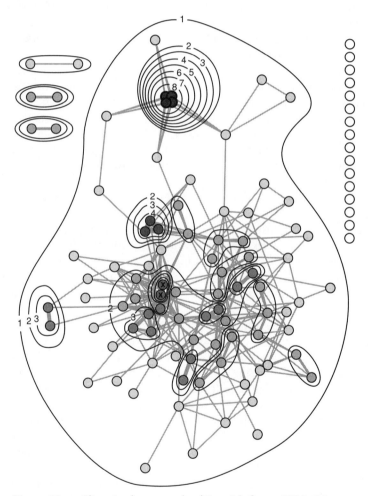

Figure 53. *m*-Slices in the network of Scottish firms, 1904–5 (contours added manually).

5.4   *m*-Slices

One-mode networks derived from two-mode affiliation networks are often rather dense. They contain many cliques, so we can analyze the structure of overlapping cliques or complete subnetworks if we want to detect cohesive subgroups (see Chapter 3, Section 3.6). Chapter 12 presents additional techniques that are useful for analyzing dense networks. In the present chapter, however, we concentrate on a technique based on line multiplicity: *m*-slices.

Multiple lines are considered more important because they are less personal and more institutional. From this point of view, we may define cohesive subgroups on line multiplicity rather than on the number of neighbors. The larger the number of interlocks between two firms, the stronger or more cohesive their tie, the more similar or interdependent they are. In Figure 53, for instance, the four gray firms share eight directors; they are connected by six lines of multiplicity eight (compare Table 8). These firms are connected much more tightly than other firms, which are connected at a multiplicity level of 5 or less.

This brings us to the concept of an *m*-slice: a subnetwork defined by the multiplicity or value of lines. In an *m*-slice, vertices are connected by lines of multiplicity *m* or higher to at least one other vertex. This concept was introduced by John Scott, who called it an *m*-core, but we prefer to rename it because we reserve the term *core* for a *k*-core.

An *m-slice* is a maximal subnetwork containing the lines with a multiplicity equal to or greater than *m* and the vertices incident with these lines.

An *m*-slice is similar to a *k*-core in several respects. A trivial point of resemblance concerns its notation. Just like a 2-core of a simple undirected network is a core in which vertices are connected to at least two neighbors, vertices in a 2-slice are connected by lines with a multiplicity of 2 or higher. Furthermore, *m*-slices are nested like *k*-cores. In Figure 53, we manually circled the components within the *m*-slices. The contours show the nesting of the slices. Look, for example, at the four dark gray vertices in the top middle of Figure 53. These firms belong to an 8-slice because they share eight directors. Because this implies that they share at least seven, six, five, and so on directors, they also belong to a 7-slice, 6-slice, 5-slice, and so on. Because of the nesting, the number of contours that surround a vertex is equal to the multiplicity value defining the *m*-slice to which it belongs. The isolated firms at the top right are not circled because they belong to a 0-slice: they share no directors with other firms.

Finally, note that an *m*-slice does not need to be connected, for instance, the 2-slice of the Scottish firms network contains several unconnected parts. Just like a *k*-core, an *m*-slice does not necessarily identify one cohesive subgroup because it does not guarantee that all vertices within the *m*-slice are connected at a minimum level of line multiplicity. Because we assume that cohesive subgroups are connected, we regard components

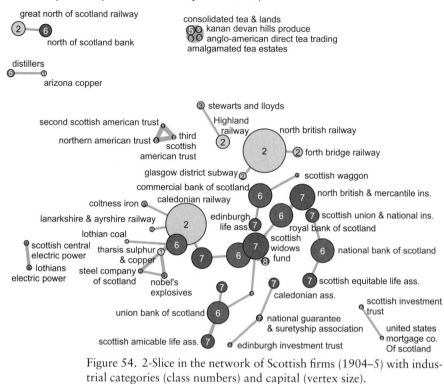

Figure 54. 2-Slice in the network of Scottish firms (1904–5) with industrial categories (class numbers) and capital (vertex size).

within an *m*-slice as cohesive subgroups rather than the *m*-slice itself. If you want to find the cohesive subgroups within a particular *m*-slice, that is, the vertices that are connected by lines of a particular minimum multiplicity, remove all lines with values lower than *m* as well as all vertices that are not part of the *m*-slice and identify the weak components in the resulting subnetwork. Each component contains vertices that are directly or indirectly linked by ties of a particular strength.

Figure 54 shows the components within the 2-slice with the industrial categories of the firms (class numbers from `Industrial_categories.clu`) and their economic value (vertex size determined by `Capital.vec`). Note that you can infer the outline of this sociogram from Figure 53: just eliminate the vertices that belong to the 1-slice and the lines that are incident with these vertices. Filtering out the weakest lines, the stronger compartments emerge from the network. The large component in Figure 53 is now broken down into a number of smaller components: several small components of firms of one type [domestic products (class 5), railways (class 2), electricity (class 4), and investments (class 8)] and one larger component mainly connected by financial institutions [banks (class 6), insurance companies (class 7), and investment banks (class 8)]. In the large component, the wealthy Caledonian Railway and the Scottish Widows Fund occupy pivotal positions. We may conclude that plural interlocks interconnect financial organizations rather than that they link the financial sphere to the heavy industries or to the production of consumer goods in this historical example.

Application

The *Net>Partitions>Valued Core* submenu contains commands that determine the *m*-slices to which the vertices belong, provided that the network contains no multiple lines or loops. Select the one-mode network of Scottish firms created earlier and make sure that the option *Use max instead of sum* is checked in the submenu before you execute either the *First Threshold and Step* or *Selected Thresholds* command in the *Net>Partitions>Valued Core* submenu, which are two different ways to group continuous line values into classes. If you want *m* to represent classes of equal width, choose the command *First Threshold and Step* and choose *Selected Thresholds* otherwise. The latter command needs a vector for input, which is a little bit complicated, so we do not discuss it here.

Net>Partitions> Valued Core> Use max instead of sum

If you use the command *First Threshold and Step*, you must choose among *Input*, *Output*, and *All*. In a directed network, *Input* takes into account incoming arcs only, *Out* focuses on outgoing arcs, and *All* uses both types of arc. In an undirected network such as our example, all three options yield the same result so it makes no difference which option you choose. In a dialog box, you must specify the first threshold, which is the upper limit of the lowest class. Note that each class includes its upper limit. The default threshold (e.g. 0) is the correct choice if you want the partition's class numbers to match the level of multiplicity. A second dialog box asks for the step value, which is the class width. It is one by default and this is a good value for *m*-slices because it creates a class for each consecutive level of multiplicity.

Net>Partitions> Valued Core> First Threshold and Step

Now, Pajek creates a partition with class numbers corresponding to the highest *m*-slice each vertex belongs to. In addition, Pajek reports a frequency table with the distribution of vertices over *m*-slices (denoted by m). Note that loops (if present) are taken into consideration in the computation, so remove them from the network first, otherwise isolated vertices may be regarded as having one or more neighbors.

As argued, the *m*-slices do not represent cohesive subgroups. We must identify the components within the *m*-slices. To this end, we have to remove all lines and vertices that do not belong to an *m*-slice first. Delete all lines with line values below *m* with the *Net>Transform>Remove>lines with value>lower than* command: enter the desired level of *m* (e.g., 2) in the dialog box issued by this command. Note that this command prompts you to create a new network. Next, remove all vertices that belong to lower *m*-slices with the *Operations>Extract from Network>Partition* command. Make sure that the *m*-core partition ("max valued core partition") is selected in the Partition drop-down menu and extract the classes from the selected value of *m* (e.g., 2) up to and including the highest value of *m*, which is 8 in this example. In the resulting network, you can easily identify the weak components with the *Net>Components>Weak* command.

Net>Transform> Remove>lines with value> lower than

Operations> Extract from Network> Partition

Net> Components> Weak

With the *m*-core partition, you can also extract the remaining vertices from the partition of industrial classes (Industrial_categories.clu) and from the vector containing the capital or deposits of the firms (Capital.vec). Use the *Partitions>Extract Second from First* (make sure that Industrial_categories.clu and the *m*-core

Partitions> Extract Second from First

Vector>Extract Subvector

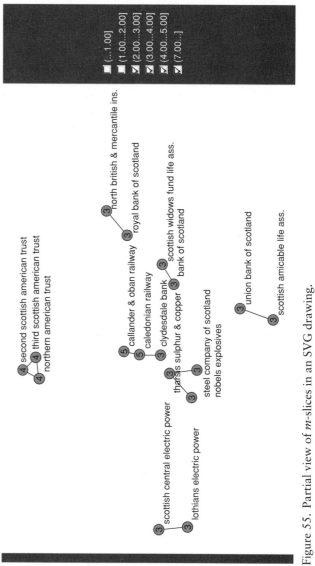

Figure 55. Partial view of *m*-slices in an SVG drawing.

112

partition are selected as the first and second partition respectively in the *Partitions* menu) and *Vector>Extract Subvector* (make sure the *m*-core partition is selected in the Partition drop list) commands discussed in Chapter 2 (Sections 2.4 and 2.5 respectively). If you draw the new network, partition, and vector (command *Draw>Draw-Partition-Vector*), you obtain a sociogram similar to the one depicted in Figure 54, provided that you obtained a layout similar to Figure 53 (see Exercise II) before you deleted lines and vertices of lower *m*-slices from the network. Note that the absolute size of the vertices depends on the size specified in the *Options>Size>of Vertices* option of the Draw screen and that small vertices may be hidden behind large ones.

Draw>Draw-Partition-Vector

Finally, Pajek offers a powerful tool to show *m*-slices interactively on the Web with the *Export>SVG* submenu. Select the one-mode network of firms and the *m*-slices partition in the drop-down menu. Then, draw the network and partition and execute the command *Nested Classes* from the submenu *Export>SVG>Line Values* in the Draw screen to obtain an HTML file and SVG file containing the drawing of the network. Dialog boxes ask for the name of the HTML (and SVG) file that stores the drawing and the number of classes from the active partition that must be represented by different layers. In the latter case, accept the default number suggested in the dialog box.

Export>SVG>Line Values>Nested Classes

If you open this file in an Internet browser with the SVG plug-in installed (see Appendix 2 for details), you will see the sociogram and a set of checkboxes to its right, such as in Figure 55. Each checkbox is associated with a class of lines. If you deselect a checkbox, all lines with values up to and including the deselected class are removed from the picture as well as the vertices that do not belong to the remaining *m*-slices. Figure 55 displays part of the 3-slice in the network of Scottish firms. With the checkboxes you can view the lines and vertices at different multiplicity levels interactively.

On the book's Web site (http://vlado.fmf.uni–lj.si/pub/networks/book/), the HTML file m-slices.htm, which loads the file m-slices.svg automatically, offers an example. Note that the class numbers and vertex colors may be different if you create the SVG image yourself. If two partitions are selected as first and second partition in the *Partitions* menu, Pajek displays the class numbers from the first partition and it determines the color of the vertices from the second partition. In Figure 55, however, vertex colors and class numbers identify the multiplicity level of the *m*-slice to which the vertices belong.

5.5   The Third Dimension

Contours around *m*-slices resemble elevation lines on a hiker's map: crossing a contour means that you go up or down one *m*-slice as if you are reaching a new level of altitude in the mountains. Can we model the network as a landscape in which the elevation of a point matches the value of its *m*-slice? In principle, this can be done but it involves techniques from geography that are not available in Pajek. We can, however, apply the principle of adding heights to points in a plane in different ways.

In previous chapters, we alluded to the possibility of drawing networks in three dimensions but we restricted ourselves to two dimensions. The third dimension is called the z axis, which points from the plane of the Draw screen toward the person in front of the computer monitor. If we use the m-slice class numbers of vertices as their scores on the z axis, the highest m-slice peaks out of the plane. If computer screens were flexible, a three-dimensional drawing of the m-slices in the network of Scottish firms would change its surface to a landscape and we would be able to feel m-slices with our fingertips.

As is, we must be satisfied with a faint sensation of depth, which is caused by the size of vertices and the darkness of vertex labels in a two-dimensional drawing. Nearby vertices are drawn larger and distant vertex labels are gray rather than black. When we rotate the network, we get a better view of the landscape of m-slices (Figure 56), which is clearly dominated by the dark gray peak of the 8-slice.

The third dimension offers another opportunity to visualize social networks. Instead of using a predetermined set of values as z scores (heights) (e.g., values of m-slices), we can energize a network in three dimensions, allowing the *Energy* procedure to locate vertices in a three-dimensional space to optimize the length of lines. Sometimes, a third dimension helps to detect patterns, for instance, a 3D model of the Scottish firms networks separates the different 3-slices better than a two-dimensional drawing

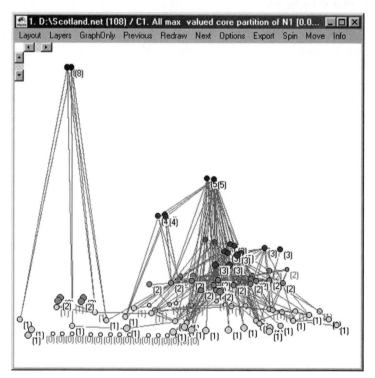

Figure 56. *m*-Slices in three dimensions.

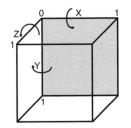

Figure 57. Coordinate system of Pajek.

but the results are often disappointing. Our graphical devices can handle two-dimensional representations much better than three-dimensional models.

Application

First, let us have a look at the coordinate system of Pajek (Figure 57). Imagine that the light gray square is the Draw screen. As we have seen before, the *x* value defines the horizontal location of a vertex (from left to right) and its *y* value specifies the vertical position (from top to bottom). The *z* value of a vertex defines its amount of protrusion from the background of the Draw screen. The arrows indicate the direction of positive rotations around the axes.

You can lift the *m*-slices out of the plane of the screen with the *Layers* menu in the Draw screen. Note that the *Layers* menu is available only if you draw a network with a partition. First, draw the network with the *m*-slices partition and energize it using line values as similarities (see Exercise II) to make sure that components within *m*-slices are drawn closely together. Next, choose option *3D* from the *Type of Layout* submenu and the *Layers* menu will show a command that displays the layers in the *z* direction. On execution of the *In z direction* command, nothing seems to happen but if you take a closer look, you will see that some vertices are drawn larger than others and some vertex labels are gray instead of black. You are looking at the peaks from above, which does not give much sense of relief.

Layers>Type of Layout

Layers>In z direction

When you rotate the structure, peaks and lowlands become more apparent. Toggle the *ScrollBar On/Off* option in the *Options* menu to add two scrollbars to the top left of the Draw screen (see Figure 56). Press the buttons on the vertical scroll bar to rotate the network around the *x* axis, which will raise or lower the peaks, and use the buttons on the horizontal scroll bar to rotate the network around the *y* axis. Continue until you are satisfied with your view. Now you can see that the dark gray 8-slice is towering high above the rest of the network. If the Draw screen is active, you can use the *x*, *y*, and *z* keys on your keyboard to spin the network around the *x*, *y*, and *z* axes, respectively. Use the capitals *X*, *Y*, and *Z* for rotation in the opposite direction.

Options>ScrollBar On/Off

You can also rotate the three-dimensional structure in any direction you wish with the *Spin* menu, but this is slightly more complicated because you have to choose the axis of rotation (command *Normal*) and the angle of rotation, which you must enter in a dialog box displayed by the *Spin*

Spin menu

around command. When you ask for a rotation over 360 degrees (or just press *s* or *S* if the Draw screen is active), you will see the network revolve for your eyes. If the rotation is too fast, lower the *step in degrees* setting. This allows you to inspect the network from all angles.

Three-dimensional optimization is accomplished with the command *3D* in the *Layout>Energy>Fruchterman Reingold* submenu. For a better view, rotate the network with the scrollbars or the *Spin* commands. The sense of depth is much greater if the model is viewed in special 3D software. To accomplish this, Pajek can export the network to a Virtual Reality Markup Language (VRML) model: just select the VRML command in the Export menu of the Draw screen. A dialog box asks for a name of the file that will contain the model. By default, the extension of this file is `.wrl`, which stands for world. VRML viewers recognize this extension, so do not change it. The VRML file can be displayed and manipulated in an Internet browser provided that a special plug-in is installed (for details see Appendix 2). You can rotate and move through the structure as if it is part of a video game, but you need a fast computer and graphics card for smooth operations. The file `m-slice.wrl` (available from the book's Web site http://vlado.fmf.uni-lj.si/pub/networks/book/), which was created by Pajek with the *Export>VRML* command, contains a model of the Scottish firms network with vertex colors indicating *m*-slices. Enjoy.

Exercise III
Create a three-dimensional energized drawing of the information network in San Juan Sur, which we analyzed in the assignment presented in Chapter 3 (`SanJuanSur_deathmessage.net`). Which family–friendship groupings (`SanJuanSur_deathmessage.clu`) are nicely clustered in this image?

5.6 Summary

Affiliation networks are typically two-mode networks, in which persons are related to organizations. The structure of these networks may be analyzed with standard network techniques, but several structural concepts have to be redefined or must be interpreted differently when applied to two-mode networks. Therefore, network analysts usually focus on the one-mode person-by-person or organization-by-organization network that can be induced from a two-mode affiliation network.

Induced one-mode networks tend to be rather dense, because all people affiliated with one organization are interrelated in the one-mode network of persons and all organizations that share a particular person are completely connected in the one-mode network of organizations. Researchers apply the techniques of overlapping cliques and *m*-slices to one-mode networks derived from affiliations. Overlapping cliques identify relatively dense sections of the network and *m*-slices identify clusters of persons or organizations that are related by multiple lines (e.g., firms sharing a number of directors).

Finally, this chapter introduces three-dimensional displays. We can use the third dimension to represent predetermined values by layers (e.g., the multiplicity level of *m*-slices), which turns a sociogram into a landscape, or we can use all three dimensions to energize a network. In subsequent chapters, we encounter more applications of the third dimension but it should be noted that two-dimensional sociograms are often easier to interpret.

5.7   Questions

1. Could the sociogram depicted below represent a two-mode network? If so, show the way in which the vertices can be divided into two modes.

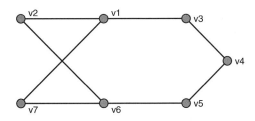

2. Add the names of the firms to the lines of the one-mode network of directors in Figure 52 (Section 5.3).
3. Which of the following statements is correct? Justify your choice.
    a. Each affiliation network is a two-mode network.
    b. Each two-mode network is an affiliation network.
4. What is the multiplicity of the tie between the two vertices marked by an X in the middle of Figure 53 (Section 5.4)?
    a. we do not know
    b. 4
    c. 5
    d. 5 or higher
5. The sociogram below depicts a one-mode network of firms derived from affiliations between multiple directors and firms. Which of the following interpretations can be incorrect?

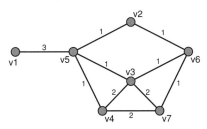

    a. Three directors sit on the boards of v1 and v5 simultaneously.
    b. No director sits on all four boards of firms v2, v3, v5, and v6.
    c. Two directors sit on the boards of v3, v4, and v7 simultaneously.
    d. No director sits on the boards of v1 and v4 simultaneously.
6. Manually add contours of *m*-slices to the sociogram of Question 5.

5.8   Assignment

In Hollywood, composers of soundtracks work on a freelance basis. For each movie, a producer hires a composer and negotiates a fee. The earnings of composers is highly skewed: a handful of composers earn a lot, whereas most of them have moderate or low revenues. This is characteristic of artistic labor markets.

Why do some composers earn much more money than their colleagues in Hollywood? Let us assume that there are two hypotheses:

1. A successful composer works for the same producer(s) on a regular basis, whereas less successful composers do not.
2. The most successful composers all work for the top producers who are responsible for the most expensive movies.

The network Movies.net contains the collaboration of forty composers and the sixty-two producers who produced a minimum of five (completed, shown, and reviewed) movies in Hollywood, 1964–76. This is a 2-mode network: a line between a composer and a producer indicates that the former created the soundtrack for the movie produced by the latter. The line values indicate the number of movies by one producer for which the composer created the music in the period 1964–76. The partition Movies_top_composers.clu identifies the five top composers, each of whom earned 1.5 percent or more of the total income of Hollywood movie score composers in the 1960s and 1970s.

Analyze the 2-mode network in order to test hypothesis 1. Then, create a 1-mode network of composers and see whether it corroborates or falsifies hypothesis 2.

5.9   Further Reading

- Georg Simmel stated his ideas about social circles in *Soziologie: Untersuchungen über die Formen der Vergesellschaftung* (Berlin: Duncker & Humblot, 1908), which was translated by Kurt H. Wolff as *The Sociology of Georg Simmel* (New York: The Free Press, 1950). It contains the often-cited chapter "The Web of Group Affiliations" (Chapter 6). Charles Kadushin used this concept and adapted it to network analysis in his book *The American Intellectual Elite* (Boston: Little, Brown and Company, 1974), using the technique of overlapping cliques. Ronald Breiger wrote a seminal article on the social meaning of affiliations: "The duality of persons and groups." In: *Social Forces* 53 (1974), 181–90.
- In the article "Analysing interlocking directorates: theory and methods" [In: *Social Networks* 1 (1979) 1–36], Meindert Fennema and Huibert Schijf survey research on interlocking directorates. Our example is taken from John Scott and Michael Hughes, *The Anatomy of Scottish Capital: Scottish Companies and Scottish Capital, 1900–1979* (London: Croom Helm, 1980).

- The concept of *m*-cores, which we renamed *m*-slices, can be found in John Scott, *Social Network Analysis: A Handbook* (London: Sage, 1991, 115–16).
- Stanley Wasserman and Katherine Faust discuss affiliation networks and some advanced techniques in Chapter 8 of their book *Social Network Analysis: Methods and Applications* (Cambridge: Cambridge University Press, 1994).
- The data of the assignment are taken from Robert R. Faulkner, *Music on Demand: Composers and Careers in the Hollywood Film Industry* (New Brunswick: Transaction Books, 1983).

5.10   Answers

Answers to the Exercises

I. Select the partition labeled "Affiliation partition of N1 [108,136] (244)" in the Partition drop-down menu before you draw the network. Note that the other partition (Industrial_categories.clu) contains information about 108 vertices (the firms), whereas there are 244 vertices in the network. Therefore, the industrial categories partition cannot be drawn with the network.

In the circular layout of the network, you may notice that all vertices in the first class of the affiliation partition (yellow or black vertices) are grouped together. These are the firms. The second class (green or gray vertices) contains the directors.

II. As explained in the Application part of Section 5.3, transform the two-mode network to a one-mode network of firms with the *Net>Transform>2-Mode to 1-Mode>Rows* command. Check that the options *Include Loops* and *Multiple lines* are not selected before you execute the *Transform* command. To obtain a layout comparable to the one shown in Figure 53, make sure that line values are regarded as measures of similarity: select the option *Options>Values of Lines>Similarities* in the Draw screen. Energy commands will now shorten lines with high multiplicity. Because the one-mode network is not connected, it is best to energize it with Fruchterman Reingold first. Then, apply Kamada–Kawai (once or repeatedly) for refined results. Perhaps, your layout is reflected or rotated – never mind that. It is very likely that you will have to rearrange the isolates and small components by hand because the energy commands do not always set them apart nicely. It is easy to locate and drag the components if you create a partition according to components (minimum size 2) with the *Net>Components>Weak* command first.

III. Energize the network with *Fruchterman Reingold>3D* and spin it around. You will see that all family–friendship groupings are clustered quite well in the three-dimensional model, with the exception of the light green family–friendship grouping consisting of families f5, f14, f17, f25, f58, and f69, which is like a thread through the middle of the sphere.

Answers to the Questions in Section 5.7

1. Yes, the sociogram may represent a two-mode network. The vertices can be divided into two modes such that all lines connect vertices from different modes (the network is bipartite): vertices v1, v4, and v6 would make up one mode and the remaining vertices the other. Vertices v1, v4, and v6 could, for example, represent firms and vertices v2, v3, v5, and v7 could be directors.

2. The sociogram should look like this (do not forget the loops!):

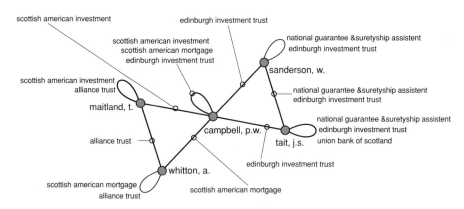

3. Answer a is correct, because affiliations are ties between people and organizations or events, there must be two subsets that cannot be linked internally. Heterosexual love ties constitute a two-mode network but not an affiliation network, so answer b is not correct.

4. Answer c is correct. There are exactly five contours around the two vertices, so their multiplicity level is five.

5. Interpretation c can be incorrect because it is possible that firms v3 and v4 share other directors than firms v3 and v7 and firms v7 and v4. The other interpretations can be correct.

6. Your answer should look like the sociogram below. Do not forget to draw two contours around the 3-slice (left) and to include a contour for the 1-slice, that is, the component, otherwise the level of multiplicity does not correspond to the number of contours.

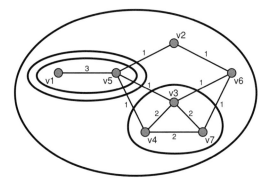

Part III

Brokerage

In quite a few theories, social relations are considered channels that transport information, services, or goods between people or organizations. In this perspective, social structure helps to explain how information, goods, or even attitudes and behavior diffuses within a social system. Network analysis reveals social structure and helps to trace the routes that goods and information may follow. Some social structures permit rapid diffusion of information, whereas others contain sections that are difficult to reach.

This is a bird's-eye view of an entire social network. However, we can also focus on the position of specific people or organizations within the network. In general, being well connected is advantageous. Contacts are necessary to have access to information and help. The number and intensity of a person's ties are called his or her *sociability* or *social capital*, which is known to correlate positively to age and education in Western societies. Some people occupy central or strategic positions within the system of channels and are crucial for the transmission process. Such positions may put pressure on their occupants, but they may also yield power and profit.

In this part of the book, we focus on social networks as structures that allow for the exchange of information. In this approach, the direction of ties is not very important, so we discuss only undirected networks (with one exception). In Chapter 6, we present the concepts of centrality and centralization. In Chapter 7, we discuss the structure of the immediate network of actors, especially the pressure or power that is connected to particular structures of this ego network. In Chapter 8, we take time into account as we study the role of network structure in the diffusion of innovations and diseases.

6

Center and Periphery

6.1   Introduction

In this chapter, we present the concepts of centrality and centralization, which are two of the oldest concepts in network analysis. Most social networks contain people or organizations that are central. Because of their position, they have better access to information and better opportunities to spread information. This is known as the *ego-centered approach* to centrality. Viewed from a *sociocentered perspective*, the network as a whole is more or less centralized. Note that we use *centrality* to refer to positions of individual vertices within the network, whereas we use *centralization* to characterize an entire network. A network is highly centralized if there is a clear boundary between the center and the periphery. In a highly centralized network, information spreads easily but the center is indispensable for the transmission of information.

In this chapter, we discuss several ways of measuring the centrality of vertices and the centralization of networks. We confine our discussion of centrality to undirected networks because we assume that information may be exchanged both ways between people or organizations that are linked by a tie. Concepts related to importance in directed networks, notably prestige, are discussed in Part IV of this book.

6.2   Example

Studies of organizations often focus on informal communication: who discusses work matters with whom and to whom do people turn for advice? Informal communication is important to the operation of the organization and it does not always coincide with the organization's formal structure. For the diffusion and retrieval of information, it is crucial to know the people who occupy central positions in the communication network.

Our example is a communication network within a small enterprise: a sawmill. All employees were asked to indicate the frequency with which they discussed work matters with each of their colleagues on a 5-point

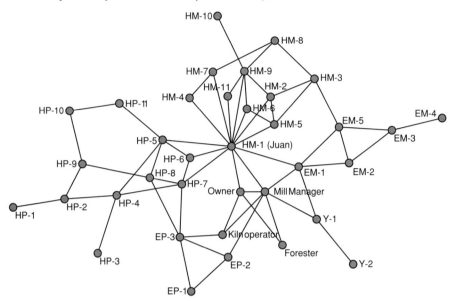

Figure 58. Communication ties within a sawmill.

scale ranging from less than once a week to several times a day. Two employees were linked in the communication network if they rated their contact as three or more. We do not know whether both employees had to rate their tie in this way or that at least one employee had to indicate a strength of three or more. The network is stored in the file Sawmill.net.

In the sawmill, the employees are Spanish speaking (H) or English speaking (E), which, of course, is relevant to their communication. The sawmill contains two main sections: the mill (M), where tree trunks are sawn into logs, and the planer section (P), where logs are planed. Then there is a yard (Y) where two employees are working and some managers and additional officials.

Figure 58 shows the communication network in the sawmill. Note that vertex labels indicate the ethnicity and the type of work of each employee, for example, HP-10 is an Hispanic (H) working in the planer section (P). In this figure, vertex labels instead of vertex colors identify the attributes of employees. It is quite easy to see that work-related communication is structured along work section (planers at the left, sawyers at the right) and ethnicity: Hispanics at the top and English-speakers at the bottom – assuming that management, forester, kiln operator, and employees in the yard are English-speakers.

Intuitively, HM-1 (Juan) is a central, perhaps the most central, person in this network. He communicates with many colleagues directly and through his direct contacts it is easy for him to reach most of the people working in the sawmill. Juan seems to occupy a pivotal position in the flow of information between the planers, the mill section, and management. This chapter presents formal measures of centrality and centralization, which capture these intuitions.

6.3   Distance

One approach to centrality and centralization is based on the simple idea
that information may easily reach people who are central in a communication network. Or, to reverse the argument, people are central if information may easily reach them.

The larger the number of sources accessible to a person, the easier
it is to obtain information; for instance, an elderly person will acquire
information about where to look for help more easily if his or her social
support network is larger. In this sense, social ties constitute a *social
capital* that may be used to mobilize social resources. Hence, the simplest
indicator of centrality is the number of its *neighbors*, which is his or her
degree in a simple undirected network (see Chapter 3). The higher the
degree of a vertex, the more sources of information it has at its disposal,
the quicker information will reach the vertex, so the more central it is.
In the sawmill network, Juan communicates with no fewer than thirteen
colleagues, whereas the manager of the mill has only seven communication
ties (Figure 58). In this respect, Juan is more central than the manager and
information from the shop floor will reach him more easily than it will
reach the manager. If degree is the simplest measure of the centrality of
a vertex, what is the associated measure of centralization for the entire
network, which expresses the extent to which a network has a center? Let
us first answer another, related question: Given a fixed number of lines,
what is the most efficient structure to exchange information? We should
note that this network must be connected, otherwise information cannot
reach all vertices. In this case, the *star-network* is known to be the most
efficient structure given a fixed number of lines. A star is a network in
which one vertex is connected to all other vertices but these vertices are
not connected among themselves (e.g., network A in Figure 59).

Compare the star-network in Figure 59 to the line-network, containing
the same number of vertices and lines (network B). It is much easier to
identify the central vertex in the star-network than in the line-network
because the difference between the central vertex (v5) and the peripheral
vertices (v1, v2, v3, and v4) is much more apparent than in the line-
network. This leads to an idea that may be counterintuitive, namely that
a network is more centralized if the vertices vary more with respect to

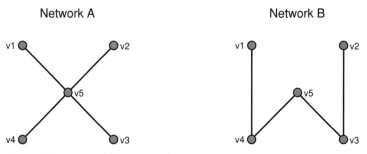

Figure 59. Star- and line-networks.

their centrality. More variation in the centrality scores of vertices yields a more centralized the network.

Now we can define degree centralization as the variation in the degree of vertices divided by the maximum variation in degree which is possible given the number of vertices in the network. In a simple network of a particular size, the star-network has maximum degree variation. The division by maximum degree variation ensures that degree centralization ranges from zero (no variation) to 1 (maximum variation) in the case of a star-network.

The **degree centrality** of a vertex is its degree.

Degree centralization of a network is the variation in the degrees of vertices divided by the maximum degree variation which is possible in a network of the same size.

Variation is the summed (absolute) differences between the centrality scores of the vertices and the maximum centrality score among them. In network A (Figure 59), for instance, one vertex (v5) has degree 4, which is the maximum degree in a simple undirected network of this size because this vertex is connected to all other vertices. The other four vertices have minimum degree, which is 1 in a connected undirected network. Hence, the degree variation amounts to 12: (vertices v1 to v4 contribute) $4 \times (4 - 1)$ and (vertex v5 contributes) $1 \times (4 - 4)$. In a simple undirected network, the degree of vertices cannot vary more than this, so 12 is the maximum variation and dividing 12 by itself, of course, yields a degree centralization of 1.00.

In network B, two vertices have a degree of 1 (v1 and v2) and the other vertices have a degree of 2. Because 2 is the maximum degree in this network, the degree variation equals $2 \times 2 - 1$ (for vertices v1, v2) and $3 \times 2 - 2$ (for vertices v3 to v5), which is 2. To obtain the degree centralization of network B, we divide 2 by 12, which is the maximum variation in a simple undirected network, and we obtain 0.17. If we add a line between v1 and v2, degree centralization becomes minimal (0.00) because all vertices have equal degree, so variation in degree is zero and degree centralization is zero.

We should issue a warning here. In a network with multiple lines or loops, the degree of a vertex is not equal to the number of its neighbors. Therefore, the star-network does not necessarily have maximum variation and we may obtain centralization scores over 1.00 if we compare the variation in a network with multiple lines or loops to the variation in a simple star-network of the same size. In this case, we advise not using degree centralization.

In a simple undirected network, degree centrality is just the number of neighbors of a vertex. In some cases, this is all we know about the network position of people, for instance, when data are collected by means of a survey in which people are asked to indicate the size of their personal network. If we want to analyze the communication structure of the network, however, we need to know who is connected to whom in the entire network and we must pay attention to indirect ties because information can flow from one person to the next and on to other people. In a communication network, information will reach a person more easily if it does not have to "travel a long way." This brings us to the concept of *distance* in networks, namely the number of steps or intermediaries needed for someone to reach another person in the network. The shorter the distance between vertices, the easier it is to exchange information.

In Chapter 3, we defined paths as a sequence of lines in which no vertex in between the first and last vertices occurs more than once. Via a path, we can reach another person in the network: we can inform our neighbor, who passes the information on to his neighbor, who in turn passes it on, until the information finally reaches its destination. We say that a person is *reachable* from another person if there is a path from the latter to the former. Note that two persons are mutually reachable if they are connected by a path in an undirected network, but that two paths (one in each direction) are needed in a directed network.

In an undirected network, the distance between two vertices is simply the number of lines or steps in the shortest path that connects the vertices. A shortest path is also called a *geodesic*. In a directed network, the geodesic from one person to another is different from the geodesic in the reverse direction, so the distances may be different. This sounds strange if you are used to geographic distances but think of a directed network as a system of one-way streets: it is easy to imagine that the route from A to B differs from the journey back. In this chapter, however, we use only undirected networks, so you do not have to worry about this now.

A *geodesic* is the shortest path between two vertices.

The *distance* from vertex u to vertex v is the length of the geodesic from u to v.

With the concept of distance, we can define another index of centrality, which is called closeness centrality. The closeness centrality of a vertex is based on the total distance between one vertex and all other vertices, where larger distances yield lower closeness centrality scores. The closer a vertex is to all other vertices, the easier information may reach it, the higher its centrality.

Just like degree centralization, we can conceptualize closeness centralization as the amount of variation in the closeness centrality scores of the vertices. Again, we compare the variation in centrality scores to the maximum variation possible, that is, the variation in closeness centrality in a star-network of the same size.

The *closeness centrality* of a vertex is the number of other vertices divided by the sum of all distances between the vertex and all others.

Closeness centralization is the variation in the closeness centrality of vertices divided by the maximum variation in closeness centrality scores possible in a network of the same size.

In star-network A (Figure 59), vertex v5 has maximum closeness centrality because it is directly linked to all other vertices. The sum of distances
to the other vertices is minimal, namely four geodesics of length 1 combine into a summed distance of 4. Because there are four vertices other
than v5, the closeness centrality of vertex v5 is maximal: $4/4 = 1.00$.
The other vertices of network A have a closeness centrality score that is
considerably lower (0.57) because three vertices are two steps away from
them.

In network B, v5 also has the highest closeness centrality because it
is in the middle, but now its closeness centrality is not maximal (0.67)
and it differs less from the other vertices, which have closeness centrality
0.57 (vertices v3 and v4) and 0.40 (v1 and v2). Because the variation
of closeness centrality scores in network B is less than in network A,
network B is less centralized. Its closeness centralization is 0.42, whereas
the maximum centralization of network A is 1.00.

Note that complications arise if the network is not (strongly) connected.
If an undirected network is not connected or a directed network is not
strongly connected, there are no paths between all vertices, so it is impossible to compute the distances between some vertices. The solution to
this problem is to take into account only the vertices that are reachable
to or from the vertex for which we want to calculate closeness centrality
and weight the summed distance by the percentage of vertices that are
reachable. This solution works fine for the closeness centrality of vertices.
However, it does not allow us to compute the closeness centralization of
the entire network because the star-network does not necessarily have
the highest variation in closeness centrality scores if the network is not
(strongly) connected. Therefore, we do not use closeness centralization in
the case of a network that is not (strongly) connected.

Application

Net>Partitions> Degree

Net>Transform> Edges→Arcs

Net>Transform> Remove> multiple lines

Net>Transform> Remove>loops

In Chapter 3, we explained how to compute the degree of vertices
in Pajek. Note that the *Net>Partitions>Degree>All* command counts
edges only once, which is fine if the network is undirected. In a network containing edges and arcs, however, you may want to count the
edges as incoming and outgoing arcs. If so, replace the edges by bidirectional arcs (*Net>Transform>Edges→Arcs*) before you calculate degree
with the *All* command. In addition, we advise removing multiple lines
(*Net>Transform>Remove>multiple lines*) and loops (*Net>Transform>
Remove>loops*) from the network before you compute degree centrality
and degree centralization.

The degree partition contains the degree centrality scores of the vertices and the normalized degree vector contains the degree centrality of
the vertices expressed as a proportion of the maximum degree, which is
the number of other vertices in the network. If you inspect these scores,
you will see that Juan has thirteen neighbors, which we already noted
in Figure 58, which is more than one-third (0.37) of all thirty-five people
with whom he can be connected. In addition to the degree partition, Pajek
automatically writes the degree centralization of the entire network to the
Report screen provided that the network contains no multiple lines and

loops. Otherwise Pajek reports a message explaining that degree central-ization is not valid for this network. Here, the degree centralization of the network is 0.289, which is meaningful only in comparison to other networks.

If you want to know the distance between one vertex (e.g., Juan) and all other vertices in the network, you can use the commands in the *Net>k-Neighbours* submenu, which create a partition of classes containing the distances between one vertex and all other vertices. The *Input* command calculates the distances *from* the selected vertex, whereas the *Output* com-mand computes distances *to* the vertex. The *All* command disregards the direction of the lines. In an undirected network, you may choose the *Input*, *Output*, or *All* commands: they yield the same results. The *From Cluster* command is useful if you want to compute distances for a subset of vertices in a large network. *Net>
k-Neighbours*

When you execute a *k-Neighbours* command, you must first specify the vertex number or the label of the vertex from which distances will be computed. In the case of Juan, enter 12 (his vertex number) or HM-1 (the start of his vertex label). Next, you can set a limit to the maximum distance that will be computed. In very large networks, setting a limit may speed up computation considerably. In this dialog box, 0 means that you want all distances, which is usually the right choice in the case of a small network. The distances are stored in a partition and unreachable vertices or vertices further away than maximum distance are placed in class number 9999998, which indicates that their distance is not known.

In Figure 60, vertex colors and class numbers indicate the distances be-tween Juan and other employees. Most employees are directly connected to Juan (black or yellow) or indirectly connected with one intermediary (light gray or green, distance 2). Two employees are four steps away from Juan, namely HP-1 and EM-4.

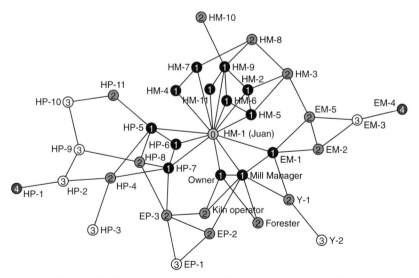

Figure 60. Distances to or from Juan (vertex colors: Default Grey-Scale 1).

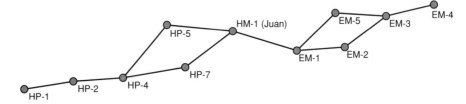

Figure 61. Geodesics between HP-1 and EM-4.

Net >Paths between 2 vertices>All Shortest

Employees HP-1 and EM-4 seem to be furthest apart in the communication network because their distance to Juan is 4. However, their geodesic does not necessarily include Juan, so they may be connected in fewer than eight steps. In Pajek, the geodesics between two vertices can be found with the command *Net>Paths between 2 Vertices>All Shortest*. In the first dialog box, enter the vertex number or label of HP-1. In the second dialog box, enter EM-4 and subsequently answer *Yes* to the question "Forget values of lines?" because you do not want to weight the lines by their values. This is the right thing to do unless line values indicate distances, for instance, geographical distances. Finally, a dialog box asks whether the paths must be identified in the source network. If you answer *Yes* to this question, Pajek produces a partition for the original network that assigns vertices on the geodesics to class 1 and other vertices to class zero. Regardless of your choice in this dialog box, Pajek creates a new network with the vertices and lines that constitute the geodesics (Figure 61). In addition, it prints the distance in the Report screen. In our example, all geodesics between HP-1 and EM-4 include Juan (see Figure 61), so the distance between HP-1 and EM-4 cannot be less than 8, which is the sum of their distances to Juan.

Net>Vector> Centrality> Closeness

In Pajek, the computation of closeness centrality is straightforward. Because closeness centrality scores are continuous rather than discrete, the centrality commands are located in the *Net>Vector* submenu. The *Net>Vector>Centrality* submenu has commands to compute closeness centrality for all vertices in the network. For undirected networks, you may choose the commands *Input*, *Output*, or *All*, which yield the same results. If the network is not (strongly) connected, Pajek creates a vector with closeness centrality scores but it does not compute closeness centralization, which is undefined in such a network. Closeness centrality of vertices that are not reachable to or from all other vertices is set to zero. For medium-sized and large networks, closeness centrality demands a lot of computing time so it should be applied with care.

Pajek creates a vector with the closeness centrality scores of the vertices. You may inspect this vector or use it for computations in the ways explained in previous chapters. In our example, closeness centrality scores range from 0.20 to 0.51 and Juan (0.51) turns out to be more central than the manager (0.42). In addition, Pajek computes the closeness centralization of the network, which is printed in the Report screen. The sawmill communication network has a closeness centralization score of 0.38, which, again, must be interpreted in comparison to other networks.

Exercise I

What will happen to the network if Juan (HM-1) disappears? Remove the vertex, compute closeness centrality and centralization, and interpret the results.

6.4   Betweenness

Degree and closeness centrality are based on the reachability of a person within a network: How easily can information reach a person? A second approach to centrality and centralization rests on the idea that a person is more central if he or she is more important as an intermediary in the communication network. How crucial is a person to the transmission of information through a network? How many flows of information are disrupted or must make longer detours if a person stops passing on information or disappears from the network? To what extent may a person control the flow of information due to his or her position in the communication network?

This approach is based on the concept of betweenness. The centrality of a person depends on the extent to which he or she is needed as a link in the chains of contacts that facilitate the spread of information within the network. The more a person is a go-between, the more central his or her position in the network. If we consider the geodesics to be the most likely channels for transporting information between actors, an actor who is situated on the geodesics between many pairs of vertices is very important to the flow of information within the network. This actor is more central.

Juan, for instance, is important to the communication between HP-1 and EM-4 in the sawmill because all (four) geodesics include Juan (Figure 61). In contrast, HP-5 and HP-7 or EM-2 and EM-5 are less important because if one fails to pass on information, the other may fulfill this role and the communication chain between HP-1 and EM-4 is still intact.

Each pair of vertices may contribute to the betweenness centrality of a vertex. HP-5 and EM-1, for example, contribute to the betweenness centrality of Juan, because their geodesic includes Juan. In contrast, the pair HP-4 and HP-5 does not contribute to Juan's betweenness centrality, because he is not included in their geodesic. In general, we may say that the betweenness centrality of a vertex is the proportion of all geodesics between other vertices in the network that include this vertex. Betweenness centralization is the ratio of the variation in betweenness centrality scores to the maximum variation.

The *betweenness centrality* of a vertex is the proportion of all geodesics between pairs of other vertices that include this vertex.

Betweenness centralization is the variation in the betweenness centrality of vertices divided by the maximum variation in betweenness centrality scores possible in a network of the same size.

It is easy to see that the center of a star network (vertex v5 in Figure 59) has maximum betweenness centrality: all geodesics between pairs of other vertices include this vertex. In contrast, all other vertices have minimum betweenness centrality (0) because they are not located between other vertices. The centrality scores of vertices in a star have maximum variation, so the betweenness centralization of the star is maximal: remove its central vertex and all communication ties are destroyed. In the line-network (B in Figure 59), removal of a vertex may also break the flow of information, but parts of the chain remain intact. Therefore, centrality indices vary less than in the star-network and betweenness centralization is lower.

Application

Net>Vector>
Centrality>
Betweenness

The *Betweenness* command in the *Net>Vector>Centrality* submenu creates a vector of betweenness centrality scores for the vertices in the network. In addition, the betweenness centralization of the network is printed in the Report screen. In directed networks, the procedure automatically searches for directed paths, so there are no separate commands for *Input*, *Output*, and *All*. Even in unconnected networks, betweenness centrality can be computed.

The sawmill communication network has a betweenness centralization of 0.55. Betweenness centrality scores of employees range from 0.00 to 0.59. In Figure 62, vertex size indicates betweenness centrality. Several vertices are invisible because they have zero betweenness centrality: they do not mediate between other vertices. In this example, the betweenness centrality of vertices varies more than their closeness centrality because vertices at the outer margin of the network have zero betweenness, whereas they are still close to part of the network. As a consequence, betweenness centralization is higher than closeness centralization.

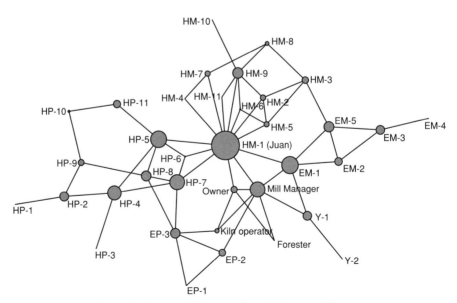

Figure 62. Betweenness centrality in the sawmill.

It is interesting to note that Juan (0.59), EM-1 (0.21), and HP-5 (0.20) are more central than the manager of the mill (0.17). Each ethnic group within the mill's departments – with the exception of the English-speaking planers – seems to have an informal spokesman who is taking care of the communication with other departments or ethnic groups. Juan, who is the spokesman of the Hispanic employees at the mill, is clearly most central.

Exercise II
Compute betweenness centrality on the sawmill network and draw it with vertex sizes corresponding to the betweenness centrality like Figure 62.

6.5   Summary

The concepts of vertex centrality and network centralization are best understood by considering undirected communication networks. If social relations are channels that transmit information between people, central people are those who either have quick access to information circulating in the network or who may control the circulation of information.

The accessibility of information is linked to the concept of distance: if you are closer to the other people in the network, the paths that information has to follow to reach you are shorter, so it is easier for you to acquire information. If we take into account direct neighbors only, the number of neighbors (the degree of a vertex in a simple undirected network) is a simple measure of centrality. If we also want to consider indirect contacts, we use closeness centrality, which measures our distance to all other vertices in the network. The closeness centrality of a vertex is higher if the total distance to all other vertices is shorter.

The importance of a vertex to the circulation of information is captured by the concept of betweenness centrality. In this perspective, a person is more central if he or she is a link in more information chains between other people in the network. High betweenness centrality indicates that a person is an important intermediary in the communication network. Information chains are represented by geodesics and the betweenness centrality of a vertex is simply the proportion of geodesics between pairs of other vertices that include the vertex.

The centralization of a network is higher if it contains very central vertices as well as very peripheral vertices. Network centralization can be computed from the centrality scores of the vertices within the network: more variation in centrality scores means a more centralized network. There is an index of network centralization for each measure of centrality but some centralization measures need special networks: degree centralization is applicable only to networks without multiple lines and loops, and closeness centralization requires a (strongly) connected network.

In this book, we apply centrality and centralization only to undirected networks. It is easy to devise centrality measures for directed networks. We could base degree centrality on the outdegree of vertices, compute closeness centrality from the distances from a vertex to all other vertices (and not in the reverse direction), and consider only shortest directed paths in the case of betweenness centrality. In fact, other books on social network analysis advocate such an approach. We think, however, that it is conceptually more clear to restrict centrality and centralization to undirected networks and to apply other concepts (e.g., prestige) to directed networks.

6.6 Questions

1. Which of the following statements is correct?
   a. The centrality of a network equals the degree of its vertices.
   b. Centralization depends on the variation of centrality scores.
   c. A single vertex is always the center of a network.
   d. The center of a network is always a cohesive subgroup.
2. Put the four networks (below) in order of ascending centralization.

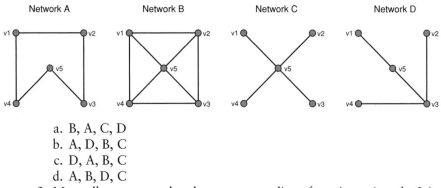

   a. B, A, C, D
   b. A, D, B, C
   c. D, A, B, C
   d. A, B, D, C
3. Manually compute the closeness centrality of vertices v1 and v3 in network D of Question 2.
4. The betweenness centrality of vertex v3 in network D of Question 2 is 0.83. List the geodesics that include v3 and the geodesics that do not.
5. The file `question5.net` contains the nominations made by thirty-two employees of an organization who were asked to name the colleagues with whom they discuss work matters. Note that not all nominations are reciprocated. Omit the unilateral nominations, which are less reliable, from the network and find out who is most central in this communication network.

6.7 Assignment

In the 1970s, Rogers and Kincaid studied the diffusion of family planning methods in twenty-four villages in the Republic of Korea. The files `Korea1.net` and `Korea2.net` contain the communication networks among women in two villages: a village with a successful family planning program (`Korea1.net`) and a village in which family planning was not adopted widely (`Korea2.net`). In both networks, a line indicates that two women discussed family planning. In addition, we know which women adopted family-planning methods at least temporarily (class 1 in the partitions `Korea1_adopters.clu` and `Korea2_adopters.clu`) and which women were members of the local Mothers' Club, which played an important role in the diffusion of family-planning methods (class 1 in the partitions `Korea1_members.clu` and `Korea2_members.clu`) in both networks. The project file `Korea.paj` contains all files.

Analyze the networks and find whether centrality and centralization are associated with the success of the family-planning program in one village and its relative failure in the other village. Explain the effects of centrality and centralization by discussing the role of communication in the adoption of family planning methods.

6.8 Further Reading

- The sawmill example is taken from J. H. Michael and J. G. Massey, "Modeling the communication network in a sawmill." In: *Forest Products Journal* 47 (1997), 25–30.
- The data on the Korean villages stem from E. M. Rogers and D. L. Kincaid, *Communication Networks: Toward a New Paradigm for Research* (New York: The Free Press, 1981), which offers an overview over network analysis from the perspective of communication studies. Note that some of the methods and software packages discussed in the book are obsolete.
- Many more measures of centrality have been proposed, notably information centrality, which considers all paths and not just geodesics in computing a betweenness score, and eigenvector centrality or power, which takes into account how central those are to whom an ego is connected. Read more about these and other measures of centrality in A. Degenne and M. Forsé, *Introducing Social Networks* (London: Sage, 1999, Chapter 6), J. Scott, *Social Network Analysis: A Handbook* (London: Sage (2nd ed. 2000), 1991, Chapter 5), and S. Wasserman and K. Faust, *Social Network Analysis: Methods and Applications* (Cambridge: Cambridge University Press, 1994, Chapter 5).
- The method for calculating closeness centrality on networks that are not (strongly) connected was proposed by G. Sabidussi ["The centrality index of a graph." In *Psychometrika* 31 (1966), 581–603].

6.9 Answers

Answers to the Exercises

I. Remove Juan by creating a partition identifying him in one class and then extracting the other vertices from the network. When Juan's vertex is deleted, the network changes considerably (see figure below). Now, the mill's manager is most central (his or her closeness centrality score is 0.29). The network's closeness centralization decreases to 0.16 and the planers (left) are clearly separated from the mill (right). It is interesting to see that the English-speaking employees are more central, because they are closer than the Spanish-speaking employees to the manager. Juan seemed to function as the informal Hispanic manager.

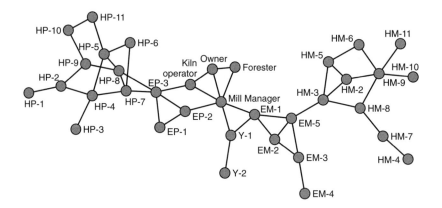

II. Section 6.4 explains how to compute betweenness centrality. To obtain a sociogram such as that in Figure 62, draw it with the command *Draw>Draw-Vector* (or *Ctrl-u*) from the Main screen.

Answers to the Questions in Section 6.6

1. Answer b is correct: network centralization measures the variation of the centrality of the vertices within the network. The more variation, the easier it is to distinguish between the center and the periphery, the more centralized the network. Answer a is incorrect because centrality is a property of a vertex, not of a network. Answers c and d are incorrect, because the center of a network, if it has one, may either be a single vertex or a cohesive subgroup (e.g., a clique) consisting of a number of vertices that are equally central.

2. Answer d is correct. The star-network is most central, so answer a is not correct. In the circle network (network A), all vertices have degree 2, each vertex is equally distant from all other vertices, and each vertex is situated on one geodesic between pairs of other vertices, so there is no variation in centrality, hence minimum centralization. Network A is least centralized, so answer c is not correct. Network D is more centralized than network B, so answer d is correct.

3. The distances between vertex v1 and vertices v2, v3, v4, and v5 are 3, 2, 3, and 1 respectively. The sum distance is 9, so the closeness centrality of vertex v1 is 4 (the number of other vertices) divided by 9, which is 0.44.

   The sum distance of vertex v3 to v1, v2, v4, and v5 is $2 + 1 + 1 + 1 = 5$, so its closeness centrality is $4/5 = 0.8$.

4. The geodesics between vertex v1 and v2 (v1-v5-v3-v2), v1 and v4 (v1-v5-v3-v4), v5 and v2 (v5-v3-v2), v5 and v4 (v5-v3-v4), and v2 and v4 (v2-v3-v4) include vertex v3, whereas the geodesic between v1 and v5

(v1-v5) does not. Five of six geodesics include v3, so its betweenness centrality is 0.83.

5. The easiest way to omit all unilateral nominations is to change bi-directional arcs into edges (*Net>Transform>Arcs->Edges>Bidirected Only*) and remove the remaining arcs subsequently (*Net>Transform>Remove>all arcs*). Now you have an undirected network and it is easy to compute the three kinds of centrality (degree, closeness, and betweenness) and display the vertices with highest scores with the *Info>Partition* and *Info>Vector* commands. Vertex v9 has highest degree (17), highest closeness centrality (0.67), and highest betweenness centrality (0.20). Person v9 consistently ranks highest on the three centrality indices.

7

Brokers and Bridges

7.1 Introduction

A person with many friends and acquaintances has better chances of getting help or information. Therefore, social ties are one measure of social capital, an asset that can be used by actors for positive advantage. Network analysts, however, discovered that the kind of tie is important in addition to the sheer number of ties. Their general argument is that strong (i.e., frequent or intense) ties with people who are themselves related yield less useful information than weak ties with people who do not know one another. Having a lot of ties within a group exposes a person to the same information over and over again, whereas ties outside one's group yield more diverse information that is worth passing on or retaining to make a profit.

As a consequence, we have to pay attention to the ties between a person's contacts. A person who is connected to people who are themselves not directly connected has opportunities to mediate between them and profit from his or her mediation. The ties of this person bridge the structural holes between others. It is hypothesized that people and organizations who bridge structural holes between others have more control and perform better.

In this chapter, we first discuss bridges at the level of the entire network (Section 7.3). Which ties (bridges) and which vertices (cut-vertices) are indispensable for the network to remain connected? If a network contains such ties and vertices, it contains bottlenecks and the flow of information through the network is vulnerable. In the remaining sections, we focus on brokerage at the level of individuals. Who is in the best position to profit from his or her social ties (Section 7.4) and how is this affected by group membership (Section 7.5)?

7.2 Example

The example in this chapter shows the importance of informal communication structures within a firm. In a wood-processing facility, a new management team proposed changes to the workers' compensation

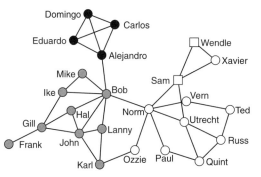

Figure 63. Communication network of striking employees.

package, which the workers did not accept. They started a strike, which led to a negotiation stalemate. Then, management asked an outsider to analyze the communication structure among the employees because it felt that information about the proposed changes was not effectively communicated to all employees by the union negotiators.

The outside consultant asked all employees to indicate the frequency with which they discussed the strike with each of their colleagues on a 5-point scale, ranging from *almost never* (less then once per week) to *very often* (several times per day). The consultant used 3 as a cutoff value. If at least one of two persons indicated that they discussed work with a frequency of 3 or more, a line between them was added to the informal communication network (`Strike.net`).

The network displays fairly stringent demarcations between groups defined on age and language (Figure 63). The Spanish-speaking young employees, who are of age 30 or younger (class 1 in the partition `Strike_groups.clu`, black or yellow vertices), are almost disconnected from the English-speaking young employees (class 2, gray or green vertices), who communicate with no more than two of the older English-speaking employees (38 years old or older, class 3: white or red vertices). These divisions mirror the homophily principle discussed in Chapter 3: people tend to relate to those who are similar.

All ties between groups have special backgrounds. Among the Hispanics, Alejandro is most proficient in English and Bob speaks some Spanish, which explains their tie. Bob owes Norm for getting his job and probably because of this, they developed a friendship tie. Finally, Ozzie is the father of Karl.

Sam and Wendle are the union negotiators; they are represented by boxes in Figure 63 (open the network data file `Strike.net` in a text editor to see how we created boxes for Sam and Wendle in the list of vertices). They were responsible for explaining the new program proposed by the managers. When the informal communication structure among employees was reported to the management, they approached two of the other employees directly (Bob and Norm) to explain the reforms to them personally. Then, they gave them some time to discuss the plans with their colleagues. Within two days, the young and old employees were willing to strike a deal with the management and they persuaded the union representatives to reopen negotiations. Soon, the labor dispute was reconciled and the strike ended.

7.3   Bridges and Bi-Components

The example shows the importance of social ties to the diffusion of information. Information is the key to the exploitation of social ties as social capital. Social ties offer access to information, which can be used to reduce uncertainty and risk and to create trust, as for instance, when information is confirmed from several sources. People in crucial positions in the information network may also spread or retain information strategically because they have control over the diffusion of information.

In a social system, for instance, an organization, the overall structure of informal ties is relevant to the diffusion of information. Can information reach all members of the organization or is it more likely to circulate in one segment of the network? Are there any bottlenecks that are vital to the flow of information, which may prohibit the spread of information because of information overload or because people pursue their private, strategic goals?

In Figure 63, the tie between Alejandro and Bob is clearly a bottleneck because it is the only channel for information exchange between the Hispanic employees and all other employees. Removing this single line will cut off the Hispanics from information circulating among the other employees. Formally, this line is a *bridge* in the network because its removal creates a new component, which is isolated from other components. The strike network consists of one component (recall that a component is a maximal connected subnetwork; see Chapter 3), so information may travel to each employee via social ties. When you remove the line between Alejandro and Bob, you disconnect the Hispanic workers from the communication network, so they become a component on their own.

> A *bridge* is a line whose removal increases the number of components in the network.

Note that there is one more bridge in the information network of striking employees: the tie between Frank and Gill. If you remove this tie, Frank becomes an isolate. Because an isolate is a component, the network consists of two components after removing Frank's tie with Gill.

The removal of a line may annul the connectedness of a network or component but the deletion of a vertex may have the same effect, because you remove the lines that are incident with the deleted vertex. After all, you cannot have a line with a single endpoint! When Bob refuses to discuss the strike any further, he is lost to the communication network and all of his ties disappear, including the bridge to Alejandro. Therefore, Bob is a *cut-vertex* or *articulation point*: its deletion disconnects the network or it disconnects a component of the network. Just as with a bridge, a

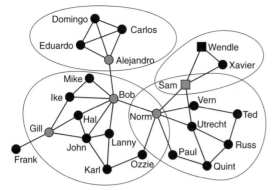

Figure 64. Cut-vertices (gray) and bi-components (manually circled) in the strike network.

cut-vertex is crucial to the flow of information in a network. It is a bottleneck in the network that controls the flow from one part to another part of the network. Norm, for example, is indispensable for exchanging information between the older and younger employees.

Deleting a vertex from a network means that the vertex and all lines incident with this vertex are removed from the network.

A *cut-vertex* is a vertex whose deletion increases the number of components in the network.

In Figure 64, all cut-vertices are gray. Note that vertices incident with a bridge may or may not be cut-vertices. Alejandro and Bob are cut-vertices, but Frank is not, because removal of Frank and his bridge to Gill does not increase the number of components.

Now that we have defined cut-vertices, it is easy to define sections of a network that are relatively invulnerable to the withdrawal or manipulation of a single vertex, namely bi-components. A *bi-component* is simply a component – a maximal connected subnetwork – of minimum size 3 without a cut-vertex. In a bi-component, no person can control the information flow between two other persons completely because there is always an alternative path that information may follow. In a bi-component, each person receives information from at least two sources (in an undirected network), so he or she may check the information. We may say that a bi-component is more cohesive than a strong or weak component because there are at least two different paths between each pair of vertices; that is, two paths that do not share a vertex in between their starting point and endpoint.

A *bi-component* is a component of minimum size 3 that does not contain a cut-vertex.

The strike network as a whole clearly is not a bi-component because it contains five cut-vertices. Within the network, however, there are four bi-components, which are manually circled in Figure 64. These are, clockwise and starting at the top, (1) a Hispanic bi-component, consisting of Alejandro, Carlos, Domingo, and Eduardo; (2) a bi-component with the two union representatives and Xavier; (3) a bi-component with all older English-speaking employees except Ozzie, Wendle, and Xavier; and (4) a bi-component with Ozzie, Norm, and all young English-speakers except Frank.

You should be puzzled now. Didn't we define a bi-component as a component (of minimum size three) without a cut-vertex? Then, how is it possible that each of the listed bi-components contains at least one gray vertex in Figure 64, that is, at least one cut-vertex? The answer is that a bi-component does not contain cut-vertices if you look at the bi-component only and ignore the rest of the network. Concentrate on the Hispanic employees, for instance: if you remove Alejandro, the other three Hispanics remain connected into one component, so the removal of Alejandro does not increase the number of components among the Hispanic employees. Looking at the entire network, however, Alejandro is a cut-vertex because he connects the Hispanic bi-component to Bob.

In other words, a cut-vertex always connects different bi-components or bridges. Norm, for example, belongs to two bi-components: to the majority of older English-speakers and to the bi-component of the young English-speaking employees. In a similar way, Sam connects two bi-components. Alejandro, Bob, and Gill, however, connect a bi-component to a bridge, namely the bridge between Alejandro and Bob or the bridge between Gill and Frank. Cut-vertices indicate the borders of bi-components and bridges. A component usually consists of overlapping bi-components and bi-components connected by bridges.

It is interesting to note that the two union representatives among the employees, Wendle and Sam, are part of a bi-component that is connected to the bi-component of older employees by Sam. So we may say that Sam controls the information exchange between the union representatives and all other employees except Xavier. If Sam does not want to strike a deal with the management of the firm, he can manipulate the information to and from the other employees.

In numerous applications, it has been shown that people with strong ties belong to cliques and strong ties tend to be located in or develop into cliques; for example, family ties are usually strong in the sense that they are intense, and family ties display cliques: several or all members of a family maintain strong ties among themselves. As a consequence, family ties are not very useful in finding new jobs because they relate you to people with whom you are already related. Usually, they do not supply information about new jobs of which you have not already heard. In contrast, less intense and irregular contacts such as former colleagues or acquaintances are better sources of information on new job opportunities. These weak ties are more likely to be bridges to distant information networks, hence the concept of "the strength of weak ties," meaning that weak ties are often more important for the dispersion of information than strong ties. The strength of a tie may be taken as a proxy of its chances of being a network bridge.

This hypothesis could apply to the Spanish-speaking employees. Strong ethnic ties develop into a clique and the only nonethnic tie (between Alejandro and Bob) is a bridge to the rest of the network. In this example, however, family ties connect employees outside cliques: Gill is Frank's cousin and Ozzie is Karl's father. We should note that the strength of weak ties depends on the situation: on the shop floor, family ties, which are usually considered strong, may fulfill the bridging role of weak ties because family ties are uncommon and they will not develop into cliques within the firm (a firm is not the natural setting for raising a family).

Remember, however, that we consider only the stronger communication ties because irregular communication ties are disregarded (scores 1 and 2 on the 5-point scale) in this example. The strength of weak ties argument predicts that strong ties will constitute cliques, which is clearly the case. Perhaps, the weaker ties cross group boundaries more often. Note that the strength of a tie may be defined in several ways, for instance, frequency versus social intensity, which is important to consider when you apply the strength of weak ties hypothesis.

Application

You may use the *Bi-Components* command in the *Net>Components* sub-menu for finding bi-components, bridges, and cut-vertices in a network. On selection of this command, you are prompted to specify the minimum size of the bi-components to be identified. The default value 3 will identify the bi-components within the network and it will only report cut-vertices that connect two or more bi-components. A minimum size of two will trace all bi-components, bridges, and all cut-vertices, including cut-vertices connecting bridges. Note that a bridge and its incident vertices constitute a component of size two without a cut-vertex in an undirected network.

Net> Components> Bi-Components

Pajek's *Bi-Components* command treats directed networks as if they were undirected, which means that it identifies weak instead of strong components without cut-vertices in directed networks. If you symmetrize a directed network before you execute the *Bi-Components* command, you will obtain exactly the same results.

In this example, we want to identify the bi-components and the bridges, so we issue the *Bi-Components* command with a minimum component size of 2. The output of the *Bi-Components* command consists of two partitions and a hierarchy. The first partition ("Vertices belonging to exactly one bicomponent") indicates the sequential number of the bridge or bi-component to which a vertex belongs. Vertices that do not belong to a bridge or bi-component (e.g., isolates) are collected in class 0 and vertices that belong to two or more bridges or bi-components – cut-vertices – are placed in class number 9999998.

The second partition ("Articulation points") indicates the number of bridges or bi-components to which a vertex belongs: 0 for isolates, 1 for a vertex that belongs to exactly one bridge or bi-component, 2 for vertices that belong to two bridges or bi-components, and so on. This partition is used in Figure 64. Finally, the hierarchy shows the bridges or bi-components to which each vertex belongs. We need a hierarchy to

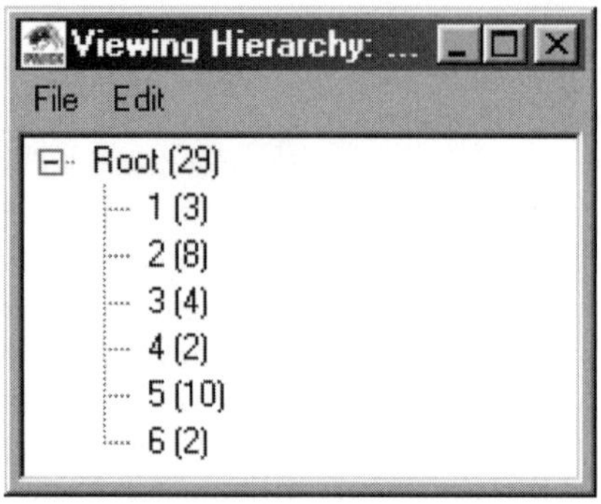

Figure 65. Hierarchy of bi-components and bridges in the strike network.

store the bridges and bi-components because cut-vertices belong to two or more bi-components. Note that bridges are not counted if the minimum size has been set to 3.

File>
Hierarchy>Edit

Because bridges are bi-components of size 2 in an undirected network without multiple lines, you can easily find the bridges in the hierarchy of bi-components: open the Edit screen with the hierarchy of bi-components (see Figure 65) with the command *File>Hierarchy>Edit* or with the Edit button on the left of the hierarchy drop-down menu. Figure 65 lists the six bridges and bi-components in the communication network among striking employees. The size of each subnetwork is reported between brackets, so it is easy to find the two bridges in this example: subnetworks four and six. Double-click them to see their vertices.

Exercise I
Detect only the bi-components in the strike network by setting the minimum component size to three in the *Bi-Components* command. How many cut-vertices does Pajek identify now. And what happens to Frank?

7.4   Ego-Networks and Constraint

In the previous section, we analyzed the structure of the entire network, which is a *sociocentered approach*. Now we turn to the *ego-network* and *ego-centered approach*: we focus on the position of one person in the network and his or her opportunities to broker or mediate between other people.

Let us first have a look at a *triad*, which consists of a focal person (ego), an alter, a third person, and the ties among them. The triad is the smallest network that contains more than two persons and it highlights the complexities of ties within a group. According to the sociologist Georg Simmel, a complete triad (A in Figure 66) reduces the individuality of its members. When three people are fully connected, they share norms and information, they create trust by feedback, and conflicts between two members may be resolved or moderated by the third person. In other words, complete connections between three persons make them behave as a group rather than as a set of individuals.

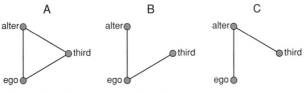

Figure 66. Three connected triads.

In an undirected triad that is connected but incomplete, for instance, networks B and C in Figure 66, people are considered less bound by group norms. One person is in an advantageous, powerful position, because he or she may broker between the other two. The person in the middle (the ego in B and alter in C, Figure 66) may profit from the competition between the other two, for example, the ego negotiates the price of a good or service to be delivered by either alter or the third party in network B. The ego makes them compete, which would not be possible if the alter and third would agree about a price among themselves. This is known as the *tertius gaudens* ("the third who benefits") or the *tertius* strategy: induce and exploit competition or rivalry between the other two, who are not directly related. The absence of a tie between an alter and the third party is known as a *structural hole*, which may be exploited by the ego.

A more malicious variant is known as *divide et impera* or the divide-and-rule strategy, in which a person creates and exploits conflict between the other two to control both of them; for example, the ego tells alter unpleasant things about the third party and the third party about alter, which results in hostility among them. This would not be possible if they could directly check the information and find out the ego's subversive strategy. Again, the structural hole allows the ego to apply this strategy.

In both strategies, an individual's advantage or power is based on his or her control over the spread of information, goods, or services, which stems from the structure of his or her network. We want to stress that brokerage is related to the absence of ties (i.e., the presence of holes) between neighbors, whereas we concentrated on the presence of ties in our chapters about cohesive subgroups in Part II.

The opportunities that a structural hole offers in an incomplete triad have a reverse side: they imply constraint in a complete triad. A complete triad is not just a triad without opportunities because it has no structural holes. The situation is even worse from the perspective of brokerage, because you cannot withdraw from any of these unrewarding ties without creating a structural hole around yourself. In network A (Figure 66), the ego is more or less obliged to maintain both ties, because if the ego ends ties with one (e.g., with the third in A, so triad C evolves), there is a structural hole around the ego that the alter may take advantage of.

> The *ego-network* of a vertex contains this vertex, its neighbors, and all lines among the selected vertices.

Now, let us focus on the *ego-network*, which consists of an ego, the ego's neighbors, and the ties among them. Alejandro's ego-network is displayed

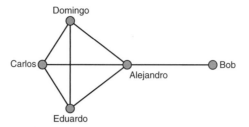

Figure 67. Alejandro's ego-network.

in Figure 67. The ego-network of a person contains all triads that include this person, so we can analyze it as a set of triads. For each triad, we can determine whether it constrains ego or whether it contains a structural hole that the ego may exploit; for instance, Alejandro (ego) has an opportunity to broker between Bob (alter) and Domingo (third) because Bob and Domingo are not directly connected. For the same reason, Alejandro may broker between Bob and Carlos or Eduardo. There are three triads in Alejandro's ego-network that give him an opportunity to broker for Bob.

In a similar way, we can compute the constraint on Alejandro that is exercised by his tie with Bob: the number of complete triads containing Alejandro, Bob, and another neighbor of Alejandro. Because no other neighbor of Alejandro is directly connected to Bob, there is no constraint on Alejandro because of his tie with Bob. A low constraint indicates many structural holes, which may be exploited. In contrast, the constraint on Alejandro's ties with Carlos, Domingo, and Eduardo is very high because these ties are involved in three complete triads. When Alejandro withdraws from any of these ties, they may start brokering for him.

The higher the constraint, the fewer the opportunities to broker and the more dangerous it is to withdraw from a tie. This constraint is known as the *dyadic constraint* associated with a tie from ego's point of view. Note that the constraint of a tie on ego may differ from the constraint experienced by alter on the same tie. The tie between Alejandro and Carlos, for instance, is more constrained for Carlos than for Alejandro, because all triads in Carlos' ego-network are complete.

In our discussion of structural holes and constraint, something is still missing: we ought to take into account the importance of a tie to a person. If a tie is very cheap in terms of investment (money, network time, and energy), it is not really a problem to be obliged to maintain it. If a tie is just one among many (low exclusivity), ego does not depend on this tie much and it is no big deal if alter threatens to break it. Besides, if the tie between the alter and the third party is not important to them, it may function like an absent tie, which can be exploited.

The *proportional strength* of a tie with respect to all ties of a person is a simple indicator of the importance or exclusivity of a tie. It is computed as the value of the line(s) representing a tie, divided by the sum of the values of all lines incident with a person. If line values express costs, time, or energy, the proportional strength of a tie is the portion of an actor's total expenditure that is invested in the ties with an alter. Just like dyadic constraint, it makes a difference from which standpoint you look at the

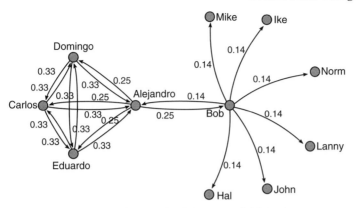

Figure 68. Proportional strength of ties around Alejandro.

network, for instance, the tie between Alejandro and Bob is one out of Alejandro's four ties (0.25) but it is only one of Bob's seven ties (0.14), so the proportional strength of a tie must be represented by a directed network (Figure 68). Note that the original network may contain multiple lines, directed and undirected lines, and line values, but the network with proportional strength ties is always simple directed and contains only bidirected arcs.

> The *dyadic constraint* on vertex u exercised by a tie between vertices u and v is the extent to which u has more and stronger ties with neighbors who are strongly connected with vertex v.

This definition describes the ideas behind dyadic constraint rather than the exact computation. For those interested in the exact computation: add the proportional strength of the tie from the ego to the alter (investment of the ego in the alter) to the products of the proportional strength of the two arcs in each path from the ego to the alter via another neighbor of the ego and take the square of this sum.

The constraint on Alejandro attached to his tie with Eduardo is equal to the square of the following sum: 0.25 (Alejandro's investment in Eduardo), plus 0.25×0.33 (Alejandro's tie to Carlos times Carlos' tie to Eduardo), plus 0.25×0.33 (idem via Domingo). All numbers are proportional strengths which can be read from Figure 68, from which we omitted arcs toward Bob that are not relevant to the constraints on Alejandro. The sum is 0.415 and the square of this sum is 0.17 (see Figure 69). As you may have expected, the constraint on Alejandro that is attached to his

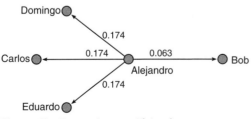

Figure 69. Constraints on Alejandro.

ties with Domingo or Carlos is also 0.17. The constraint on his tie with Bob is just the square of the proportional strength of this tie (0.0625) because there are no indirect paths from Alejandro to Bob in Alejandro's ego-network.

We may conclude that the constraint on Alejandro's tie with Bob is about one-third of the constraint of his ties within the Hispanic cluster. Clearly, the structural holes in Alejandro's network are attached to his link with Bob: he is able to play the *tertius gaudens* strategy between Bob and the other Hispanics because he may act as a representative of the Hispanics to Bob.

If we have the dyadic constraint on all ties of a person, we can simply add them to obtain the *aggregate constraint* on this person. The aggregate constraint is a nonnegative number that is usually between 0 and 1 but it can be greater than 1. The aggregate constraint on Alejandro, for instance, is $0.174 + 0.174 + 0.174 + 0.063 = 0.585$. The higher the aggregate constraint, the less "freedom" a person has to withdraw from existing ties or to exploit structural holes.

In general, more direct links between an ego's neighbors yield a higher aggregate constraint on that ego because each link between neighbors creates a complete triad with the ego. For this reason, network analysts have used the *density of the ego-network* without the ego as an indicator of the constraint on an ego. In the case of Alejandro, there are three lines among his four neighbors (see Figure 67) (viz. between Carlos, Domingo, and Eduardo). The *egocentric density* is 0.5: three of the six possible lines exist among Alejandro's four neighbors. In contrast, Carlos' egocentric density is maximal because all of his neighbors (Domingo and Eduardo) are directly linked.

People or organizations with low aggregate constraint are hypothesized to perform better. It has been shown that employees with low constraint in an organization have more successful careers and that business sectors with lower constraint on firms are more profitable. In general, researchers compare the constraint on an actor to one or more indicators of its (economic) success. In our example, this could be the success in resolving the conflict between employees and management or personal influence on the conditions specified in the final agreement. Bob and Norm negotiated the proposal with the management before they called in the union representatives, so they may have been successful in changing the conditions according to their interests.

Application

Net> Vector> Structural Holes

In Pajek, one command computes the proportional strength of ties, the dyadic constraint, and the aggregate constraint for all vertices in a network. This command is aptly called *Structural Holes* and you can find it in the *Net>Vector* submenu. The proportional strength of ties is output as a new network and so is dyadic constraint. In these networks, the line values express the strength and constraint on ties, respectively. Note that these networks are always directed and that all arcs are reciprocated, no matter whether the original network is directed or undirected and valued or unvalued or contains multiple lines and loops.

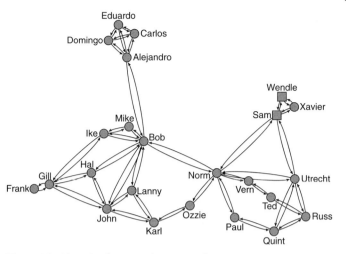

Figure 70. Energized constraint network.

There is an easy way to visualize the structural holes in a network. Take the network of dyadic constraint and, using the line values as similarities (option *Options>Values of Lines>Similarities* in the Draw screen), energize it. Now, vertices that are tied by links of high constraint are drawn closely together, whereas ties of low constraint are long, so they create a lot of space between the vertices that looks like a hole (Figure 70 – energized with Kamada–Kawai).

Options >Values of Lines> Similarities

Aggregate constraint is output as a vector. You may inspect this vector in the usual ways with the *Info>Vector* command or by editing it. If you want the size of the vertices to represent their aggregate constraint in the Draw screen, we advise multiplying the vector by 10 (command *Vector>Transform>Multiply by*) or using the *Autosize* option in the *Options>Size>of Vertices* submenu of the Draw screen, otherwise the vertices are drawn too small.

Info>Vector

Vector> Transform> Multiply by

[Draw]Options> Size>of Vertices

To calculate the egocentric density of a vertex, that is, the density of ties among its neighbors, you must extract the subnetwork of the neighbors from the overall network. First, select the neighbors of a particular vertex with the *Net>k-Neighbours>All* command. In the first dialog box, specify the number or label of the vertex for which you want to compute egocentric density (e.g., Alejandro). In the second dialog box, enter 1 as the maximum distance. The command now creates a partition with the ego in class zero and its neighbors in class 1. Second, extract the neighbors from the network with the *Operations>Extract from Network>Partition* command, selecting class 1 as the only class to be extracted. Now that you have created the network of neighbors, you can inspect its density with the *Info>Network>General* command in the Main screen.

Net>k-Neighbours>All

Operations> Extract from Network> Partition

[Main] Info> Network> General

For a simple undirected network you can compute the egocentric density of all vertices with the *Net>Vector>Clustering Coefficients>CC1* command. This command produces two vectors; the first vector – "Clustering Coefficients CC1" but *not* "Clustering Coefficients CC1'" – contains the egocentric density. The results for directed networks

Net>Vector> Clustering Coefficients> CC1

represent egocentric density only if the network does not contain loops or bidirectional arcs.

Exercise II
Compute the aggregate constraint on Norm and Bob in the strike network as well as their egocentric density. Do aggregate constraint and egocentric density match in this case?

7.5   Affiliations and Brokerage Roles

Group affiliation is often important in brokerage processes. A union representative mediates between the management and the workers. He or she can negotiate with one manager or another and choose whom of his or her colleagues to consult. To some extent, his or her contacts are replaceable by someone else from the same group. Moreover, the union representative himself must belong to a particular group, namely the workers. In our example, the union representatives Sam and Wendle are a subgroup of workers and the management is supposed to negotiate with them. This restricts the managers' choice of negotiation partners enormously, so they have little opportunity to play off one negotiator or worker against another. In this case, the opportunity to broker depends not only on the position of people in the network but also on their group affiliations.

The easier it is to replace your contact by someone else from his or her group, the stronger your position is to negotiate and the higher the chance of striking a good deal or of getting things done your way. The replacement does not have to be one of your present contacts; it may be someone outside of your present ego-network whom you include at the expense of someone else. Is there someone else in your contact's group who is at least as central as your contact but who is not directly linked to your contact so including him or her in your ego-network would create a structural hole between your present contact and the new contact? Such a structural hole is called a *secondary structural hole*.

Let us illustrate this with an example. Suppose Alejandro wants to play a divide-and-rule strategy against Bob because he feels too constrained by him. Bob is in a good structural position to negotiate on behalf of the English-speaking young employees because he is directly connected to most members of this group. It is very difficult to spread discord among members of his group by spreading rumors about Bob, because the other members of the group are likely to inform Bob when they maintain direct ties. Alejandro's best choice seems to be Gill, because he is not directly connected to Bob and it is very likely that Frank will team up with him, after which Gill may try to play Ike versus Hall and John, although these colleagues are constrained by Bob. Frank and Karl, the only other English-speaking young employees who are not directly related to Bob, are less suited as an alternative to Bob because they are less central in the group.

Because secondary structural holes concern the ties within one group, namely the opportunities to exploit structural holes within that group, the aggregate constraint within a group seems to be a useful

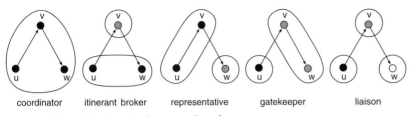

Figure 71. Five brokerage roles of actor v.

indicator of whom to contact and persuade as an alternative to your present contact in the group: the person who is least constrained and who is not constrained by your present contact because he is not directly tied to him or her (see Figure 73 in the Application section).

For another approach to brokerage and affiliations, we have to turn to triads again. A triad in which person *v* mediates transactions between persons *u* and *w* can display five different patterns of group affiliations, which are indicated by vertex color as well as contours in Figure 71. Each pattern is known as a *brokerage role*. Research into brokerage roles is concerned with describing the types of brokerage roles that dominate a transactional or exchange network. In addition, individual positions within the network may be characterized by the dominant type of brokerage role and hypotheses may be tested about the personal characteristics of individuals with certain types of brokerage roles.

Two brokerage roles involve mediation between members of one group. In the first role, the mediator is also a member of the group. This is known as the *coordinator role*. In the second role, two members of a group use a mediator from outside, an *itinerant broker*. The other three brokerage roles describe mediation between members of different groups. In one role, the mediator acts as a *representative* of his group because he regulates the flow of information or goods from his or her own group. In another role, the mediator is a *gatekeeper*, who regulates the flow of information or goods to his or her group. Finally, the *liaison* is a person who mediates between members of different groups but who does not belong to these groups himself or herself.

The five types of brokerage roles have been conceived for directed networks, namely transaction networks. Note, however, that the direction of relations is only needed to distinguish between the representative and the gatekeeper. The other brokerage roles are also apparent in undirected relations, so we can apply the brokerage roles to undirected networks if we do not distinguish between representatives and gatekeepers. In an undirected network, each representative is also a gatekeeper and vice versa.

Now, let us have a look at the brokerage roles in the strike network. We use the groups according to language and age (see Figure 63) and we assume that a line is equivalent to a bidirectional arc: discussing work implies the possibility of disseminating and receiving information. Employees who are isolated or whose ties are contained within a clique (e.g., Carlos, Domingo, and Eduardo, but also Wendle and Xavier) have no opportunity to mediate because all of their contacts are directly connected. As a result, none of the brokerage roles apply to them.

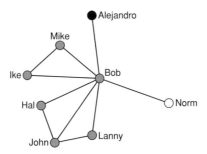

Figure 72. Bob's ego-network.

Most of the other employees have ties only within their own group, so they can play only the coordinator role. In the network, brokerage is clearly dominated by the coordinator role. It is easy to see that Alejandro, Bob, Norm, and Ozzie are the only employees who also have other types of brokerage roles because they are the only ones who are connected to members of different groups.

Let us have a closer look at Bob (Figure 72), who combines several types of brokerage roles. There are several structural holes among Bob's ties within the group of English-speaking young employees (e.g., between Ike and Mike, on the one hand, and Hal, John, and Lanny, on the other hand). To them, Bob plays the coordinator role. In addition, Bob bridges many structural holes between his group of English-speaking young employees and the Hispanic workers or the older employees. For information about his group, Bob is a representative and for information flowing toward members of his group, he is a gatekeeper. Finally, he may mediate between Alejandro and Norm, that is, between the Hispanics and the older workers. In this role, he is a liaison.

The only brokerage role that Bob cannot play given the ties in the network, is the role of an itinerant broker because he has no ties with two or more members of any group other than his own. Actually, none of the employees can play this role – this role is absent in the strike network.

Bob was the first employee whom the management contacted directly. Perhaps, this was justified not only by the amount of structural holes in his ego-network but also by the variety of brokerage roles that Bob may play.

Application

Secondary structural holes are related to constraint within a group, so we may delete the ties between groups and calculate the constraint within each group. If there is another member of the group with equal or less constraint than the one you are already connected to, you may play him or her off against your present contact provided that they are not strongly and directly connected. In a similar manner, you may evaluate your position within your own group to see whether you may easily be replaced by someone else.

Operations>
Transform>
Remove Lines>
Between Clusters

The detection of secondary structural holes consists of two steps. In the first step, we delete the lines between groups. Because the groups are defined as classes in a partition (in our example `Strike_groups.clu`),

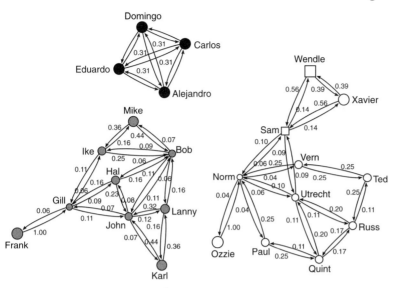

Figure 73. Constraint inside groups.

we must make sure that this partition is selected in the partitions drop-down menu. Then we can remove the lines between clusters with the command *Operations>Transform>Remove Lines>Between Clusters*.

In the second step, we apply the *Structural Holes* command to the network without lines between clusters to obtain the constraint of vertices within their groups (Figure 73). We can see that Gill is even less constrained within the class of young English-speaking employees than Bob. Because there is no direct tie between Gill and Bob, Gill seems to be a good candidate to be played off against Bob. In the Hispanic group, there is no real alternative to Alejandro because he is directly connected to all others. Among the older employees, Norm is clearly less constrained than any other employee, so there is no good alternative in this group. Judging from their structural positions and ignoring their linguistic abilities or special relationships, we conclude that Norm and Alejandro are less likely to be replaced as representatives or gatekeepers of their groups than Bob because there is a good alternative to Bob only.

Pajek contains a command that counts the brokerage roles in a network. Make sure that the strike network and the appropriate partition (`strike_groups.clu`) are selected in the drop-down menus of the Main screen. Then, execute the command *Operations>Brokerage Roles* to obtain five new partitions, one for each brokerage role, which are added to the Partition drop-down menu. The class number of a vertex in a partition specifies the number of incomplete triads in which this vertex plays the corresponding brokerage role. A frequency table of a partition is obtained in the usual way (*Info>Partition*). Table 9 shows the results for the coordinator role, which is stored in the partition labeled "Coordinators in N1 according to C1."

We can see that ten employees have no coordinator roles. The number of coordinator roles per person is unevenly distributed: some employees

Net>Vector>
Structural Holes

Operations>
Brokerage Roles

Info>Partition

Table 9. *Frequency Tabulation of Coordinator Roles in the Strike Network*

Class	Freq	Freq%	CumFreq	CumFreq%	Representative
0	10	41.6667	10	41.6667	Frank
1	5	20.8333	15	62.5000	Hal
2	3	12.5000	18	75.0000	Ike
4	2	8.3333	20	83.3333	Utrecht
5	1	4.1667	21	87.5000	Gill
6	1	4.1667	22	91.6667	John
7	1	4.1667	23	95.8333	Bob
9	1	4.1667	24	100.0000	Norm
SUM	24	100			

have one or two coordinator roles, whereas Norm has no less than nine coordinator roles. If we sum the roles (five employees with one coordinator role plus three with two roles, etc.), we count forty-six coordinator roles. In the representative roles partition we count twenty-one roles and there is just one liaison role. As noted, the coordinator role occurs most frequently in this network because most employees have direct ties only within their own subgroup.

7.6   Summary

In a connected social network, information may reach anybody through their ties. Holes in this network, that is, absent ties, are obstacles to flows of information. Information is less likely to reach anybody easily in a connected network with large holes. In this chapter, we focus on the holes in a network. The information flow is especially vulnerable in networks with bridges and cut-vertices because the removal of a bridge or cut-vertex disconnects the network. Actors who are cut-vertices in a network control the flow of information from one part of the network to another. They may decide to retain information when it suits their personal purposes.

From the perspective of the communication system as a whole, bridges and cut-vertices are undesirable. From the individual point of view, however, being a cut-vertex is attractive because it offers opportunities for brokering information and for profiting from brokerage in one way or another. The advantage of the broker position in an ego-network, which is the network of one actor and its neighbors, is that you can play a *tertius* strategy: you can induce competition or conflict between neighbors who are not linked directly. The gap between the neighbors is called a structural hole and each structural hole represents an opportunity to broker.

There is a drawback, however: you must avoid becoming the object of a *tertius* strategy yourself. This implies that you cannot end ties with neighbors who are directly linked. This is called the constraint on your tie with a neighbor. The constraint on a tie is inversely related to the structural holes associated with it: low constraint means many structural holes and vice versa. The constraint on each tie as well as on each vertex in the network may be calculated to find the segments that have most opportunities to broker, which are hypothesized to be more successful and profitable.

In many social contexts, brokerage is connected to group affiliations and the people involved can be replaced only by other persons from their groups. Threatening a contact to replace him or her by another contact is also a *tertius* strategy. This strategy is successful only if there is a good alternative to the present contact in the group, someone who is also quite central in the group but who is not directly linked to the present contact so the (secondary) structural hole between them can be exploited.

When we consider brokerage in the context of group membership, there are five brokerage roles. We can characterize a network or an actor in a network by the kinds of brokerage roles that occur. The brokerage signature of a network or actor can be compared to other characteristics to determine whether certain types of actors or types of social relations develop particular brokerage roles.

7.7 Questions

1. List the bridges in the network depicted below (ignore contours and vertex colors).

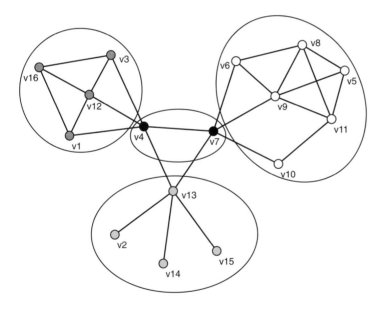

2. How many bi-components and cut-vertices does the network of Question 1 contain?
   a. Three bi-components and two cut-vertices
   b. Three bi-components and three cut-vertices
   c. Six bi-components and two cut-vertices
   d. Six bi-components and three cut-vertices
3. Let the network of Question 1 represent the communication network within an organization. If you would like to reduce the power of

cut-vertices to control the flow of information, which pair of vertices would you urge to establish a communication tie? Justify your answer.

4. Which of the following statements is correct?
   a. Vertices incident with a bridge are cut-vertices if and only if they have two or more neighbors.
   b. Vertices which are part of a bi-component cannot be cut-vertices.
   c. A bi-component is a subnetwork without cut-vertex.
   d. If there are two paths between all pairs of vertices in a component, this component is a bi-component.

5. Which of the following statements about the strength of weak ties hypothesis is correct?
   a. Strong family ties cannot be bridges in a communication network.
   b. A tie is weak if and only if it is a bridge in a communication network.
   c. In general, weak ties are more likely to be bridges in a communication network.
   d. A tie is strong if and only if it is part of a clique in a communication network.

6. In the network of Question 1, which vertex is least constrained: v4, v7, or v13? Justify your answer.

7. When vertex v7 wants to reduce the number of ties that he is maintaining in the network of Question 1, which tie would you advise him to end?

8. In the network of Question 1, vertex colors and contours indicate the group to which a vertex is affiliated. Count each brokerage role that vertex v7 may play in this network.

7.8   Assignment

In our discussion of the triad, we compared complete and nearly complete triads. We stressed the opportunities that the incomplete structure offers to the person in the middle and the constraint exercised by the complete triad. Especially in the case of public behavior, that is, behavior that cannot be concealed from people in other groups, it has been argued that membership in several different cliques is very stressful because it obliges a person to conform to the (supposedly different) sets of norms of the different cliques. In this position, a person has very little room to maneuver.

In particular instances, this hypothesis contradicts the structural holes argument. If a person is a member in several different cliques, there are structural holes between the cliques, which may be exploited. In the network depicted in Figure 74, for example, vertex v3 may exploit structural holes between the other members in the 3-clique (v1 and v2) and the other members in the 4-clique (v4, v5, and v6). According to the structural holes hypothesis, vertex v3 is least constrained. According to the hypothesis of overlapping cliques, however, v3 is most constrained because it is a member in two cliques.

Having two competing hypotheses, it is interesting to see which one applies in a particular situation. The case is a small hi-tech computer firm

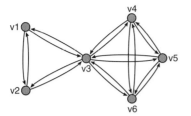

Figure 74. Two overlapping cliques.

that sells, installs, and maintains computer systems. The data file `hi-tech.net` contains the friendship ties among the employees, which were gathered by means of the question: Who do you consider to be a personal friend? Three employees (Fran, Quincy, and York) did not return the questionnaire. Note that most friendship nominations are reciprocated, but not all (112 of 147).

Some months later, employees tried to unionize the firm: they sought support among the employees to let the union have a say in the firm. The three top managers (class 3 in the partition `hi-tech.union.clu`) and three employees who were not directly involved (class 2) were opposed to union certification of the firm. Five employees (class 1) were pro-union, but two of them (Chris and Ovid) did not actively advocate the pro-union position. At the end, the proposal to unionize the firm was voted down. Chris resigned from the firm ten days before the vote because he did not want to participate in it. He rejoined the firm two days after the vote.

Analyze these data, which are joined in the project file `Hi-tech.paj`, and argue whether they support the structural holes argument or the overlapping cliques hypothesis. For the analysis of cliques, review Section 3.6 in Chapter 3. Pay attention to the position and behavior of Chris in particular. In addition, analyze the brokerage roles if the groups are defined by their stance toward unionization (`hi-tech.union.clu`) and find out whether this explains Chris's behavior.

7.9   Further Reading

- The example is taken from J. H. Michael, "Labor dispute reconciliation in a forest products manufacturing facility." In: *Forest Products Journal* 47 (1997), 41–5.
- G. Simmel explains his ideas about triadic configurations in "Individual and society" in *The Sociology of Georg Simmel* (New York, London: The Free Press, 1950, a translation of *Soziologie: Untersuchungen über die Formen der Vergesellschaftung*, Berlin: Duncker & Humblot, 1908). A recent approach from a different angle can be found in H. C. White, *Identity and Control. A Structural Theory of Social Action* (Princeton, New Jersey: Princeton University Press, 1992).
- Read more on social capital in Chapter 5 of A. Degenne and M. Forsé's *Introducing Social Networks* (London: Sage, 1999) or

N. Lin's *Social Capital: A Theory of Social Structure and Action* (Cambridge: Cambridge University Press, 2001).

- Mark Granovetter's article "The strength of weak ties" [*American Journal of Sociology* 78 (1973), 1360–80] is the source of the strength of weak ties hypothesis. The second edition of his book *Getting a Job: A Study of Contacts and Careers* (Chicago: The University of Chicago Press, 1974, 1995) includes an appendix which surveys and analyses research based on this hypothesis.

- The theory of structural holes was introduced by R. S. Burt in his book *Structural Holes: The Social Structure of Competition* (Cambridge/London: Harvard University Press, 1992), which contains applications of this theory to careers of managers and to the profitability of business sectors. We use the formulae presented in the second chapter of this book.

- The five types of brokerage roles were proposed by R. V. Gould and R. M. Fernandez in "Structures of mediation: a formal approach to brokerage in transaction networks." In: *Sociological Methodology 1990*. San Francisco: Jossey-Bass (1989), 89–126.

- The example used in the assignment as well as the theory of constraint by overlapping cliques stems from D. Krackhardt's "The ties that torture: Simmelian tie analysis in organizations" [*Research in the Sociology of Organizations* 16 (1999), 183–210].

7.10   Answers

Answers to the Exercises

I. When Pajek detects the bi-components but ignores bridges, it identifies a cut-vertex only if it belongs to two or more bi-components, that is, if bi-components intersect at this vertex. In the strike network, this is the case only for Norm and Sam, as one can tell from the contours in Figure 64. Frank is not part of a bi-component, so he is put in class zero in both partitions produced by the *Bi-Components* command and he is not included in the hierarchy of bi-components.

II. The aggregate constraint on Norm and Bob can be determined with the *Net>Vector>Structural Holes* command. This command produces a vector containing the aggregate constraint on vertices. Open this vector in an Edit screen (e.g., use the writing hand button left of the Vector droplist) and look for Norm and Bob. Their aggregate constraint is 0.20 and 0.24, respectively.

Extracting the subnetwork of Norm's neighbors, we find one link among six neighbors, so a density of 0.07. The subnetwork of Bob's seven neighbors contains three links: a density of 0.14. Both Bob's constraint and his egocentric density are higher than Norm's, so they match in this respect. Norm has more opportunities to broker.

Answers to the Questions in Section 7.7

1. The lines between v13 and v2, v14, and v15 are bridges. If you remove one of these lines, v2, v14, or v15 becomes an isolate, so the network contains two components instead of one.

2. Answer b is correct. The network contains three cut-vertices: v4, v7, and v13. Removal of any of these vertices disconnects the network. Cut-vertex v4 belongs to two bi-components: one bi-component contains vertices v1, v3, v4, v12, and v16, and the other bi-components consists of v4, v7, and v13. Cut-vertex v7 belongs to the latter bi-component and to the third bi-component with vertices v5, v6, v7, v8, v9, v10, and v11. Cut-vertex v13 is part of the second bi-component and links it with the bridges (see Exercise 1) toward vertices v2, v14, and v15. These bridges and the vertices incident to them, however, are not bi-components, so the total number of bi-components is three, not six.

3. To reduce the control of a cut-vertex, you must join two or more bi-components into one bi-component. A tie between members of the two largest bi-components, which are not cut-vertices, produces this effect, for instance, between vertices v3 and v6. Now v4 and v7 are no longer cut-vertices.

4. Statement a is correct. A vertex that is incident to a bridge can have only fewer than two neighbors if its only neighbor lies at the other side of the bridge. The vertex, then, is a "hanger," such as v2 in the network of Question 1. If you remove this vertex, you create no new components. If the vertex has two or more neighbors, however, it mediates between the vertex at the other side of the bridge and its other neighbor(s). When you remove the vertex, the latter neighbor is disconnected from the network, so the number of components in the network increases.

   Statement b is not correct because a vertex in a bi-component may well be a cut-vertex in the network at large (e.g., vertices v4, v7, and v13 in the network of Question 1). Statement c is not correct because a subnetwork is not necessarily connected. It may consist of several components that are not one bi-component by definition. Finally, statement d is not correct because the two paths between a pair of vertices may share a vertex in between the endpoints, for instance, the paths v16-v3-v4-v7 and v16-v1-v4-v13-v7 in the network of Question 1. This vertex (v4) is a cut-vertex, so the component is not a bi-component. Statement d would be correct if it read "two distinct paths," meaning that the two paths share no vertex between the endpoints.

5. Answer c is correct. It is not ruled out that a strong family tie is a bridge in an information network, for instance, the tie between Frank and Gill in the strike network, so answer a is not correct. Strong and weak ties are defined on the basis of their frequency or intensity, not on their structural features, so it is not ruled out that strong ties occur outside cliques and weak ties occur inside cliques, so answers b and d are incorrect. However, there is a statistical association between the property (strength) of a tie and its structural location, so we may

say that weak ties are more likely to be bridges in general, which is answer c.

6. Vertex v13 is less constrained than vertices v4 and v7. Note, first, that these three vertices have the same degree: each has five neighbors. As a consequence, the proportional strength of their ties is equal, namely 0.20. Therefore, we do not have to bother with the proportional strength of ties and we can simply count the number of structural holes around each vertex to find out who is least constrained. We count only one direct tie among the five neighbors of vertex v13, namely between v4 and v7, so nine of the ten possible pairs of neighbors are not directly linked: they are separated by structural holes. Among the neighbors of v7, two pairs are directly linked, which leaves eight structural holes. Finally, three pairs of v4's neighbors are directly linked, so there are seven structural holes. More structural holes means less constraint, so vertex v13 is least constrained.

7. It is not wise to withdraw from ties that are part of a complete triad because that allows a neighbor to play the *tertius* strategy against you. Vertex v7 has only one tie outside a complete triad, namely the tie with vertex v10. He may safely withdraw from this tie because he is already connected to vertex v9, which is the most central member of the white group.

8. Vertex v7 does not broker between members of its own group, so he cannot play the coordinator role. V7 is connected to three vertices in the white group, two of whom are directly connected, so he is an itinerant broker between v10 on the one hand and v6 and v9 on the other hand. V7 may mediate between v4, who is a member of his group, and three vertices in the white group: v6, v9, and v10. Here, v7 plays the representative or gatekeeper role, which occurs three times. Finally, v7 may mediate between three white neighbors and v13, who is in the light gray group, which yields three liaisons.

8

Diffusion

Diffusion is an important social process. Administrators are interested in the diffusion of information and opinions manufacturers seek the adoption of new techniques and products, and all of us have a vivid interest in not acquiring contagious diseases. Diffusion processes are being studied in the communication sciences, social psychology and sociology, public administration, marketing, and epidemiology.

In this chapter, we present diffusion processes from a network point of view. Diffusion is a special case of brokerage, namely brokerage with a time dimension. Something – a disease, product, opinion, or attitude – is handed over from one person to another in the course of time. We assume that social relations are instrumental to the diffusion process: they are channels of social contagion and persuasion.

If personal contacts are important, then the structure of personal ties is relevant to the diffusion process and not just the personal characteristics that make one person more open to innovations than another. We investigate the relation between structural positions of actors and the moment at which they adopt an innovation.

8.1 Example

Educational innovations have received a lot of attention in the tradition of diffusion research. Our example is a well-known study into the diffusion of a new mathematics method in the 1950s. This innovation was instigated by top mathematicians and sponsored by the National Science Foundation of the United States as well as the U.S. Department of Education. The diffusion process was successful because the new method was adopted in a relatively short period by most schools.

The example traces the diffusion of the modern math method among school systems that combine elementary and secondary programs in Allegheny County (Pennsylvania, U.S.A.). All those school superintendents who were in office at least two years were interviewed. They are the gatekeepers to educational innovation because they are in the position to make the final decision. The researchers obtained data from sixty-one of sixty-eight superintendents, fifty-one of whom had adopted by 1963 (84%).

161

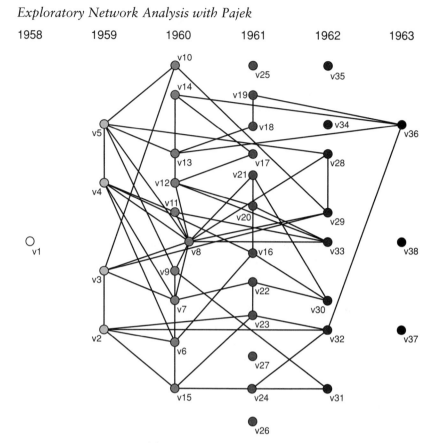

Figure 75. Friendship ties among superintendents and year of adoption.

Among other things, the superintendents were asked to indicate their friendship ties with other superintendents in the county with the following question: Among the chief school administrators in Allegheny County, who are your three best friends? The researcher analyzed the friendship choices among the thirty-eight interviewed superintendents who adopted the method and were in position at least one year before the first adoption, so they could have adopted earlier. Unfortunately, the researcher did not include the friendship choices by superintendents who received no choices themselves; they are treated as isolates. In the original network, some friendship choices are reciprocated and others are not (ModMath_directed.net) but we use the symmetrized network (ModMath.net), which is depicted in Figure 75. A line in this network indicates that at least one superintendent chooses the other as his friend.

As you may infer from Figure 75, adoption started in 1958 and all the schools researched had adopted by 1963. The year of adoption by a superintendent's school is coded in the partition ModMath_adoption.clu: 1958 is class (time) 1, 1959 is class (time) 2, and so on. The first adopter (v1) is a superintendent with many contacts outside Allegheny County but few friends within the county. He is a "cosmopolite" and cosmopolites usually are early adopters but they are often too innovative to be influential in a local network.

Application

For a first visual impression of a diffusion process, open the Pajek project file ModMath.paj and draw the sociogram in the order of adoption time (see Figure 75; we manually added the years to the top of this figure). To do this, the adoption time of vertices must be specified in a partition (e.g., ModMath_adoption.clu). Draw the sociogram with vertex colors defined by the partition (*Draw>Draw-Partition* or *Ctrl-p*) and select the command *Layers>in y direction* to arrange the vertices by adoption time. Note that this procedure is available only when a network with partition is drawn.

Draw>Draw-Partition

Layers>in y direction

In most cases, the vertices are not optimally placed within each level. To improve their positions, use the *Optimize layers in x direction* command. You can let this command adjust all levels (i.e., classes) or you can restrict the optimization to a range of levels. Play around with the options (*Forward, Backward, Complete*) until you obtain a layout without lines that cross vertices with which they are not incident. In Figure 75, this was not possible because superintendent v8 is connected to too many vertices in his adoption class, so we decided to move him away from the line of his class. Even for our small diffusion network, the sociogram needs a lot of fine-tuning, so you should not expect a clear picture if you are working with large networks.

Layers>Optimize layers in x direction

Sometimes it helps to rearrange the vertices within a layer by hand. If you do this but you want to be sure that the vertices within a class remain aligned, activate the option *y* in the *Fix* menu of the Draw screen. Now, you can move vertices horizontally only.

Move>Fix>y

The layers are drawn in the *y* direction: from the top down. In Figure 75, however, time flows from left to right on the *x* axis, which is the standard way to represent time. We obtained this figure by rotating the standard layout of layers by 90 degrees. Select the command *Rotate 2D* from the *Options>Transform* submenu in the Draw screen. Type 90 in the dialog box captioned *Angle in degrees* and press the OK button.

[Draw screen] Options> Transform> Rotate 2D

8.2   Contagion

Information is important to the diffusion of new opinions, products, and the like. In most societies, the mass media are central to the spreading of information, so we ought to pay attention to mass communication. Several models have been proposed for the process of mass communication, one of which is consistent with a network approach: the two-step flow model. According to this model, mass communication consists of two phases. In the first phase, mass media inform and influence opinion leaders. In the second phase, opinion leaders influence potential adopters within their communities or social systems.

Network models of diffusion focus on the second phase, assuming that opinion leaders use social relations to influence their contacts. Social ties are thought to be important because innovations are new, hence risky. Personal contacts are needed to inform and persuade people of the benefits associated with the innovation. Note that salient social relations for

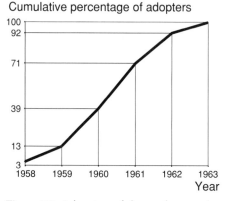

Figure 76. Adoption of the modern math method: diffusion curve.

spreading information may be different from relations used for persuasion. The relations most commonly investigated are advice and friendship relations.

Basically, network models see diffusion as a process of contamination, just like the spread of an infectious disease. Therefore, passing on an innovation via social ties is called *social contagion*. This perspective is backed by the empirical fact that many innovations diffuse in a pattern that is similar to the spread of infectious diseases. First, an innovation is adopted by few people but their number increases relatively fast. Then, large numbers adopt but the growth rate decreases. Finally, the number of new adopters decreases rapidly and the diffusion process slowly stops. This diffusion pattern is characteristic for a chain reaction in which people contaminate their contacts, who contaminate their contacts in the next step, and so on.

The adoption of the modern math method is represented by a *diffusion curve* (Figure 76). The *x* axis shows the moment of adoption and the *y* axis represents the *prevalence* of the innovation, which is the percentage of all interviewed superintendents who have adopted the modern math method by that year. Note that prevalence is represented by cumulative percentages, that is, the sum of all percentages of previous adopters: in 1958, 3 percent of the superintendents adopt and in 1959 another 10 percent adopt, so the cumulative percentage of adopters is 13 percent in 1959.

The diffusion curve has the logistic S-shape, which is characteristic of a chain reaction. We find a similar curve when we take a random network and choose a vertex as a source of contamination (the white vertex in Figure 77). When we assume that a vertex contaminates its neighbors at time 1, who contaminate their neighbors at time 2, and so on, we obtain the typical diffusion curve of Figure 78 (bold line). Note that the number of new adopters increases faster and faster in the first three steps (vertices with numbers 1, 2, and 3) and that the absolute number of new adopters decreases sharply after the fourth step. This example illustrates that contagion through network ties may explain the logistic spread of an

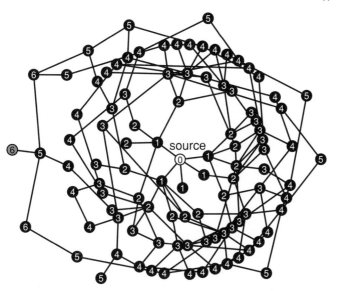

Figure 77. Diffusion by contacts in a random network ($N = 100$, vertex numbers indicate the distance from the source vertex).

innovation or a disease. If we find a diffusion curve that does not have the typical S shape, it is quite unlikely that network ties are important to the diffusion process and diffusion is probably propelled predominantly by other forces such as mass media campaigns.

When contagion drives the diffusion process, the structure of an information or contact network conditions the diffusion of information, innovations, diseases, and so on. Using the measures introduced in previous chapters, some broad hypotheses are easily derived as follows:

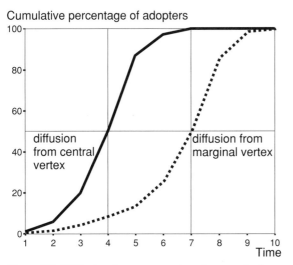

Figure 78. Diffusion from a central and a marginal vertex.

- In a dense network an innovation spreads more easily and faster than in a sparse network,
- In an unconnected network diffusion will be slower and less comprehensive than in a connected network,
- In a bi-component diffusion will be faster than in components with cut-points or bridges,
- The larger the neighborhood of a person within the network, the earlier s/he will adopt an innovation,
- A central position is likely to lead to early adoption,
- Diffusion from a central vertex is faster than from a vertex in the margins of the network.

The *adoption rate* is the number or percentage of new adopters at a particular moment.

The speed of the diffusion process is measured by the *adoption rate*, which is the number or percentage of new adopters at a particular moment. It is easy to see that the adoption rate is higher when an innovation spreads from a central vertex than when it starts at a marginal vertex. Figure 78 shows the diffusion curves for the diffusion from the central white source vertex in Figure 77 (bold line) and from the peripheral gray vertex (dotted line). Both curves have the typical S shape but it takes considerably more time for a diffusion to reach half or all of the population when it is triggered by a vertex in the periphery.

The hypotheses presented above highlight the impact of network structure on the diffusion process. We should note, however, that personal characteristics and the type of innovation also influence the rate of adoption. The perceived risk of an innovation, its perceived advantage over alternatives, and the extent to which the innovation complies with social norms that govern the target group determine whether it is adopted quickly, reluctantly, or not at all. A risky innovation, for instance, will diffuse slower regardless of the network's density and connectivity.

Application

Info>Partition

The diffusion curve is constructed from a simple frequency tabulation of adoption time, which is displayed by the *Info>Partition* command (Table 10). The table shows the cumulative relative frequencies that are plotted on the *y* axis in the chart of Figure 76. The class numbers represent the moments that are displayed on the *x* axis. Note that the table and chart are basic statistical techniques, which may be produced in any statistical software package or spreadsheet.

Exercise I

Net>Random Network> Vertices Output Degree

Create a simple random network with fifty vertices that have an outdegree of 1 or 2 (use the *Net>Random Network>Vertices Output Degree* command with a minimum outdegree of 1 and a maximum outdegree of 2 and no multiple lines). Pick a vertex as the source of a diffusion process

Table 10. *Adoption in the Modern Math Network*

Class	Freq	Freq%	CumFreq	CumFreq%	Representative
1	1	2.63	1	2.63	v1
2	4	10.53	5	13.16	v2
3	10	26.32	15	39.47	v6
4	12	31.58	27	71.05	v16
5	8	21.05	35	92.11	v28
6	3	7.89	38	100.00	v36
SUM	38	100.00			

and determine the adoption time of all vertices and the adoption rate at each point in time, assuming that a vertex will adopt at the first time point after it has established direct contact with an adopter. Note that the adoption time of a vertex is equal to its distance (see Chapter 7) from the source vertex under this assumption. Ignore the direction of the lines in the network.

8.3 Exposure and Thresholds

In the previous section, we assumed that every person is equally suscepti-ble to contagion. One infected neighbor is enough to get infected; friend-ship with one adopter is enough to persuade someone to adopt. This is not very realistic because some people are more receptive to innovations than other people. There are two different ways to conceptualize the inno-vativeness of people, namely relative to the system and relative to their personal networks: adoption categories and threshold categories.

Adoption categories classify people according to their adoption time relative to all other adopters. These typologies are very popular in prod-uct marketing. A standard classification distinguishes between the early adopters (the first 16 percent who adopt), the early majority (the next 34 percent), the late majority (the next 34 percent), and late adopters or laggards (the last 16 percent to adopt). To classify people, we have to know only their adoption time. Then, we can simply mark the first 16 percent of all adopters as early adopters, and so on. This classification is useful for marketing purposes because it enables the marketing manager to identify the social and demographic characteristics of early adopters.

In the modern math example, early adopters are characterized by higher professionalism ratings and more accurate knowledge about the spread of educational innovations in their district. In addition, the superintendents who adopted early were not recruited from the school staff but they came from outside.

We concentrate on the second approach to innovativeness, *threshold categories*, which considers the personal network of actors. The network model of diffusion is based on contagion: an adopter spreads the innova-tion to his or her contacts. It is quite natural to assume that the chance that a person will adopt increases when he or she is linked to more people who

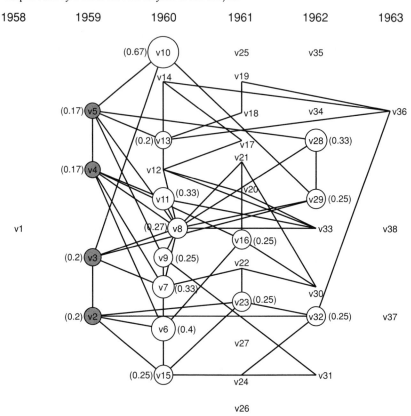

Figure 79. Adoption (vertex color) and exposure (in brackets) at the end of 1959.

already have adopted, that is, when he or she is exposed to more adopters. Hearing about the benefits of an innovation from different sources will persuade a person to adopt. The amount of exposure varies over time and among individuals, which explains that some people adopt early although they are not close to the sources in a diffusion process. The exposure of a person is expressed as a proportion so it may be the thought of as a chance to adopt.

The *exposure* of a vertex in a network at a particular moment is the proportion of its neighbors who have adopted before that time.

Figure 79 shows the modern math network with the exposure of vertices in 1959 indicated by vertex size and by the numbers in brackets. Note that invisible vertices have zero exposure: none of their neighbors adopted in or before 1959. Eight of the ten superintendents who adopted in 1960 had friends among the 1959 adopters, so they were exposed. Clearly, superintendent v10 was most exposed: two of his three friends adopted in 1959, so his exposure was 0.67 at the end of 1959. However, not all exposed superintendents adopted in 1960: superintendents v16 and v23 adopted in 1961 and v28, v29, and superintendent v32 adopted in 1962. They were not less exposed than several superintendents who adopted immediately in 1960, for instance, v8, v9, v13, and v15, so we would expect them also to adopt in 1960. They contradict the simple contagion model which presupposes that all actors need the same amount of exposure to adopt.

In fact, statistical analyses of diffusion data do not always find a systematic relation between exposure and adoption. This means that either exposure and contagion are irrelevant to adoption or people need different levels of exposure before they adopt. If we pursue the latter option, we assume that some people are easily persuaded (e.g., they need only one contact with an adopter), whereas others are talked into adopting an innovation with difficulty. Some people are more susceptible than others, which is an established fact for media exposure as well as social exposure.

In the network model of diffusion, the *innovativeness* of a person is perceived as his or her threshold to exposure. An individual's threshold is the degree of exposure that he or she needs to adopt an innovation. Now, differences between individual thresholds may account for the fact that only part of the people adopt who are equally exposed.

The *threshold* of an actor is his or her exposure at the time of adoption.

In our example, four superintendents (gray vertices in Figure 79) adopted the new math method in 1959. They exposed thirteen superintendents (white vertices) to their experience with this method and eight of them adopted the method in the next year. However, five superintendents adopted two or three years later. Why? Each of the exposed superintendents who adopted after 1960 has one or two friends among the colleagues who adopted in 1960 or 1961. By the time they adopted, these friends had also adopted, so their exposure was higher than at the end of 1959. According to the threshold hypothesis, their exposure had not reached the required threshold in 1959 but it did in 1960 or 1961. This explains why they adopted later.

At the end of 1959, for example, one of the four friends of superintendent v23 had adopted the modern math method, so his exposure was 0.25. In 1960, one more friend (v15) adopted and his exposure increased to 0.5. Then, superintendent v23 adopted, so we assume that his threshold was 0.5 or somewhere between 0.25 and 0.5.

We should note that individual thresholds are computed from the diffusion network after the fact: they are predictions with hindsight and they are not very informative by themselves. It is important to make sense of them or to validate them, which means that they should be associated with other indicators of innovativeness, for instance, adoption time or personal characteristics.

Thresholds indicate personal innovativeness, a lower threshold means more innovative, and we expect innovative people to adopt an innovation earlier than noninnovative people. Therefore, individual thresholds must be related to adoption time: innovative people have low thresholds and adopt early. If we find such a relation, we obtain some support for the assumption that individual thresholds indicate innovativeness.

At least to some extent, however, a positive relation between adoption time and individual thresholds is an artifact of the contagion model that we use. The first adopters cannot be exposed to previous adopters, so their thresholds are zero by definition. Within the network of adopters, the last adopters are very likely to be connected to previous adopters, so their exposure and thresholds are high at the time of adoption. When measurement of adoption time is restricted to a small number of moments, this will automatically produce a relation between individual thresholds and adoption time.

Therefore, it is also important to compare individual thresholds to external characteristics of the actors that usually indicate innovativeness. In general, innovativeness and low thresholds are supposed to be related to broad media use, many cosmopolitan contacts (contacts outside your local community), a high level of education, and high socioeconomic status.

Application

*Net>Transform>
Arcs→Edges>
All*

Let us compute exposure levels in the modern math network at one moment, for instance, at time 2, 1959 (see Figure 79). The procedure consists of several steps, which illuminate the calculation and exact meaning of the exposure concept. We assume that the network is undirected. If not, symmetrize it (*Net>Transform>Arcs→Edges>All* and remove any multiple lines, e.g., take the sum or minimum line value).

*Partition>
Binarize*

*Partition>Make
Vector*

First, we identify the adopters in the network at the selected time, which is 1959 or time 2 in our example. Make a binary partition from the adoption time partition where adoption times 1 and 2 are assigned a score of 1 (adopted) and others are assigned a score of zero (notadopted yet) with the *Partition>Binarize* command, selecting classes 1 through 2 in the dialog boxes. In Figure 79, the adopters are gray and the nonadopters are white. Then turn this partition into a vector to use it for computation (*Partition>Make Vector* or simply press *Ctrl-v*).

*Operations>
Vector>
Summing up
Neigbours*

Second, compute the number of adopters in each actor's neighborhood with the command *Operations>Vector>Summing up Neigbours>Input, Output,* or *All*. A dialog box appears that asks whether a vertex should be included in its own neighborhood; answer no. Pajek does not count the number of neighbors but it sums the class numbers of the neighbors of a vertex. Because we use a binary partition in which an adopter has class number 1 and a nonadopter has class number zero, this sum is equal to the number of adopters in the neighborhood. It is a little trick, but it works.

*Vectors>First
Vector*

*Vectors>Second
Vector*

*Vectors>Divide
First by Second*

Third, the number of adopters in the neighborhood of a vertex must be divided by its total number of neighbors because we defined exposure as the percentage of neighbors who have adopted. The division can be done in the *Vectors* menu. The vector we just made must be selected as the first vector in this menu (*Vectors>First Vector*). Next, we must make a vector with the total number of neighbors of a vertex. Recall that the degree of a vertex in a simple undirected network specifies the number of neighbors of a vertex, so we can make a degree partition in the usual way (*Net>Partitions>Degree*) and turn it into a vector (*Partition>Make Vector* – do not use the Normalized Indegree vector!). This vector must be used as the second vector in the *Vector* menu (*Vector>Second Vector*). Finally, we divide the number of adopters in a vertex's neighborhood by the total number of neighbors with the *Vectors>Divide First by Second* command. Now, we obtain a vector with the exposure of vertices at the end of 1959 (time 2).

[Main]
*Options>Read/
Write>0/0*

Note that the computation of exposure is not straightforward if the network contains isolated vertices. An isolated vertex has no neighbors, so its degree is zero. The division described in the previous paragraph would ask Pajek to divide by zero, which is mathematically incorrect. In this case, Pajek assigns the value zero to the exposure of the vertex, that is, if the default setting of *0/0* to zero was not changed in the *Options>Read/Write* submenu of the Main screen.

Macro>Play

The calculation of exposure consists of a considerable number of steps. If you want to compute exposure at several points in time, you have to repeat these steps over and over again. This is not very efficient, so Pajek contains the possibility of executing a number of steps in one command, which is called a *macro*. A macro is a file that consists of a list of commands that are executed when you play the macro in Pajek. We prepared the macro `exposure.mcr`, which you can execute by clicking on the *Play* command in the *Macro* menu and selecting the file `exposure.mcr`, which is located in the directory with the data accompanying this chapter. Make sure that the original undirected network and the adoption time partition are selected before you execute the macro. When you open this file, Pajek starts to execute the commands. It displays the dialog boxes that allow you to select the first time of adoption (*Select clusters from*), which is 1 in our example, and the time for which you want to compute exposure (*Select clusters from 1 to*), for instance, time 3. Upon completion of the macro, several new partitions and vectors have been created and the last vector contains the exposure at the requested time.

Macro>Record

*Macro>Add
message*

Creating a macro yourself is fairly simple. In essence, Pajek records all commands that you execute between the first and second time you click the *Record* command in the *Macro* menu. It prompts for a filename with the extension `.mcr` in which to store the recorded commands. While recording, you can add messages to the macro (*Macro>Add message*) that will be displayed in the Report screen when the macro is played afterwards. Make sure that you have the relevant network, partition, and vector selected in the drop-down menus before you record the macro and check the results when you play it for the first time.

Now that we have computed the exposure at one time, let us turn our attention to the calculation of thresholds. The *threshold* of a vertex is the proportion of its neighbors who have adopted before ego does, so we have to divide the number of prior adopters among the neighbors of a vertex by the size of its neighborhood. The computation of thresholds is fairly simple once you realize that the number of neighbors who have adopted prior to ego is equal to the indegree of ego in a directed network in which each line points from an earlier adopter to a later adopter. Figure 80,

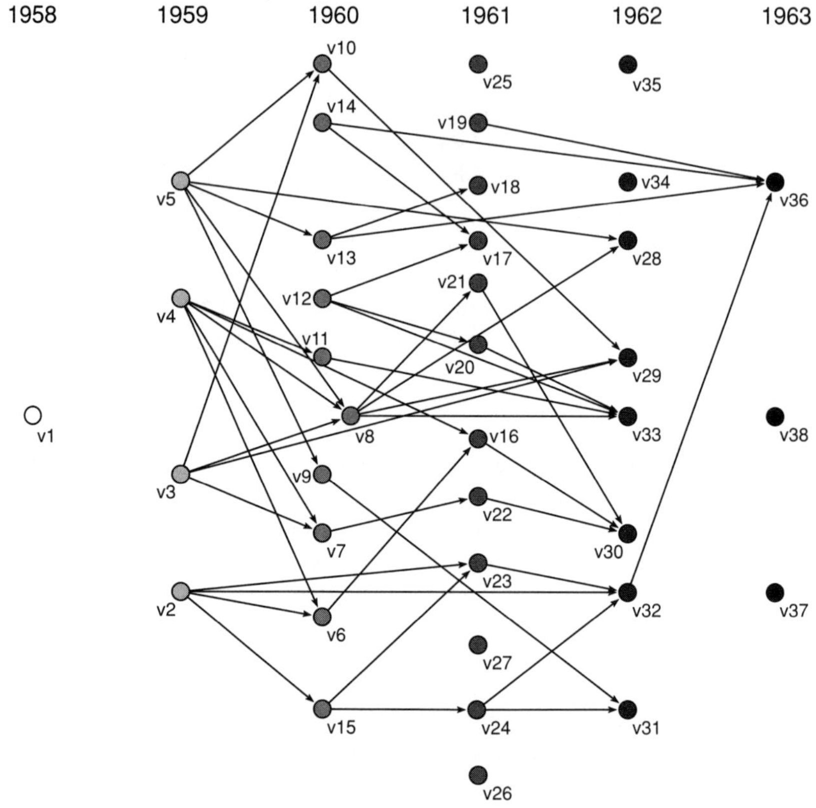

Figure 80. Modern math network with arcs pointing toward later adopters.

for instance, shows the modern math network if edges are replaced by arcs that point to later adopters. If social ties are used to spread the innovation, the arcs represent the direction of the spread. Note that ties within an adoption class are omitted because they are not supposed to spread the innovation.

Operations>
Transform>
Direction

In Pajek, we can change an undirected network (e.g., the modern math network) into a directed network with all arcs pointing from an earlier adopter to a later adopter with the commands in the *Operations> Transform>Direction* submenu. The commands are located in the *Operations* menu, so you need a network and something else, namely a partition that specifies the (adoption) classes to which the vertices belong. There are two commands: *Lower→Higher* and *Higher→Lower*. The first command replaces an edge in an undirected network by an arc that points toward the vertex with the higher class number. In our case, the partition contains adoption time classes so the *Lower→Higher* command produces arcs toward later adopters. This command issues a dialog box asking whether lines within classes must be deleted. In a directed diffusion network, we do not want to have lines within adoption classes normally, so answer yes. Now, we obtain the network shown in Figure 80. Applied to a directed network, the *Direction* procedure selects the arcs that conform to the selected option (lower to higher or higher to lower).

Now, we can simply compute the thresholds of all vertices in the diffusion network by dividing the indegree of vertices in the transformed directed network by their degree in the original undirected network provided that both networks contain neither multiple lines nor loops. Select the vector with normalized indegree in the directed network as the first vector in the *Vectors* menu, select the corresponding vector for the undirected network as the second vector, and divide the first by the second to obtain a vector with the individual thresholds. Make sure that a division of zero by zero (no neighbors) yields zero in the *Options>Read/Write* menu.

Net>Partitions> Degree>Input

Vectors>Divide First by Second

Exercise II
Compute the thresholds of the vertices in the modern math diffusion network as explained in this section. Is the threshold higher for vertices that adopt later as one would expect when thresholds really matter?

8.4   Critical Mass

Some diffusion processes are successful because almost everybody in the target group adopts the innovation. For instance, the modern math method was adopted by fifty-one of sixty-one superintendents in Allegheny County within a period of six years. Diffusion, however, may also fail because too few people adopt and spread the innovation. Once again, a biological metaphor is illuminating: a bacteria may either succeed to overcome the resistance of the human body and develop into a disease or does not gain the upper hand and is oppressed and finally eliminated by antibodies. The spread of a disease has a critical limit: once it is exceeded, the bacteria multiplies quickly.

> The *critical mass* of a diffusion process is the minimum number of adopters needed to sustain a diffusion process.

In the diffusion of innovations theory, a similar limit is hypothesized to exist. It is called the critical mass of a diffusion process and it is defined as the minimum number of adopters needed to sustain a diffusion process. In the first stage of a diffusion process, outside help is needed (e.g., an advertisement campaign) but once a sufficient number of opinion leaders have adopted, social contagion fuels the process and causes a chain reaction that ensures wide and rapid diffusion. Then, no more outside input to the diffusion process is required.

The critical mass of a particular diffusion process is difficult to pinpoint, so it is hard to prove that it exists and when it occurs. Recall that the two-step flow model combines contagion with external events. We need detailed information about the effects of external events, such as media

Table 11. *Adoption Rate and Acceleration in the Modern Math Diffusion Curve*

Time	Cum% of Adopters	Cum # of Adopters	Adoption Rate	Acceleration
↓			1	
1958 (1)	2.63	1		3
↓			4	
1959 (2)	13.16	5		6
↓			10	
1960 (3)	39.47	15		2
↓			12	
1961 (4)	71.05	27		−4
↓			8	
1962 (5)	92.11	35		−5
↓			3	
1963 (6)	100.00	38		−3
↓			0	

campaigns, versus the effect of social contagion on the diffusion process to know when critical mass is reached. Only afterwards, we may evaluate whether a diffusion process was successful. We present some approaches that try to overcome this problem.

There is an empirical rule of thumb that tells us something about the number of people who will eventually adopt an innovation. In many diffusion processes, a particular phenomenon occurs when the innovation has been adopted by 16 (or 10 to 20) percent of all people who will adopt eventually: the acceleration of the adoption rate decreases although the adoption rate still increases in absolute numbers. This is known as the first *second-order inflection point* of the S-curve.

In the modern math network, for instance, the number of new adopters (adoption rate) rises from 1 to 4 from 1958 to 1959 (see the fourth column in Table 11), which is three more than the number of adopters in 1958, so there is an acceleration of 3 (see the fifth column in Table 11). Note that adoption rates are placed between the moments because they reflect the change between two measurements. In the next year, ten superintendents adopt, which is an even larger acceleration, but in 1961 the acceleration drops to 2 because the number of new adopters grows only from 10 to 12; the number of new adopters still rises but it rises less sharply. In 1959, we may conclude, the acceleration of the adoption rate is highest and we can see that 13 percent of all adopters have adopted (see the column "Cum% of adopters" in Table 11) as predicted by the rule of thumb.

Because of this empirical relation between the first second-order inflection point of the diffusion curve and the final spread of an innovation, diffusion analysts say that critical mass is attained when the diffusion curve reaches this inflection point. In this approach, any diffusion process in which the adoption rate first accelerates and then declines is thought to be driven by the chain reaction characteristic for contagion models. Social contagion is assumed to take over the diffusion process at this point, so we may conclude that the process has reached its critical mass.

A similar argument has been made for the first-order inflection point of the logistic diffusion curve, which is the period with the highest adoption rate, that is, the largest absolute increase in new adopters. Usually, the first-order inflection point occurs when approximately 50 percent of all eventual adopters have adopted. In the modern math network, the highest adoption rate is 12 and it was realized between 1960 and 1961. In this period, the percentage of adopters rose from 39 to 71 percent.

We ought to realize that this approach completely presupposes the relation between contagion and critical mass; it does not prove that critical mass occurs, it merely assumes so. Nevertheless, it is useful for practical purposes. We may monitor the diffusion process and watch out for the moment in which the first decline in growth acceleration occurs (but we should ignore incidental declines). When it occurs, we may estimate the final number of adopters at about five to ten times the number of adopters at the time of the largest increase because about 10 to 20 percent has adopted then. If this estimated number of adopters is not enough according to our target, we can try to boost the diffusion process with additional media campaigns and the like. If this leads to acceleration of the diffusion, the critical mass becomes larger and the diffusion process will probably reach more people in the end. However, we have no guarantee that this will actually happen. After all, we are working with a simple rule of thumb.

In another perspective, a diffusion process is assumed to attain its critical mass when the most central people have adopted. Once they have adopted, so many actors in the network are exposed to adopters that many individual thresholds have been reached and an avalanche of adoptions occurs. Betweenness-centrality seems to be associated with critical mass in particular. Targeting the actors with highest betweenness-centrality is a good strategy for launching an innovation. In general, the position of the first adopters in the network is relevant to the diffusion process. If the first adopters are central and directly linked, their neighbors have higher exposure rates, so they are more likely to adopt.

Why does critical mass boost the diffusion of an innovation? On the one hand, the reason may be purely quantitative: once a sufficient number of well-connected people have adopted, enough people are exposed to the innovation to adopt, after which even more people are exposed. This is the mechanism we described for the case that the central actors adopt. On the other hand, reaching the critical mass has been thought of as a qualitative change to the system, namely a sudden lowering of individual thresholds. During the diffusion process, individual thresholds may be lowered as a consequence of the rate of adoption in the entire social system. People are supposed to monitor their social system. If they perceive wide acceptance of an innovation, they feel confident or even obliged to adopt it. Lower thresholds lead to easier adoption, so the diffusion process strengthens itself and it will most probably not wither away.

The lowering of thresholds is expected to occur particularly when actors are interdependent with regard to an innovation. New communication technology products (e.g., buzzers or SMS) are a case in point. When more people have one, their benefits and value increase. The first adopters can reach few people with the new communication products but the late majority can contact many more users. This kind of innovation is called an *interactive innovation*. Even in the case of noninteractive innovations, such as the modern math method, the qualitative mechanism may be operative. Superintendents may be persuaded to adopt the new method because they know that most of their peers have adopted, regardless of the number of adopters in their circle of friends.

A *threshold lag* is a period in which an actor does not adopt although he or she is exposed at the level at which he or she will adopt later.

The lowering of thresholds when critical mass is attained in the diffusion process may explain the occurrence of a threshold lag, that is, a period in which the exposure has reached the individual threshold but the individual does not adopt. In this case, adoption occurs after the critical mass is reached, and the individual's threshold is lowered. In the modern math network, superintendents v28 and v29 reached the level of exposure at which they would eventually adopt in 1960 because all of their friends had adopted by that year. However, they did not adopt immediately in 1961. There is a delay of one year, which is their threshold lag. Perhaps, the diffusion process reached its critical mass in 1961, which lowered their thresholds and induced them to adopt in 1962.

We should note that this approach to thresholds and threshold lags does not prove that individuals have certain thresholds and threshold lags; it merely defines them in a particular way. In an empirical diffusion network, we can always compute an actor's exposure at the moment of adoption (threshold) and how long this actor had been exposed at this level before he or she adopted (threshold lag). But this does not rule out the possibility that the individual threshold was actually lower and his or her threshold lag was longer. We should also consider the possibility that the individual's original threshold was even higher than the exposure at the time of adoption, so there was no threshold lag at all, namely when the diffusion process reached a critical mass lowering individual thresholds or when outside events (e.g., a media campaign) convinced individuals to adopt before they reached their thresholds. The launching of Sputnik I in October, 1957, for example, is known to have spurred a wave of innovations in science and education in the United States.

Therefore, we need empirical data supplementing the diffusion network data to validate the actors' thresholds, notably, psychological information, relevant social characteristics, or a record of past adoptions. Then we can estimate the most likely adoption time and compare it to the actual adoption time to determine threshold lags and critical mass effects. If threshold lags coincide with external events, it is likely that these events have an impact on the diffusion process. In contrast, if a media campaign does not coincide with the end of relatively many lags, it is probably not very influential.

Table 12. *Fragment of Table 11*

Time	Cum% of Adopters	Cum # of Adopters	Adoption Rate	Acceleration
↓			1	
1958 (1)	2.63	1		3
↓			4	
1959 (2)	13.16	5		6
↓			10	
1960 (3)	39.47	15		2

Application

The absolute adoption rates and their acceleration can be calculated from the frequency tabulation of adoption times, discussed in Section 8.2. The absolute growth or adoption rate is just the number of new adopters between two moments (e.g., ten superintendents adopt the modern math method between the end of 1959 and the end of 1960). In Table 12, adoption rates are again placed between the moments because they reflect the change between two measurements. The acceleration of the adoption rate at a particular moment is the difference between the adoption rate directly before and after this moment: subtract two successive adoption rates. In 1959, the acceleration is 6, because ten schools adopted in the year after the end of 1959 and four adopted in the year before. It is easy to spot the moment in which the acceleration starts to decrease while the absolute growth (adoption rate) is still increasing.

Info>Partition

If the critical mass is the first moment at which the most central vertices have adopted, we may simply calculate the betweenness centrality of the vertices and check at which time all or most of the central actors have adopted (*Net>Vector>Centrality>Betweenness*). We advise computing betweenness-centrality in the undirected network, so symmetrize a directed network first (*Net>Transform>Arcs→Edges>All*, avoid multiple lines). List the most central vertices with the *Info>Vector* command by entering a positive number in the dialog box captioned *Highest/lowest or interval of values*. You can check their adoption time in the adoption time partition or in the layered sociogram (see Section 8.1). In our example, the most central superintendents (v8, v13, and v12) are found among the adopters in 1960 or 1959 (v5), so critical mass was reached in 1960. Note, however, that not all central actors have adopted then: the fifth (v36) and sixth (v32) most central superintendents adopted as late as 1963 and 1962.

Net>Vector>Centrality>Betweenness

Net>Transform>Arcs→Edges>All

Info>Vector

For the calculation of threshold lags, it is important to note that a vertex reaches its threshold when all prior adopters in its neighborhood have adopted. In the modern math network, for instance, superintendent v28 reached his threshold of 0.67 in 1960, when superintendent v8 adopted. At the end of 1960, all prior adopters in his neighborhood had adopted (superintendents v5 and v8). The third contact in his friendship network, superintendent v29, is irrelevant to the threshold of v28 because he or she adopted at the same time as v28. The threshold lag is calculated as the difference between the time of adoption of an actor (his or her class number in the adoption partition) and the maximum adoption time of the neighbors that adopted before him or her. We have to subtract 1 from the threshold lag if we consider exposure at one moment to cause adoption at the next moment. The threshold lag of v28 is equal to 1962–1960–1, which is one year.

threshold
lag.mcr
In Pajek, the last contact of a vertex to adopt prior to this vertex is easily found in the directed network that we introduced to calculate thresholds. When all lines point from earlier to later adopters, the neighbor with the highest adoption time on the input side of a vertex is its closest predecessor. However, the computation of thresholds includes some tricks we do not want to discuss here, so we prepared a macro (Threshold_lag.mcr) you can use to obtain threshold lags from the original undirected network and adoption time partition. When you play this macro (see Section 8.3), some new networks, partitions, and vectors are created. The last vector contains the threshold lags.

In the modern math network, we find threshold lags only for superintendents v28 and v29 (one-year lag). This small number of lags does not suggest that external events or critical mass influenced the diffusion process. Most vertices have adopted right after one or more of their friends had adopted, which is in line with the simple exposure and threshold model.

8.5   Summary

Innovations and infectious diseases diffuse in a particular manner that is represented by the typical S shape of the diffusion curve. At first, few actors adopt the innovation but the adoption rate accelerates. When 10 to 20 percent of the actors have adopted, the acceleration levels off while the absolute number of new adopters is still increasing, causing a sharp rise of the total number of adopters. Finally, the number of new adopters decreases and the diffusion process slowly reaches its end.

This growth pattern is typical for a chain reaction caused by contagion. Therefore, network models approach diffusion as a contagion process in which personal contacts with adopters expose people to an innovation. They learn about the innovation and their contacts persuade them to adopt. Once exposure reaches their threshold for adopting the innovation, which depends on their personal characteristics and on characteristics of the innovation, they will adopt the innovation and start infecting others. As a consequence, the network structure and the positions of the first adopters in the network, who are usually opinion leaders, influence the rate at which an innovation diffuses. This is a very likely mechanism but it is difficult to prove that diffusion actually works this way.

At a particular moment in time, a successful diffusion process is hypothesized to reach a critical mass, which means that the diffusion process can sustain or even accelerate itself without help from outside (e.g., media campaigns). Even with hindsight it is not easy to pinpoint the moment when critical mass is reached, but according to an empirical rule of thumb this happens when the innovation has spread to 10 to 20 percent of the actors who adopt eventually. This is the first second-order inflection point of the S-shaped diffusion curve: the moment when the adoption rate no longer accelerates although it is still increasing. Alternatively, the critical mass may be placed at the moment when the most central actors have adopted or when relatively many actors adopt although their exposure is not increasing. In the latter case, the critical mass or external events are thought to lower individual thresholds.

We are not sure whether critical mass occurs and whether it has the hypothesized impact on the diffusion process. Ongoing research in the diffusion of innovations tradition must clarify this matter. Nevertheless, the concept offers some practical tools for monitoring and guiding a diffusion process.

In theory, knowledge about other people's adoption without personal contact may count as exposure too, especially in the case of status similarities. Knowing that people with similar network positions have adopted although you are not directly linked to them may persuade you to also adopt. In this chapter, we have presented contagion by contact only and not by status imitation. Structural approaches to status and roles will be introduced in Part V of this book.

8.6 Questions

1. If we use a simple contagion by contact model without individual thresholds and one source of contamination, which vertex is the source in diffusion curve 1 and which vertex is the source in curve 2 in the network below?

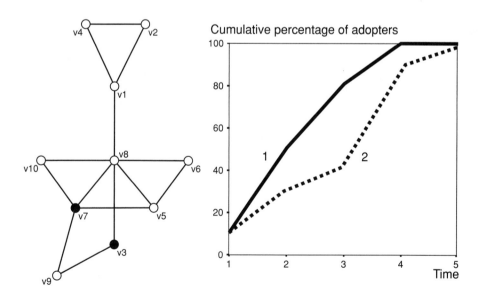

    a. v8 is the source in curve 1 and v1 is the source in curve 2.
    b. v7 is the source in curve 1 and v2 is the source in curve 2.
    c. v6 is the source in curve 1 and v3 is the source in curve 2.
    d. v5 is the source in curve 1 and v4 is the source in curve 2.

2. In the network of Question 1, which vertex would you choose to introduce an innovation (e.g., a new product)? Justify your choice.

3. In the network of Question 1, assume that the black vertices have adopted an innovation at time one. Calculate the exposure of the remaining vertices by hand.

4. Take the situation of Question 3 as your starting point. At time 2, vertices v9 and v10 adopt. What can you say about the thresholds of vertices v10, v9, and v8?

5. Take the situation of Question 4 as your starting point. If vertices v5, v6, and v8 adopt at time three, which vertices have threshold lags?
    a. None of the three vertices.
    b. Only vertex v5.
    c. Vertices v5 and v6.
    d. All three vertices.

6. Considering your answer to Question 5, can you identify the critical mass of this diffusion process? Justify your answer.

7. Estimate the total number of adopters from the following data on the start of a diffusion process.

Time	1	2	3	4	5	....
Cumulative number of adopters	21	74	251	635	1176	....

8.7   Assignment

In a famous study, known as the Columbia University Drug Study, the diffusion of a new drug (gammanym) was investigated. The researchers collected data on the first subscription of this drug by physicians in several communities. In addition, they investigated friendship ties and discussion links between the physicians, asking them to name three doctors they considered to be personal friends and to nominate three doctors with whom they would choose to discuss medical matters.

The file `Galesburg.net` contains a network of friendship (blue) and discussion ties (red) between seventeen physicians who adopted the new drug in Galesburg (Illinois) in the 1950s. The partition `Galesburg_adoptiontime.clu` specifies the number of months since the introduction of the new drug at which the physician first prescribed the drug. This is considered to be their adoption time.

Analyze the diffusion process visually and numerically. Do you think the innovation diffused by a simple contagion process or by a contagion process with individual thresholds? Is it probable that external events or a critical mass effect influenced the diffusion process?

8.8   Further Reading

- The example is taken from R. O. Carlson, *Adoption of Educational Innovations* (Eugene: University of Oregon, Center for the Advanced Study of Educational Administration, 1965). Friendship choices and year of adoption are coded from the sociogram on page 19 of the book.
- The Columbia University Drug Study was reported in J. S. Coleman, E. Katz, and H. Menzel, *Medical Innovation: A Diffusion Study* (Indianapolis: Bobbs-Merrill, 1966). The data, however, are taken from D. Knoke and R. S. Burt, "Prominence." In R. S. Burt and M. J. Minor (Eds.), *Applied Network Analysis: A Methodological Introduction* (Beverly Hills: Sage, 1983, 195–222).
- E. M. Rogers's *Diffusion of Innovations* (New York: The Free Press, 1995, 4th edition) offers a general overview of diffusion theory and research. He uses the modern math case as an example (see pages 65–6 and Chapter 8).
- M. Granovetter introduced the concept of threshold as the percentage of previous adopters in a person's ego-network in "Threshold models of collective behavior" (*American Journal of Sociology* 83 (1978), 1420–43).
- T. W. Valente's *Network Models of the Diffusion of Innovations* (Creskill, NJ: Hampton Press, 1995) presents and evaluates different diffusion network models.

8.9   Answers

Answers to the Exercises

I. After producing the random network, you must use the *Net>k-Neighbours>All* command to obtain a partition with the distances between the selected source vertex and all other vertices ignoring the direction of lines. Under the current assumptions the distance to the source vertex is the adoption time of a vertex, so this partition specifies all adoption times and a tabulation of this partition, which may be obtained with the *Info>Partition* command, shows the adoption rate at each moment (see the columns CumFreq or CumFreq%). It is worthwhile playing around a little with central and peripheral vertices as source vertices and with different random networks (e.g., with outdegree fixed at one or outdegree varying from one to three or more).

II. In the sociogram below, the sizes of the vertices (*Draw>Draw-Vector* command) and the numbers in brackets (*Options>Mark Vertices Using>Vector Values* in the Draw screen) show the thresholds of all vertices. If we ignore the actors without contacts to previous adopters, which cannot have adopted by direct contagion, the thresholds seem to increase from left to right. The mean thresholds per year (excluding the actors without links to prior adopters) illustrate this: 0.34 (1960), 0.47 (1961), 0.86 (1962), and 1.00 (1963).

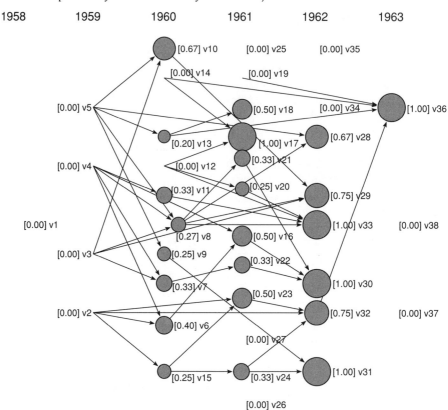

Answers to the Questions in Section 8.6

1. Answer b is correct. Recall that the simple contagion model without individual thresholds assumes that an adopter persuades his neighbors to adopt at the next time, who transmit the innovation to their neighbors, and so on. This means that the adoption time of a vertex is directly related to its distance from the source of contagion. If we assume that the source adopts at time 1, the cumulative percentage of adopters is one of ten (the number of vertices) or 10 percent. This is correct because both diffusion curves start at 10 percent. At time 2, the neighbors of the source adopt. In the solid line, 50 percent or five of ten vertices have adopted at the second moment. One of them is the source, so there are four new adopters who are neighbors of the source. There is only one vertex in the network with four neighbors, namely vertex v7, so this must be the source of the diffusion process represented by the solid curve.

From the dotted curve, we can infer that two vertices adopt at time 2, one vertex adopts at time 3, five vertices adopt at time 4, and one vertex adopts at time 5. The source has two neighbors, so it can be vertex v2, v4, v6, v3, v9, or v10. At distance 2, it is connected to one vertex. This is true for vertices v2 and v4 but not for the other possible sources. As is shown, the diffusion process is identical whether it starts from v2 or v4, so the dotted line may represent the diffusion from both vertices.

2. For optimal diffusion, you must choose the most central vertex in a network because it exposes most vertices to the innovation. Vertex v8 is most central and has the largest degree, so it is a good choice.

3. Vertices v1, v2, v4, and v6 are not directly linked to the adopters (v3 and v7) in the network, so their exposure is zero. Vertex v9 is only linked to adopters, so its exposure is maximal: 1.00. One of v10's two neighbors is an adopter, so its exposure is 0.5. One of v5's three neighbors and two of v8's six neighbors are adopters, so they have an exposure of 0.33.

4. If we calculate the exposure of a vertex as the number of vertices that adopted previously, the threshold of v9 and v10, who adopt at time 2, is equal to their exposure to the vertices that adopted at $T1$. Hence, the threshold of v9 is 1.00 and the threshold of v10 is 0.5. The exposure of vertex v8 is 0.33 at $T2$ but this vertex does not adopt, so we may conclude that its threshold is higher than 0.33.

5. Answer c is correct. At $T2$, vertices v9 and v10 adopt (see Question 3). This changes the exposure of vertex v8: now half of its neighbors are adopters. The new degree of exposure may surpass its threshold, hence v8 adopts at the next time. In contrast, the exposure of vertices v5 and v6 does not change at $T2$ because neither vertex is directly linked to v9 or v10, so they could have adopted earlier. These vertices have threshold lags.

6. Threshold lags may be caused by critical mass. When a substantive number of vertices adopt at a moment when their exposure does not increase, their thresholds may be lowered due to critical mass. If we think that two threshold lags ending at $T3$ is a substantive amount for this small network, we may propose that the diffusion process reached its critical mass at $T2$.

7. To estimate the total number of adopters, we need to know the number of adopters at the first second-order inflection point of the diffusion curve, that is, the last time that the acceleration of the adoption rate increases. Because this moment often occurs when 10 to 20 percent of all adopters have espoused the innovation, the total number of adopters may be estimated as five to ten times this number.

   Between successive measurements, the number of new adopters specifies the adoption rate, which increases over all five moments (see the third row in the table below). To calculate the acceleration, we must subtract the number of new adopters by the number of new adopters at the previous moment. The results are presented in the fourth row.

   Now, we can see that the acceleration decreases after $T3$, so we assume that $T3$ represents the inflection point. The total number of adopters may be estimated at five to ten times the (cumulative) number of adopters at $T3$, which is five to ten times 251: 1255 to 2510 adopters.

Time	$\rightarrow$	1	$\rightarrow$	2	$\rightarrow$	3	$\rightarrow$	4	$\rightarrow$	5	...
Cumulative number of adopters		21		74		251		635		1176	
Adoption rate (number of new adopters)	21		53		177		384		541		
Acceleration		31		124		207		157			

Part IV

Ranking

Previous chapters paid little attention to the direction of social relations. In matters of cohesion or brokerage, it is more important to know that a tie exists than to know who initiates it. In this part, however, direction is central, especially asymmetry in social relations. Which choices are not reciprocated? Asymmetry in social relations points to social prestige and ranking.

9

Prestige

9.1 Introduction

In directed networks, people who receive many positive choices are considered to be prestigious. Prestige becomes salient especially if positive choices are not reciprocated, for instance, if everybody likes to play with the most popular girl or boy in a group but he or she does not play with all of them or, in the case of sentiments, if people tend to express positive sentiments toward prestigious persons but receive negative sentiments in return. In these cases, social prestige is connected to social power and the privilege of not having to reciprocate choices.

In social network analysis, prestige is conceptualized as a particular pattern of social ties. We discuss techniques to calculate the *structural prestige* of a person from his or her social ties, notably sociometric choices. We do not compute a prestige score for an entire network.

Structural prestige is not identical to the concept of *social prestige* in the social sciences or in ordinary speech. For example, the medical profession is thought to be prestigious, but it is difficult to consider professions as a network in which many arcs point toward the medical profession. The prestige of an art museum may depend on the value and origins of its collection rather than on the number of art works it attracts (receives) from other museums. However, social prestige is probably related to structural prestige. In community studies, for example, a physician is more often nominated in advice seeking relations than members of many other professions, and a prestigious art museum receives more attention from art critics than less prestigious ones.

In this chapter, we compare the structural prestige of families within a network of visiting ties to their social prestige. As is shown, the two kinds of prestige are related but far from identical. Therefore, be careful not to equate structural prestige to social prestige. Instead, find out whether structural prestige scores on a social relation match indicators of social prestige that are measured by external variables. In a particular setting, which social relation is connected to social prestige?

9.2 Example

Let us have a look at the visiting ties in another village in the Turrialba region of Costa Rica: the village of San Juan Sur containing seventy-five *haciendas* (SanJuanSur.net). In Chapter 3, we analyzed cohesive subgroups in the network of Attiro. Now, we concentrate on status and prestige. Members of the San Juan Sur community who were well informed about its population were asked to rank order all heads of households according to their importance to the community. Social status was computed for each family farm in this area as the average importance of its inhabitants and grouped into fourteen classes (partition SanJuanSur_status.clu). Prestige leaders were identified as those people who received more than ten nominations within the community on the question: Which persons would you pick to represent you and the people of this place on a commission? In Figure 81 the prestige leaders are black (partition SanJuanSur_leaders.clu, the data are collected in SanJuanSur2.paj). In this chapter, we use these scores as indicators of social prestige or status.

Figure 81 depicts the simple network of visiting ties. Note that bidirectional arcs are replaced by lines for the sake of clarity. There are three types of visiting ties, indicated by the color of arcs as well as line values in

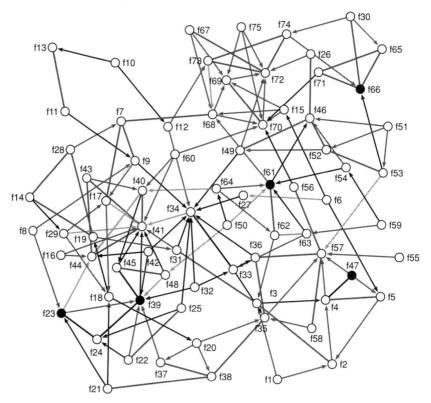

Figure 81. Visiting ties and prestige leaders in San Juan Sur.

the data file: dark gray (or red) arcs (line value 2) represent visits among kin, light gray (or blue) arcs (line value 3) are visits among families bound by godparent or godchild ties (church relations), and other types of ties are drawn in black arcs (line value 1). Note that the grays in Figure 81 do not show the different types of visiting ties as clearly as the colors on your computer screen. In this chapter, we calculate the structural prestige of the families from these visiting relations to find out whether social prestige (status) matches structural prestige.

9.3 Popularity and Indegree

At a first glance, this sociogram tells us little about the structural positions of prestige leaders. The leaders are dispersed over the network. They are situated in dense areas (e.g., family f39) as well as in the margins (families f23, f49, and f66). We need some calculations to get a better view of structural prestige.

> The *popularity* or indegree of a vertex is the number of arcs it receives in a directed network.

The simplest measure of structural prestige is called popularity and it is measured by the number of choices a vertex receives: its indegree. Nominations on a positive social relation (e.g., liking) express prestige; more nominations indicate higher structural prestige, for example, in an election or a popularity poll. In this example, receiving more visitors indicates higher structural prestige. Note that the indegree of a vertex can be determined only in a directed network. In undirected networks, we cannot measure prestige; instead, we use degree as a simple measure of centrality (see Chapter 6). In fact, several centrality measures are equal or similar to prestige measures applied to undirected networks.

Of course, a high indegree on a relation such as "lend money to someone" does not reflect the popularity of an actor: it merely identifies someone who owes money to many persons. We should note that indegree does reflect prestige if we *transpose* the arcs in such a network, that is, if we reverse the direction of arcs. In the transposed network, arcs represent the "owe money to" relation and someone with a large indegree has lend money to many other people. Probably, this actor is quite rich compared to the other actors and more prestigious.

In the original network, the direction of the arcs depends on the way the researcher has defined the relation and worded the sociometric question. In the analysis, it is sometimes better to change the direction of the arcs. You are allowed to do this, because no information is lost in the transposed network: just transpose it again and you obtain the original network. It is interesting to note that several structural properties of a network do not change when the arcs are transposed (e.g., the components

Table 13. *Indegree Listing in Pajek*

Cluster	Freq	Freq%	CumFreq	CumFreq%	Representative
0	13	17.3333	13	17.3333	f1
1	17	22.6667	30	40.0000	f11
2	11	14.6667	41	54.6667	f13
3	15	20.0000	56	74.6667	f2
4	5	6.6667	61	81.3333	f3
5	6	8.0000	67	89.3333	f35
6	2	2.6667	69	92.0000	f44
7	1	1.3333	70	93.3333	f70
8	3	4.0000	73	97.3333	f39
10	1	1.3333	74	98.6667	f34
12	1	1.3333	75	100.0000	f41
SUM	75	100.0000			

remain unchanged) and other properties are just swapped (e.g., outdegree becomes indegree and vice versa).

Application

Net>Partitions> Degree>Input

In Chapter 3, you have learned to compute the indegree of vertices in a directed network by means of the *Input* command in the *Net>Partitions>Degree* submenu. This command creates a new partition that can be displayed with *Info>Partition*. Table 13 shows the frequency count of the indegree of family farms in San Juan Sur. Thirteen families were not visited, so their indegree is zero. They have minimal structural prestige. Family number f41 is most popular because it is visited by twelve families (see entry of class 12 in Table 13). Note that the indegree is equal to the number of visiting families because there are no multiple arcs. In Figure 81, we can see the high number of visits that family f41 receives. This simple frequency tabulation summarizes the distribution of popularity better than the sociogram. The table shows that half of the families receive two visits at most. No more than one-fifth of all families receive five or more visits (see column CumFreq%).

File>Partition> Edit

How about the prestige leaders? May we conclude that families containing prestige leaders are structurally prestigious? Inspecting the sociogram or the indegree partition (use *File>Partition>Edit*), we note that prestige leaders f23, f39, f47, f61, and f66 have indegree 3, 8, 1, 5, and 5, respectively. All prestige leaders except for family f47 have indegree above average and three of five families belong to the top 20 percent because they receive five or more visits. Therefore, we conclude that the prestige leaders are visited quite often, but there are other families that receive even more visits. Structural prestige measured by indegree does not distinguish between prestige leaders and other frequently visited families in this example.

Net>Transform> Transpose

If the relation points from more to less prestigious vertices, as in the case of "lend money to," you should change the direction of all ties in a network. This can simply be done by means of the *Net>Transform>Transpose* command.

9.4   Correlation

Does structural prestige indicated by indegree match social status as it was rated by experts within the community? To answer this question, we have to use standard statistical analysis to the results from our network analysis, which are the structural prestige scores. Because this is not a course in statistics, we keep it as simple as possible. It is our primary goal to show that social network analysis and statistical analysis are two sets of techniques that work very well together in social research.

In statistics, the association between two phenomena is usually measured by *correlation coefficients*. Correlation coefficients range from 1 to −1. A positive coefficient indicates that a high score on one feature is associated with a high score on the other (e.g., high structural prestige occurs in families with high social status). A negative coefficient points toward a negative or inverse relation: a high score on one characteristic combines with a low score on the other (e.g., high structural prestige is found predominantly with low social status families). As a rule of thumb, we may say that there is no correlation if the absolute value of the coefficient is less than .05. If the absolute value of a coefficient is between .05 and .25, association is weak, coefficients from .25 to .60 (and from −.25 to −.60) indicate moderate association, and .60 to 1.00 (or −.60 to −1.00) is interpreted as strong association. Usually, a coefficient of 1 or −1 is said to display perfect association, but it is very unlikely that you will find this unless you correlate a characteristic to itself.

In Pajek, two kinds of correlation coefficients can be computed: Spearman's rank correlation and Pearson's correlation. *Spearman's rank correlation* determines whether the ranking of vertices on one characteristic (e.g., indegree) matches the ranking on another characteristic (e.g., status). The magnitude of differences between ranks is unimportant. Of course, both characteristics must have scores that can be ranked. Spearman's rank correlation is a robust measure of association provided that few cases have equal ranks.

Pearson's correlation coefficient uses the exact numerical scores on both characteristics. It assumes a linear association between two characteristics, which means that a unit increase in one characteristic will be associated with a fixed increase (or decrease) in the other. In our example, Pearson's correlation assumes that one extra indegree of structural prestige is accompanied by a fixed amount of additional social status (e.g., 2.4 extra points of social prestige).

Pearson is more precise and more sensitive than Spearman. This can be an advantage as well as a disadvantage. If a linear association exists among two features of vertices in the network, Pearson's correlation coefficient describes it more accurately than that of Spearman. However, the assumption that unit change on one feature is associated with a fixed change in another is very strict and often not met. For example, one extra indegree may involve substantial extra social status for families in the classes with low indegree, whereas it may be associated with little extra status for families in the middle or upper indegree classes. In this case, Pearson's coefficient underestimates the actual association, whereas that of Spearman does not. Therefore, it is important to use Pearson's correlation coefficient only if its results do not diverge too much from Spearman's coefficient. If results are very different, the data contain irregularities.

Application

To compute a correlation coefficient, we need two characteristics of each vertex in the network. As learned in Chapter 2, features of vertices are stored in partitions and vectors. A partition contains integers, a vector is a list of numbers with decimals. Because Spearman's rank correlation coefficient takes only the (discrete) rank order of scores into account, it operates on partitions. To calculate Spearman, you need two partitions. Hence, Spearman can be found in the *Partitions* menu. However, Pearson's correlation coefficient uses the exact magnitude of scores. In Pajek, Pearson needs two vectors as input data and the procedure is to be found in the *Vectors* menu.

Partitions>First Partition

Partitions> Second Partition

Partitions>Info> Spearman Rank

Social status scores are available as a partition (SanJuanSur_status.clu) which must be opened in Pajek to compute its correlation with the indegree partition. Load both partitions in the *Partitions* menu by selecting the partition in the drop-down menu and clicking on the commands *First Partition* and *Second Partition*, respectively. It does not matter which partition is first. When both partitions are selected, choose the command *Spearman Rank* on the *Info* submenu (see Figure 82) and Pajek computes the rank correlation coefficient. In this case, it is .40, meaning that there is a moderate positive rank correlation between indegree and social status. Families with larger indegree tend to be families with higher status. Hence, we may conclude that structural prestige is moderately associated with status in this example.

Vectors>First Vector

Vectors>Second Vector

Vectors>Info

Pearson's correlation coefficient is computed in a similar way. Select a first and second vector in the *Vectors* menu and choose the *Info* submenu, which has no options other than Pearson's coefficient. In this example, you may use the normalized input degree vector created by the *Network>Partitions>Degree>Input* command but you have to translate the status partition (SanJuanSur_status.clu) to a vector first with the *Partition>Make Vector* command. Pearson's correlation coefficient is .35, which is slightly lower than Spearman's correlation, indicating that

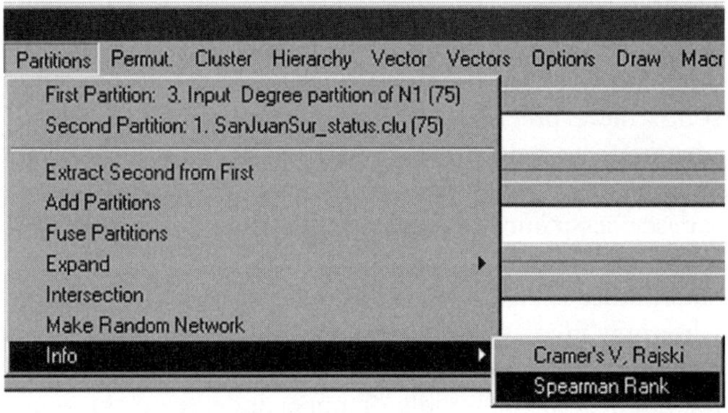

Figure 82. Partitions menu in Pajek.

the association is not linear. Using the rule of thumb specified above, however, we reach the same conclusion about the association between indegree and social status.

Exercise I
Split the visiting relations network into three separate networks: one for each type of visiting relation (note that the type of visiting relation is indicated by line values). For each new network, determine the popularity of the vertices and the correlation between popularity and status (SanJuanSur_status.clu). Which type of visiting relation matches the status hierarchy best?

9.5 Domains

Popularity is a very restricted measure of prestige because it takes only direct choices into account. With popularity it does not matter whether choices are received from people who are not chosen themselves or from popular people. The overall structure of the network is disregarded.

Several efforts have been made to extend prestige to indirect choices. The first idea that comes to mind is to count all people by whom someone is nominated directly or indirectly, that is, without or with go-betweens. This is the input domain of an actor, which has been called the influence domain because structurally prestigious people are thought to influence people who regard them as their leaders. The larger the input domain of a person, the higher his or her structural prestige.

> The *input domain* of a vertex in a directed network is the number or percentage of all other vertices that are connected by a path to this vertex.

Note that the output domain is more likely to reflect prestige in the case of a relation such as "lend money to." It is easy to define the output domain of a vertex and we guess that you understand that the output domain of a vertex is identical to the input domain of the vertex in the transposed network. In fact, we may distinguish between three domains: input domain, output domain, and (overall) domain, which is the union of the input and the output domain.

Let us have a look at the visiting relations network again to understand the concept of an input domain. Figure 83 contains the vertices in the input domain of family f47 and the paths toward this family. The numbers inside the vertices indicate the distance to family f47. Clearly, family f47 has zero distance to itself. This family is visited only by family f4: its distance to family f47 is 1. Families f2, f3, and f5 visit family f4, so they can reach family f47 via family f4 (distance 2). They are visited by three families (distance 3), and so on. Ultimately, family f47 can be reached by sixty-four of the remaining seventy-four families (86%) in San Juan Sur. The input domain of family f47 equals sixty-four vertices or 86 percent.

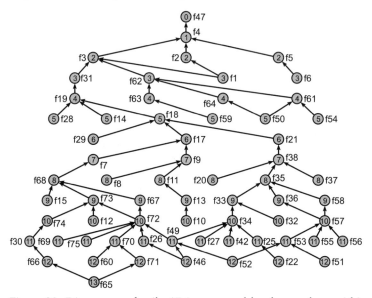

Figure 83. Distances to family 47 (represented by the numbers within the vertices).

The ten families outside the input domain of family f47, which are not drawn in Figure 83, include prestige leaders f23 and f39, and several families from the densest part of the network (e.g., f40, f43, f44, f45, and f48), among them family f41 with highest indegree. Family f47, which is also a prestige leader, turns out to be unreachable for the prestige leaders in the center of the network. This family was probably nominated as a representative by a relatively isolated group of families, including families f2, f3, f4, and f5. In this case, prestige leadership does not necessarily imply high overall social or structural prestige. The prestige leader is probably just a little more prestigious than the subgroup he or she represents.

In a well-connected network with many reciprocal ties, vertices are reachable from most other vertices. Hence, input domain scores display little variation. In this case, it is more interesting to capture the network structure in a prestige index that does not consider the entire input domain. For example, we can count the vertices that are able to reach a person in one or two steps: direct choices and indirect choices with one go-between. This *restricted input domain* takes into account only the direct popularity of the people by whom one is nominated. The input domain of family f47 restricted to two steps (distance 2) is four (or 5%): one family at distance 1 (f4), and three families at distance 2 (f2, f3, and f5) (see Figure 83).

Application

Net>
k-Neighbours>
Input

Info>Partition

The input domain of a particular vertex can be found with the *Net>k-Neighbours>Input* command, which is discussed in Chapter 6. In the first dialog box, enter the number or label of a vertex (e.g., f47), and in the second dialog box accept the default value (zero) to compute all distances. Then, the command creates a partition specifying the distances of all vertices to the selected vertex. From a frequency tabulation, created with

Table 14. *Input Domain of f47*

Cluster	Freq	Freq%	Valid%	CumFreq	CumFreq%	CumValid%	Representative
0	1	1.3333	1.5385	1	1.3333	1.5385	f47
1	1	1.3333	1.5385	2	2.6667	3.0769	f4
2	3	4.0000	4.6154	5	6.6667	7.6923	f2
3	4	5.3333	6.1538	9	12.0000	13.8462	f1
4	4	5.3333	6.1538	13	17.3333	20.0000	f19
5	6	8.0000	9.2308	19	25.3333	29.2308	f14
6	3	4.0000	4.6154	22	29.3333	33.8462	f17
7	3	4.0000	4.6154	25	33.3333	38.4615	f7
8	6	8.0000	9.2308	31	41.3333	47.6923	f8
9	7	9.3333	10.7692	38	50.6667	58.4615	f13
10	7	9.3333	10.7692	45	60.0000	69.2308	f10
11	12	16.0000	18.4615	57	76.0000	87.6923	f25
12	7	9.3333	10.7692	64	85.3333	98.4615	f22
13	1	1.3333	1.5385	65	86.6667	100.0000	f65
SUM	65	86.6667	100.0000				
UNKNOWN	10	13.3333					
TOTAL	75	100.0000					

the *Info>Partition* command (Table 14), you can calculate the number of vertices (CumFreq) in the input domain of the selected vertex at a particular maximum distance; for instance, the input domain at maximum distance two contains four vertices: the five vertices at maximum distance 2 minus family f47 itself. The entry identified by "Unknown" in the table shows the number of vertices that are not connected by a path to the selected vertex: they do not belong to its input domain. In our example, ten of seventy-four vertices (do not count the selected vertex itself!) are outside the input domain of family f47, which is 14 percent; the remaining 86 percent of the vertices are inside its input domain. Note that you cannot find these percentages in the table because all percentages there include family f47.

It is quite cumbersome to repeat this command for each vertex in a network, so Pajek contains a command that calculates the size of the input domains of all vertices in one go: *Net>Partitions>Domain>Input*. Use the command *Input* to restrict the analysis to incoming arcs only. A dialog box, which is similar to the one displayed by *k-Neighbours*, allows you to specify a maximum distance for the input domain.

Net>Partitions> Domain>Input

The *Domain>Input* command produces three new data objects: one partition and two vectors. The partition specifies the number of vertices within the input domain of each vertex. The vector labeled "Normalized Size of input domain" lists the size of input domains as a proportion of all vertices (minus the vertex itself) and the second vector gives the average distance to a vertex from all vertices in its input domain. Of course, it is impossible to compute average distance in the case of a vertex with an empty input domain, that is, a vertex that is not chosen at all. In this case, average distance is set to 999998, which represents infinity. The average distances vector is very useful, as shown in the following section.

Table 15 lists the size of input domains in the visiting relations network. Nine families have maximal input domains; they are reachable from all

Table 15. *Size of Input Domains in the Visiting Relations Network*

Class	Freq	Freq%	CumFreq	CumFreq%	Representative
0	13	17.3333	13	17.3333	f1
1	7	9.3333	20	26.6667	f12
2	2	2.6667	22	29.3333	f11
6	3	4.0000	25	33.3333	f61
12	5	6.6667	30	40.0000	f26
64	36	48.0000	66	88.0000	f2
74	9	12.0000	75	100.0000	f23
SUM	75	100.0000			

seventy-four other vertices. Prestige leaders f23 and f39 are among them. As noted, the third prestige leader, family f47, is situated in the class of families with an input domain of size 64. Inspecting the partition with input domain sizes with the *File>Partition>Edit* procedure, we find that prestige leader f66 belongs to this class too. Family f61 is the only prestige leader that has a small input domain of size 6. We may conclude that most prestige leaders have large input domains, but many families with equally large input domains are not prestige leaders.

The rank correlation between structural prestige measured as the size of the input domain and social prestige indicated by social status scores can easily be computed (see Section 9.4). Spearman's rank correlation coefficient is .36, which is a little less than the rank correlation between popularity (indegree) and social status. Nevertheless, it points to a positive, moderate association between input domain and social status: larger input domains occur among families of higher social status.

Exercise II
Produce a sociogram such as that in Figure 83 from the network of visiting relations in San Juan Sur. Let vertex colors indicate the distance to family f47 in Pajek's Draw screen. Note that this sociogram requires many steps. You must combine several techniques that you have learned in the current and previous chapters.

9.6   Proximity Prestige

In the previous section, we noted that the input domain of a vertex is not a perfect measure of prestige. In a well-connected network, the input domain of a vertex often contains all or almost all other vertices, so it does not distinguish very well between vertices. In this case, we proposed to limit the input domain to direct neighbors or to neighbors at maximum distance two on the assumption that nominations by close neighbors are more important than nominations by distant neighbors. An indirect choice contributes less to prestige if it is mediated by a longer chain of intermediaries.

Of course, the choice of a maximum distance from neighbors within a restricted input domain is quite arbitrary. The concept of proximity prestige overcomes this problem. This index of prestige considers all vertices within the input domain of a vertex but it attaches more importance to a nomination if it is expressed by a closer neighbor. In other words, a nomination by a close neighbor contributes more to the proximity prestige of an actor than a nomination by a distant neighbor, but many "distant nominations" may contribute as much as one "close nomination."

To allow direct choices to contribute more to the prestige of a vertex than indirect choices, proximity prestige weights each choice by its path distance to the vertex. A higher distance yields a lower contribution to the proximity prestige of a vertex, but each choice contributes something. In the calculation of proximity prestige, this is accomplished by dividing the input domain of a vertex (expressed as a proportion of all vertices that may be part of the input domain) by the average distance from all vertices in the input domain. A larger input domain (larger numerator) yields a higher proximity prestige because more vertices are choosing an actor directly or indirectly. In addition, a smaller average distance (smaller denominator) yields a higher proximity prestige score because there are more nominations by close neighbors.

Maximum proximity prestige is achieved if a vertex is directly chosen by all other vertices. This is the case, for example, in a star-network in which all choices are directed to the central vertex. Then, the proportion of vertices in the input domain is 1 and the mean distance from these vertices is 1, so proximity prestige is 1 divided by 1. Vertices without input domain get minimum proximity prestige by definition, which is zero.

> The *proximity prestige* of a vertex is the proportion of all vertices (except itself) in its input domain divided by the mean distance from all vertices in its input domain.

In Figure 84, all vertices at the extremes of the network (v2, v4, v5, v6, and v10) have empty input domains, hence they have a proximity score of zero. The input domain of vertex v9 contains vertex v10 only, so its size is 1 out of 9 (.11). Average distance within the input domain of vertex v9 is one, so the proximity prestige of vertex 9 is .11 divided by 1. You can see that the proximity prestige of vertices increase if they have a longer "tail" from vertex v10 to v1. Vertex v1 has a maximal input domain, because it can be reached by all nine vertices (a proportion of 1.00). Average distance is 2.0, so proximity prestige amounts to 1.00 divided by 2.0, which is .5.

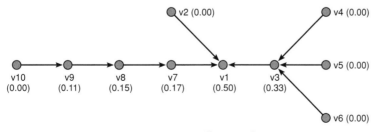

Figure 84. Proximity prestige in a small network.

Application

In the previous section, we have learned how to compute the size of input domains and average distance from all vertices within the input domain (command *Net>Partitions>Domain>Input*). Thus, we obtain the two vectors we need to compute proximity prestige: the size of the input domain expressed as a proportion ("Normalized Size of input domain") and the average distance from vertices within the input domain ("Average distance from input domain").

To calculate proximity prestige, we just divide the input domain size by the average distance. Select the vector with the normalized size of the input domain in the vectors drop-down menu and click command *First Vector* in the *Vectors* menu to use it as the numerator in the division operation. Select the vector with average distances as the second vector in a similar manner and click on the command *Divide First by Second* in the *Vectors* menu. This creates a new vector containing the proximity prestige scores of all vertices. Inspect them with the command *Info>Vector* or browse with *File>Vector>Edit*. Proximity prestige scores must range from zero to 1. If they do not, you probably specified the wrong vectors in the *Vectors* menu.

In the network of visiting ties at San Juan Sur, proximity prestige ranges from 0.0 to .33. Family f41 has the highest proximity prestige. Three of five prestige leaders have a proximity prestige above average (.12). However, the proximity prestige of families f47 (.11) and f61 (.07) is below average. We must conclude that prestige leaders are not characterized by high proximity prestige. In Section 9.5, we noted that family f47 occupies a special position in the network. Inspection of the average distances confirms this: family f47 has the largest average distance (8.03). This family is difficult to reach in the network.

Finally, let us see whether proximity prestige is associated with social status in San Juan Sur. Before we can compute Spearman's rank correlation, we must turn the vector with proximity prestige scores into a partition. As learned in Chapter 2, this can be done in several ways. In this case, the easiest way to convert the vector into a partition is to create classes of equal width with the procedure *Vector>Make Partition>by Intervals>First Threshold and Step*. Specify 0.01 as the first threshold (the upper limit of the lowest class) and enter this number also as the step (the class width) to obtain a partition with classes between 0 and 100.

The newly created partition with proximity prestige scores can be correlated to the existing partition with social status (SanJuanSur_status.clu) in the manner described in Section 9.4. Spearman's correlation coefficient is .26, indicating a low or moderate association between proximity prestige within the network and social status rated separately by members of the community. In this example, social status is related less to proximity prestige than to popularity (indegree), which has a rank correlation of .40 (see Section 9.4).

9.7 Summary

This is the first chapter of the book to deal with asymmetry in social networks. We present the simplest way to take the direction of ties into account, which is to pay attention to incoming ties only. Structural indices that do this are called measures of prestige. Actors who receive a lot of choices are popular provided, of course, that the choices express a positive social relation. Popularity, which is measured as the indegree of a vertex, is the first index of prestige we discuss. More advanced measures of prestige also take indirect choices into account. We present two advanced measures: the input domain of a vertex and proximity prestige.

It is important to distinguish between structural prestige and social prestige. The indices introduced in this chapter assess structural prestige, that is, a pattern of ties that network analysts call prestige. They are called prestige because actors in prestigious network positions often enjoy high social prestige. However, the example we use shows that structural prestige and social prestige do not match perfectly; we find moderate association only. We use correlation coefficients to establish the strength of the association between structural prestige and social status scores measured independently from the network. This is an example of an important research strategy, namely using structural indices such as prestige scores in statistical analysis.

9.8   Questions

1. In the network below, which vertex or vertices have the highest proximity prestige?

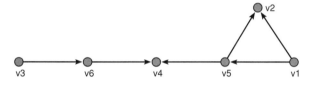

   a. Vertex v2.
   b. Vertex v4.
   c. Vertices v2 and v4 have equal proximity prestige.
   d. It is impossible to tell from this sociogram.
2. In the network below, which vertex or vertices have minimal structural prestige?

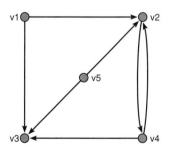

   a. Vertex v5.
   b. Vertices v5 and v1.
   c. All vertices have equal structural prestige.
   d. It is impossible to tell from this sociogram.

3. In the network presented in Question 2, which vertex or vertices have the highest social prestige?
   a. Vertex v3.
   b. Vertices v2 and v3.
   c. Vertices v2, v3, and v4 have approximately equal prestige.
   d. It is impossible to tell from this sociogram.
4. What is the correct interpretation of a correlation coefficient of size −.20?
   a. Weak negative association
   b. Medium association
   c. Medium positive association
   d. No association
5. Which prestige indices take indirect ties into account?
   a. Proximity prestige only
   b. Proximity prestige and input domain
   c. Proximity prestige and popularity
   d. Input domain and popularity
6. For which of the networks below is it useless to compute structural prestige as the full input domain of a vertex?

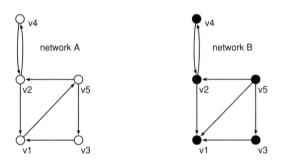

   a. A
   b. B
   c. A and B
   d. A nor B
7. In an undirected network, is proximity prestige equal to closeness centrality?
   a. Yes, because proximity prestige is equal to mean distance to all other vertices in an undirected network.
   b. Yes, because a prestige index applied to an undirected network is equal to a centrality index.
   c. No, unless the network is connected.
   d. No, because the calculation of an input domain is meaningless in an undirected network.

9.9   Assignment

In Chapter 8, we learned that the diffusion of innovations resembles a contagion process because social contacts are needed to persuade people to adopt innovations. It is hypothesized, therefore, that prestige is associated with adoption time: less prestigious actors adopt later because they wait for more prestigious opinion leaders to adopt first.

The file `Galesburg_discussion.net` contains a network of discussion ties among thirty-one physicians in Galesburg (Illinois) in the 1950s. The researchers asked each physician to name three doctors with whom they would choose to discuss medical matters. For seventeen physicians, the date that they first prescribed a new drug (gammanym) was recorded. The partition `Galesburg_adoptiontime31.clu` measures the adoption time as the number of months since the introduction of the drug. Note that the adoption time is unknown (code 9999998) for fourteen physicians. For most of them, the new drug was not relevant.

Investigate whether adoption time is associated with the structural prestige rather than the centrality of doctors in the discussion network. Compute the indices of prestige presented in this chapter (indegree, restricted input domain with a maximum distance of 2, and proximity prestige) as well as the corresponding centrality measures in the undirected network. Use rank correlation and note that adoption time is higher when a doctor adopts later.

Another hypothesis states that friendship relations are more important than discussion relations for the adoption of a new drug because it is easier to persuade friends than people you only know professionally. Physicians with many direct or indirect friends would adopt sooner than physicians with less central positions in the friendship network. The file `Galesburg_friends.net` contains the friendship network between the doctors. Is the adoption time of the new drug related to prestige or centrality in the friendship network rather than in the discussion network?

9.10   Further Reading

- The data on San Juan Sur are taken from Charles P. Loomis, Julio O. Morales, Roy A. Clifford, and Olen E. Leonard, *Turrialba: Social Systems and the Introduction of Change* (Glencoe, Ill.: The Free Press, 1953). Consult this book to learn more about the research project.
- The medical innovation project is taken from James S. Coleman, Elihu Katz, and Herbert Menzel, *Medical Innovation: A Diffusion Study* (Indianapolis: Bobbs-Merrill, 1966). David Knoke and Ronald S. Burt reanalyzed the data in a chapter on prominence in R. S. Burt and M. J. Minor (Eds.), *Applied Network Analysis: A Methodological Introduction* (Beverly Hills: Sage, 1983, pp. 195–222). This article contains the basic argument to distinguish between directed prestige and undirected centrality.
- To learn more about prestige indices, use Chapter 5 of Stanley Wasserman and Katherine Faust, *Social Network Analysis: Methods and Applications* (Cambridge: Cambridge University Press, 1994).

9.11 Answers

Answers to the Exercises

I. Remove the lines with line values lower than 3 (with the *Net> Transform>Remove>lines with value>lower than* command) to obtain a network of visits among kin. Compute the indegree partition and select it as the first partition in the Partitions menu. Select the status partition (SanJuanSur_status.clu) as the second partition in this menu and calculate Spearman's rank correlation by means of the *Partitions>Info* submenu. Spearman's rank correlation between the status partition and the indegree partition is 0.52 in this network.

In a similar way you can create a network of church relations (select the *lower than* command with 2 as the limit and subsequently the *higher than* command with two again as the limit) and a network of other relations (select *higher than* with a threshold value of 1). Spearman's rank correlation between the indegree partition and the status partition is 0.33 and 0.22, respectively.

Visits among kin seem to follow status differences best in that the less prestigious family comes to visit the more prestigious but note that the network contains very few lines, so we should not rely too much on this correlation coefficient.

II. When you compute the input domain of family f47 with the *Net>k-Neighbours>Input* command, as shown in Section 9.5, you will find that the families outside the input domain are attributed to class 9999998 in the input neighbors partition. Extract all classes (do not forget class zero) except 9999998 from the network (*Operations>Extract from Network>Partition* – see Chapter 2, Section 2.4.3) to obtain a new network without the vertices outside f47's input domain. Compute the distances toward f47 again for the new network. Now you can draw this network in layers according to the vertices' distances to family f47 and optimize it as you have learned in Section 8.1 (Chapter 8).

In Figure 83, all arcs that do not point up toward f47 have been eliminated because they are not relevant to the shortest paths to f47. This was achieved with the *Operations>Transform>Direction>Higher Lower* command, deleting lines within clusters too. Note that the input k-neighbors partition must be selected in the Partition drop-down menu. After deleting these lines, optimize the positions of the vertices within the layers again (see Section 8.1).

Answers to the Questions in Section 9.8

1. Answer b is correct. Vertex v4 has the largest input domain, which contains all vertices except for v2, and paths to v4 are quite short for all vertices in its input domain. A large numerator (size of input domain) and a relatively small denominator (average distance) yields high proximity prestige. Vertex v2 is second best because it has an even lower average distance from vertices in its input domain (it is directly chosen by both vertices in its input domain), but its input domain is a lot smaller.

2. Answer b is correct. Vertices v1 and v5 are not chosen. They have zero indegree, hence no input domain and minimum proximity prestige. Both vertices have minimal scores on all prestige indices presented in this chapter.

3. Answer d is correct. Because structural prestige is not necessarily equal to social prestige, we cannot tell which actor has the most social prestige from this sociogram.

4. Answer a is correct. According to the rule of thumb presented, the association is weak. The sign of the coefficient tells us that there is a negative or inverse relation between the two characteristics.

5. Answer b is correct. Input domain counts direct choices as well as indirect choices of vertices at distance two or higher, so it definitely takes indirect ties into account. Proximity prestige uses the input domain, so it uses indirect ties too. Popularity is just the indegree of a vertex, the direct choices it receives. Clearly, it does not use indirect ties.

6. Answer a is correct. In network A, each vertex is reachable for all other vertices, so each vertex has an input domain of size 4. In other words, the network is one strong component. Because there are no differences between vertices with respect to the size of their input domain, this prestige index is useless. Network B differs from network A in the tie between v1 and v5. Changing the direction of this tie breaks the strong component: v5 is no longer reachable for any other vertex and as a consequence v1 can no longer reach v2 and v3. Now, the size of the input domain varies between vertices; it is a useful prestige index.

7. Answer c is correct. Proximity prestige is calculated as the average distance from all vertices in the input domain of a vertex divided by the size of the input domain as a proportion of the maximum number of vertices it can hold. Closeness centrality is similar to the numerator of this fraction: average distance. In an undirected network, proximity prestige is only equal to closeness centrality if the denominator of the fraction is 1, which means that all other vertices are part of the input domain. This is the case if the network is connected because each vertex is reachable from all other vertices in a connected undirected network.

10

Ranking

10.1 Introduction

In the social sciences, society is regarded as a set of social layers or strata. Instead of ranking people, groups, or organizations on a continuous scale of prestige, they are usually classified into a limited set of discrete ranks, for instance, working class, lower middle class, upper middle class, and upper class. Within a group of humans, discrete ranking also occurs, for instance, leaders, followers, and outcasts. The stratification of art worlds into stars, settled artists, and mediocre artists is likely another example. In this chapter, we discuss techniques to extract discrete ranks from social relations.

Social ranking may be formal or informal and the two types of ranking may coexist. In a formal ranking, it is written down who commands whom and insignia or symbols minimize the ambiguity of the ranking and preclude any confusion about a person's rank. The army is an obvious example with its elaborate hierarchy. In contrast, an informal ranking is neither written down nor expressed by official symbols. It manifests itself in the opinions and behavior of people toward each other: respect and acts of deference versus disrespect and dominance.

The creation and maintenance of an informal ranking is a very important social process. Social network analysis is needed to investigate it and to assess the positions that individuals occupy within the informal ranking. If a formal ranking exists, it is interesting to compare it to the informal ranking because they do not need to match, just like informal communication patterns often deviate from the official communication structure.

The structural concept of social ranking is an extension to balance theory presented in Chapter 4. Balance theory assigns people to clusters that are not ranked with respect to one another. Within a cluster, people tend to like each other but people do not like members of other clusters. Within clusters as well as between clusters, ties are supposed to be symmetric: you are supposed to reciprocate the sentiment or choices that you receive. Elaborating on this perspective, asymmetric ties, for instance, A reports to B but B does not report to A, indicate ranking: B is ranked over A.

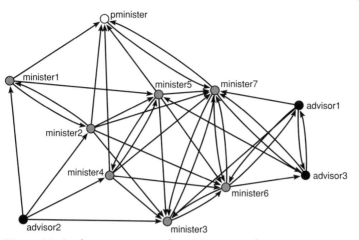

Figure 85. Student government discussion network.

10.2   Example

Our example is a network of a discussion relation among the eleven students who were members of the student government at the University of Ljubljana in Slovenia (Student_government.net). The students were asked to indicate with whom of their fellows they discussed matters concerning the administration of the university informally. We suppose that this relation indicates esteem: students will choose fellows whom they respect. Therefore, we expect this network to display informal ranking.

Within the parliament, students have positions that convey formal ranking: the prime minister, the ministers, and the advisors. In Figure 85, vertex color indicates the formal position of a student in the parliament (partition student_government.clu). We compare the formal ranking to the informal ranking we derive from network analysis of the discussion relation.

10.3   Triadic Analysis

Before we can analyze the ranks in the student government discussion network, we must discuss balance theory once more. In Chapter 4, we learned that a balanced or clusterable network can be partitioned into clusters such that all positive choices occur within clusters and all negative choices are found between clusters. If we replace negative choices by absent choices, it follows that positive choices are found within clusters but choices do not occur between clusters: people tend to choose members from their own group instead of members from other groups. Because absent choices should not occur within a group, each positive choice must be reciprocated.

As a consequence, we can rephrase balance theory for the type of tie between two vertices (dyads) in a simple directed network: mutual choices

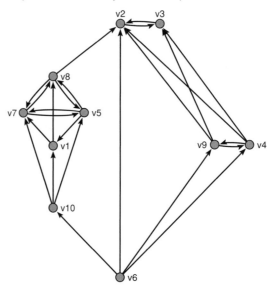

Figure 86. An example of a network with ranks.

indicate group membership and mutual absent or null choices indicate membership of different groups. Of course, this presupposes that the social relation under investigation implies a positive choice and that an absent choice is equivalent to a negative choice.

> A *dyad* is a pair of vertices and the lines between them.

In the directed network of Figure 86, vertices v5, v7, and v8 constitute a cluster because they are connected by mutual choices (*complete dyads*) and vertices v4 and v9 constitute another cluster. The two clusters are separated by absent lines or *null dyads*.

Both mutual choices and mutual absent choices are symmetric: you give as good as you get. Symmetric dyads indicate equivalence so we assume that vertices which are linked by symmetric ties belong to the same rank. The third type of dyad, however, is the *asymmetric dyad*: one person chooses the other but this choice is not reciprocated. Asymmetric dyads indicate ranking. In an asymmetric dyad, it is assumed that the receiver of the positive choice is ranked over the sender provided that being chosen expresses esteem or appreciation: the former can afford not to reciprocate the choice of the latter. In Figure 86, vertex v6 is ranked under v9 and v4 among others, which are ranked under v2 and v3.

To capture the structure of a directed network, we must proceed from dyads to *triads*. In a simple directed network, sixteen types of triads may occur, which are listed in Figure 87. As proposed by Davis, Holland, and Leinhardt, triad type is identified by a M-A-N number of three digits and, occasionally, a letter. The first digit indicates the number of mutual positive dyads (M), the second digit is the number of asymmetric dyads (A), and the third digit is the number of null dyads (N). Sometimes

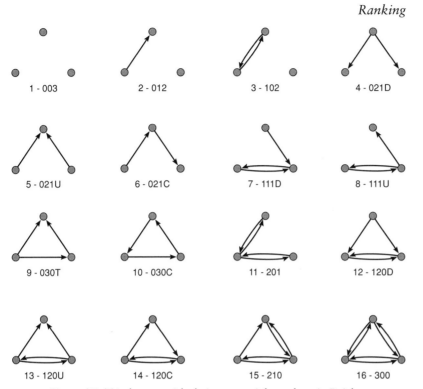

Figure 87. Triad types with their sequential numbers in Pajek.

a letter that refers to the direction of the asymmetric choices is added to distinguish between triads with the same M-A-N digits: D for down, U for Up, C for cyclic, and T for transitive (which is explained later).

It has been shown that the overall structure of a directed network (or a complete signed network) can be inferred from the types of triads that occur. It is very important to understand the consequences of this discovery: it suffices to analyze small subnetworks (of size 3) to understand the structure of the overall network! We do not have to check all semicycles to determine whether a network conforms to a balance theoretic model as we did in incomplete signed networks (Chapter 4).

If a directed network is balanced, for example, only two of the sixteen types of triads occur, namely, triads 300 and 102. Each cluster is a clique, so each subset of three vertices from a cluster is a complete triad like triad 300 (e.g., vertices v5, v7, and v8 in Figure 86). If two vertices belong to one cluster and the third belongs to the other cluster, we encounter a triad in which two vertices are symmetrically linked because they belong to the same clique (e.g., vertices v5 and v8 in Figure 86), but they are not connected to the third vertex, which belongs to the other clique (e.g, vertex v9 in Figure 86). This is represented by triad 102. There are no other possibilities, so the two triad types identify the *balance model* for the structure of the entire network. If a network contains just these two types of triads then we know that the network consists of two cliques that are not interrelated.

In the course of time, four additional models for the overall structure of a directed network have been discovered, which we present now. These models have a very important property, namely that they progressively allow for more types of triads to occur. In other words, each model that we present is less restrictive than the previous one. The second model, the *model of clusterability*, for instance, relaxes the demand of the balance model that the network consists of no more than two cliques. A clusterable network may contain three or more clusters. As a consequence, triad 003 is allowed to occur in a clusterable network because it contains vertices which belong to three different clusters. The two balanced triads (300 and 102) are also permitted because they still refer to vertices within one cluster or vertices of two clusters. The clusterability model is more permissive than the balance model: it allows for one more triad type.

In a similar way, the *model of ranked clusters* extends the clusterability model because it allows clusters to be spread over different ranks. Clusters at different ranks are connected by asymmetric dyads: each vertex in a lower cluster sends unilateral choices toward all vertices in a higher cluster. As a consequence, five triads are permitted that contain asymmetric dyads: 120D, 120U, 021D, 021U, and 030T. In triad 120U, for instance, the bottom two vertices belong to one cluster because they are linked by mutual choices. The top vertex is connected to them by asymmetric ties: it is chosen but it does not reciprocate the choices, so it must belong to a higher rank.

If a network contains these triads in addition to balanced or clusterable triads, the network can be partitioned into ranks and clusters according to the criteria that mutual choices are found within clusters, asymmetric choices point up to a higher rank, and null choices occur between clusters within a rank. In our example of a ranked network (Figure 86), vertices v4, v6, and v9 constitute a 120D triad and a 030T triad contains vertices v1, v5, and v10.

There are two models that relax the criteria of the ranked clusters model. The first model is the *transitivity model*. In a transitive triad, each path of length 2 is closed by an arc from the starting vertex to the end vertex of the path. If actor A obeys actor B, and actor B obeys actor C, actor A also obeys actor C in a transitive triad. In a hierarchy, relations are usually transitive but transitivity is an effect that is also found in many other social relations, for instance, the relation "to know someone" is often transitive.

The balanced, clusterable, and ranked clusters triads are transitive, but the 012 triad, which contains a single asymmetric choice, is also transitive because it does not violate the rule that an indirect choice is paralleled by a direct choice; the 012 triad simply does not contain an indirect choice. Under the ranked clusters model, the 012 triad would mean that the three vertices belong to different clusters within a rank because of the two null dyads and, at the same time, that two vertices are ranked as a result of the asymmetric dyad. Clearly, this is a contradiction. Under the transitivity model, however, null choices are allowed between ranks. It is not necessary that someone at a lower rank chooses all people of higher rank, for instance, boys and girls may have separate rank systems that are perfect ranked clusters but boys may ignore girls and vice versa.

Table 16. *Balance-Theoretic Models*

Model	Ties within a Cluster	Ties between Ranks	Permitted Triads
Balance	Symmetric ties within a cluster, no ties between clusters max. two clusters	None	102, 300
Clusterability	Idem no restriction on the number of clusters	Idem	+003
Ranked Clusters	Idem	Asymmetric ties from each vertex to all vertices on higher ranks	+021D, 021U, 030T, 120D, 120U
Transitivity	Idem	Null ties may occur between ranks	+012
Hierarchical Clusters	Asymmetric ties within a cluster allowed provided that they are acyclic	Idem	+120C, 210
No Balance-Theoretic Model ("Forbidden")			021C, 111D, 111U, 030C, 201

Note: A + sign indicates that all triads in previous rows are also permitted.

The other model that relaxes the criteria of the ranked clusters model is the *hierarchical clusters model*, which is also called the hierarchical m̄-clusters model. This model permits asymmetric dyads within a group as long as they are acyclic. Within a cluster, asymmetric dyads are supposed to express a mild form of ranking within a group and, like any kind of ranking, this ranking must be acyclic. The set of vertices v1, v5, v7, and v8 (Figure 86) is an example of a hierarchical cluster. Vertex v1 is connected to the other vertices by two 120C triads. Vertex v7 does not reciprocate the choice by v1, who does not reciprocate v5's choice, so these three vertices are ranked but vertices v5 and v7 are also part of a cluster with vertex v8 because of the symmetric dyads.

The remaining five types of triads do not occur under any of the models. We may say that they are forbidden: they contradict all balance-theoretic models and the assumptions about symmetric and asymmetric dyads on which the models are based. If these triads occur often, we ought to doubt whether we can cluster and rank the data according to balance-theoretic principles. Table 16 summarizes the models.

Let us apply the balance-theoretic models to the example network (Figure 86). Table 17 shows the number of triads found in this network arranged by the balance theoretic model to which they belong. Such a distribution is known as the *triad census*. The models are less restrictive in the order in which they are listed in Table 17 and it is standard practice to characterize the overall structure of a network by the least restrictive model that applies. After all, a less restrictive model covers all more restrictive models because it also permits their triads.

Unfortunately, social networks hardly ever conform perfectly to a balance-theoretic model. Each type is likely to occur at least once, so the

Table 17. *Triad Census of the Example Network*

	Type	Number of Triads	Expected	Model
3	102	*22*	7.56	Balance
16	300	*1*	0.06	
1	003	*7*	17.0	Clusterability
4	021D	*3*	7.56	Ranked
5	021U	*3*	7.56	Clusters
9	030T	4	5.81	
12	120D	*5*	1.12	
13	120U	2	1.12	
2	012	*58*	39.3	Transitivity
14	120C	2	2.24	Hierarchical
15	210	0	0.86	Clusters
6	021C	*7*	15.12	Forbidden
7	111D	4	5.81	
8	111U	2	5.81	
10	030C	0	1.94	
11	201	0	1.12	
TOTAL		120		

presence of one triad does not mean that the associated model must apply. We must compare the triad census to the distribution of triad types which is expected by chance. If a particular triad type occurs clearly more often than expected by chance, the corresponding model may be said to guide or influence the relations: there is a tendency toward balance, clusterability, ranked clustering, transitivity, or hierarchical clusters in the network. If the models explain network structure, the forbidden triads should occur less frequently than predicted by chance.

Table 17 shows the triad census of the example network. The column headed "Number of triads" shows the triad counts in the example network and the column "Expected" lists the numbers of triads that are expected by chance in a network of this size containing this number of arcs. If the actual frequencies are close to the expected frequencies, the network conforms to none of the balance-theoretic models and we may conclude that its structure is random from the point of view of balance theory. This, however, does not seem to be the case in our example.

In the example network, some types of triads occur substantially more often or less frequently than expected by chance. These frequencies are printed in italics in the table. The example network seems to contain relatively few clusterable triads but many balanced ones, some ranked clustering (120D) although other ranked clusters triads occur less often than expected (021D and 021U), and a tendency toward transitivity but not a surprising number of hierarchical cluster triads. The forbidden triads occur at chance level or less (021C and 111U), so we do not have to discard all balance-theoretic models. The most appropriate model for this network seems to be the transitivity model, which allows for clustering and ranking but which does not require that all ties between ranks are asymmetric.

We should note that our expected frequencies take into account only the number of vertices and arcs in the network. Standard statistical tests of the triad census condition on indegree, outdegree, and number of mutual choices, which expresses the tendency to reciprocate choices at the level of the dyad. These statistical tests may produce different results but they fall outside the scope of the present book.

The triad census is an example of a research strategy that concentrates on local structure because it accounts only for ties within triads. The implications for the overall structure of the network are usually taken for granted and not much effort is made to assign vertices to clusters and ranks. Triadic analysis is the basis of statistical models that test hypotheses about the ties of individual actors: why do they establish some ties and not others? Are their choices motivated by balance, transitivity?

Application

In Pajek, it is very easy to compute the triad census: simply use the *Triadic Census* command in the *Info>Network* submenu. A dialog box asks whether the models should be reported and if you choose this option, the triad types ("Type"), their actual frequencies ["Number of triads (ni)"], and the frequencies expected by chance ["Expected (ei)"] are reported. In addition, the relative difference between the actual and the expected number of triads is shown ["(ni-ei)/ei"] and a chi-square statistic testing the hypothesis that the actual frequencies are equal to the expected frequencies. This statistic is not reliable if expected frequencies are low. The triad counts and expected frequencies are also stored in two vectors.

Info>Network>
Triadic Census

Table 18 contains the triad census for the student government network. Three of the five forbidden triads appear less frequently than expected by chance in the student government network (triads 021C, 111U, and 030C), which is also signaled by the negative value of the actual versus expected ratio, so there is some support that the underlying ideas of symmetric and asymmetric ties apply here.

Then, which structure characterizes the network? The student government network contains more between groups triads (triad 102) than expected by chance but the number of clusterability triads (003) is predicted by chance, so a partition into two clusters seems to suffice. Some ranked clusters triads appear as often as expected by chance but the number of 120D triads, which signal asymmetric choices toward mutually connected pairs, is much higher than the expected frequency (the ratio of actual to observed number of triads is 2.72), so we should conclude that the network is ranked. Finally, the number of triads identifying the transitivity model (012) matches the amount expected in a random network and the hierarchical cluster triads also do not appear more often than expected by chance.

A ranked clusters model seems to be the best choice for this data set because it permits triads 120D, 120U, and 021U, which appear substantially more often than chance, but it also permits the triads associated to more restrictive models (viz., the two balanced triads 300 and 102). In this way,

Table 18. *Triad Census of the Student Government Network*

	Type	Number of Triads (ni)	Expected (ei)	(ni-ei)/ei	Model
3	102	20	10.65	0.88	Balance
16	300	1	0.44	1.26	
1	003	10	10.05	−0.01	Clusterability
4	021D	9	10.65	−0.15	Ranked
5	021U	15	10.65	0.41	Clusters
9	030T	7	12.65	−0.45	
12	120D	14	3.76	2.72	
13	120U	6	3.76	0.60	
2	012	37	35.84	0.03	Transitivity
14	120C	1	7.52	−0.87	Hierarchical
15	210	5	4.47	0.12	Clusters
6	021C	16	21.29	−0.25	Forbidden
7	111D	13	12.65	0.03	
8	111U	6	12.65	−0.53	
10	030C	1	4.22	−0.76	
11	201	4	3.76	0.06	

Chi-square = 55.7613***.
Six cells (37.50%) have expected frequencies less than 5.
The minimum expected cell frequency is 0.44.

the ranked clusters model contains all types of triads that occur clearly more often than expected by chance in the student government network.

The chi-square statistic is highly significant: the three stars indicate that it is statistically significant at the .001 level (one star represents statistical significance at the .05 level, and two stars signal the .01 level), so the tendency toward ranked clustering is higher than expected by chance given the density of the network. We should note, however, that the expected frequency of six triads is less than five and one triad (300) is expected to occur less than once. This casts some doubt on the reliability of the chi-square measure.

10.4   Acyclic Networks

In directed networks, ranking is associated with asymmetry: arcs that represent an "ego obeys alter" relation point up, not down. Triadic analysis applies this principle to triads, that is, to local structure, but it can also be applied to the overall structure of a directed network. In a network that perfectly reflects a hierarchy, all arcs should point up and no arc should point down from a higher rank to a lower rank. This is called an acyclic network. It is important to note that such a network cannot contain cycles because a cycle would include arcs pointing up *and* arcs pointing down to return to its starting point.

An *acyclic network* contains no cycles.

We associate ranking with acyclic structures; for example, the soldier is subordinate to the sergeant, who is subordinate to the captain, who is subordinate to the colonel, and so on. An arc pointing in the wrong direction (e.g., the colonel obeys the soldier for whatever mysterious reasons) contradicts our idea of a hierarchy. This arc creates a cycle in the network and it may even make the whole network cyclic in the sense that in the end everyone obeys everybody.

When acyclic structures point to ranking, cyclic structures are associated with clusters within one rank because they suggest equality among its vertices. In the short run (e.g., in a symmetric dyad) or in the long run (e.g., in a feedback loop that includes many vertices) a choice is reciprocated. From this point of view, we may partition a directed network into ranks: cyclic subnetworks represent a cluster within a rank and acyclic structures link ranks into a hierarchy.

Fortunately, it is easy to detect the cyclic parts of a network and you have already mastered the technique to do it. Recall that a strong component is a maximal subnetwork in which each vertex is reachable to each other vertex (Chapter 3). There are paths in both directions between all pairs of vertices within a strong component, so a strong component is a cyclic (sub)network by definition. The arcs that are not part of a strong component cannot belong to a cycle, so they are part of an acyclic structure. In fact, if we shrink the strong components of a network, the network becomes acyclic.

Figure 88 shows the strong components in the student government discussion network (for the sake of clarity we replaced bidirectional arcs by fat edges). There are three components and, if you look carefully, the arcs between strong components all point in the same direction: from the white (red) component to the gray (green) component to the black (yellow) component. This is very clear in Figure 89, which shows the network with shrunk strong components. Note that the prime minister is included in the strong component in the top of the hierarchy, which is in line with his formal position.

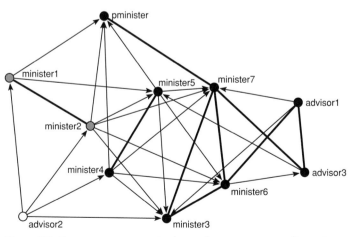

Figure 88. Strong components in the student government discussion network.

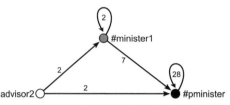

Figure 89. Acyclic network with shrunk components.

Application

Net>
Components>
Strong

In Chapter 3, we learned to identify the strong components in a network with the command *Net>Components>Strong*. This command creates a partition with a class for each strong component. We advise to set the minimum size of a component to one, otherwise the "red" component of advisor2 is not recognized.

Operations>
Shrink
Network>
Partition

Chapter 2 presented the command to shrink a network. The present case offers no complications: make sure the student government discussion network and the strong components partition are selected in the drop-down menus and execute the *Operations>Shrink Network>Partition*. In the dialog boxes, require a minimum of one connection between clusters and do not shrink cluster number zero or any other nonexistent cluster. If the network is shrunk according to a strong components partition, we obtain three vertices as shown in Figure 89.

Exercise I

Remove the arc from advisor3 to minister5 in the student government discussion network (right-click the vertex of advisor3 in the Draw screen and double-click the arc toward minister5 in the list). Determine the strong components in the modified network and shrink the components. Which new rank appears now?

10.5   Symmetric-Acyclic Decomposition

In triadic analysis (Section 10.3), clusters within a rank must be complete. In many social networks, this criterion is too strict. Usually, social networks contain a limited number of choices made by each individual as a result of measurement techniques and social or cognitive limitations on the part of the investigated people. Respondents who are asked to recall with whom they discussed a particular matter informally, for instance, are likely to mention their most salient contacts rather than everyone with whom they have merely touched on the subject. A network constructed from these data will not yield complete clusters.

Conversely, the strong components do not seem to be sufficiently strict to identify a cluster within a rank (Section 10.4). In the student government discussion network, it would be nice if we could subdivide the black (yellow) component, which contains a heterogeneous group of actors at present: advisors, ministers, and the prime minister.

The *symmetric-acyclic model* is a suitable alternative. It uses a version of the symmetry versus asymmetry principle that is less strict than the balance-theoretic assumptions but stricter than the acyclic character of

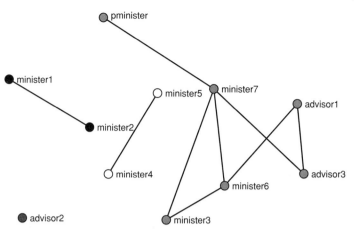

Figure 90. Clusters of symmetric ties in the student government network.

strong components. It assumes that vertices that are linked by symmetric (i.e., mutual) choices directly or indirectly belong to one cluster, hence to one rank. Clusters that are linked by asymmetric ties only are ranked.

This model is especially less restrictive with respect to the internal structure of clusters because it allows for asymmetric and null dyads within a cluster, for example, if vertex u is linked to vertices v and w by symmetric ties, they belong to one cluster regardless of the tie between v and w, which may be symmetric, asymmetric, or null. Balance-theoretic models never allow null dyads within a cluster and asymmetric dyads may occur only under special conditions in the hierarchical clusters model.

It is easy to identify clusters of vertices that are connected by mutual choice: just delete all unilateral arcs from the network and compute components. Each component is a cluster of vertices, which are linked by symmetric dyads. Figure 90 shows the four clusters in the student government network. Note that the dark gray (blue) and black (yellow) symmetric clusters of Figure 90 are strong components in the overall network (Figure 88).

The largest strong component of the original network, however, combines two symmetric clusters: the cluster of minister4 and minister5 with the cluster of the prime minister. The two symmetric clusters are linked into one strong component because the arcs between these clusters do not point in the same direction. In Figure 91, we can see that the symmetric cluster of minister4 and minister5 predominantly sends asymmetric ties to the cluster of the prime minister but they receive one asymmetric choice from that cluster [viz., the arc from advisor3 to minister5 (check Figure 88)]. When we ignore this arc, we obtain smaller strong components that match the symmetric clusters perfectly.

Clusters of vertices which are reachable through symmetric ties are preferable over strong components because mutual choice is a clear indication of group membership and equality with respect to ranking. We therefore recommend to pay close attention to strong components in which not all vertices are linked by paths of mutual choices. Elimination of a single arc may split this component into smaller clusters which are asymmetrically ordered.

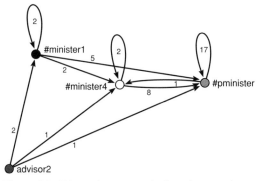

Figure 91. Discussion network shrunk according to symmetric clusters.

A stricter interpretation of the symmetric-acyclic model forbids all asymmetric ties inside clusters. In other words, vertices within a cluster are either tied by a symmetric tie or no tie at all (a null tie) and all asymmetric choices are situated between clusters. In the largest cluster of the student government network, which contains the prime minister, three asymmetric ties are found and all of them involve the advisors. The ministers and the prime minister are linked by symmetric ties only. If we would delete advisor3, who is offending the ranking between two symmetric clusters and who is also involved in an asymmetric tie within the top cluster, and we ignore the arc from minister6 to advisor1, we obtain a decomposition that satisfies the strictest criteria of the symmetric-acyclic model (see Figure 92).

Note that this decomposition nicely reflects the formal positions of the students: the advisors are on the lower ranks, the prime minister is on the highest rank, and the ministers are in the middle or top ranks. If the prime minister had not chosen minister7, he would have had the top rank for himself or herself. In this case, the informal ranking is more differentiated than the formal ranking because the ministers are spread over three ranks.

Figure 92 illustrates an important characteristic of the symmetric-acyclic model. Often, the order of the symmetric clusters is not completely determined. Advisor1, for example, must be ranked below the black

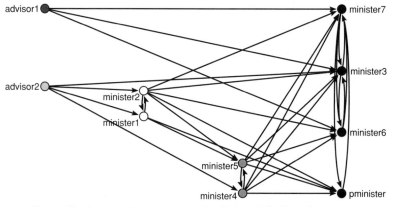

Figure 92. Symmetric components in the (modified) student government discussion network.

cluster containing the prime minister. It is unclear, however, whether this advisor should be ranked with advisor2, minister2, or minister5 or whether it occupies a rank of its own. There is no path of asymmetric ties between advisor1 and advisor2, minister2, or minister5 that defines his or her position with respect to them. This is called a *partial order*: we know the order of some pairs of vertices but not of all pairs. As a result, the classification of vertices according to rank does not necessarily yield a single result. In Figure 92, advisor2 could have been drawn at several other levels.

Application

Pajek contains a command to find clusters of symmetrically linked vertices and ranks: *Net>Hierarchical Decomposition>Symmetric-Acyclic*. This command follows the logic outlined above.

Net> Hierarchical Decomposition> Symmetric-Acyclic

First, the command finds the components of symmetrically linked vertices. It produces a new network with edges instead of bidirected arcs like Figure 88. Then it creates a network without the remaining (unilateral) arcs and it computes a partition of weak components. Each weak component is a cluster of vertices that are reachable through symmetric ties. When you draw the network and partition, you obtain Figure 90.

Second, the procedure shrinks the clusters of symmetrically linked vertices. The shrunk network is very convenient for finding symmetric clusters that are linked by asymmetric ties in both directions. If you draw this network, you obtain a sociogram that is similar to that in Figure 91. In this drawing, you may detect symmetric clusters that are nearly asymmetrically linked, such as the #minister4 and #pminister clusters.

Finally, the procedure repeats the first and second steps until it does not encounter any symmetrically linked vertices or clusters. Then, all strong components have been shrunk and the network is acyclic by definition. After the first shrinking of the student government discussion network (see Figure 91), the #pminister and #minister4 clusters are connected by a bidirectional arc: they are symmetrically linked. In the next step, they are concatenated into one new symmetric cluster and shrunk. In the resulting network, no vertices or clusters are symmetrically linked, so the procedure stops. Note that in this example the last network created by the *Symmetric-Acyclic* command contains no lines. You should select the last shrunk network (labeled something like "Shrinking N5 according to C3") as the final result of the analysis.

The shrunk network that results from the symmetric-acyclic decomposition is acyclic, so we may determine the order of the ranks with the *Depth>Acyclic* command from the *Net>Partitions* submenu provided that you delete the loops first (*Net>Transform>Remove>loops*), which are created when the network is being shrunk. Draw the shrunk network and its depth partition according to layers (*Layers>In y direction*) to obtain a graphical representation of the ranks. It will look like Figure 93: advisor2 advises the symmetric cluster of minister1, who advise the symmetric cluster of the prime minister. When you move the gray vertex manually in the Draw screen, you will see that there is also a direct arc from the advisor to the cluster of the prime minister.

Net> Transform> Remove>loops

Net>Partitions> Depth>Acyclic

If you want to draw the original network in layers that represent the ranks, you have to expand the depth partition to the original network.

Net> Components> Strong

Figure 93. The order of symmetric clusters acording to the depth partition (acyclic).

Because the shrunk vertices in the acyclic network are the strong components (size one and larger) in the original network, you can use a strong components partition of the original network to expand the depth partition. Create this partition with the *Net>Components>Strong* command making sure that the original network is selected in the Network dropdown menu.

Partitions>
Expand>First
according to
Second (Shrink)

Net>Transform>
Arcs→Edges>
Bidirected only

[Draw]
Options>
Transform>
Rotate 2D

Now, you can expand the depth partition of the shrunk network to the original network. Select the depth partition of the shrunk network as the first partition in the *Partitions* menu and select the strong components partition as the second partition. Then choose the *First according to Second (Shrink)* command from the *Partitions>Expand* submenu. Pajek asks which class in the strong components partition was not shrunk (zero or a number that does not occur in the strong components partition will do) and it creates a new partition that assigns each vertex in the original network to its depth in the symmetric-acyclic decomposition. You may draw this partition in layers and move vertices within each layer to obtain an image of the ranking. In Figure 94, we replaced all bidirected arcs by edges (*Net>Transform>Arcs→Edges>Bidirected only*) and we rotated the layout (*[Draw] Options>Transform>Rotate 2D*), so the ranks increment from left to right. Note that we cannot see all arcs within the white rank but it is clear that all arcs between ranks point in the same direction (right).

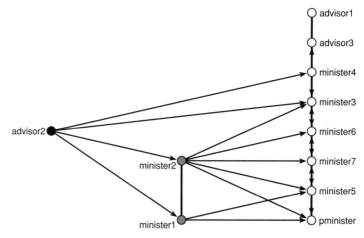

Figure 94. Ranks in the student government discussion network.

In the symmetric-acyclic decomposition, the resulting strong components are not necessarily symmetric clusters. In the student government network, for example, a strong component combines the two symmetric clusters #pminister and #minister4 (Figure 91). We have found a decomposition that satisfies the weak version of the symmetric-acyclic model.

Operations> Transform> Remove Lines>Between Clusters

The stronger version of this model does not allow asymmetric ties within clusters, so we have to inspect the ties within each cluster to find out whether the stronger model applies. Because the strong components are the clusters, we may simply remove all lines between strong components and check whether the resulting network contains bidirected arcs only. Select the original network and the strong components partition to this network and remove the lines between components with the *Operations>Transform>Remove Lines>Between Clusters* command. Now, replace bidirected arcs by edges (command *Net>Transform>Arcs→ Edges>Bidirected only*) and check the number of arcs in the network (*Info>Network>General*). If there are no arcs, all strong components are symmetric clusters. Strong components containing arcs, however, are not symmetric clusters, so they do not satisfy the stronger version of the symmetric-acyclic model. In our example, the strong component containing the prime minister contains several unilateral arcs. This network does not satisfy the requirements of the strong symmetric-acyclic model.

Exercise II
In Exercise I, you removed the arc from advisor3 to minister5. In this network, do the symmetric clusters conform to the weak or strong symmetric-acyclic model?

10.6 Summary

Society and, in more detail, the human group is characterized by clustering and ranking. Like-minded people cluster into cohesive groups on the basis of mutual positive ties. Rivalry between groups is expressed by negative or absent ties. In addition, social groups are usually ranked such that dominant groups occupy higher ranks or strata. Asymmetric ties indicate ranking: a positive choice received from a lower ranked group is not reciprocated.

Society and the social group are generally considered to contain a limited number of discrete ranks. In this chapter, we present structural models of discrete ranks that have evolved from balance theory. The first two balance-theoretic models – balance and clusterability (see Chapter 4) – are confined to the clustering of social entities; they tacitly assume that there is no ranking, so asymmetric ties and unclusterable semicycles are not allowed. A third model, the ranked clusters model, regards a social system as a set of ranks where each rank contains one or more clusters. Positive arcs connect entities within a cluster but no arcs connect different clusters at one level, as in the clusterability model. In addition, asymmetric dyads connect clusters at different ranks, where arcs point from lower to higher levels.

The ranked clusters model represents a simple hierarchy in which each pair of clusters or vertices is unambiguously ranked. Often, social systems are more complicated, containing incomplete hierarchies or even different hierarchies that are not compatible. The social cleavage between girls and boys is a simple example. There is a hierarchy of boys and a hierarchy of girls but nobody is interested in the members of the other gender regardless of their ranking. This phenomenon is captured in the fourth balance-theoretic model, which is known as the transitivity model. A fifth model, called the hierarchical clusters model, is even more permissive because it allows for ranking within a group. Asymmetric dyads within a cluster of otherwise symmetrically connected people indicate ranking in this model.

In a simple directed network, a balance-theoretic model is identified by the types of triads that it permits, so we may count the number of times each triad type occurs in the network – this is called the triad census – and find the appropriate model. Unfortunately, social networks seldom fit a balance-theoretic model perfectly, so we need statistical tests to determine which triad types and models occur more often than expected by chance. Triadic analysis is the basis for statistical modeling rather than exploring the structure of clusters and ranks.

By definition, ranking is acyclic, so cyclic parts of the network either represent clustering within a rank or they contain complicated or imperfect ranking. Recall that a strong component contains vertices that are connected by paths in both directions, so strong components are cyclic subnetworks. If we shrink the strong components, the resulting network is acyclic and can be partitioned into ranks. Next, we inspect each strong component for clusters and complicated or imperfect ranking. In a simple directed network, mutual (positive) choices are the backbones of clusters, so we look for clusters of vertices that are directly or indirectly linked by symmetric ties. The ties between the clusters tell us whether they belong to one rank or to different ranks.

This is an exploratory procedure for detecting the clusters and ranks that best fit a network but it does not tell us whether the fit is satisfactory. With enough effort and modification, we can probably find clusters and ranks that even fit a random network. As elsewhere in this book, we must make sense of our results. The clusters and ranks should be meaningful with respect to other information that we have about the social entities in the network.

10.7   Questions

1. How many dyads does the network depicted below contain and how many types of dyads?

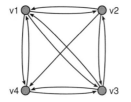

a. Six dyads and one type
b. Six dyads and two types
c. Eleven dyads and one type
d. Eleven dyads and two types

2. Assemble the triad census (type of triad and frequency of occurrence) of the network shown above by hand.

3. Which balance-theoretic model characterizes the network of Question 1?
   a. The balance model
   b. The hierarchical clusters model
   c. The balance and hierarchical clusters models
   d. No balance-theoretic model fits this network

4. The table below shows the triad census of a directed network. Choose the appropriate balance-theoretic model for this network and justify your choice.

No.	Type	Number of Triads (n_i)	Expected (e_i)	$(n_i-e_i)/e_i$	Model
3	102	41	10.7	2.83	Balance
16	300	2	0.1	15.63	
1	003	8	19.4	−0.59	Clusterability
4	021D	0	10.7	−1.00	Ranked
5	021U	3	10.7	−0.72	Clusters
9	030T	7	9.2	−0.24	
12	120D	14	2.0	6.13	
13	120U	6	2.0	2.05	
2	012	77	49.9	0.54	Transitivity
14	120C	0	3.9	−1.00	Hierarchical
15	210	0	1.7	−1.00	Clusters
6	021C	2	21.4	−0.91	Forbidden
7	111D	3	9.2	−0.67	
8	111U	2	9.2	−0.78	
10	030C	0	3.1	−1.00	
11	201	0	2.0	−1.00	

5. Explain why triad 201 is not allowed under the hierarchical clusters model.

6. Assign the vertices of the network depicted below to clusters and ranks. Vertex colors indicate strong components. Does your decomposition satisfy the weak or the strong symmetric-acyclic model?

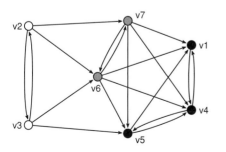

7. Which of the following statements about symmetric-acyclic decomposition is correct?

   a. In the strong symmetric-acyclic model, clusters do not contain asymmetric dyads.

   b. In the strong symmetric-acyclic model, vertices in different ranks are always connected by asymmetric dyads.

   c. In the weak symmetric-acyclic model, clusters contain mutual or null dyads only.

   d. In the weak symmetric-acyclic model, all asymmetric dyads point from a lower rank to a higher rank.

10.8   Assignment

In 1976, a literary critic published an essay about contemporary Dutch prose. In his essay, he distinguished among four trends or movements: narrators, including the authors Donkers, Kooiman, Matsier, and Meijsing; alienators, including Van Marissing, Robberechts, and Vogelaar; petty realism, including Hart, Hiddema, Luijters, Meinkema, Plomp, and Sijtsma; and decadence, including Siebelink and Joyce & Co. Find out whether this classification matches the ranks and clusters in the networks of critical attention in 1976. The simple directed network literature_1976.net contains an arc between two people if the first has paid attention to the second in an interview or review. Hint: create a partition reflecting the classification of the authors according to literary movement.

10.9   Further Reading

- Chapters 6 and 14 of S. Wasserman and K. Faust's *Social Network Analysis: Methods and Applications* (Cambridge: Cambridge University Press, 1994) provide an excellent overview over balance-theoretic models and the analysis of triads. An overview over the work of Davis, Holland, and Leinhardt on triads can be found in J. A. Davis' article "The Davis/Holland/Leinhardt Studies: An Overview." In P. W. Holland and S. Leinhardt (Eds.), *Perspectives on Social Network Research*. New York: Academic Press, 1979." C. Flament, in *Applications of Graph Theory to Group Structure* (Englewood Cliffs, N.J.: Prentice Hall, 1963), proved that triads suffice for detecting balance in complete signed graphs and Davis ["Clustering and structural balance in graphs." In: *Human Relations*, 20 (1967), pp. 181–7] did this for clusterability. For more information on the hierarchical m̄-clusters model, see E. C. Johnsen, "Network macrostructure models for the Davis-Leinhardt set of empirical sociomatrices" [in *Social Networks* 7 (1985), 203–24].

- For more information on the student government data, consult V. Hlebec, "Recall versus recognition: comparison of two alternative procedures for collecting social network data." In

A. Ferligoj and A. Kramberger (Eds.), *Developments in Statistics and Methodology*. (Ljubljana: FDV, 1993). Results of an analysis of the Dutch literary criticism data are reported in W. de Nooy, "A literary playground. Literary criticism and balance theory." In: *Poetics* 26 (1999), 385–404.

10.10   Answers

Answers to the Exercises

I. When the arc from advisor3 to minister5 has been removed, four strong components are found. Now, minister4 and minister5 constitute a strong component on their own, which is separated from the component containing the prime minister. This may be regarded as a new rank in the student government discussion network, between the rank of minister1 and minister2, who send arcs to minister4 and minister5, and the rank including the prime minister, three ministers, and two advisors, who receive only arcs from them. The arc from advisor3 to minister5 created a cycle containing minister4 and minister5 in the original network.

II. Without the arc from advisor3 to minister5, you obtained four strong components. When you remove the lines between clusters with the *Operations>Transform>Remove Lines>Between Clusters* command in the Main screen and change the bidirectional arcs into edges (*Net>Transform>Arcs→Edges>Bidirected only*), you can easily see that three components contain edges only, but the largest component (including the prime minister) still contains three arcs (see the figure below). All arcs involve ties between a minister and an advisor. We must conclude that the weak symmetric-acyclic model applies.

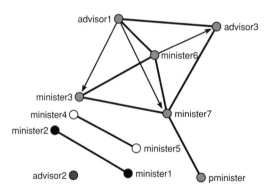

Answers to the Questions in Section 10.7

1. Answer b is correct. A dyad is a pair of vertices and the lines among them. In a network with four vertices, such as the example, there are six different pairs of vertices, so there are six dyads. In a simple directed network, a dyad is mutual (arcs in both directions), asymmetric (an arc in one direction), or null (no arcs). In the example, five dyads are

mutual and the sixth (v2 and v4) is asymmetric, so there are two types of dyad.

2. The table below shows the triad census.

No.	Type	Number of Triads	Model
3	102	0	Balance
16	300	2	
1	003	0	Clusterability
4	021D	0	Ranked
5	021U	0	Clusters
9	030T	0	
12	120D	0	
13	120U	0	
2	012	0	Transitivity
14	120C	0	Hierarchical
15	210	2	Clusters
6	021C	0	"Forbidden"
7	111D	0	
8	111U	0	
10	030C	0	
11	201	0	
TOTAL		4	

3. Answer b is correct. In Question 2, you have found two balanced triads (300) and two hierarchical cluster triads (210). The hierarchical clusters model allows for balanced triads but the reverse is not true. Therefore, the hierarchical clusters model is the appropriate model for this network.

4. The transitivity model is appropriate here. The forbidden triads do not occur (030C and 201) or occur less often than in random networks, so a balance-theoretic model characterizes this network. The hierarchical cluster triads do not occur, but the network contains far more transitivity triads (012) than expected by chance. Two ranked clusters triads (120D and 120U) and both balanced triads appear more often than expected by chance, but they are also permitted by the transitivity model, so we may conclude that the transitivity model characterizes this network.

5. Triad 201 contains two symmetric choices and one null dyad. In the hierarchical clusters model, vertices connected by symmetric ties belong to one (hierarchical) cluster. A null dyad means that two vertices belong to different clusters. Therefore, two vertices belong to different clusters because of the null dyad and to the same cluster because of the path of symmetric choices at the same time. This is a contradiction, so this triad is not allowed.

6. Arcs between strong components point from the white to the gray component and from the gray to the black component. Clearly, there are three ranks, the black rank is the top rank and the white rank is at the

bottom. The vertices in the white and gray component are connected by mutual arcs but two black vertices (v1 and v5) are connected by an asymmetric tie, so the decomposition does not satisfy the criteria of the strong symmetric-acyclic model for all strong components.

7. Statement a is correct. In the strong symmetric-acyclic model, clusters contain no asymmetric dyads, hence all asymmetric dyads are found between ranks. This is not the case in the weak symmetric-acyclic model, where asymmetric dyads may occur within clusters (answers c and d). Answer b is not correct because vertices at different ranks can also be connected by null dyads.

11

Genealogies and Citations

11.1 Introduction

Time is responsible for a special kind of asymmetry in social relations, because it orders events and generations in an irreversible way. Social identity and position is partially founded on common ancestors, whether in a biological sense (birth) or in an intellectual manner: citations by scientists or references to predecessors by artists. This is social cohesion by common descent, which is slightly different from cohesion by direct ties (see Part II). Social communities and intellectual traditions can be defined by a common set of ancestors, by structural relinking (families which intermarry repeatedly), or by long-lasting cocitation of papers.

Pedigree is also important for the retrospective attribution of prestige to ancestors. For example, in citation analysis the number of descendants (citations) is used to assign importance and influence to precursors. Genealogy is the basic frame of reference here, so we discuss the analysis of genealogies first.

11.2 Example I: Genealogy of the Ragusan Nobility

Ragusa, which is now known as Dubrovnik (Croatia), was settled on the coast of the Adriatic Sea in the seventh century. For a time, it was under Byzantine protection, becoming a free commune as early as the twelfth century. Napoleon, having destroyed the Venetian Republic in 1797, put an end to the Republic of Ragusa in 1806. It came under Austrian control until the fall of the Austro-Hungarian monarchy in 1918.

In Ragusa, all political power was in the hands of male nobles older than eighteen years. They were members of the Great Council (*Consilium majus*) who had the legislative authority. Every year, eleven members of the Small Council (*Consilium minus*) were elected. Together with a duke, the Small Council had both executive and representative authority. The main power was in the hands of the Senate (*Consilium rogatorum*), which contained forty-five members elected for one year. This organization prevented any single family, such as the Medici in Florence, from prevailing. Nevertheless historians agree that the Sorgo family was among the most influential.

226

The Ragusan nobility evolved from the twelfth century to the fourteenth century and was finally established by statute in 1332. After 1332, no new family were accepted until the large earthquake in 1667. A major problem facing the Ragusan noble families was that, because of their decreasing numbers and the lack of noble families in the neighboring areas, which were under Turkish control, they became more and more closely related – marriages between third and fourth removed relatives were frequent. It is interesting to analyze how families of a privileged social class organized their relations by marriage and how they coped with the limited number of potential spouses for their children.

The file `Ragusan.ged` contains the members of the Ragusan nobility from the twelfth to the sixteenth centuries, their kinship relations (parent–child), their marriages, and their (known) years of birth, marriage and death. Note that this is not an ordinary network file, because it contains attributes and ties of vertices. The extension `.ged` indicates that it is a GEDCOM-file, which is the standard format for genealogical data as explained in the next section. The genealogy is large, it contains 5,999 persons. For illustrative purposes, we selected the descendants of one nobleman, Petrus Gondola, in the file `Gondola_Petrus.ged` (336 persons).

11.3   Family Trees

Across the world, many people are assembling their family trees. They visit archives to collect information about their ancestors in registers of births, deaths, and marriages. Because in most Western societies family names are the usual entries in these registers and family names are the father's surname, a patrilineal genealogy is reconstructed, in which father–child relations rather than mother–child relations connect generations. In addition, marriages are included in the family tree.

Figure 95 shows a part of the Gondola family tree, which includes three generations of descendants to Petrus Gondola, who was born in 1356. Note that children born to a Gondola father are included because they receive the Gondola surname. Children of a Gondola mother are not included because their surname assigns them to another family in this historiography of a family name. An exception would be a Gondola mother who married a Gondola father, but, as shown in Figure 95, this does not occur among the descendants.

In principle, genealogies contain persons as units and two types of relations among persons: birth and marriage. A person may belong to two nuclear families: a family in which it is a child and a family in which it is a parent. The former is called the *family of child or orientation* (FAMC) and the latter is the *family of spouse or procreation* (FAMS). Petrus Gondola's family of procreation, for example, contains his wife and eight children and it is identical to the family of orientation of each of his children. A husband and wife have the same family of procreation, but they have different families of orientation unless they are brother and sister.

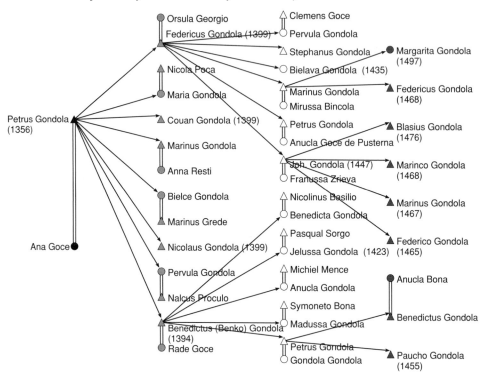

Figure 95. Three generations of descendants to Petrus Gondola (years of birth).

The standard data format for genealogies (GEDCOM) uses the double coding according to family of orientation and family of procreation. In addition, it has facilities to store all sorts of information about the persons and events (e.g., about their marriage) so we advise using this data format for the collection and storage of genealogical data. On the Internet, excellent free software and several databases of genealogical data are available (see Further Reading).

In a representation of a genealogy as a network, family codes are translated to arcs between parents and children. In a sociogram of kinship ties that is known as the *Ore graph* (Figure 96) men are represented by triangles, women by ellipses, marriages by (double) lines, and parent–child ties by arcs. Note that the arcs point from parent to child following the flow of time.

In contrast to the family tree, fathers *and* mothers are connected to their children in an Ore graph. This greatly simplifies the calculation of kinship relations because the length and the direction of the shortest semi-path between two individuals defines their kinship tie, for instance, my grandparents are the vertices two steps up from me in the Ore graph. They are relatives in the second remove because two births are included in this path. In a patrilineal family tree, relatives from my mother's side (e.g., her parents and brother) are not included so it is impossible to establish my kinship tie with them. In the Ore graph, it is possible to distinguish

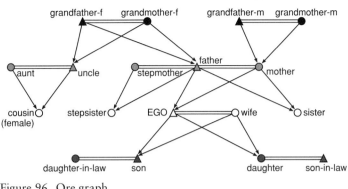

Figure 96. Ore graph.

between blood relations and marriage relations, so we may calculate the remove in a strict sense, that is, ignoring marital relations, or in a loose sense, including them and considering them relations with zero distance.

In the standard display of a kinship network, marriages and siblings are drawn at the same layer and layers are either top-down (Figure 96) or ordered from left to right (Figure 95). A layer contains a *genealogical generation*: grandparents versus parents, uncles and aunts versus children, nieces, and nephews. Such are the generations that we experience during our lives. From a social point of view, however, we define generations as birth cohorts (e.g., the generation of 1945–1960). In contemporary Western societies, *social generations* contain people who were born within a period of approximately fifteen years. Genealogical generations overlap with social generations to a limited extent. For four or more generations, genealogical generations may group people of very different ages as a result of early marriage and childbearing in one branch of the family and late marriage in another branch. The birth years of the great-grandchildren of Petrus Gondola, for instance, range from 1455 (Paucho) to 1497 (Margarita, see Figure 95). Biologically, the former could have been the latter's grandfather. As a consequence, Paucho's grandson could have married Margarita, causing a *generation jump* in the genealogy because it would connect a third-degree descendant of Petrus Gondola (viz., Margarita) to a fifth-degree descendant (Paucho's grandson).

The Ore graph is a very useful instrument for finding an individual's *ancestors* (*pedigree*) and *descendants* from both the father's side and the mother's side. In addition, it is easy to count *siblings* and trace the *closest common ancestor* of two individuals.

Application

Genealogical data in GEDCOM format can be read directly by Pajek. To obtain the Ore graph, make sure that the option *GEDCOM - Pgraph in the Options>Read/Write* submenu is *not* selected before you open the GEDCOM file. When you check the option *Ore: 1-Male, 2-Female links*, marriages receive line value zero (drawn as double lines), father–child ties have a line value of 1 (solid lines), and mother–child ties have a value of 2 (dotted lines). This is particularly useful if you want to extract patrilineal ties from the Ore graph. In all other cases, it is better not to

[Main]
Options>
Read/Write>
GEDCOM -
Pgraph,
Ore: 1-Male,
2-Female links

check this option, so all parent–child ties have line a value of 1. Then, open a GEDCOM file in the usual way with the *File>Network>Read* command, but select the option *Gedcom files (*.ged)* in the *File Type* drop-down menu of the Read dialog screen.

Info>Vector

Reading the GEDCOM file, Pajek translates family numbers to parent–child ties and it creates a partition and four vectors. The partition identifies vertices that are brothers and sisters, that is, children born to the same father and mother. Stepbrothers and stepsisters from a parent's remarriage are grouped separately and vertices without parents in the network are collected in class zero. The vectors contain each person's sequential number in the GEDCOM file and his or her year of birth, marriage, and death. Unknown dates are represented by vector value 9999998. You may inspect the dates with the *Info>Vector* procedure in the usual way (see Section 2.5 in Chapter 2).

*Net>Partitions>
Depth>
Genealogical*

The *genealogical generations* of the Ore graph can be obtained with the command *Genealogical* from the *Net>Partitions>Depth* submenu. An acyclic depth partition is not possible because the marriage edges are cyclic: a husband is married to his wife and a wife is married to her husband at the same time. Draw the network in layers according to the genealogical depth partition (*Layers>In y direction* in the Draw screen) and optimize it in the usual way (*Layers>Optimize layers in x direction*). To focus on the distinct branches in the genealogy rather than the vertices, use the *Averaging x coordinate* command from the *Layers* menu. Usually, the *Forward* option works well but you may have to apply it more than once to clearly separate distinct branches as in Figure 97.

*Layers>In y
direction*

*Layers>
Optimize layers
in x direction*

*Layers>
Averaging x
coordinate*

*[Main]
Options>
Read/Write>
Ore: 1-Male,
2-Female links*

The length of the shortest semipath in a symmetrized Ore graph is the *remove* or *degree of a family relation*, provided that all parent–child ties have a line value of 1 and marriage lines have a line value of zero. Therefore, you must open the GEDCOM file with the option *Ore: 1-Male, 2-Female links* not checked in the *Option>Read/Write* submenu.

*Net>Transform>
Remove>all
edges*

First, decide whether you want to include marital relations in the calculation. If not, remove the edges from the network (*Net>Transform>Remove>all edges*). Then, symmetrize the Ore graph (*Net>Transform>Arcs→Edges>All* and do not remove multiple lines) and use the *Paths between 2 vertices>All Shortest* command to obtain the geodesics between two individuals in the network. When asked, do not ignore (forget) the values of the lines, because a marriage link should not contribute to the length of the semipath and hence to the remove of the relation. The length of the shortest paths, which is the distance between the vertices in the symmetrized network, is printed in the Report screen. Among the descendants of Petrus Gondola (Figure 95), for instance, Paucho Gondola (born in 1455) is a relative of Margarita Gondola (born in 1497) in the sixth remove.

*Net>Transform>
Arcs→Edges>
All*

*Net>Paths
between 2
vertices>All
Shortest*

Pajek creates a new network of the geodesics it has found and a partition that identifies the vertices on the geodesics in the original network provided that you requested this in one of the dialog boxes. If we extract these vertices from the original directed network (*Operations>Extract from Network>Partition* and choose class 1) and relocate the vertices, we obtain that shown in Figure 98. Note the triangles containing two

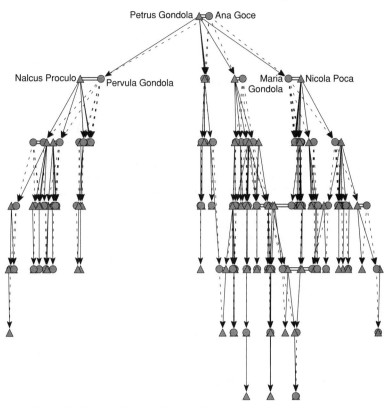

Figure 97. Descendants of Petrus Gondola and Ana Goce.

parents and one child. The direct path from child to father is just as long as the indirect path via the child's mother because a marriage line counts as zero distance. If we had ignored line values, the shortest paths would not have included the mothers (except for Ana Goce) in this example.

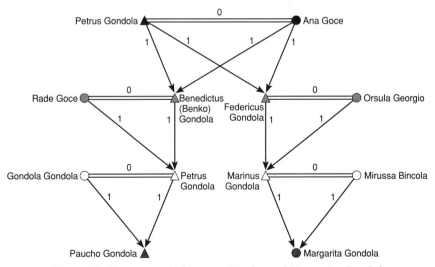

Figure 98. Shortest paths between Paucho and Margarita Gondola.

In Figure 98, it is easy to see that Petrus Gondola and his wife Anna Goce are the closest common ancestors of Paucho and Margarita. Of course, we could already see that in the original family tree (Figure 95), but we need the shortest paths command in large networks such as the genealogy of the entire Ragusan nobility, because this is too complicated to analyze by eyeballing.

Net>k-Neighbours

The *ancestors* (*pedigree*) or *descendants* of a person are easily found with the *k-Neighbours* procedure in the Ore graph. Ancestors are connected by paths toward an individual, so they are its input neighbors. Descendants are reachable from the individual: they are output neighbors in the Ore graph. You may restrict the selection of ancestors to a limited number of generations in the *Maximal distance* dialog box of the *k-Neighbours* procedure. Note that the number of generations that you select is one more than the largest distance that you specify because the selected person, who also represents a generation, is placed in class zero. For example, the family tree in Figure 95 contains a number of output neighbors (descendants) of Petrus Gondola at maximum distance of 3.

Info>Partition

The Ore graph is most suited for finding brothers and sisters and for counting the size of sibling groups in a genealogical network. Pajek automatically creates a brothers/sisters partition, which identifies children of the same parental couple. Each class is a sibling group, except for class zero, so the number of vertices within a brothers and sisters class represents the size of a sibling group. Unfortunately, it is not easy to obtain a frequency distribution of the size of sibling groups from this partition in Pajek because the *Info>Partition* command lists each sibling group (class) separately.

It is possible, however, to obtain a frequency distribution of the size of sibling groups that have the same father or the same mother. In the Ore graph, the outdegree of a vertex is equal to the number of its children provided that marriage lines are disregarded. Ideally, every child has a father and a mother in the genealogical network, so we may count the number of children for each father or mother. In the case of a single marriage, the father and mother have the same number of children but these numbers may differ in the case of remarriages. In the little example (Figure 96), my father remarried: he has three children (my stepsister, sister, and me), whereas my mother has only two children (my sister and me). Therefore, we must look at the outdegree of fathers or mothers, not at both.

Net>Transform>Remove>all edges

Net>Partitions>Degree>Output

Net>Partitions>Vertex Shapes

Partitions>Extract Second from First

This is achieved in the following way. First, remove the marriage lines (*Net>Transform>Remove>all edges*) from the Ore graph. Now, the outdegree of a vertex is equal to an actor's number of children, so create an outdegree partition with the *Net>Partition>Degree>Output* command and select it as the first partition in the *Partitions* menu.

Next, create a partition on vertex shape (*Net>Partitions>Vertex Shapes*). Recall that in the Ore graph men are represented by triangles and women by ellipses. In the vertex shape partition, one class contains the men and another contains the women. Inspect this partition (e.g., edit it) to find out which class represents the men or the women. Finally, select the partition according to vertex shape as the second partition in the

Table 19. *Number of Children of Petrus Gondola and His Male Descendants*

Cluster	Freq	Freq%	CumFreq	CumFreq%	Representative
0	131	67.5258	131	67.5258	4
1	14	7.2165	145	74.7423	15
2	15	7.7320	160	82.4742	3
3	11	5.6701	171	88.1443	1
4	7	3.6082	178	91.7526	2
5	4	2.0619	182	93.8144	29
6	1	0.5155	183	94.3299	120
7	3	1.5464	186	95.8763	23
8	4	2.0619	190	97.9381	13
9	1	0.5155	191	98.4536	114
11	2	1.0309	193	99.4845	85
12	1	0.5155	194	100.0000	171
SUM	194	100.0000			

Partitions menu and execute the command *Extract Second from First.* In the dialog boxes, choose the class identifying the gender that you want to select and Pajek will create a new partition with the outdegree of the selected vertices (viz., the men).

The *Info>Partition* command will produce the desired frequency tabulation (see Table 19). Among Petrus Gondola's descendants, one man had twelve children and the others had fewer. Two-thirds (67.5%) of the men did not have children. Note, however, that they include the youngest men of the genealogy, who may have had children who were not included in the data set.

Info>Partition

Exercise I

From the genealogical data in `Gondola_Petrus.ged`, construct a network containing Petrus Gondola (born in 1356) and all his descendants who received the Gondola surname at birth. In other words, create a patrilineal genealogy for Petrus Gondola's offspring.

11.4   Social Research on Genealogies

Kinship is a fundamental social relation that is extensively studied by anthropologists and historians. In contrast to people who assemble their private family trees, social scientists are primarily interested in the genealogies of entire communities, such as the nobility of Ragusa.

These genealogies, which are usually very large, enable the study of overall patterns of kinship ties which, for instance, reflect cultural norms for marriage: who are allowed to marry? Property is handed over from one generation to the next along family lines, so marriages may serve to protect or enlarge the wealth of a family; family ties parallel economic exchange. Demographic data on birth, marriage, and death reflect economic and ecological conditions (e.g., a famine or deadly disease causes high mortality rates).

Table 20. *Size of Sibling Groups* in 1200–1250 and 1300–1350*

Size of Sibling Group	1200–50		1300–50	
0 (no children)	18	16.4%	386	54.5%
1	22	20.0%	87	12.3%
2	18	16.4%	73	10.3%
3	19	17.3%	53	7.5%
4	11	10.0%	38	5.4%
5	10	9.1%	29	4.1%
6–10	12	10.9%	40	5.6%
11–21	—	—	2	0.3%
TOTAL (# sibling groups)	110	100%	708	100%

* The number of children from one father.

The number of marriages and the age of the marital couple, the size of sibling groups, nuclear families, or extended families are determined and compared across different societies or different periods. Differences are related to external conditions and internal systems of norms or rules.

Table 20 compares the number of children of Ragusan noblemen across two periods: men born in 1200–1250 and 1300–1350. Unfortunately, many birth dates are unknown, so we added the parents' children and the children's in-laws from the kinship network assuming that they belong to the same generation. In the Ore graph, the simple outdegree of a vertex specifies the number of children of a person. Table 20 summarizes the output degree frequencies. In the first half of the fourteenth century and in comparison to the previous century, a large proportion of the noblemen had no children. Perhaps fewer men got married because no new families were admitted to the nobility as of 1332. Conversely, some men may have died young as a consequence of the black death epidemic, which struck the town in 1348.

This type of research may use network analysis but it can also be done by database counts, for instance, calculations on a GEDCOM genealogy database. A second type of research, however, is inherently relational and must use network analysis as a tool. It focuses on structural relinking between families and the economic, social, and cultural reasons or rules for structural relinking. *Structural relinking* refers to the phenomenon that families intermarry more than once in the course of time. Intermarriage or *endogamy* is an indicator of social cohesion within a genealogy. If families are linked by more kinship ties, they are more likely to act as a clan: sharing cultural norms, entertaining tight relations, and restricting ties to families outside the clan.

There are two types of structural relinking: *blood marriages* and *non-blood relinking*. A blood marriage is the marriage of people with a close common ancestor, for instance, a marriage between a brother and sister or between a granddaughter and a grandson. The occurrence of this type of relinking tells us which types of intermarriages are culturally allowed and which are not. In the Ragusan nobility, a grandson of Benko Gondola (Benedictus Gondola) married a granddaughter (Anucla Bona), who was a fourth-degree relative (see Figure 99). Blood marriages between closer

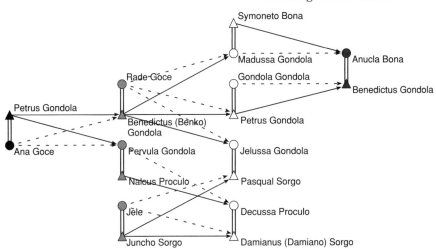

Figure 99. Structural relinking in an Ore graph.

relatives – a son who married a daughter, a child who married a grand-child – did not occur among the Ragusan nobility. Apparently, these marriages were not allowed.

Nonblood relinking refers to multiple marriages between families without a close common ancestor. This type of relinking often serves economic goals, namely to keep the wealth and power within selected families. Figure 99 shows nonblood interlinking between the Gondola and Sorgo families: two granddaughters of Petrus Gondola and Ana Goce (Jelussa and Decussa) marry brothers from the Sorgo family (Pasqual and Damianus), who were acknowledged to be the most influential family among the Ragusan nobility.

Structural relinking produces semicycles within a genealogical network, for instance, the blood marriage between Benedictus Gondola and Anucla Bona closes the paths from Benko Gondola to his granddaughter Anucla and his grandson Benedictus (Figure 99). The nonblood relinking between the Gondola and Sorgo families also yields a semicycle (Petrus Gondola–Benko–Jelussa Gondola–Pasqual Sorgo–Jele–Damianus Sorgo–Decussa Proculo–Pervula Gondola–Petrus Gondola, among other semicycles).

However, in the Ore graph not all semicycles represent structural relinking. A father, mother, and child also create a semicycle (e.g., Ana Goce–Petrus Gondola–Pervula Gondola in Figure 99). In addition, parents and two or more children create larger semicycles (e.g., Ana Goce–Pervula Gondola Petrus Gondola–Benko Gondola–Ana Goce). Remarriages yield even more complicated semicycles that do not point to structural relinking.

Because it is troublesome to distinguish between semicycles that represent structural relinking and semicycles that do not, D. R. White and P. Jorion developed a special kind of genealogical network: the *parentage graph* or *P-graph*. In the P-graph, couples and unmarried individuals are the vertices and arcs point from children to parents. The type of arc shows

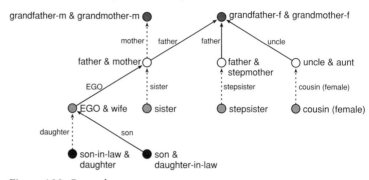

Figure 100. P-graph.

whether the descendant is male (full arc) or female (dotted arc). In Figure 100, for instance, my son and his wife are connected by a full arc to me and my spouse; my daughter and her husband are connected by a dotted arc.

The P-graph has several advantages. It contains fewer vertices but the path distance in a symmetrized P-graph still shows the remove of a relation, although it is not possible to exclude marital ties from the calculation. The main advantage of the P-graph, however, is the fact that it is acyclic – there are no edges between married people – and there are no separate arcs from mother and father to child. As a result, every semicycle and bicomponent indicates structural relinking, which is either a blood marriage or another type of relinking. Figure 101 shows the P-graph associated with the Ore graph of Figure 99. The two semicycles represent structural relinking: the blood marriage of Benedictus Gondola and Anucla Bona and the nonblood relinking between the Gondola and Sorgo families.

Apart from specific cases of relinking, social network analysts are interested in the amount of relinking in a genealogy. In a P-graph, this is measured by the *relinking index*. To understand this index, we must introduce the concept of a tree in graph theory: a connected graph that contains no semicycles. A tree has several interesting properties but for our purposes the fact that it does not contain cycles and semicycles is most important.

A *tree* is a connected graph that contains no semicycles.

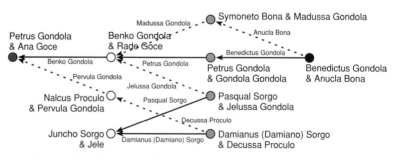

Figure 101. Structural relinking in a P-graph.

In a P-graph, every semicycle indicates structural relinking because the people or couples on the semicycle are linked by (at least) two chains of family ties (e.g., common grandparents on the father's side and on the mother's side). As a consequence, a P-graph which is a tree or a set of distinct trees (a *forest*) has no relinking and its relinking index is zero. Given the number of people and the assumption that a marriage links exactly one man and one woman, the maximum amount of relinking within the P-graph of a genealogy can be computed so the actual number of relinking can be expressed as a proportion of this maximum. This is the relinking index, which is 1 in a genealogy with maximum relinking and zero in a genealogy without relinking.

We advise calculating the relinking index on bi-components within the P-graph rather than on the entire P-graph. Genealogies have no natural borders; kinship ties extend beyond the boundaries of the data collected by the researcher, but boundary setting is important to the result of the relinking index. The largest bi-component within a genealogy is a sensible boundary because it demarcates families that are integrated into a system by at least one instance of relinking. In general, structural relinking may be used to bound the field of study, which means that you limit your analyses to the families within the largest bi-component of a genealogy.

Let us calculate the amount of structural relinking among the Ragusan nobility in the period 1200–1350, in which new families were admitted to the nobility, and 1350–1500, when the nobility was chartered and no new families were admitted. Because we lack birth dates, we add the parents' children and children's in-laws to the couples in which at least one spouse is known to be born in the selected period. Between 1200 and 1350, a small number of the couples (137 of 1412 vertices or 9.7 percent) were connected by two or more family ties, so the relinking index is low for the network in this period (0.02). Within this bi-component, the relinking index is higher (0.24), so there is a small core of families, the Sorgo family among them, who are tightly related by intermarriages.

In the period 1350–1500, the bi-component is larger, containing 476 couples (23.7 percent) and featuring many members of the Goce, Bodacia, and Sorgo families. The relinking index of the entire network is 0.20 and within the bi-component the proportion of relinking is 0.69. Both values are much larger than in the period before 1350, which shows increased endogamy among the Ragusan nobility.

In the P-graph, each person is represented by one arc except in the case of multiple marriages: remarriages and polygamy. Because each marriage is a separate vertex (e.g., my father and mother or my father and step-mother in Figure 100), men and women who remarry are represented by two or more arcs. In the P-graph, it is impossible to distinguish between a married uncle and a remarriage of a father or between stepsisters and (female) cousins. This problem is solved in the bipartite P-graph, which has vertices for individuals and vertices for married couples. However, the bipartite P-graph has the drawback of containing considerably more vertices and lines than the P-graph and path distance does not correspond to the remove of a kinship relation. We do not use bipartite P-graphs in this book.

Application

*Options>Read/
Write>
GEDCOM-
Pgraph*

*Options>Read/
Write>
Bipartite Pgraph*

*Options>Read/
Write>
Pgraph+labels*

The format of a genealogy that is read from a GEDCOM data file depends on the options checked in the *Options>Read/Write* menu. As noted, Pajek transforms a GEDCOM data file into an Ore graph if the option *GEDCOM-Pgraph* is *not* checked. A regular P-graph is created if this option is checked but the option *Bipartite Pgraph* is not. If the option *Pgraph + labels* is also checked, the name of a person is used as the label of an arc. All P-graphs have a line value of 1 for male lines and a value of 2 for female lines.

Pajek does not create a brothers and sisters partition in conjunction with a P-graph because siblings can easily be identified as the input neighbors (remember: arcs point from children to parents!) of a vertex representing a married couple or an unmarried mother or father. It stores the years of birth of men and women in separate vectors because a couple has two birth dates. This also applies to the years of death. In addition, Pajek lists the year of marriage (9999998 for unmarried individuals), the family of spouse number (FAMS) for each couple, the family of child numbers (FAMC), and the sequential number (INDI) for the men and women separately.

We advise opening the entire Ragusan nobility genealogy (Ragusan.ged) as a P-graph (check option *GEDCOM-Pgraph* in the *Options>Read/Write* submenu) and making sure that names are used as labels of the arcs (also check the option *Pgraph + labels*). Note that reading the arc labels takes more time and uses more computer memory, so you may want to omit them if your network is very large and you do not really need the labels.

*Info>Network>
Indices*

The relinking index is calculated by the *Info>Network>Indices* command and it is printed in the Report screen. Note that the index is valid only for P-graphs. On request, Pajek will compute it for any network, but then its value is meaningless. In the P-graph with the entire Ragusan nobility, the relinking index is 0.23.

*Net>
Components>
Bi-Components*

*File>Hierarchy>
Edit*

If you want to calculate the relinking index for the largest bi-component in this P-graph, you have to identify the bi-components and extract the largest bi-component first. The *Net>Components>Bi-Components* command, introduced in Chapter 7, identifies the bi-components. Make sure that the minimum size of a bi-component is set to 3 in the dialog box issued by this command. As you have learned in Chapter 7, bi-components are stored as a hierarchy, so inspect the hierarchy (*File>Hierarchy>Edit*) to find the sequential number and size of the largest bi-component. In the Ragusan nobility genealogy, we find two bi-components: the first contains five vertices and the second 1446.

*Hierarchy>
Extract Cluster*

*Operations>
Extract from
Network>
Cluster*

*Info>Network>
Indices*

Extract the second bi-component from the network in the following way: translate the required class of the hierarchy into a cluster with the *Hierarchy>Extract Cluster* command, specifying the sequential number of the bi-component in the hierarchy, and execute the *Extract from Network>Cluster* command from the *Operations* menu. Finally, calculate the relinking index with the *Info>Network>Indices* command. The relinking index is 0.74, which is quite high. If you would like to draw this bi-component in layers, remember that the arcs point from children to parents in a P-graph, so the oldest generations are drawn at the bottom of the Draw screen.

Particular types of relinking can be found with the *Fragments* commands in the *Nets* menu, which we also used to trace complete subnetworks (Chapter 3). Create a network that represents the relinking structure that you want to find (e.g., a marriage between two grandchildren of the same grandparents) (see Figure 102), with the *Net>Random Network* command and manual editing in the Draw screen. This fragment is also available in the file `relinking grandchildren.net`. Select this fragment as the first network in the *Nets* menu and select the P-graph of the Ragusan nobility genealogy as the second network. In the *Nets>Fragment (1 in 2)>Options* dialog box, make sure that *Induced* is not checked because additional lines among the vertices in the fragment are allowed now. Finally, find the fragments with the *Nets>Fragment (1 in 2)>Find* command. Pajek encounters three instances of this fragment, among which the marriage of the two grandchildren of Benko Gondola and Rade Goce.

Nets>Fragment (1 in 2)> Options> Induced

Nets>Fragment (1 in 2)>Find

If you want to find a fragment with a particular pattern of male and female lines, make sure that the lines have the right values in the fragment (1 for male and 2 for female; the female lines do not have to be dotted) and select the *Check values of lines* option in the *Nets>Fragment (1 in 2)>Options* menu. In the Ragusan network, there are only two instances of a marriage among grandchildren to the same grandparents where the grandson is a descendant along patrilineal lines and the granddaughter descended along matrilineal lines as in the fragment of Figure 102.

Nets>Fragment (1 in 2)> Options>Check values of lines

When you want to restrict your analysis to a particular birth cohort, you need a network with a selection of the genealogical data. Because the vertices of a P-graph may represent couples, you have to take into account the years of birth of the men and women, which are stored in separate vectors. You may decide either that both husband and wife must be born in the selected period or that at least one of them must be in that period. We should note, however, that vertices may also represent unmarried individuals, in which case husband or wife is irrelevant. In addition, missing birth dates, which are to be expected in historical data, may cause problems if you demand that both husband and spouse are known to be born in the selected period. Given these complexities, we

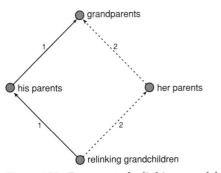

Figure 102. Fragment of relinking grandchildren.

advise to select the right period in your genealogical database software, produce a separate GEDCOM data file, and have Pajek translate it into a P-graph. Then, skip the remainder of this section.

Vector>Make Partition>by Intervals> Selected Thresholds

If this is not possible, however, you may extract the subnetwork in Pajek by combining information from different vectors. First, translate the vectors with birth dates of men and women to partitions with the *Vector>Make Partition>by Intervals>Selected Thresholds* command. In the dialog box, enter the limits of the required period (e.g., 1349 and 1500 if you are interested in the people born in 1350 up to and including 1500). Note that each threshold is included as the upper limit of the interval. In addition, include the threshold 9999997 to obtain a separate class with the 9999998 code, which represents either unknown or irrelevant birth dates (e.g., the male birth date in the case of an unmarried woman). Separate the thresholds by a blank.

Info>Partition

If we execute the command, Pajek creates a partition with four classes. If we inspect the partition with male birth dates (*Info>Partition*), we see that 1,025 men were born before 1350, 1,493 were born between 1350 and 1500, and 46 were born after 1500 and we have no information on 1,812 couples or individuals. The partition with female birth dates shows that 401 women are known to be born between 1350 and 1500.

Partitions>Info> Cramer's V/Rajski

The four classes in the men and women partitions yield sixteen combinations, which are listed in Table 21. This table is part of the output produced by the *Partitions>Info>Cramer's V/Rajski* command after selecting the male birth dates partition as the first partition and the female birth dates partition as the second partition in this menu. Note that the men are in the rows and the women in the columns and that the second class represents the period 1350–1500, whereas the fourth class contains the unknown and irrelevant birth dates.

In Table 21, the second row contains the men who were born between 1350 and 1500 (1,493 in total) and the second column shows the (401) women born in this period. Only 83 couples are known to consist of a husband and wife born in the selected period. In a majority of cases, we deal with unmarried men or unknown birth date of the wife (1,407 cases) and unmarried women or unknown birth date of the husband (317 cases). In very few cases, one spouse is known to be born in the right period, whereas the other is born in another period, namely before 1350

Table 21. *Birth Cohorts among Men and Women*

Rows: 10. From Vector 1 [1349 1500 9999997] (4376)
Columns: 11. From Vector 2 [1349 1500 9999997] (4376)
Crosstabs

	1	2	3	4	Total
1	51	1	0	973	1025
2	3	83	0	1407	1493
3	0	0	0	46	46
4	268	317	19	1208	1812
TOTAL	322	401	19	3634	4376

(period 1): in one case the husband was born before 1350 and in three cases the wife was born before 1350.

It seems reasonable to select all vertices in which either the man or the woman was born in the right period. This can be done if we create a new partition identifying the vertices for which the male birth date and/or the female birth date is coded as class 2. First we have to binarize the two birth dates partitions such that the period 1350–1500 (class 2 in these partitions) becomes class 1 in the new partitions, whereas all other classes become zero. Simply execute the *Partition>Binarize* command on each of the birth dates partitions and select class 2 in the dialog boxes. Do this for both partitions: male and female birth dates.

Partition> Binarize

Then select the two binarized partitions as first and second partition in the *Partitions* menu and sum them (*Partitions>Add Partitions*). The resulting partition has three classes: class zero containing (2,565) individuals or couples without known birth between 1350 and 1500, class 1 containing (1,728) individuals and couples containing a husband or wife born in this period, and class 2 with (83) couples with both spouses known to be born between 1350 and 1500. Now we can extract the desired subnetwork from the Ragusan nobility genealogy by executing the *Operations>Extract from Network>Partition* command, selecting clusters from one to two in the dialog boxes. This subnetwork contains 1,811 vertices.

Partitions>First Partition, Second Partition

Partitions>Add Partitions

Operations> Extract from Network> Partition

In the Ragusan nobility genealogy, many birth dates are missing. Assuming that all children of the same parents and all parents and in-laws of children belong approximately to the same birth cohort, we may add them to the people we know were born in the required period. We need these indirect neighbors to preserve the structure of the genealogical network. The procedure is stored in the macro expand_generation.mcr, which can be executed with the *Macro>Play* command. A genealogical network (Ore graph or P-graph) must be selected in the Network dropdown menu and a binary partition identifying the selected birth cohort must be selected in the Partition drop-down menu. Note that the partition that we used to extract the birth cohort is not binary, because it contains classes zero, 1, and 2. We must first binarize it such that all selected couples and individuals are in class 1. Execute the *Partition>Binarize* command and select classes 1 and 2 in the dialog boxes if you want to expand this birth cohort. The macro creates a new partition with the extended birth cohort in class 1: in our example 2,007 bachelors and couples.

Macro>Play

The macro can be executed several times to increase the number of selected vertices but *generation jumps* may extend the range of birth dates enormously. We advise applying the macro only once and checking the range of known birth years among the selected vertices afterwards. To this end, extract the vertices selected in the expanded partition from the year of birth vector(s): make sure the expanded birth cohort partition is selected in the Partition drop-down menu and a year of birth vector in the Vector drop-down menu and execute the *Vector>Extract Subvector* command (select class 1 only). You may inspect the extracted years with the *Info>Vector* command, which reports the lowest and highest values: there should not be years that fall widely outside the selected period. In

Vector>Extract Subvector

Info>Vector

the case of a P-graph, you must check the birth dates of men and women separately. With the men, the known birth dates range from 1280, which is seventy years before the selected period, to 1500. The women were born between 1298 and 1498. Even in its first step, the expansion macro lengthens the range of birth dates considerably.

Exercise II

What kind of structural relinking does the small bi-component in the Ragusan nobility genealogy represent: a blood marriage or nonblood re-linking? Extract this bi-component from the network and draw it to find the answer to this question.

11.5   Example II: Citations among Papers on Network Centrality

In several social domains, genealogical terminology is used as a metaphor for nonbiological affinity. Artists who were trained by the same master or who are influenced by the same predecessors are considered to belong to the same family or tradition. A work of art has a pedigree: a list of former owners. In a similar way, scientists are classified according to their intellectual pedigree: the theories and theorists they use as a frame of reference in their work.

In science, citations make explicit this frame of reference, so they are a valuable source of data for the study of scientific development and scientific communities in scientometrics, history, and the sociology of science. They reveal the impact of articles and their authors on later scientific work and they signal scientific communities or specialties which share knowledge.

In this chapter, we analyze the citations among articles that discuss the topic of network centrality. In 1979, Linton Freeman published an article that defined several kinds of centrality. His typology has become the standard for network analysis, so we used it in Chapter 6 of this book. Freeman, however, was not the first to publish on centrality in networks. His article is part of a discussion that dates back to the 1940s. The network depicted in Figure 103 (centrality_literature.net) shows the articles that discuss network centrality and their cross-references until 1979. Arcs represent citations; they point from the cited article to the citing article.

In principle, articles can cite only articles that appeared earlier, so the network is *acyclic*. Arcs never point back to older articles just as parents cannot be younger than their children. However, there are usually some exceptions in a citation network: articles that cite one another (e.g., articles appearing at about the same time and written by one author). We eliminate these exceptions by removing arcs that are going against time or by shrinking the articles by an author that are connected by cyclic citations. In the centrality literature network, we used the latter approach (e.g., two publications by Gilch denoted by #GilchSW-54 in Figure 103).

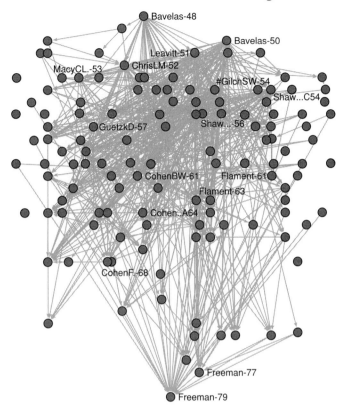

Figure 103. Centrality literature network in layers according to year of publication.

There are important differences between genealogical data and citation data. A citation network contains one relation, whereas genealogical data concern two relations: parenthood and marriage. In addition, an article may cite all previous articles notwithstanding their distance in time. In a genealogical network, children have two (biological) parents and parenthood ties always link two successive generations. The concept of a generation is not very useful in the context of a citation network, so we order the articles by publication date. In Figure 103, layers represent the year of publication (the `centrality_literature_year.clu` partition), which is also indicated by the last two digits in the label of a vertex.

11.6   Citations

Nowadays, citations are being used to assess the scientific importance of papers, authors, and journals. In general, an item receiving more citations is deemed more important. Databases of citations, for instance, the *Science Citation Index* and the *Social Science Citation Index* compiled by the Institute for Scientific Information (ISI) list the citations in a large number of journals. Simple calculations yield indices of scientific standing, for instance, the *impact factor* of a journal (the average number of citations to papers in this journal) and the *immediacy index* (the average number of citations of the papers in a journal during the year of its publication). In each year, journals are ranked by their scores on these indices. Compared over longer periods, these indices show differences between scientific disciplines. In the liberal arts, for instance, it is rare for authors to cite recent publications, whereas this is very common in the natural sciences.

Citation analysis is not exclusively interested in the assessment of scientific standing. It also focuses on the identification of specialties, the evolution of research traditions, and changing paradigms. Researchers operating within a particular subject area or scientific specialty tend to cite each other and common precursors. Citation analysis reveals such cohesive subgroups and it studies their institutional or paradigmatic background. Scientific knowledge is assumed to increment over time: previous knowledge is used and expanded in new research projects. Articles that introduce important new insights are cited until new results modify or contradict them. Citation analysis, therefore, may spot the articles that influence the research for some time and link them into a research tradition that is the backbone of a specialty. Scientific revolutions, that is, sudden paradigmatic changes resulting from new insights, are reflected by abrupt changes in the citation network.

Network analysis is the preferred technique for extracting specialties and research traditions from citations. Basically, specialties are cohesive subgroups in the citation network, so they can be detected with the usual techniques. Weak components identify isolated scientific communities that are not aware of each other or who see no substantial overlap between their research domains. Within a weak component, a bi-component identifies sections where different lines of citations emanating from a common source text meet again. This is similar to the concept of relinking in genealogical research.

In most citation networks, however, these criteria are not strong enough because almost all articles are linked into one bi-component. k-Cores (Chapter 3) offer a more penetrating view. The centrality literature network, for example, contains one large weak component and eleven isolates. There is one large bi-component and twelve vertices are connected by one citation. The network contains a 10-core of twenty-nine papers that is the central summit of this network (the black vertices in Figure 104). Each of the articles in this core is connected to at least ten other articles by citations but we do not know which are cited often and cite others often.

The cohesion concept (as discussed in Chapters 3–5) does not take time into account. It does not reflect the incremental development of knowledge, nor does it identify the articles that were vital to this development. Therefore, a special technique for citation analysis was developed that explicitly focuses on the flow of time. It was proposed by N. Hummon and colleagues and it is called *main path analysis*.

Let us think of a citation network as a system of channels which transport scientific knowledge or information. An article that integrates information from several previous articles and adds substantial new knowledge receives many citations and it will make citations to previous articles more or less redundant. As a consequence, it is an important junction of

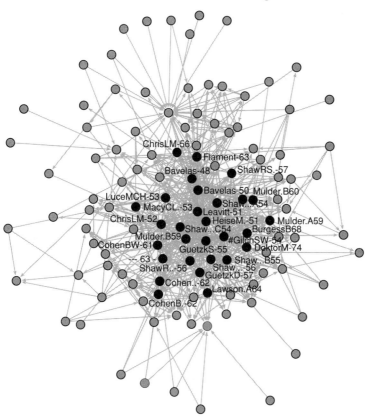

Figure 104. *k*-Cores in the centrality literature network (without isolates).

channels and a great deal of knowledge flows through it. If knowledge flows through citations, a citation that is needed in paths between many articles is more crucial than a citation that is hardly needed for linking articles. The most important citations constitute one or more main paths, which are the backbones of a research tradition.

Main path analysis calculates the extent to which a particular citation or article is needed for linking articles, which is called the traversal count or traversal weight of a citation or article. First, the procedure counts all paths from each source (an article that is not citing within the data set) to each sink (an article that is not cited within the data set) and it counts the number of paths that include a particular citation. Next, it divides the number of paths that use a citation by the total number of paths between source and sink vertices in the network. This proportion is the traversal weight of a citation. In a similar way, you can obtain the traversal weight of each article.

In an acyclic network, a *source vertex* is a vertex with zero indegree.

In an acyclic network, a *sink vertex* is a vertex with zero outdegree.

The *traversal weight* of an arc or vertex is the proportion of all paths between source and sink vertices that contain this arc or vertex.

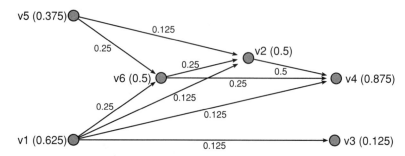

Figure 105. Traversal weights in a citation network.

For example, Figure 105 shows a citation network of six articles ordered in time from left to right. There are two sources (v1 and v5) and two sinks (v3 and v4). One path connects source v1 and sink v3 but there is no path from v5 to v3. Four paths reach v4 from v1 and three paths from v5. In sum, there are eight paths from sources to sinks. The citation of article v1 by article v3 is included in one of the eight paths, so its traversal weight is 0.125. The citation of v2 in article v4 is contained in exactly half of all paths. The traversal weights of the vertices, which are reported between brackets, are calculated in a similar way.

Now that we have defined and calculated the traversal weights of citations, we may extract the paths or components with the highest traversal counts on the lines, the main paths or main path components, which are hypothesized to identify the main stream of a literature. We can analyze their evolution over time and search for patterns that reflect the integration, fragmentation, or specialization of a scientific community.

In a citation network, a *main path* is the path from a source vertex to a sink vertex with the highest traversal weights on its arcs. Several methods have been proposed to extract main paths from the network of traversal weights. The method we follow here consists of choosing the source vertex (or vertices) incident with the arc(s) with the highest weight, selecting the arc(s) and the head(s) of the arc(s), and repeating this step until a sink vertex is reached. In the example of Figure 105, the main paths start with vertex v1 and vertex v5 because both source vertices are incident with an arc carrying a traversal weight of 0.25. Both arcs point toward vertex v6, which is the next vertex on the main paths. Then, the paths proceed either to vertex v2 and on to vertex v4 or directly from vertex v6 to vertex v4. We find several main paths, but they lead to the same sink, so we conclude that the network represents one research tradition.

A *main path component* is extracted in a way which is similar to the slicing procedure used for *m*-slices (Chapter 5). Choose a cutoff value between zero and 1, and remove all arcs from the network with traversal weights below this value. The components in the extracted networks are called main path components. Usually, we look for the lowest cutoff value that yields a component that connects at least one source vertex to one sink vertex. This value is equal to the lowest traversal weight on the main paths. In our example, this cutoff value is 0.25 and we obtain a main path component that includes all articles except v3, which is a marginal article in the research tradition represented by this data set.

Of course, article v3 may be very important in another research tradition. The choice of the articles to be included in the data set restricts the number and size of research traditions that can be found. Like a genealogy, a citation network is virtually endless so it cannot be captured entirely in a research project. The researcher has to set limits to the data collection, but this should be based on sound substantive arguments.

Application

In Chapters 3 and 7, we discussed the commands for detecting components, bi-components, and *k*-cores, which identify cohesive subgroups in a network. In principle, a citation network is directed and acyclic, so you should search weak components instead of strong components and find *k*-cores on input and output ties (command *All* in the *Net>Partitions>Core* submenu).

Net>Partitions> Core>All

Main path analysis is very easy in Pajek. The commands in the *Net> Citation Weights* submenu compute the traversal weights for lines and vertices in an acyclic network. There are three commands: *Search Path Count (SPC)*, *Search Path Link Count (SPLC)*, and *Search Path Node Pair (SPNP)*. The *Search Path Count (SPC)* command counts the paths between all source and sink vertices as explained above. The *Search Path Link Count (SPLC)* command traces paths from all vertices to the sink vertices. In the latter procedure, citations of early articles receive lower weights because they cannot be part of paths emanating from later articles, so we advise to use it only in special cases where early articles are relatively unimportant. In the *Search Path Node Pair (SPNP)* command, each vertex is considered as a source and as a sink. As a result, vertices and edges in the middle will receive higher traversal weights.

Net>Citation Weights

There are several ways of normalizing the traversal weights of lines and vertices in a citation network. Above, we discussed the normalization according to flow (*Net>Citation Weights>Normalization of Weights>Normalize–Flow*) for the *Search Path Count* method: the number of paths that include a line or vertex divided by the total number of paths between sources and sinks. This normalization yields the percentage of all paths between sinks and sources that include a vertex or line and it is the recommended normalization. Other options include dividing the number of paths containing a vertex or line by the maximum found among the vertices or lines (option *Normalize–Max*), which is useful when all traversal weights according to flow are low, and taking the logarithm of the number of paths containing a vertex or line before dividing it by the highest (log) score found (option *Logarithmic Weights*), which is useful when the variation among traversal weights are very high. Finally, it is possible not to normalize the raw counts (option *Without Normalization*). Note, however, that normalization does not affect the main paths that are retrieved from the citation network. It merely changes the range and variation among transversal weights.

Net>Citation Weights> Normalization of Weights

The traversal weights of the papers (the original vertices) are stored in a vector and the weights of the citations (lines) are saved as line values in a new network (labeled "Citation weights"), which can be inspected with the *Info>Network>Line Values* command.

Info>Network> Line Values

Table 22. *Traversal Weights in the Centrality Literature Network*

Line Values	Frequency	Freq%	CumFreq	CumFreq%
(.... 0.0000]	90	14.68	90	14.68
(0.0000 .... 0.0515]	465	75.86	555	90.54
(0.0515 .... 0.1030]	45	7.34	600	97.88
(0.1030 .... 0.1545]	8	1.31	608	99.18
(0.1545 .... 0.2059]	2	0.33	610	99.51
(0.2059 .... 0.2574]	2	0.33	612	99.84
(0.2574 .... 0.3089]	0	0.00	612	99.84
(0.3089 .... 0.3604]	0	0.00	612	99.84
(0.3604 .... 0.4118]	1	0.16	613	100.00
TOTAL	613	100.00		

When we apply the *Search Path Count (SPC)* command to the centrality literature network, about 90 percent of the lines have a traversal weight of 0.05 or less and thirteen lines have a value exceeding 0.103 (Table 22: be sure the network labeled "Citation weights (SPC)" is selected in the drop-down menu when you execute the *Info>Network>Line Values* command and request #9 clusters). Clearly, one citation is very important to the development of the centrality literature: it has an extremely high traversal weight of 0.41. This is the citation of Bavelas' 1948 article by Leavitt in 1951. Bavelas (1948) and Leavitt (1951), as well as Freeman (1979) and Flament (1963) are the vertices with the highest traversal weights. These are the crucial articles in the centrality literature.

The *Citation Weights* commands automatically identify the main paths in the citation network. The commands create a partition identifying the vertices on the main paths (cluster one) in the original citation network and they produce a new network that contains the main paths (labeled "Main path"). In the centrality literature, the main paths start with Bavelas (1948), proceed to Leavitt (1951), and, finally, end with Freeman (1977 and 1979), see Figure 106.

Net>Transform> Remove> lines with value> lower than

The lowest traversal weight of the arcs in the main path is 0.05, but it is interesting to use a slightly lower cutoff value to obtain the main path component here. Let us delete all arcs with traversal weights lower than 0.03. This can be done with the *Remove>lines with value>lower than* command in the *Net>Transform* submenu. Now, determine the weak components of minimum size 2 with the *Net>Components>Weak* command. The network contains two weak components, one large component

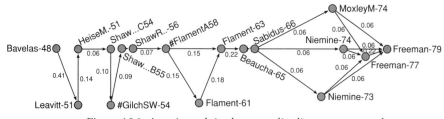

Figure 106. A main path in the centrality literature network.

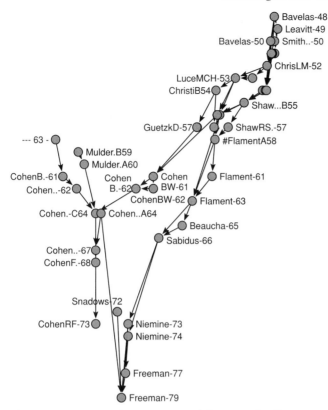

Figure 107. Main path component of the centrality literature network (not all names are shown here).

with forty-six articles and a small component with three articles by Lawson and Burgess and eighty isolated vertices.

Let us concentrate on the largest component and extract it with the *Operations>Extract from Network>Partition* command, using the citation network with lines of minimum value 0.03 and the partition according to weak components. If we also extract the publication years of the forty-six articles in this component from the publication years partition (`centrality_literature_year.clu`) – select this partition as the first partition and the weak components partition as the second partition in the *Partitions* menu, and extract the first weak component (class 1) with the *Partitions>Extract Second from First* command – we can draw this component into layers.

The resulting sociogram may look like Figure 107 if we optimize it with the *Layers>Averaging x coordinate* command (*Forward* or *Backward*). This figure reveals that the literature on network centrality was split into two lines between 1957 and 1979. One line was dominated by Cohen and the other by Flament and Nieminen. In 1979, Freeman integrated both lines in his classic article.

Mutual references among articles appearing at approximately the same time (e.g., two 1954 articles by Gilch in the original centrality network) or erroneous references to later articles by mistakes during data collection

*Operations>
Extract from
Network>
Partition*

*Partitions>
Extract Second
from First*

*Layers>
Averaging x
coordinate*

*Operations>
Transform>
Direction>
Lower→Higher*

and coding may prevent the citation network from being acyclic. Then, the *Citation Weights* commands issue a warning and stop; the network must first be made acyclic. References to later publications can be removed with the *Operations>Transform>Direction>Lower→Higher* command (do not delete lines within clusters) provided that the partition according to publication dates was selected in the Partition drop-down menu.

Net>
Components>
Strong

In the centrality literature network, however, this solution did not work because both articles by Gilch appeared in 1954. In this case, we had to merge the articles. We computed the strong components of minimum size 2 (*Net>Components>Strong*) because they contain cyclically connected vertices in a directed network (see Chapter 10). We shrank each strong component to one vertex in a new network with the *Operations>Shrink Network>Partition* command selecting zero as the class that should not be shrunk because that class contained the vertices outside the strong components. We removed the loops with the *Net>Transform>Remove>loops* command to obtain an acyclic network that allows the computation of citation weights.

Operations>
Shrink
Network>
Partition

Net>Transform>
Remove>loops

11.7   Summary

This was the last chapter that presented methods that cope with the dynamics of time in network analysis. Over time, social relations branch off into a gamut of independent strands. Kinship relations, for instance, create family trees that expand rapidly over generations. Sometimes, however, these strands merge after some time, for instance, people with common ancestors marry. This is called structural relinking, which is a measure of social cohesion over time. A social system with much relinking is relatively cohesive because relinking shows that people are oriented toward members of their own group or family.

In a genealogy, the amount of structural relinking can be assessed provided that we use a special kind of network: the P-graph. In contrast to an Ore graph, which represents each person by a vertex, parenthood by arcs, and marriage by (double) lines, couples and bachelors are vertices and individuals are arcs in a P-graph. Because symmetric marriages and parallel mother–child and father–child arcs are not represented by lines in the P-graph, each bi-component is an instance of structural relinking.

Methods for analyzing citation networks handle the time factor in a slightly different way. Here, we want to identify the publications that are the crucial links in the literature on a particular topic. Scientific articles contain knowledge, and citations indicate how knowledge flows through a scientific community. Each flow follows a path of citations and citations that occur in many paths are important to the transmission of knowledge: they have high traversal weights. Citations with high traversal weights are linked into main paths, which represent the main lines of development in a research area. The articles and authors connected by citations of some minimum traversal weight constitute main path components, which are hypothesized to identify scientific specialties or subspecialties.

11.8 Questions

1. The Ore graph depicted below shows part of the family ties of Louis XIII, king of France (1601–43). Calculate the remove of his relation with Henrietta Anne Stuart.

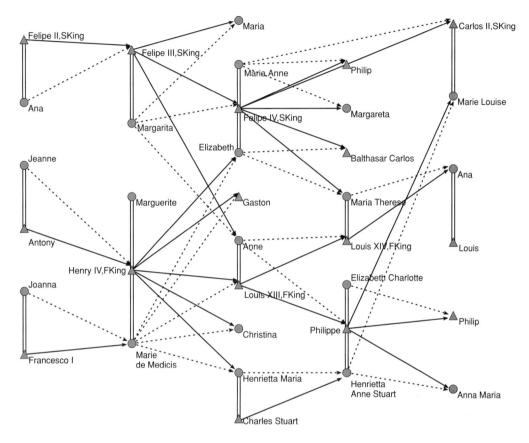

2. Which people constitute the family of orientation of Louis XIII and what is his family of procreation?
3. What is a generation jump? Indicate one in the Ore graph of Question 1.
4. Draw a P-graph that contains the same information as the Ore graph of Question 1.
5. How can we distinguish between a blood marriage and a relinking nonblood marriage in a P-graph? Give an example of both types of relinking in the genealogy of Louis XIII.
6. Explain why the relinking index of a tree is zero.
7. List all paths from sources to sinks in Figure 105 and show that the citation weight of the arc from v2 to v4 is correct.
8. Identify the source and sink vertices, the paths between them, and the traversal weight of the arcs in the citation network depicted below. What is the main path?

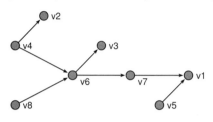

11.9   Assignment 1

The GEDCOM file Isle_of_Man.ged contains the combined genealogies of approximately twenty families from the British Isle of Man. Describe the overall structure of this network and the sections with structural
relinking. Which types of relinking do occur?

11.10   Assignment 2

Publications and citations pass on scientific knowledge and traditions, so
do advisors to their students. The file PhD.net contains the ties between
Ph.D. students and their advisors in theoretical computer science; each
arc points from an advisor to a student. The partition PhD_year.clu
contains the (estimated) year in which the Ph.D. was obtained. Search
for separate research traditions in this network and describe how they
evolve.

11.11   Further Reading

- The genealogical data of the Ragusan nobility example were
  coded from the Ph.D. thesis of Irmgard Mahnken (1960): *Das
  Ragusanische Patriziat des XIV. Jahrhunderts*. For an analysis of
  a part of the genealogy, see V. Batagelj, "Ragusan families marriage networks" [in: A. Ferligoj and A. Kramberger (Eds.), *Developments in Data Analysis* (Ljubljana: FDV, 1996, 217–28)] and
  P. Doreian, V. Batagelj, A. Ferligoj, "Symmetric-acyclic decom-
  positions of networks" [in *Journal of Classification* 17 (2000),
  3–28].
- For the collection and storage of genealogical data, we advise
  to use the GEDCOM 5.5 standard (http://www.gendex.com/
  gedcom55/55gcint.htm). Good free software is the Genealogical Information Manager, available at http://www.mindspring.
  com/~dblaine/gimhome.html, and Personal Ancestral File, which
  is produced and distributed by the Church of Jesus Christ
  of Latter-day Saints (www.familysearch.org). This organization
  compiles a large database of genealogical information from
  which downloads can be made. The genealogies from the Isle
  of Man (Assignment 1) were downloaded from http://www.isle-
  of-man.com/interests/genealogy/gedcom/index.htm.

- The P-graph was presented by D. R. White and P. Jorion in "Representing and analyzing kinship: A network approach" [in: *Current Anthropology* 33 (1992), 454–62] and in "Kinship networks and discrete structure theory: Applications and implications" [in *Social Networks* 18 (1996), 267–314].

- For additional reading on the analysis of kinship relations in the social sciences, we refer to T. Schweizer and D. R. White, *Kinship, Networks, and Exchange* (Cambridge: Cambridge University Press, 1998).

- The centrality literature example was taken from N. P. Hummon, P. Doreian, and L. C. Freeman, "Analyzing the structure of the centrality-productivity literature created between 1948 and 1979". In: *Knowledge-Creation Diffusion Utilization* 11 (1990), 459–80. The different types of main path analysis stem from N. P. Hummon and P. Doreian, "Connectivity in a citation network: The development of DNA theory." In: *Social Networks* 11(1989), 39–63. E. Garfield's *Citation Indexing: Its Theory and Application in Science, Technology, and Humanities* (New York: Wiley, 1979) is a classic text on citation analysis.

11.12   Answers

Answers to the Exercises

I. You should realize that a surname was passed on from father to child in Ragusa. Mother–child ties and marriages do not matter (we are only concerned with the name given at birth). Therefore, you should eliminate all marriages and mother–child ties from the Gondola_Petrus.ged data. This can be done easily if you open the GEDCOM file with the option *Options>Read/Write>Ore: 1-male, 2-Female links* selected. In this network, you can remove the marriages by deleting all lines (*Net>Transform>Remove>all edges*) and you can delete all mother–child ties by removing lines with a value of 2 (choose *Net>Transform>Remove>lines with value>higher than* and enter 1 as the upper limit).

In the resulting network, the descendants of Petrus Gondola are all people who received his surname. Identify them with the *k-Neighbours>Output* command (Petrus Gondola has a vertex number of 94) and extract them from the network with the *Operations> Extract from Network>Partition* command (in the dialog boxes enter 0 and 3, respectively), making sure that the *k*-neighbors partition is selected in the partition drop-down menu. If you determine the genealogical depth partition of the new network (*Net>Partitions> Depth>Genealogical*), draw it in layers (*Layers>In y direction*), optimize it (*Layers>Optimize layers in x direction>Forward*), and rotate it 90 degrees (*[Draw] Options>Transform>Rotate 2D*) it should look like the sociogram that follows.

II. In the Application part of Section 11.4, you learned how to determine the bi-components in a P-graph (command: *Net>Components>
Bi-Components*), how to create a cluster from a bi-component in the
hierarchy of bi-components (*Hierarchy>Extract Cluster*), and how
to extract this component from the original P-graph (*Extract from
Network>Cluster*). In this way, you can obtain the subnetwork of
the small bi-component in the Ragusan nobility genealogy consisting
of five vertices. With the vertices relocated, this network may look
like the sociogram depicted below. From this layout, it is clear that
the marriages closing the semicycle are not blood marriages. Neither
Pasqua Merguncho nor Maria Proculo have a close common ancestor,
nor have Gregorius Proculo and Stana Merguncho. This structural relinking is an instance of repeated mariages between two families: the
Proculo and Mernuch/Merguncho families swap a son.

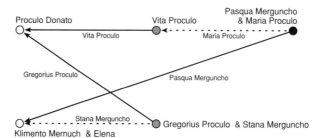

Answers to the Questions in Section 11.8

1. Louis XIII is the uncle (mother's brother) of Henrietta Anne Stuart, so she is a relative in the third degree if we restrict ourselves to blood relations. Louis XIII is also her stepfather, so the degree is 1 if we include marital ties.

2. The family of orientation of Louis XIII include his parents Henry IV and Marie de Medicis, his brother Gaston, and his sisters Elizabeth, Christina, and Henrietta Maria. Marguerite, the other wife of Henry IV, may or may not belong to the family of orientation. His family of procreation contains his wife Anne and their children Louis XIV and Philippe.

3. A generation jump in a genealogy refers to a relinking marriage that connects people of different genealogical generations, which are calculated from the point of view of their common ancestor. The marriage between Carlos II and Marie Louise creates a generation jump, because Carlos is a grandson of Felipe III and Margarita (second remove) and Marie Louise is the granddaughter of the daughter (Anne) of Felipe III and Margarita (third remove).

4. The P-graph should look like the following figure. Do not forget to draw different arcs for men and women and to reverse the direction of arcs.

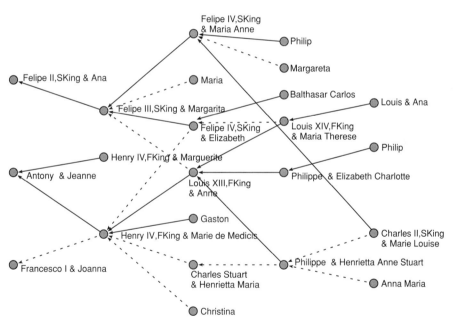

5. In a P-graph, the husband and wife involved in a blood marriage share at least one ancestor: there are two paths from the blood marriage to an ancestor, for instance, from Philippe and Henrietta Anne Stuart to Henry IV, king of France, and his spouse Marie de Medicis. Both Philippe and Henriette Anne Stuart are their grandchildren. A relinking nonblood marriage is a marriage between descendents of families that are already linked by intermarriage, for example, the Spanish king

Felipe III and the French king Henry IV are linked by two marriages among their children: Felipe IV and Elizabeth, Louis, XIII, and Anne. In a P-graph, this type of relinking is characterized by two semipaths (or one path and one semipath) between couples.

6. Structural relinking involves semicycles: vertices are connected by two paths or semipaths. Because trees contain no semicycles by definition, there is no relinking and the relinking index is zero.

7. The eight paths are as follows: (1) v1 → v3, (2) v1 → v4, (3) v1 → v2 → v4, (4) v1 → v6 → v4, (5) v1 → v6 → v2 → v4, (6) v5 → v6 → v4, (7) v5 → v6 → v2 → v4, and (8) v5 → v2 → v4. Four paths include the arc v2 → v4 (viz., paths 3, 5, 7, and 8), which is half of all paths, so the traversal weight of this arc is 0.5.

8. The source vertices are v4, v8, and v5; v2, v3, and v1 are sink vertices. There are six paths from sources to sinks as follows: (1) v4 → v2, (2) v4 → v6 → v3, (3) v4 → v6 → v7 → v1, (4) v8 → v6 → v3, (5) v8 → v6 → v7 → v1, and (6) v5 → v1. The arcs v4 → v2 and v5 → v1 are included in one of these paths, so their traversal weight is 1 divided by 6 as follows: 0.167. The other arcs are included in two paths, so their traversal weights are 0.333. There are four main paths: (1) from v4 to v3, (2) from v4 to v1, (3) from v8 to v3, and (4) from v8 to v1.

Part V

Roles

Cohesion, brokerage, and ranking are connected to social roles: being a member of a group, being a mediator, or being a superior. Each of these roles is associated with a particular pattern of ties. A blockmodel describes the social roles and associated patterns of ties in the network at large. Blockmodels offer a different perspective on the concepts discussed in previous chapters.

12

Blockmodels

12.1   Introduction

In previous parts of this book, we have presented a wide range of techniques for analyzing social networks. We have discovered that one structural concept can often be measured in several ways (e.g., centrality). We have not encountered the reverse, that is, a single technique that is able to detect different kinds of structures (e.g., cohesion *and* centrality). In this final chapter, we present such a technique, which is called blockmodeling.

Blockmodeling is a flexible method for analyzing social networks. Several network concepts are sensitive to exceptions, for instance, a single arc may turn a ranking into a rankless cluster (Chapter 10). Empirical data are seldom perfect, so we need a tool for checking the structural features of a social network that allows for exceptions or error. Blockmodeling and hierarchical clustering, which are closely related, are such tools.

Although blockmodeling is a technique capable of detecting cohesion, core-periphery structures, and ranking, it does not replace the techniques presented in previous chapters. At present, blockmodeling is feasible and effective only for small dense networks, whereas the other techniques work better on large or sparse networks. In addition, blockmodeling is grounded on different structural concepts: equivalence and positions, which are related to the theoretical concepts of social role and role sets. Blockmodels group vertices into clusters and determine the relations between these clusters (e.g., one cluster is the center and another the periphery). In contrast, the techniques discussed in previous chapters, such as the measures of centrality, compute the structural position of each vertex individually.

Blockmodeling uses matrices as computational tools and for the visualization of results. Therefore, we introduce the matrix as a means for representing social networks before we will proceed to the concept of equivalence and the technique of blockmodeling.

12.2   Matrices and Permutation

In social network analysis, matrices have been used in addition to sociograms for a long time. A matrix is an efficient tool for representing a

259

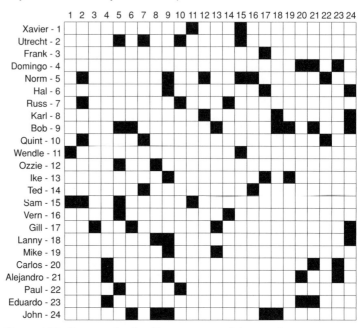

Figure 108. Communication lines among striking employees.

small social network and for computing results on its structure. In addition, matrices offer visual clues on the structure of small and dense networks, which is what we use them for in the present section.

A matrix is a two-way table containing *rows* and *columns*. The intersection of a row and a column is called a *cell* of the matrix. Figure 108 displays the matrix of the communication network of striking employees in a wood-processing facility (see Chapter 7). In this matrix, each row and column represent one vertex of the network, for instance, the first (highest) row and the first (left) column feature Xavier. The cells in this row or column show Xavier's ties. In Figure 108, a black cell indicates that Xavier communicates with another employee (or with himself) and a white (empty) cell means that there is no communication. Note that a matrix usually contains numbers, for instance, 1 for the presence of a tie and 0 if there is no tie. In Figure 108, we replaced the numbers by black or white squares to highlight the pattern of communication ties.

This type of matrix is called an *adjacency matrix* because we can tell from it which vertices are neighbors (adjacent) in the network, for instance, the black cells in the first row mean that Xavier (vertex 1) communicates with Wendle (vertex 11) and Sam (vertex 15). To be more precise, these black cells indicate that there is a tie *from* Xavier *to* Wendle and Sam. The row entry contains the sender of the tie and the column entry its recipient, so the first row contains ties *from* Xavier and the first column shows the ties *to* Xavier (e.g., from Wendle and Sam). It is not a coincidence that Xavier has the same neighbors in his row and column: the network is undirected, so Xavier's communication with Wendle implies that Wendle communicates with Xavier, and so on. An edge is equivalent to a bidirectional arc, so an edge is represented by two arcs in an adjacency matrix. In general, the adjacency matrix of an undirected network is symmetric around the diagonal running from the top left to the bottom right of the matrix, which is usually referred to as the diagonal of the matrix.

The adjacency matrix of Figure 108 contains no black cells on the diagonal because these cells represent the relation of a vertex to itself and the employees were not considered to communicate with themselves. Cells on the diagonal of an adjacency matrix often receive special treatment because they feature loops.

Because the same vertices define the rows and columns of an adjacency matrix, the adjacency matrix is square by definition. In contrast, a two-mode network such as the network of multiple directors in Scotland (Chapter 5), is represented by a matrix that is rectangular but not necessarily square. We can place the firms in the rows and the directors in the columns and still include all ties in the cells of this matrix because firms can only be directly related to directors. Such a matrix is called an *incidence matrix*. In an incidence matrix, diagonal cells do not represent loops.

The pattern of black cells in a matrix offers visual clues on the structure of the network because we see which lines are present (black) or absent (white). Just like a sociogram, however, a matrix discloses network structure only if its vertices are carefully placed. Figure 108, for instance, shows a seemingly random pattern of black cells. It does not reveal the structure of the network because the employees are listed in an arbitrary order. If we order them by their language (English or Spanish) and age (below or over thirty years), the black cells display a much more regular pattern (Figure 109). Now, it is easy to see that lines occur predominantly within the

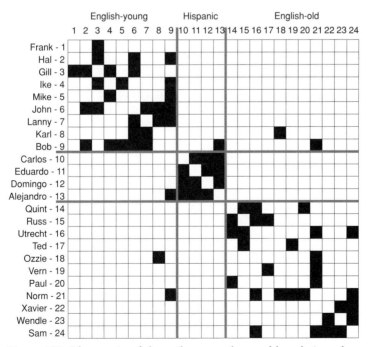

Figure 109. The matrix of the strike network sorted by ethnic and age group.

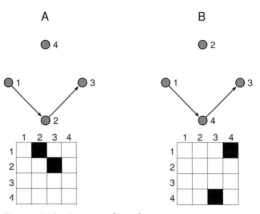

Figure 110. A network and a permutation.

ethnic and age groups: no more than three lines (Karl–Ozzie, Bob–Norm, and Bob–Alejandro) exist between the groups.

A reordering or sorting of vertices is called a permutation of the network. Essentially, a permutation is a list with an entry for each vertex in the network, specifying its new vertex number. In other words, a permutation is a renumbering of the vertices in the network.

A *permutation* of a network is a renumbering of its vertices.

If we assign new numbers to the vertices, the structure of the network does not change. Compare, for example, networks A and B in Figure 110. We exchanged the numbers of vertices 2 and 4, but this does not affect the structure of the network: networks A and B are *isomorphic*; that is, they have the same structure. In the matrix, we exchanged vertex numbers in the rows *and* the columns and we reordered the matrix obtaining a different matrix for the same structure.

The matrices look different but they describe the same structure. This means that we can represent the same network by a number of different matrices, just as we can draw many different sociograms for one network. A permutation rearranges a matrix just like an energy command redraws a sociogram. Therefore, we can use permutations to find matrices that reveal the structure of a network. Subsequent sections show how to do this.

The strike network permuted by ethnic and age groups (Figure 109) shows the pattern that characterizes cohesive subgroups: the black (nonempty) entries cluster around the diagonal of the matrix, where they form clumps. The clumps identify subgroups of actors who maintain ties predominantly within their groups. In our example, the clumps nicely reflect the ethnic and age groups.

Application

Because a matrix can represent a network, it is possible to store network data in matrix format. For small networks, a matrix is a traditional and useful alternative to the lists of arcs and edges that we have used so far as

```
                              1 1 1 1 1 1 1 1 1 1 2 2 2 2 2
                  1 2 3 4 5 6 7 8 9 0 1 2 3 4 5 6 7 8 9 0 1 2 3 4
        --------------------------------------------------------------
        Xavier    1.  . . . . . . . . . # . . . # . . . . . . . . . .
        Utrecht   2.  . . . . # . # . . # . . . # . . . . . . . . . .
        Frank     3.  . . . . . . . . . . . . . . # . . . . . . . . .
        Domingo   4.  . . . . . . . . . . . . . . . . . # # . # . . .
        Norm      5.  . # . . . . . # . . # . . # # . . . . . # . . .
```

Figure 111. Partial listing of the strike network as a binary matrix.

our format for network data files. Pajek can read data in matrix format, see Appendix 1, Sections 1.2 and 1.3, for details, which also discuss some disadvantages of the matrix format.

In Pajek, you can display the matrix of a network by double-clicking its name in the Network drop-down menu. In the dialog box that appears, enter a 1 if you want to display a binary matrix, that is, a matrix that tells only whether a line is present (#) or absent (.). Figure 111 shows part of the original strike network (included in the Pajek project file `strike.paj`) displayed as a binary matrix. Note that the listing consists of raw unformatted text, so it should be displayed in a fixed wide type font such as Courier. If you want to display the line values in the adjacency matrix, type a 2 in the dialog box to obtain a valued matrix. In a valued matrix, an absent line is represented by a 0 in the cell. *Network drop-down menu*

In Pajek, networks of 100 vertices or more cannot be displayed in this way, because they yield enormous matrices. Therefore, the options "binary" and "valued" are not available for larger networks, which are automatically reported as lists of arcs and edges. In these lists, each line represents a vertex, which is identified by its number and label followed by the numbers of all vertices which receive a line from it. This type of listing is also the third option ("Lists") for displaying small networks.

The raw text matrices are not suited for high-quality printing. To this end, the matrix can be saved with the command *File>Network>Export Matrix to EPS>Original* in PostScript format. Line values are automatically translated to the darkness of cells, as in Figure 108 and Figure 109. Larger networks can be exported in this way, but large matrices are usually not very helpful visualizations for detecting the structure of a network. *File>Network> Export Matrix to EPS>Original*

As we have argued, a matrix is usually more informative if it is reordered. In the example of the strike network, we must reorder the vertices according to their membership of the ethnic and age groups, which is available to us as a partition (`strike_groups.clu` included in the project file `strike.paj`). It is easy to derive a permutation from a partition such that vertices in the same class receive consecutive numbers: select the partition in the Partition drop-down menu and execute the *Make Permutation* command, which is located in the *Partition* menu. Pajek creates a new permutation assigning the lowest vertex numbers to the vertices in the first class of the partition, and so on. *Partition>Make Permutation*

The permutation is displayed in the Permutation drop-down menu of Pajek's main screen. You may inspect and edit a permutation in the usual ways. When you edit a permutation, you will see one line for each vertex containing two numbers. The first number is the new vertex number and the second number is the original vertex number. If a compatible *Permutation drop-down menu*

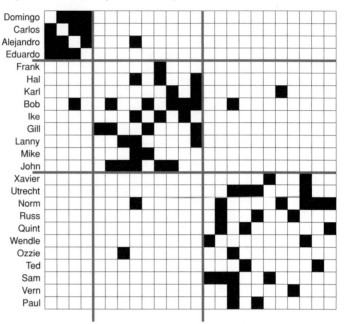

Figure 112. The strike network permuted according to ethnic and age groups.

network is active in the Network drop-down menu, the vertex label is also displayed.

File>Network>
Export Matrix to
EPS>Using
Permutation

When the network, the partition, and the permutation are selected in their respective drop-down menus, you can export the adjacency matrix to an Encapsulated PostScript file with the command *File>Network>Export Matrix to EPS>Using Permutation*. A dialog box prompts for a name of the file in which the matrix must be saved and another dialog box asks whether (blue) lines should be drawn between classes according to the active partition. In a viewer capable of reading PostScript (see Appendix 2), the result should look like that in Figure 112.

Operations>
Reorder>
Network

Operations>
Reorder>
Partition

The permutation of ethnic and age groups can also be used to reorder the network itself. If the network and permutation are selected in their drop-down menus, the *Operations>Reorder>Network* command creates a new permuted network. Display the reordered network as a binary matrix by double-clicking its name in the drop list and you will see that the four Hispanic employees have received vertex numbers from 1 to 4 (Figure 113). Note that the original partition according to ethnicity and age is

```
                                1 1 1 1 1 1 1 1 1 2 2 2 2
                    1 2 3 4 5 6 7 8 9 0 1 2 3 4 5 6 7 8 9 0 1 2 3 4
          -------------------------------------------------------------
Domingo   1.    . # # # . . . . . . . . . . . . . . . . . . . .
Carlos    2.    # . # # . . . . . . . . . . . . . . . . . . . .
Alejandro 3.    # # . # . . . # . . . . . . . . . . . . . . . .
Eduardo   4.    # # # . . . . . . . . . . . . . . . . . . . . .
Frank     5.    . . . . . . . . # . . . . . . . . . . . . . . .
```

Figure 113. Part of the permuted strike network displayed as a binary network.

not compatible with the permuted network but it can also be reordered: make sure that the original partition and permutation are active in their drop-down menus and execute the command *Operations>Reorder> Partition*.

12.3   Roles and Positions: Equivalence

In social theory, positions and roles are important and related theoretical concepts. A position, for instance, the position of being an instructor at a university, is usually connected to a social role or a role set, namely tutoring students and conferring with colleagues. It is hypothesized that this role or role set involves a particular pattern of ties and relations toward students, colleagues, and superiors. Sociologists, social psychologists, and other social scientists investigate the nature of social roles and role sets by observing interactions and by interviewing people about their motives and their perceptions of the roles they play.

In social network analysis, we concentrate on the patterns of ties. We want to identify actors that have similar patterns of ties to find whether they are associated with a particular role or role set, or we want to check whether people with similar role sets are involved in characteristic patterns of ties. In social network analysis, a *position* is equated to a particular pattern of ties. Actors with similar patterns of ties are said to be relationally *equivalent*, to constitute an *equivalence class*, or to occupy *equivalent positions* in the network.

Figure 114 offers a simple example illustrating these ideas. Two instructors (i1 and i2) within one department supervise three students (s1 to s3). They contact the students and they are contacted by the students. The instructors interact, so they are a cohesive subgroup and their interaction may cause them to behave in a similar way. The three students, however, do not necessarily interact. Nevertheless, they are in the same position with respect to the supervisors, hence they may act similarly toward them. They are relationally equivalent although they are not a cohesive subgroup. It is important to note that the external ties to members of other positions are just as important to the concept of equivalence as internal ties within a position.

Figure 114 is an example of a small core-periphery structure in which the two instructors constitute the core (one position) and the students the periphery (the other position). Ties occur predominantly within the core

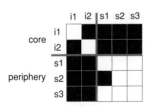

Figure 114. Hypothetical ties among two instructors (i) and three students (s).

and between the core and the periphery, so we see a horizontal and a vertical strip of ties in the permuted matrix.

So far, we have loosely described the concept of equivalence. Now let us define one type of equivalence formally, namely structural equivalence: two vertices are structural equivalent if they have identical ties with themselves, each other, and all other vertices. This definition implies that structural equivalent vertices can be exchanged with no consequences to the structure of the network.

> Two vertices are *structural equivalent* if they have identical ties with themselves, each other, and all other vertices.

In our example, in which arcs are either present or absent, let us compare the two vertices in the core (instructors i1 and i2). Clearly, the two instructors have identical ties to themselves and to each other: none of them communicates with himself or herself (no loops), and the tie among them is symmetric. In addition, their ties with vertices in the other position – the students – are also identical. If instructor i1 is connected to a student (e.g., student s2), then the other instructor is also connected to this student. As a consequence, the rows of the two instructors are identical, except for the cells on the diagonal because they are not supposed to contact themselves. The same is true for their columns, which represent the ties received by the instructors. We may exchange the two instructors without changing the structure of the network.

In general, we can say that vertices that are structural equivalent have identical rows and columns (except for the cells on the diagonal) in the adjacency matrix. With this in mind, it is easy to see that the three students in the periphery (s1, s2, and s3) are not completely structural equivalent because vertex s2 is related to vertex s1 but the reverse is not true, so they have no identical ties to each other. Student s3 is not related to s1, so he or she is not structural equivalent to s2.

Structural equivalence is based on the similarity or dissimilarity between vertices with respect to the profile of their rows and columns in the adjacency matrix. The dissimilarity of two vertices can be calculated and expressed by an index that ranges from zero (completely similar) to 1 (completely different). In Figure 114, the row and column of instructor i1 is perfectly similar to the row and column of instructor i2, so their dissimilarity score is zero (see Table 23). Students s1, s2, and s3 are not

Table 23. *Dissimilarity Scores in the Example Network*

	i1	i2	s1	s2	s3
i1	0.0000	0.0000	0.1875	0.1875	0.2500
i2	0.0000	0.0000	0.1875	0.1875	0.2500
s1	0.1875	0.1875	0.0000	0.1250	0.0625
s2	0.1875	0.1875	0.1250	0.0000	0.0625
s3	0.2500	0.2500	0.0625	0.0625	0.0000

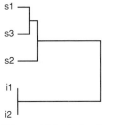

Figure 115. A dendrogram of similarities.

completely similar in this respect, so their dissimilarity score is larger than zero (ranging from 0.0625 to 0.125) but they are more similar to each other than to the instructors in the core (dissimilarities of 0.1875 or 0.25).

Knowing the dissimilarities between all pairs of vertices, how can we cluster vertices which are (nearly) structural equivalent into positions? This can be achieved with a well-known statistical technique, which is called *hierarchical clustering*. First, this technique groups vertices that are most similar. In our example, instructors s1 and s2, who are completely similar with respect to their ties, are merged into a cluster. Then, hierarchical clustering groups the next pair of vertices or clusters that are most similar and it continues until all vertices have been joined.

Figure 115, which is called a *dendrogram*, visualizes the clustering process. You must read it from left to right. First, instructors i1 and i2 are joined because they are perfectly similar: their dissimilarity is zero. Then, students s1 and s3 are joined (at dissimilarity level 0.06, see Table 23). In the third step, student s2 is added to the cluster of s1 and s3. Finally, this cluster is merged with the cluster of core vertices (i1 and i2) in the last step of the clustering process.

In the dendrogram, the length of a horizontal branch represents the dissimilarity between two vertices or clusters at the moment when they are joined, so you can see that the last step merges two very different clusters. If you want to partition the vertices into two clusters, you should separate instructors i1 and i2 from the students. In general, a hierarchy of clusters is split at the place or places where the branches make large jumps. In this way, you can detect clusters of vertices that are structural equivalent or nearly structural equivalent.

Application

Let us apply the concept of structural equivalence to the world trade network, which we introduced in Chapter 2. The Pajek project file `world_trade.paj` contains the network and a partition identifying world system positions in 1980. Figure 116 shows the matrix containing the countries with known world system position in 1980 (we extracted classes 1 to 4 of the partition from the network with the *Operations>Extract from Network>Partition* command). Line values indicate the gross value of imports of miscellaneous manufactures of metal; they are represented by the color of the cells in the PostScript matrix: higher values are represented by darker cells. The distribution of gross

Operations> Extract from Network> Partition

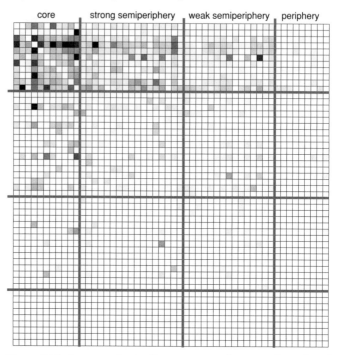

Figure 116. Imports of miscellaneous manufactures of metal and world system position in 1980.

imports is highly skewed because a couple of countries trade very high volumes of goods. We changed all imports over 1 billion U.S.$ to 1 billion to obtain slightly darker cells for trade ties with lower gross value. Note that these adjustments are made only for a better display of the matrix. We use the original trade network in the remainder of this section.

The network is directed, so the matrix is not symmetric although the values of imports are often in the same range as the values of exports. The matrix reveals some characteristics of a core-periphery structure that we have noted before: many and strong ties within the core and between the core and the semiperiphery but few and weak ties within the semiperiphery and the periphery. As a result, the ties concentrate in the horizontal and vertical strip which is associated with the core countries.

Cluster>Create
Complete
Cluster

Now, let us calculate the dissimilarity of the rows and columns of the countries in the original trade network. First, we must make a preliminary step. The dissimilarity method is computationally complex, so it should be used for small networks or for a small part of a large network. Therefore, the method requires that we indicate which vertices it should use. We must identify them in a special data object, which is called a *cluster*. In our example, we want to include all countries, so we create a cluster containing all vertices with the *Cluster>Create Complete Cluster* command. The total number of vertices in the network is shown by default in the dialog box issued by this command, so you may simply press the OK button. The cluster created by this command is listed in the Cluster drop-down menu and it can be edited in the usual way.

If you want to restrict your analysis to a part of the network, however, identify the vertices for which you want to compute dissimilarities in a partition and translate the desired class or classes from this partition into a cluster with the *Partition>Make Cluster* command. Dialog boxes will prompt you for the class number or range of class numbers of the partition that must be selected. For example, you may restrict the calculation of dissimilarities to the core countries of 1980 by translating class 1 of the world system positions partition to a cluster. In this case, the *Dissimilarities* command, which we discuss next, calculates dissimilarities for the core countries only but it takes into account the ties of the core countries to noncore countries.

Partition>Make Cluster

Because we need a network and a cluster to compute dissimilarities in Pajek, the *Dissimilarity* commands are located in the *Operations* menu. There are several dissimilarity indices but we present and use only the index *d1*. Consult a handbook on numerical taxonomy to learn more about the other indices (see Further Reading). The dissimilarity d1 of two vertices is simply the number of neighbors that they do not share (normalized to the interval 0–1). This index may be restricted to input neighbors (*Input*; the columns are compared) or output neighbors (*Output*; the rows are compared), or it may consider both input and output neighbors (*All*). Choose the *All* command unless you have good reasons for concentrating on input or output neighbors.

Operations> Dissimilarity> d1>All

Operations> Dissimilarity> Options> Report Matrix

The d1 dissimilarity index examines the neighborhoods of vertices, so it does not consider the values of lines. If you want the dissimilarity scores to reflect line values, you should select the Euclidean or Manhattan distance indices (d5 and d6). In the world trade example, using Euclidean or Manhattan distance would require structural equivalent countries not merely to export to and import from the same countries but, on top of that, have trade ties of comparable intensity. This, however, might be too harsh a criterion because the value of imports vary dramatically among countries. We therefore recommend the d1 index here.

Now execute the *Operations>Dissimilarity>d1>All* command. Pajek calculates the dissimilarities and reports them in the Report screen if the option *Operations>Dissimilarity>Options>Report Matrix* has previously been selected (note: do not select the other options in this submenu). The command stores the dissimilarities as line values in a new network, which you may list or print in the usual ways (see Section 12.2). Note that this network is directed and very dense because each pair of vertices that are not completely similar (hence: have a dissimilarity larger than zero) are connected by a pair of arcs. As a rule, do not attempt to draw and energize this network.

While executing a dissimilarities command, Pajek automatically tries to apply hierarchical clustering to the newly created network of dissimilarities. It prompts the user to specify the name of a file in which the dendrogram of the clustering is stored. The dendrogram is saved and not shown because it is in Encapsulated PostScript format. You can view it (Figure 117) with a PostScript interpreter (see Appendix 2) or print it on a PostScript printer. In addition, the results of the hierarchical clustering are saved as a permutation and a hierarchy.

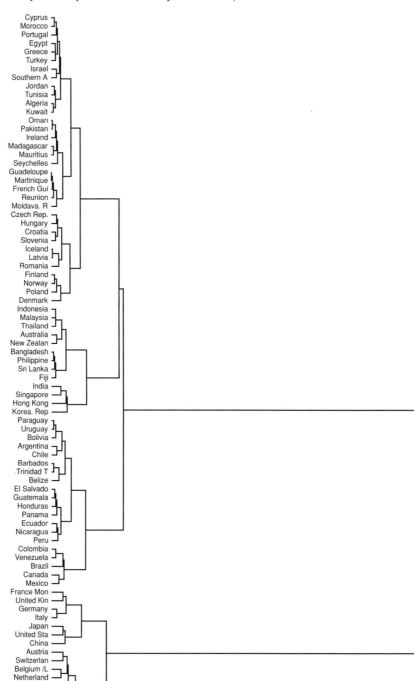

Figure 117. Hierarchical clustering of the world trade network.

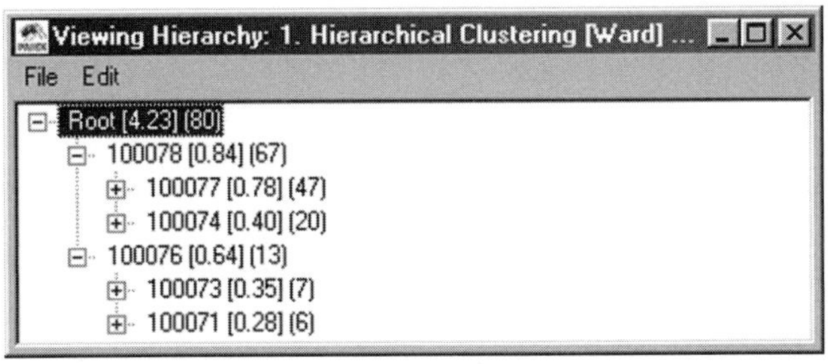

Figure 118. Hierarchical clustering of countries in the Hierarchy Edit screen.

The dendrogram of the world trade network, which is depicted in Figure 117, shows two very dissimilar clusters of countries in the world trade network: ten Western European countries, the United States, Japan, and China are clearly separated from the remaining sixty-seven countries, most of which are poorer countries.

This can also be inferred from the hierarchy created as a result of the *Dissimilarity* command, which is labeled "Hierarchical Clustering [Ward]." Note that "Ward" refers to the default hierarchical clustering method in Pajek. Other methods are accessible from the *Net>Hierarchical Decomposition>Clustering>Options* dialog screen. Open the hierarchy in an Edit screen (click on the button with the writing hand at the left of the Hierarchy drop-down menu) and expand the root as well as the next layer of clusters by clicking on them to obtain the listing depicted in Figure 118. The root unites the two principal clusters. The figures in square brackets tell you the dissimilarity of the clusters or vertices that are joined; a larger value means that they are more dissimilar. The cluster of thirteen countries is internally more similar (0.64) than the larger cluster (0.84), which corresponds to the fact that the first split within the larger group is more to the right than the split within the smaller group in the dendrogram (Figure 117). *(margin: Net> Hierarchical Decomposition> Clustering> Options / Hierarchy Edit screen)*

How do we know which countries belong to a particular cluster? We can find the names of the countries in the Hierarchy Edit screen in the following way, provided that a compatible network is active in the Network drop-down menu. First, make sure that the option *Show Subtree* is selected in the *Edit* menu of the hierarchy's Edit screen. Otherwise, Pajek displays only the names of the vertices that were added to the cluster in the present step of hierarchical clustering. Second, select a cluster in the Edit screen by left-clicking it and right-clicking it subsequently. In a new window, the numbers and labels of the vertices in this cluster and all of its subclusters are listed. If you apply this to the cluster labeled "100071," for example, you will see that it contains Austria, Switzerland, Belgium/Luxembourg, The Netherlands, Sweden, and Spain. *(margin: [Hierarchy Edit screen] Edit>Show Subtree)*

Hierarchical clustering gradually merges vertices into clusters and small clusters into larger clusters. Which clusters represent structural equivalence classes and which do not? Under a strict approach to structural equivalence, vertices with zero dissimilarity are structural equivalents. In real social networks, however, such vertices are seldom found, so we consider clusters of vertices that are not very dissimilar to represent structural equivalence classes.

Which vertices are not very dissimilar? There is no general answer to this question. It is up to you to decide on the number of equivalence classes that you want, that is, how many times you want to cut up the dendrogram, but you should always cut it from "right to left": separate the most dissimilar clusters first. In the world trade example, you should separate the thirteen rich countries from the other countries first. Then, you could make a subdivision within the latter cluster because these countries are more dissimilar (0.84) than the thirteen rich countries (0.64), and so on, until you reach the desired number of equivalence classes or further subdivisions seem to be arbitrary or meaningless.

Let us divide the trade network into four structural equivalence classes, because we have a partition into four world system positions (core, strong semiperiphery, weak semiperiphery, and periphery). We split the cluster of sixty-seven countries (dissimilarity is 0.84) and its largest subcluster (dissimilarity is 0.78). Now, we can create a partition from the hierarchy that identifies these four clusters. This is done in two steps.

[Hierarchy Edit screen] Edit> Change Type

First, we must close the clusters in the hierarchy that we want to split no further. Select a cluster by left-clicking it in the Hierarchy Edit screen and select *Change Type* from the *Edit* menu of the Hierarchy Edit screen or press *Ctrl-t*. Now, the message (close) appears behind the selected cluster. Repeat this for the other clusters that must be closed but do *not* apply it to any cluster that must be subdivided.

Hierarchy>Make Partition

Second, execute the *Make Partition* command from the *Hierarchy* menu in the Main screen. This command creates a partition in which each closed cluster is represented by a class. When you draw this partition in the original world trade network, you will notice that the equivalence classes represent a mixture of trade position and geography; the core countries, which are Western European countries, the United States, Japan, and China, are delineated from three regional positions: the Americas, Asia with Oceania, and Europe (including former colonies) with the Middle East.

File>Network> Export Matrix to EPS>Using Permutation

So far, we have discussed the dendrogram and the hierarchy created by the *Dissimilarities* command but not the permutation. The permutation is labeled "Hierarchical Clustering Permutation [Ward]" and it identifies the order of the vertices as represented in the dendrogram. When you want to print the matrix reordered by the results of hierarchical clustering, you can use this permutation. It is compatible with the partition that you created from the hierarchy, so you can obtain a matrix with blue lines indicating the splits that you have made in the hierarchy of clusters (see Section 12.2).

Exercise I

Apply hierarchical clustering to the strike network (Pajek project file `strike.paj`) and delineate the most likely clusters. To what extent do these clusters reflect the groups according to age and ethnicity?

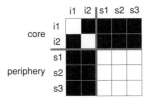

Figure 119. An ideal core-periphery structure.

12.4   Blockmodeling

In previous sections, we have drawn adjacency matrices with (blue) lines demarcating classes of vertices, for example, ethnic/age groups among the striking employees (Section 12.2), advisors versus students in a small example network, and world system positions of countries in the trade network (Section 12.3). By now, we should note that these lines divide the adjacency matrix into rectangles and these rectangles are called *blocks*.

> A *block* contains the cells of an adjacency matrix that belong to the cross section of one or two classes.

We can describe the structure of the network (within and between positions) by analyzing the blocks of the adjacency matrix. The blocks along the diagonal express the ties within a position. In an ideal core-periphery structure (e.g., Figure 119), vertices are linked within the core (vertices i1 and i2), whereas the peripheral vertices (s1 through s3) are not directly linked. The blocks off the diagonal represent the relations between classes, namely the relations between the core and periphery. The students derive their identity from their dependence on the instructors but not from their internal ties (instead, their identity is based on the absence of internalties).

12.4.1   Blockmodel

Adjacency matrices of networks containing structural equivalence classes have a very remarkable feature, namely their blocks are either complete or empty (null blocks), if we disregard cells on the diagonal. This results from the criterion of structural equivalence that equivalent vertices have identical rows and columns.

To understand this, imagine that there is one tie among the students of Figure 119, for instance from s2 to s1. Structural equivalent vertices must have identical ties to each other, so s1 must also be connected to s2. If all students are structural equivalent, s3 must have identical ties as s1 and s2, so it must be linked with s1 and s2. Now, the block is complete, except for the diagonal. This is also true for ties between positions.

Now that we know that the adjacency matrix of a network with structural equivalence classes contains only complete and null blocks, we may simplify the adjacency matrix by shrinking each class of vertices to one

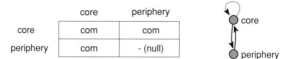

	core	periphery
core	com	com
periphery	com	- (null)

Figure 120. Image matrix and shrunk network.

new vertex (entry in the matrix) and mark the block type of each cell in the new matrix, which is either complete (com) or empty (– or null) in the case of structural equivalence. This shrunken matrix is called an *image matrix* and it contains all information that was present in the original adjacency matrix. Figure 120 shows the image matrix of a simple core-periphery structure and a graphical representation of the relations within and between equivalence classes (positions) in which an arc indicates a complete block and the absence of an arc signifies a null block.

A *blockmodel* assigns the vertices of a network to classes and it specifies the permitted type(s) of relation within and between classes.

The image matrix is the last ingredient we need to define a blockmodel. A *blockmodel* for a network consists of a partition and an image matrix. The partition assigns vertices to equivalence classes and it divides the adjacency matrix of the network into blocks. The image matrix specifies the types of relations within and between the classes because it says which kinds of blocks are allowed and where they may occur. The blockmodel of the core-periphery structure of Figure 119, for instance, consists of a partition which assigns instructors i1 and i2 to one class and the three students (s1, s2, and s3) to another class and the image matrix specifying the relations between the blocks shown in Figure 120.

A blockmodel describes the overall structure of a network and the position of each vertex within this structure. In the example of the instructors and students, the image matrix shows the type of equivalence that applies to the network. This network contains structural equivalence classes because there are only complete and empty blocks. In addition, the image matrix reveals the core-periphery structure of the network because the complete blocks are arranged within one horizontal strip and one vertical strip. Class 1 represents the core, which is internally linked, and class 2 identifies the periphery. Finally, the partition tells us which actors are part of the core (the two instructors, who constitute class 1) and which actors belong to the periphery (the three students in class 2). A blockmodel is an efficient devise for characterizing the overall structure of a network and the positions of individual vertices.

12.4.2   Blockmodeling

Until now, we have assumed that we knew the blockmodel of a network, that is, the partition of vertices into classes and the image matrix specifying the permitted types of blocks. In a research project, naturally, we work the other way around: we have a network and we want to find the blockmodel that captures the structure of the network. The technique to obtain this blockmodel is called *blockmodeling*.

In general, blockmodeling consists of three steps. In the first step, we specify the number of classes in the network, for instance, two classes or positions if we hypothesize a simple core-periphery structure. In the second step, we choose the types of blocks that are permitted to occur and, optionally, the locations in the image matrix where they may occur. In the case of structural equivalence, for instance, we permit only complete and empty blocks to occur and we expect one complete block (the core) and one empty block (the periphery) along the diagonal. Finally, the computer partitions the vertices into the specified number of classes according to the conditions specified by the model and, if necessary, it chooses the final image matrix for the model. In this third step, the blockmodel is completed.

The first two steps define the image matrix: we fix the number of classes and the types of blocks (relations) but we do not yet know which vertices belong to a particular class and sometimes we do not know exactly which block type will be found in which part of the image matrix. That is settled in the third step. It goes without saying that we must have some knowledge or expectations about the network to choose an appropriate number of classes and to specify types of relations among classes that make sense. We should have reasons or clues for expecting a core-periphery structure and structural equivalence in the example of contacts between instructors and students.

Empirical networks, however, seldom match the ideal represented by the image matrix. Errors occur but they can be checked easily. Suppose you know which vertices belong to each class, then you can check whether each block of the adjacency matrix is of the right type according to the image matrix. In fact, you compare an ideal matrix (Figure 119) to the real matrix (Figure 114). In the case of structural equivalence, count the missing lines within the blocks that should be complete (none in this example) and count the number of lines that occur in the blocks that should be empty (one error: the arc from student s1 to student s2, see Figure 121) to obtain an error score that indicates how well the ideal matrix fits the real network.

In this approach, the third step of blockmodeling boils down to finding the partition of vertices into equivalence classes that yields the lowest error score, that is, that fits the ideal matrix best. First, the computer assigns vertices at random to the specified number of classes. Then, it calculates the error score of this solution by comparing the actual matrix to an ideal matrix represented by the image matrix. Next, it tries to decrease the

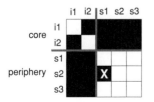

Figure 121. Error in the imperfect core-periphery matrix.

error score by moving a randomly selected vertex from one to another cluster or by interchanging two vertices in different clusters. It continues this process until it can no longer improve the error score.

This optimization approach to blockmodeling has the advantages and disadvantages of all optimization techniques (e.g., the *Balance* command) namely, if applied repeatedly, it is likely to find the optimal solution but most of the time you cannot be sure that no better solution exists. In addition, you must be aware that another number of classes or other permitted types of blocks may yield blockmodels that fit better. Usually, it is worthwhile to apply several slightly different blockmodels to the data set, namely with another number of classes or other constraints on the relations within or between blocks. This underlines the importance of careful considerations on the part of the researcher concerning the image matrix that is hypothesized. Moreover, trees are troublesome in exploratory blockmodeling because they contain many vertices that may be exchanged between classes without much impact on the error score, so apply blockmodeling only to rather dense (sections of) networks.

In this optimization technique, errors can be weighted and line values can be used. We do not go into details here, but it should be noted that lower error scores indicate better fit and an error score of zero always represents a perfect fit.

Application

As noted, blockmodeling consists of three steps. In the first two steps, the image matrix is specified: the number of classes and the types of blocks or relations within and between classes that are allowed. Then, the computer completes the blockmodel by searching the partition of vertices into classes that match the hypothesized image matrix best. If several image matrices are possible, it chooses the one which fits best. The error score shows how well the selected image matrix fits the network.

The blockmodeling commands of Pajek reflect these three steps. Before we discuss these commands, however, we must warn you that the method, like all optimization techniques, is time-consuming, so it should not be applied to networks with more than some hundreds of vertices, in which case the computer may need a full day to execute the command. For this reason the command is marked by a star in the menu.

Operations>
Extract from
Network>
Partition

In Pajek, there are two blockmodeling methods: one searches for the best fitting partition from scratch (*Random Start*), whereas the other only tries to improve an existing partition (*Optimize Partition*). Let us start with the latter method and apply it to the world trade network, using the world system positions in 1980 as the starting partition. Both files are available in the Pajek project file `world_trade.paj`. Delete the countries with unknown world system position in 1980 (*Operations>Extract from Network>Partition* classes 1–4, see Section 12.3) and remove them from the world system partition (selecting this partition as the first and second partition in the *Partitions* menu and extracting classes 1–4 with the *Extract Second from First* command). Thus, we have selected fifty-two of eighty countries.

Partitions>
Extract Second
from First

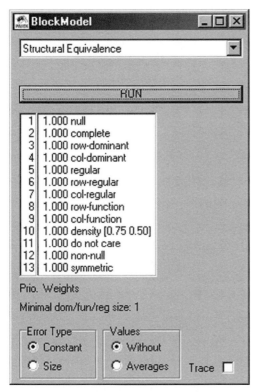

Figure 122. *Optimize Partition* dialog box.

Operations>
Blockmodeling>
Optimize
Partition

When you select the *Optimize Partition* command from the *Operations>Blockmodeling* submenu, the active partition specifies the number of equivalence classes you are looking for, which is the first step of blockmodeling. On selection of the command, a dialog box opens (Figure 122). The selection box shows the last selected type of equivalence. We want to apply structural equivalence so select this type of equivalence if the list box does not yet read "Structural Equivalence." Change none of the other options, just press the *Run* button to execute the command.

Pajek lists the initial settings in the Report screen, as well as the initial image matrix, the initial error matrix, and the error score of the initial partition. In our example, 366 initial errors are reported: in 366 (of the $52 \times 51 = 2652$) cells, imports are absent where they should be present and vice versa. By default, Pajek does not take into consideration line values, so it pays no attention to the value of imports here. Next, Pajek tries to improve the partition and creates the best fitting partition it has found and reports the final image matrix, the final error matrix, and the associated error score (see Figure 123). The optimal partition fits a little bit better than the world system positions in 1980 because the error score has decreased from 366 to 339. However, we do not know whether this is a small or large error score for a network like this and maybe another number of classes or other permitted block types would yield a better solution.

```
Image Matrix:

          1   2   3   4
      1  com com com com
      2   -   -   -   -
      3   -   -   -   -
      4   -   -   -   -


Error Matrix:

          1    2    3    4
      1    7   28   32   39
      2   36   50   55   28
      3    6   13   17   14
      4    0    0    1   13


Final error =      339.000
```

Figure 123. Output of the *Optimize Partition* procedure.

Note that the final image matrix has a very clear structure: the cells in the first row are all complete, whereas all other cells are empty. This means that every core country (class 1) exports miscellaneous manufactures of metal to all other countries but no other country exports these products in the blockmodel: their rows only contain empty (null) cells. The error score indicates that some of these countries do export miscellaneous manufactures of metal, but the blockmodel assumes that they are not.

Partitions>First Partition

Partitions> Second Partition

Partitions> Info>Cramer's V, Rajski

The best fitting partition is equal to the initial world system partition except for one country that has been moved from the core to the strong periphery. You may check this by selecting the initial partition and the new partition as first and second partition in the *Partitions* menu and execute the *Partitions>Info>Cramer's V, Rajski* command. Table 24 shows the cross-tabulation of the original (rows) and optimized partition (columns). Almost all countries are on the diagonal, indicating that they remain in their original class. Just one country moves from the first row (core) to the second column (strong semiperiphery).

Operations> Blockmodeling> Random Start

The second method searches for the best fitting partition without taking into account an initial partition provided by the user of the program. Therefore, no initial partition is needed for the *Random Start* command. The dialog box displayed by this command offers the possibility to specify the number of classes (step 1), the kind of equivalence or blockmodel (step 2), and the number of repetitions (see Figure 124). Each repetition uses a new, random partition as a starting point to avoid settling on a local optimum. Change these choices by clicking on the buttons and

Table 24. *Cross-Tabulation of Initial (Rows) and Optimal Partition (Columns)*

	1	2	3	4	Total
1 (core)	10	1	0	0	11
2 (strong semiperiphery)	0	17	0	0	17
3 (weak semiperiphery)	0	0	15	0	15
4 (periphery)	0	0	0	9	9
TOTAL	10	18	15	9	52

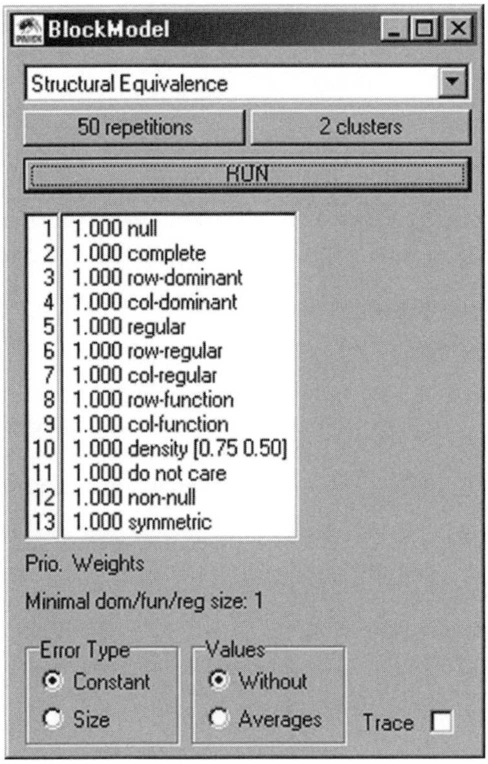

Figure 124. *Random Start* dialog box.

entering the required numbers, for instance, change the number of clusters to 4 (core, strong semiperiphery, weak semiperiphery, and periphery) and the number of repetitions to 100.

Applied to the fifty-two classified countries in the world trade network, looking for four clusters and structural equivalence, the *Random Start* command finds a partition with 281 errors. This is quite an improvement in comparison to the solution with the world system positions in 1980 as equivalence classes. Now, the procedure does not settle on the image matrix fitting the initial partition best (Figure 123) but it finds another image matrix (Table 25, note that you may get a permutation of this image matrix) in which countries of class 1 export miscellaneous manufactures of metal to all other countries except for the countries in class 3, whereas class two countries export to all other countries. Countries of classes 3

Table 25. *Final Image Matrix of the World Trade Network*

	1	2	3	4
1	com	com	—	com
2	com	com	com	com
3	—	—	—	—
4	—	—	—	—

and 4 are just importing and not exporting miscellaneous manufactures of metal.

Exercise II

Draw the image matrix that you expect to fit the strike network (strike.paj), using structural equivalence. Then, check your expectations by fitting a structural equivalence blockmodel to this network.

12.4.3   Regular Equivalence

Structural equivalence requires that equivalent actors have the same neighbors. In several applications of social network analysis, this criterion is too strict because it does not cluster actors who fulfill the same role in different locations, for instance, teachers at different universities, who have different students, so they have ties with similar people but not with the same people.

For these situations, another type of equivalence has been defined: *regular equivalence*. Vertices that are regular equivalent do not have to be connected to the same vertices, but they have to be connected to vertices in the same classes. This sounds like a circular argument but it is not. In the student government discussion network (Chapter 10), for instance, all advisors are expected to choose ministers for discussing student politics because they are supposed to advise the ministers. However, they do not have to advise the same ministers and they do not have to advise all ministers (e.g., advisor2 chooses minister1 to minister4 but advisor3 selects minister5 and minister7) (Figure 125). In reverse, each minister is supposed to use the services of at least one advisor but he or she is not obliged to take advice from all advisors. This is also true for ties within a class: if one minister selects another minister, each minister must select a peer and must be selected by a peer. One peer, however, suffices: they do not have to be related to all peers, so their block is not necessarily complete.

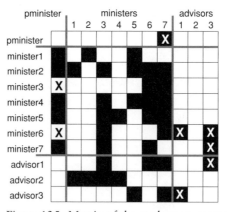

Figure 125. Matrix of the student government network.

We can detect regular equivalence by means of blockmodeling because there is a special block type associated with regular equivalence, which is called a *regular block*. A regular block contains at least one arc in each row (everyone selects at least one actor) and in each column (everyone is selected at least once). Regular equivalence allows regular blocks and null blocks. Note that a complete block is always a regular block, so structural equivalence is a special kind of regular equivalence or, in other words, regular equivalence is more general than structural equivalence.

A *regular block* contains at least one arc in each row and in each column.

In the student government network with three classes (one class for each formal position – see Figure 125), two blocks are regular: the choices of advisors among ministers and the choices among ministers. The block containing choices from ministers to the prime minister would have been complete (thus, regular) if ministers three and six had also chosen the prime minister. The two missing choices are represented by black crosses in Figure 125; they contribute two units to the error score of the regular equivalence model for this network.

In Figure 125, two blocks are empty: the choices from advisors to the prime minister and vice versa. The social distance between these two classes seems to be too large to be spanned by direct consultation. The remaining three blocks are neither null nor regular, so they contain at least one violation against the regular equivalence model. The number of errors is minimal if we assume these blocks to be empty, so all six choices in these blocks are errors (white crosses) and we assume that the ideal matrix contains null blocks here. In our image matrix, we merely specified that all blocks should be empty or regular. While evaluating the error score, we discover that it is least erroneous to expect empty blocks here. Thus, we fix the type of these blocks to null blocks.

Figure 126 shows the image matrix and the number of errors in each block (the error matrix), which summarize the results. Class 1 contains the prime minister, class 2 contains the ministers, and the advisors are grouped in class 3.

The student government discussion network is an example of a ranked structure that entails a particular location of block types. In a ranked structure, actors are supposed to choose up. If the ranks are ordered such that the highest rank is in the first rows (and columns) and the lowest rank occupies the last rows (and columns), we should not encounter choices

	image matrix					error matrix		
	1	2	3			1	2	3
1	- (null)	- (null)	- (null)		1	0	1	0
2	com	reg	- (null)		2	2	0	3
3	- (null)	reg	- (null)		3	0	0	2

Figure 126. Image matrix and error matrix for the student government network.

in the blocks above the diagonal of the matrix because they would point from a higher rank (rows) toward a lower rank (columns). Indeed, we find empty (null) blocks only above the diagonal in the image matrix of the student government network, which is a general property of a ranked structure.

Instead of using a particular type of equivalence to define the block types which are allowed, we may use any combination of permitted block types to characterize a network by specifying the type(s) allowed for each individual block, for instance, a complete block for the ministers to prime minister block, a regular block for the ministers themselves, and an empty block for the ministers to advisors block. This is known as *generalized blockmodeling*. Note that there are more block types than the three presented here. Some patterns of block types are known to contain classes of networks, namely core-periphery models and models of ranks. These classes have a particular substantive meaning, so it is easy to interpret them. In the near future further applications to empirical social networks will probably reveal more classes of blockmodels.

In exploratory social network analysis, we are mainly interested in detecting the blockmodel that fits a particular network. The blockmodel tells us the general structure of the network and the equivalence classes that we find can be used as a variable in further statistical analysis. But we should issue a warning here. We will always find a best fitting blockmodel, even on a random network that is not supposed to contain a regular pattern. Therefore, we should restrict ourselves to blockmodels that are supported by theory or previous results. We should start out with a motivated hypothesis about the number and types of blocks in the network. As in other cases of exploratory network analysis, we should try to validate the result, e.g., by linking the equivalence classes to external data, such as actor attributes. If equivalence classes of actors have different properties, tasks, or attitudes, this corroborates the interpretation that the blockmodel identifies social roles or role sets.

Application

*Operations>
Blockmodeling>
Random Start*

In Pajek, a blockmodel satisfying *regular equivalence* is found in the same way as a structural equivalence blockmodel (see the previous section): just replace structural equivalence by regular equivalence in the equivalence type drop-down menu (see Figure 122 and Figure 124). If we apply the *Random Start* blockmodeling procedure to the student government discussion network (available in the Pajek project file student_government.paj), we find eight solutions with seven errors (under regular equivalence with three classes and hundreds of repetitions). This is a minimal improvement in comparison to the solution with the formal roles as equivalence classes, discussed above, and it has the disadvantage that a choice must be made among seven alternative solutions. None of the solutions matches the formal roles but the image matrix resembles the image matrix in Figure 126 or one of its permutations.

Note that another number of classes and another type of equivalence may yield even better solutions, for example, we find four errors in regular equivalence solutions with two classes but the interpretation is difficult:

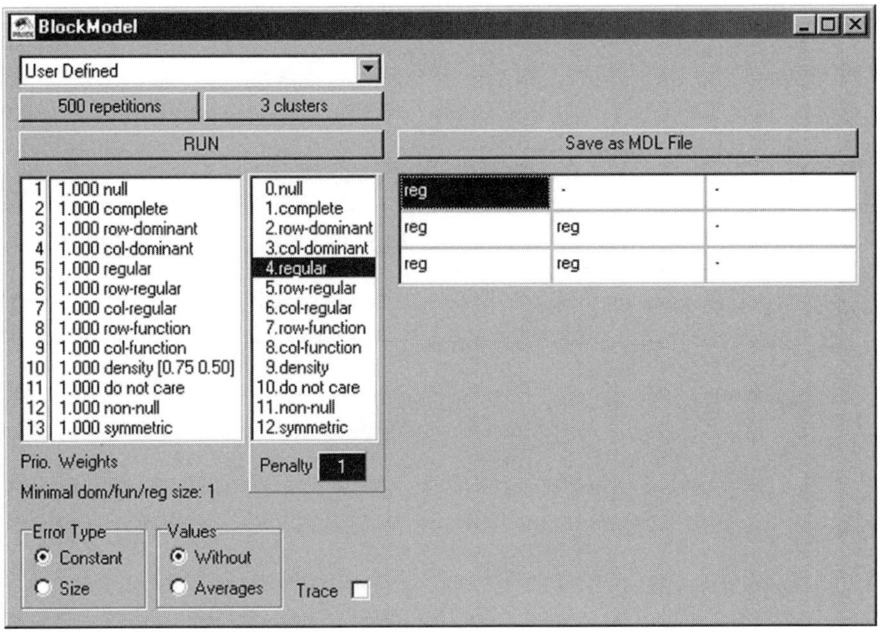

Figure 127. Assembling a blockmodel in Pajek.

in one solution advisor2 is separated from the rest of the network, which seems to be a trivial solution, and in the other solution, advisor1 and advisor2 are joined by minister4. Therefore, we prefer the original classification according to formal role within the student government.

In blockmodeling, the option *Structural Equivalence* tells Pajek that each block must be either complete (com) or empty (null). In regular equivalence, each block must be either complete, empty, or regular. The user has no control over the location of complete, empty, and regular blocks in the image matrix. In contrast, *generalized blockmodeling* offers the possibility of specifying (and fixing) the equivalence type of each block in the image matrix. For example, we may want to test whether a regular equivalence blockmodel matches the student government discussion network with three classes in which each class advices higher classes (if any) and all except the lowest class advice members in their own class.

The required image matrix is depicted in Figure 127 and it is shown underneath the "Save as MDL File" button if the *User Defined* option is picked in the selection box. If you click on one of the cells (blocks) of this matrix, a list is opened showing thirteen kinds of equivalence. In this list, you can select one or more (press the *Alt* key to add another choice) types of equivalence that you prescribe for the selected cell. In the example, five cells are forced to be regular equivalent and the remaining four cells must be empty. In addition, you may raise or lower the penalty of an error in the selected cell if you think that errors in one cell are more or less important than errors in another cell. Just click on the number after "Penalty" and enter a new number.

When you have defined your own blockmodel, you may save it for future use. Press the "Save as MDL File" button and enter a name for the file in which the model must be stored. By default, Pajek gives these files the extension .mdl (model) and we strongly advise using this file name extension. In another blockmodeling session, you can open this file by picking the *Load MDL File* option in the selection box. After loading the model, you can inspect it by selecting the *User Defined* option again. Finally, you can run the blockmodeling command.

The number of blockmodels that you can try to fit to a network is immense, especially when you design your own generalized blockmodels. Therefore, we advise the following strategy for exploratory blockmodeling: (1) use the results of other analyses and theoretical considerations to assemble an image matrix, (2) try stricter blockmodels and block types first (structural equivalence is more strict than regular equivalence), and (3) try a smaller number of classes first. Select the blockmodel with the lowest error score, but if a model with a slightly higher error score yields a single solution which is easy to interpret, you should prefer the latter.

Exercise III
Apply the generalized blockmodel described above to the student government discussion network and evaluate the results.

12.5   Summary

With this chapter, we conclude our book on social network analysis. The families of networks presented in previous parts of this book were reviewed once more: cohesive subgroups, core-periphery structures (brokerage), and systems of ranks. We presented a technique capable of detecting each of these structures, namely blockmodeling.

In the case of blockmodeling, we need a new representation for networks: the matrix. The adjacency matrix of a network contains its structure: each vertex is represented by a row and a column and arcs are located in the cells of the matrix: the first row and column belong to the first vertex, the second row and column to the second vertex, and so on. When sorted in the right way, the adjacency matrix offers visual clues on the structure of the network. Such a sorting is called a permutation of the network, which is actually a renumbering of the vertices.

Blockmodeling is not an easy technique to understand. Basically, this technique compares a social network to an ideal social network with particular structural features: a model. The researcher must suggest the model and the computer checks how well this model fits the actual data.

The model, which is called a blockmodel, contains two parts: a partition and an image matrix. The partition assigns the vertices of the network to classes, which are also called equivalence classes or positions. In the adjacency matrix of the network, the classes demarcate blocks: rectangles of cells. Blocks along the diagonal of the adjacency matrix contain ties within classes, whereas off-diagonal blocks represent relations between classes.

In the image matrix, which is the second part of a blockmodel, each cell represents a block of the adjacency matrix. It is a shrunk and simplified model of the adjacency matrix. If the vertices within a class are structurally similar – equivalent, we say – the blocks in the adjacency matrix have particular features: they are empty, complete, or regular, which means that there is at least one tie from and to each vertex in a block. More types of blocks exist but we do not present them here.

The image matrix shows which block types are allowed and, possibly, where to expect them. In addition, the distribution of nonempty blocks in the image matrix reveals the overall structure of the network. If the network contains cohesive groups, the nonempty blocks are found along the diagonal of the image matrix. If the network is dominated by a core-periphery structure, we find all nonempty blocks in one horizontal and one vertical strip in the image matrix. Finally, if there is a system of ranked clusters and the vertices are sorted according to their ranks, we find the nonempty blocks in the lower or upper half of the image matrix.

In exploratory blockmodeling, we search for the partition and image matrix that fit a social network best. Empirical social networks seldom match a blockmodel perfectly: arcs that should be present are absent or some absent arcs should be present. The number of errors expresses how well a blockmodel fits the network. This error score is used to evaluate different blockmodels for the same network.

Blockmodeling is a powerful technique for analyzing rather dense networks but it needs the right input from the researcher to produce interesting results. The number of blockmodels that may be fitted to a social network is large, so it is not sensible to embark on blockmodeling without clear conceptions of and expectations on the overall structure of the network. A researcher needs an informed hypothesis about network structure for a fruitful application of blockmodeling. In this sense, blockmodeling is used for hypothesis testing rather than exploration. Here, we reach the limits of the domain we want to cover in this book.

12.6   Questions

1. Below, one adjacency matrix and three sociograms are presented. Which adjacency matrix belongs to the sociogram?

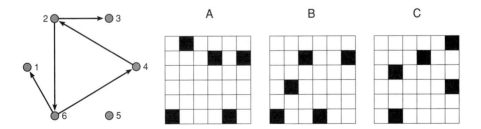

a. Matrix A.
b. Matrix B.

    c. Matrix C.
    d. Each matrix.
2. Which of the following statements is correct?
    a. An adjacency matrix may contain more rows than columns.
    b. An adjacency matrix is always symmetric with respect to the diagonal.
    c. An incidence matrix may contain more columns than rows.
    d. An incidence matrix is always symmetric with respect to the diagonal.
3. Of the three adjacency matrices in Question 1, which are isomorphic? It may help to draw the sociograms of the matrices.
    a. Matrices A and B.
    b. Matrices A and C.
    c. Matrices B and C.
    d. All three matrices are isomorphic.
4. Write down the permutation that reorders one matrix of Question 1 into another matrix of that question.
5. According to the adjacency matrix below, which vertices are structural equivalent?

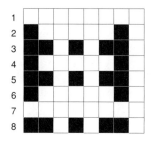

6. The dendrogram below displays the results of hierarchical clustering. Which equivalence classes would you make?

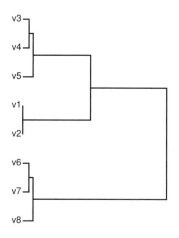

7. Which statement is correct?
    a. Regular equivalence allows for regular and empty blocks, but not complete blocks.

b. Structural equivalence allows for complete and empty blocks, but no kind of regular blocks.

c. Regular equivalence is a special case of structural equivalence.

d. Structural equivalence is a special case of regular equivalence.

8. Assign the vertices of the adjacency matrix depicted below to a minimum number of regular equivalence classes.

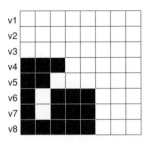

9. What kind of structure does the adjacency matrix of Question 8 represent?

a. No particular structure

b. Cohesive subgroups

c. A core-periphery structure

d. A system of ranks

12.7 Assignment

In Mexico throughout most of the twentieth century, political power has been in the hands of a relatively small set of people who are connected by business relations, family ties, friendship, and membership of political institutions. A striking case in point is the succession of presidents, especially the nomination of the candidates for the presidential election. Since 1929, each new president was a secretary in the previous cabinet, which means that he worked closely together with the previous president. Moreover, the candidates always entertained close ties with former presidents and their closest collaborators. In this way, a political elite has maintained control over the country.

The network `mexican_power.net` contains the core of this political elite: the presidents and their closest collaborators. In this network, edges represent significant political, kinship, friendship, or business ties.

Notwithstanding the fact that one political party (the Partido Revolucionario Institucional) won all elections in the period under consideration, two (or more) groups within this party have been competing for power. The main opposition seems to be situated between civilians and members of the military (`mexican_military.clu`: the military in class 1 and civilians in class 2). After the revolution, the political elite was dominated by the military but gradually the civilians have assumed power. The partition `mexican_year.clu` specifies the first year (minus 1900) in which the actor occupied a significant governmental position. All data are available in the project file `mexican_power.paj`.

Draw the network into layers according to the year of "accession to power" and use it to see when the civilians assume power. Use hierarchical clustering and blockmodeling to assess whether the political network consists of two (or more) cohesive subgroups and check whether these subgroups match the distinction between military and civilians or whether they cover a particular period.

12.8   Further Reading

- For an introduction to matrices, see Chapter 3 in J. Scott, *Social Network Analysis: A Handbook* (London: Sage, 1991), Chapter 3 in A. Degenne and M. Forsé, *Introducing Social Networks* (London: Sage, 1999), and Section 4.9 in S. Wasserman and K. Faust, *Social Network Analysis: Methods and Applications* (Cambridge: Cambridge University Press, 1994).
- M. S. Aldenderfer and R. K. Blashfield's, *Cluster Analysis* (London: Sage, 1984) offers a helpful introduction to hierarchical clustering. A comprehensive overview of (dis-)similarity measures can be found in P. Sneath and R. Sokal, *Numerical Taxonomy* (San Francisco: Freeman, 1973).
- Blockmodeling is explained in Chapters 9, 10, and 12 in S. Wasserman and K. Faust (see earlier reference) and in Chapter 4 of A. Degenne and M. Forsé (see earlier reference). For generalized blockmodeling, consult Doreian, Batagelj, and A. Ferligoj, *Generalized Blockmodeling* (Cambridge: Cambridge University Press, in press).
- The example analyzed in the assignment is taken from J. Gil-Mendieta and S. Schmidt, "The political network in Mexico." In: *Social Networks* 18 (1996), 355–81.

12.9   Answers

Answers to the Exercises

I. Create a complete cluster (*Cluster>Create Complete Cluster*) and determine the dissimilarities in the strike network (*Operations> Dissimilarity>d1>all*). The dendrogram is depicted below; inspect the hierarchy in the Hierarchy Edit screen if you have no PostScript viewer for the dendrogram. The largest split distinguishes between the eleven older English-speaking employees (Russ to Sam, cluster 100021 in the hierarchy) and the other employees (cluster 100022). The latter cluster is internally more heterogeneous than the former, according to their values in the hierarchy (3.58 versus 1.62). Therefore, the next great split occurs in the first cluster and it separates the young English-speakers (cluster 100020) from the Hispanic employees (cluster 100005). These two splits exactly yield the three age–ethnic groups. Further splits occur at a far lower level (more to the left in the dendrogram) and may be ignored.

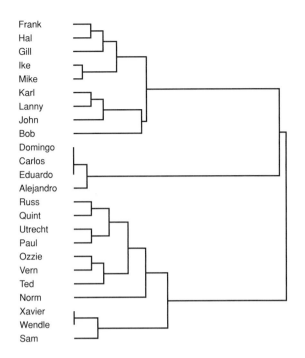

II. In previous analyses, we found three cohesive groups according to age and ethnicity in the strike network, so we may assume that there are three equivalence classes in the blockmodel. In addition, we may expect a cohesive group to be a complete block: everyone is connected rather than not connected to everyone else within the group. Links between groups are sparse, so we may expect off-diagonal blocks to be empty (null) rather than complete in the image matrix. The hypothesized image matrix is depicted below.

	1	2	3
1	com	—	—
2	—	com	—
3	—	—	com

Now, execute the *Operations>Blockmodeling>Random Start* command, choosing structural equivalence, three clusters, and a sufficiently large number of repetitions (some hundreds). Pajek finds two partitions with an error score of 56. Both are saved as a partition but none of them nicely delineates the three groups according to age and ethnicity. The final image matrix resembles the hypothesized image matrix except for the fact that the third equivalence class is internally not connected (null block) rather than completely connected. In the error matrix, we can see that most mistakes (thirty-eight of fifty-eight) occur here. The young and older English-speaking employees are simply connected too loosely to be recognized as a complete subnetwork (clique).

III. Following the steps outlined in the application part of Section 12.4.3, the special ranked generalized blockmodel can be constructed. Run this model many times on the student government discussion network and you will obtain two optimal partitions with seven errors each. The model fits the network just as well as the regular equivalence model computed in Section 12.4.3 but now there are just two optimal partitions compared to eight under the regular equivalence model. That is a step forward. Drawing the network and the partitions, we see that two advisors are placed in the third equivalence class, and the first class contains the prime minister and ministers three and seven. The results suggest a split among the ministers.

Answers to the Questions in Section 12.6

1. By convention, the first (top) row and the first (left) column represents the vertex with number 1. Vertex 2 is identified by the second row and column, and so on. The sociogram contains an arc from vertex 2 to vertex 3, so the cell at the intersection of the second row and the third column must contain an arc. In adjacency matrix B, this is the case so this is the only matrix which may represent the sociogram. Check the remaining arcs and black cells: they match. Answer b is correct.

2. Answer c is correct. In an incidence matrix, the rows represent actors and the columns contain the events to which the actors can be affiliated. The number of actors (rows) is not necessarily equal to the number of events (columns), so the number of columns may be larger than the number of rows (and vice versa). In an adjacency matrix, the rows as well as the columns represent all vertices in the network, so their numbers must be equal (answer a is not correct). The adjacency matrix of an undirected network is always symmetric with respect to the diagonal, but this is not necessarily so in the case of a directed network (answer b is incorrect). Finally, it is a coincidence and not a necessity if for each actor u who is affiliated to event v, there would be an actor v who is affiliated to event u. Incidence matrices are seldom symmetric (answer d is incorrect).

3. In matrices A and B, three vertices do not send arcs (their rows are empty), one vertex sends one arc, and two vertices send two arcs. These matrices may describe isomorphic networks. The vertices of matrix C,

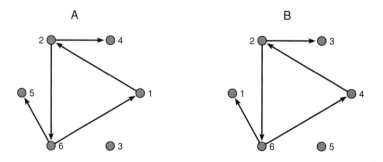

however, have different outdegree: one vertex has zero outdegrees and the remaining five have one outdegree. The network of matrix C cannot be isomorphic to the networks of matrices A and B. Are the networks of matrices A and B isomorphic? If we draw them, we can see that their structures are identical. Answer a is correct.

4. The permutation that transforms matrix A into matrix B can be read from the sociograms drawn in the answer to Question 3 (clockwise): vertex 2 remains vertex 2, 4 becomes 3, 1 becomes 4, 3 becomes 5, 6 remains 6, and 5 becomes 1.

5. Vertices with identical rows and columns are structurally equivalent. In the adjacency matrix, vertices 1and 7 are structurally equivalent, because their rows are empty and their columns contain six arcs send by the remaining six vertices. Vertices 2, 4, and 6 are also structurally equivalent, and this is also true for vertices 3, 5, and 8.

6. In the first step, vertices v6, v7, and v8 must be separated from the rest. Then, vertices v1 and v2 can be split from vertices v3, v4, and v5. At this stage, the dissimilarities between vertices within a cluster are low, so it is not sensible to further subdivide the three equivalence classes.

7. Answer d is correct. A complete block is also a regular block because each row and each column contains at least one entry (arc) within the block. Structural equivalence is a special type of regular equivalence (answer d). The reverse is not true (answer c is incorrect). Therefore, complete blocks are allowed under regular equivalence (answer a is incorrect) and a special type of regular block, namely the complete block, is allowed under structural equivalence (answer b is incorrect).

8. A regular equivalence block is regular (at least one arc in each row and column) or empty. The rows of vertices v1, v2, and v3 are empty, so their horizontal blocks are null blocks. No other vertex has an empty row, so we cannot add a vertex to this cluster because we would get blocks in the rows of these vertices that are not empty and not regular because not every row contains an arc. For similar reasons, we may cluster vertices v6, v7, and v8: they have empty columns. If we cluster the remaining vertices v4 and v5, we obtain a solution with three regular equivalence classes: (1) v1, v2, and v3, (2) v4 and v5, and (3) v6, v7, and v8. In the adjacency matrix with gray lines separating classes, we can easily check that each block is either empty or regular.

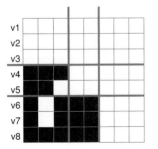

9. Answer d is correct because all entries are situated at one side of the diagonal, which means that vertices consistently choose up (or down). It is clearly not a structure of cohesive subgroups or a core-periphery structure because the blocks on the diagonal are empty.

Appendix 1

Getting Started with Pajek

A1.1   Installation

Pajek software for network analysis can be installed on all computers operating under Windows 95, 98, 2000, NT, or XP. The software can be installed on the computer's hard disk: double-click the file named Pajek.be.exe (Pajek book edition) and follow the instructions.

Pajek can be started by double-clicking the file Pajek.exe, which you will find in the directory where you installed the program. The subdirectory *Doc* contains additional information about the software in several hypertext files (.htm), which can be opened in an Internet browser, and Portable Document Files (.pdf), which can be read with (Adobe) Acrobat Reader.

A1.2   Network Data Formats

*File>Network
>Read*

Pajek can read network data in several plain text formats, that is, files containing unformatted text (ASCII). We briefly discuss them in the order in which they appear on the dialog box issued by the *File>Network>Read* command (Figure 128).

The first two data formats are indigenous Pajek formats: Pajek networks and Pajek matrices. The *Pajek network* format (the filename extension is .net) is explained in Chapter 1 (Section 1.3.1) and additional features for longitudinal networks are discussed in Chapter 4 (Section 4.5). Basically, it is a list of vertices followed by a list of arcs and edges. It is the most flexible format because it allows for multiple lines and many (layout) properties of the vertices and lines can be specified, which are explained in the file DrawEPS.htm on the book's Web site. The Pajek network format is in line with the logic of relational databases. See Section A1.3.3 for more information on organizing your network data as a relational database and exporting from database software to Pajek. There are three network formats: Arcs/Edges, ArcsList/EdgesList, and ArcsList/EdgesList (min). In Section A1.3, we discuss only the first type (Arcs/Edges) because it is most flexible.

The *Pajek matrix* format (with the filename extension .mat) is slightly different. The list of vertices is the same as in the Pajek network format

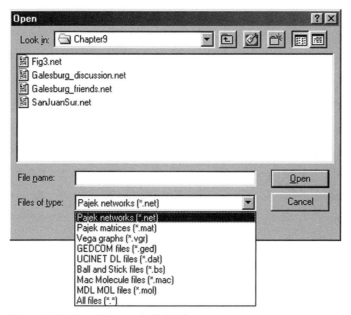

Figure 128. *Read Network* dialog box.

but the list of edges and arcs is replaced by a matrix consisting of integers or real numbers, which are separated by blanks (Figure 129). This is an ordinary adjacency matrix (see Chapter 12, Section 12.2). The Pajek matrix format is useful for importing network data in matrix format.

The third data format is the *Vega* format devised by Pisanski. The fourth format, *GEDCOM*, is the standard data format for genealogical data, which is discussed in Chapter 11 (Section 11.3, see also Further Reading). The fourth format, *UCINET DL files*, is the raw data format of another widely used program for network analysis: UCINET. Both UCINET and Pajek can read networks exported in this format, so this is the format for exchanging data between the two software packages. For more information about UCINET, consult the Web site http://www.analytictech.com/.

The last three data formats (*Ball and Stick*, *Mac Molecule*, and *MDL MOL*) were developed for chemistry. These formats are not widely used in social network analysis.

```
*Vertices      6
    1 "Ada"                   0.1646    0.2144    0.5000
    2 "Cora"                  0.0481    0.3869    0.5000
    3 "Louise"                0.3472    0.1913    0.5000
    4 "Jean"                  0.1063    0.5935    0.5000
    5 "Helen"                 0.2892    0.6688    0.5000
    6 "Martha"                0.4630    0.5179    0.5000
*Matrix
0.000 1.000 1.000 0.000 0.000 0.000
1.000 0.000 0.000 1.000 0.000 0.000
0.000 0.000 0.000 0.000 0.000 0.000
0.000 0.000 0.000 0.000 1.000 0.000
0.000 0.000 0.000 1.000 0.000 0.000
0.000 0.000 0.000 0.000 0.000 0.000
```

Figure 129. A network in Pajek matrix format.

A1.3   Creating Network Files for Pajek

There are several ways to create data files that can be read by Pajek. We distinguish between three methods: creating data files manually within Pajek, creating them in a word processor, and exporting them from a relational database. We present the methods in this order, from the simple and inflexible to the complicated and versatile.

A1.3.1   Within Pajek

Net>Random Network>Total No. of Arcs

In Pajek, you can create new networks, partitions, and vectors manually by means of a number of commands and tricks, which have been presented in the chapters of this book. Let us start with creating a new network. We suppose that you have the data on the vertices and lines at hand (e.g., on paper). Start Pajek and use the *Net>Random Network>Total No. of Arcs* command to create a new network (see Chapter 1, Section 1.4). Enter the desired number of vertices in the first dialog box and request zero arcs in the second dialog box because you are going to add the lines manually.

Partition>Create Null Partition

File>Partition> Edit

As a first step, add labels to the vertices so they can be identified more easily. Here, the trick is to create a new partition with the *Partition>Create Null Partition* command (see Chapter 2, Section 2.3) and then open it in an Edit screen (the *File>Partition>Edit* command, see Chapter 2, Section 2.3). The result may look like that in Figure 130. In this screen, you can manually edit the labels of the vertices. Now you have defined the labels of the vertices.

File>Network> Edit

Editing Network screen

As a next step, you must add lines to the network. This can be done in the Editing Network screen (Figure 131), which can be opened either from the Main screen with the *File>Network>Edit* command specifying a vertex number or label or from the Draw screen by right-clicking a vertex. Double-click the word *Newline* to add an edge (enter the number of the vertex that must be connected to the selected vertex) or an arc [enter the vertex number preceded by a plus sign (arc toward the selected vertex) or a minus sign (arc from the selected vertex)]. This is discussed in more detail in Chapter 1, Section 1.4.

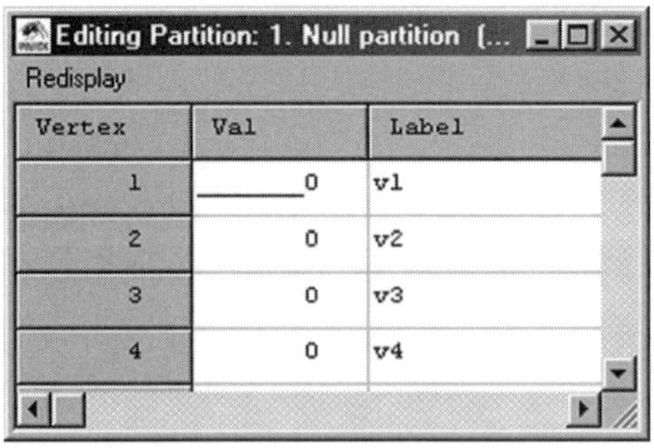

Figure 130. Editing vertex labels.

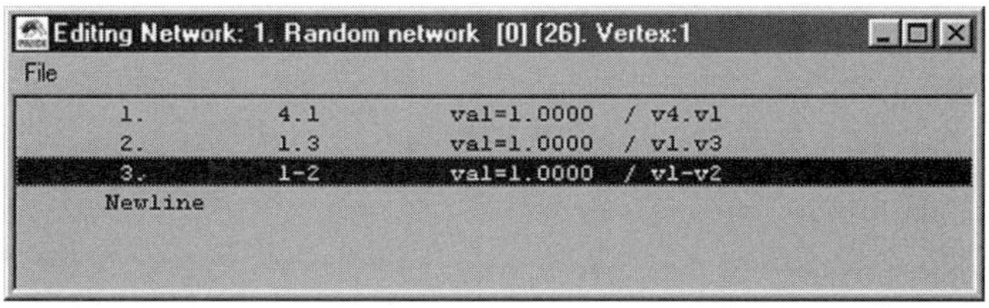

Figure 131. Edit Network screen.

If you have a discrete characteristic of the vertices (e.g., the sex of persons), you can store this in a new partition. Create a new empty partition and open it in an Edit screen as discussed above. Then give each person (vertex) the appropriate sex code in the Edit Partition screen. Just enter the right code in the "Val" column (see Figure 130 and Chapter 2, Section 2.3). Note that Pajek accepts only numerical codes. As an alternative, you can draw the network with a new empty partition by executing the *Draw>Draw-SelectAll* command (see Chapter 2, Section 2.3). Now, you can respectively raise and lower the class associated with a vertex by left-clicking the vertex while pressing the *Shift* key, which is equivalent to clicking with the middle mouse button, or left-clicking it while holding down the *Alt* key (see Chapter 2, Section 2.3).

File>Partition>Edit

Draw>Draw-SelectAll

Change the class number of vertices

Vectors, which specify continuous characteristics of vertices, may be created in a similar way. Create a new vector with the *Vector>Create Identity Vector* command and edit it manually in the Editing Vector screen, which opens on execution of the *File>Vector>Edit* command. Initially, all vertices have one as their vector value. You can manually change it to the desired number.

Vector>Create Identity Vector

File>Vector>Edit

Don't forget to save the data files before you exit from Pajek, otherwise your work will be lost. Pajek does not save data files automatically. Save the data files by means of the diskette button to the left of the drop-down menus or with the *Save* command in the appropriate submenu of the *File* menu: *Network*, *Partition*, or *Vector*. You can save the network in any of Pajek's formats as well as in UCINET's DL format.

File>Network>Save

File>Partition>Save

File>Vector>Save

A1.3.2 Word Processor

It is possible to create a network data file in Pajek, but adding lines by means of the Editing Network screen (Figure 131) is quite tedious. Usually, it is more efficient to create a network with the right number of vertices but without lines in Pajek with the *Net>Random Network>Total No. of Arcs* command and to change vertex labels and add lines in a word processor. Note: never use tabs!

Net>Random Network>Total No. of Arcs

Figure 132 shows an empty network consisting of six vertices, which was created with the *Net>Random Network>Total No. of Arcs* command and saved from Pajek as a Pajek Arcs/Edges network file. It is a plain text file so it can be opened in any word processor (e.g., NotePad and WordPad). Its first line specifies the number of vertices. This number may never be lower than the highest vertex number in the network.

```
*Vertices        6
         1  "v1"           0.1000    0.5000    0.5000
         2  "v2"           0.3000    0.1536    0.5000
         3  "v3"           0.7000    0.1536    0.5000
         4  "v4"           0.9000    0.5000    0.5000
         5  "v5"           0.7000    0.8464    0.5000
         6  "v6"           0.3000    0.8464    0.5000
*Arcs
```

Figure 132. An empty network in Pajek Arcs/Edges format.

The first line is followed by the list of vertices: each vertex has one line containing the vertex number (here: 1 to 6), the vertex label, which is the letter *V* followed by a number by default, and the *x*, *y*, and *z* coordinates of the vertex in a layout. In a word processor, you can easily change these properties of the vertices but it is wise not to meddle with the vertex numbers even though Pajek allows vertices to be out of order or some vertex numbers to be absent in the list. Empty lines, however, are not allowed in the list of vertices.

In Figure 132, the last line reads *Arcs, which signals the start of the list of arcs. In this example, the list is still empty. You may add arcs manually, using one line for each arc. First, specify the number of the sending vertex. Next, add one or more spaces and the number of the receiving vertex. Optionally, you can add the line value after one or more spaces. If you do not specify the line value, it is considered to be 1 (e.g., the arc from vertex one to vertex two in Figure 133). For undirected lines, first add the line *Edges and then use a line for each edge just like the arcs. The only difference is that it does not matter which vertex is specified first. There is no limit to the number of arcs or edges, and multiple arcs and edges are allowed. The order of the lines does not matter.

If you prefer to enter the data as a matrix, as in Figure 129, replace the line *Arcs with *Matrix and type in a square matrix, that is, a matrix with as many rows as columns. Use one line for each row and at least one space between the cells in different columns. You may use any number of spaces between two numbers within a row. Now, the network data file may look like that in Figure 134: there is an arc from vertex 1 to vertex 2 (second number or cell in the first row of the matrix) with a line value of 1. Line values may have decimal places and negative signs.

```
*Vertices        6
         1  "v1"           0.1000    0.5000    0.5000
         2  "v2"           0.3000    0.1536    0.5000
         3  "v3"           0.7000    0.1536    0.5000
         4  "v4"           0.9000    0.5000    0.5000
         5  "v5"           0.7000    0.8464    0.5000
         6  "v6"           0.3000    0.8464    0.5000
*Arcs
1  2
2  5  2.5
4  5
*Edges
3  4  -1
5  6
```

Figure 133. A network in the Pajek Arcs/Edges format.

```
*Vertices        6
        1 "v1"        0.1000      0.5000      0.5000
        2 "v2"        0.3000      0.1536      0.5000
        3 "v3"        0.7000      0.1536      0.5000
        4 "v4"        0.9000      0.5000      0.5000
        5 "v5"        0.7000      0.8464      0.5000
        6 "v6"        0.3000      0.8464      0.5000
*Matrix
0    1    0    0    0    0
0    0    0    0    2.5  0
0    0    0   -1    0    0
0    0   -1    0    1    0
0    0    0    0    0    1
0    0    0    0    1    0
```

Figure 134. A network in the Pajek matrix format.

There are some disadvantages to the matrix data format. First of all, Pajek cannot distinguish between an edge and a bidirectional arc. Therefore, a matrix read by Pajek only contains arcs. Second, Pajek cannot distinguish between a line with a value of zero and an absent line, so Pajek replaces all zeros with arcs with a line value of zero unless it is instructed to ignore lines with a value of zero in the *Threshold* field of the *Options>Read/Write* dialog box. The threshold must be set to zero before a network is opened. Note that the threshold applies to absolute values: negative line values (e.g., -1 in Figure 134) are not eliminated if the threshold is zero. Finally, it is impossible to have multiple lines in matrix format.

[*Main*]
*Options>Read/
Write>Threshold*

Until now, we have considered only one-mode networks. Section 5.3 in Chapter 5, however, introduced *two-mode networks*: networks consisting of two sets of vertices such that all lines are found between the sets (e.g., affiliations of people to organizations). Pajek network data files have a special arrangement for two-mode networks. You can split the list of vertices into two sets or modes in the *Vertices statement by specifying the total number of vertices followed by one or more spaces and the number of vertices in the first mode. This requires that the list of vertices is sorted such that the vertices in the first mode have the lowest vertex numbers and the vertices in the second mode have the highest numbers. Figure 135 shows the data file of a two-mode network consisting of two organizations and four persons. Note that Pajek will issue a warning if it encounters lines within a mode, which should not occur in a two-mode network.

```
*Vertices        6 2
        1 "org1"         0.1000      0.5000      0.5000
        2 "org2"         0.3000      0.1536      0.5000
        3 "person1"      0.7000      0.1536      0.5000
        4 "person2"      0.9000      0.5000      0.5000
        5 "person3"      0.7000      0.8464      0.5000
        6 "person4"      0.3000      0.8464      0.5000
*Arcs
1 3
2 5 2.5
1 4
*Edges
2 4 -1
1 6
```

Figure 135. A two-mode network in the Pajek Arcs/Edges format.

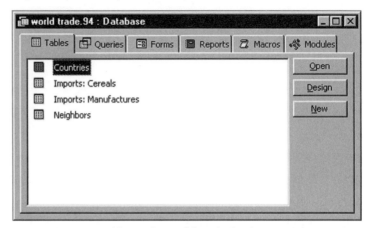

Figure 136. Four tables in the world trade database (MS Access 97).

A1.3.3   Relational Database

Data on large networks are optimally stored as relational databases. In a relational database, two tables can represent a *one-mode network* (Figure 136): one table contains the vertices of the network (e.g., countries) and another table stores the lines between the vertices (e.g., trade relations such as imports). This matches the basic structure of the Pajek Arcs/Edges network format: a list of vertices and a list of lines.

This book's Web site contains a Microsoft Access database with the world trade data of Chapter 2 (see Section 2.10 for the data sources): `world_trade_94.mdb`. The database is made with MS Access version 97, so you have to convert the database if you open it in a newer version of this software. The *Countries* table is the heart of the database, containing one record (row) for each country (Figure 137). Each country has a numerical code, which is its vertex number in the network. In addition to the country's name, several properties are listed, including its GDP, geographic location, and population growth. The table provides the data for the list of vertices in a network data file and the data for partitions

vertexnr	vertexlabel	x	y	continent	trade bloc	position
1	Algeria	0.4380682	0.4957265	1	0	999998
2	Argentina	0.2159091	0.7749288	6	3	2
3	Australia	0.8636364	0.7008547	5	0	2
4	Austria	0.46875	0.411396	3	0	2
5	Barbados	0.2670454	0.5766382	6	4	999998
6	Bangladesh	0.7301137	0.5071225	2	8	999998
7	Belgium, Lux.	0.45	0.3931624	3	1	1
8	Belize	0.1352273	0.5259259	4	4	999998
9	Bolivia	0.2215909	0.6951567	6	3	999998
10	Brazil	0.2897727	0.6780627	6	3	2
11	Canada	0.1363636	0.3304843	4	2	1
12	Chile	0.1931818	0.7635328	6	3	3
13	China	0.75	0.4643874	2	0	999998

Record: 62 of 80

Figure 137. Contents of the *Countries* table (partial).

tail	head	value	valperc
Belgium, Lux.	Southern Africa	9931	2.136122
France	Southern Africa	12892	2.773022
Germany	Spain	29006	6.239084
United Kingdom	Sri Lanka	20081	4.319349
Australia	Sweden	7514	1.616234
Canada	Switzerland	25318	22.98711
United States	Thailand	70774	64.25822
Chile	Trinidad Tobago	1902	1.726893
Colombia	Tunisia	4836	4.390775
Germany	Ecuador	5062	4.595969

Figure 138. A Lookup to the *Countries* table.

and vectors (e.g., GDP and population size of the countries). In principle, any relevant characteristic of the countries can be added to this table. For instance, we added the coordinates of the country in a map (fields x and y), which we used to create the geographical layout of the trade network in Figure 10 (see Chapter 2).

The network lines are stored in separate tables. We collected the information on two kinds of trade: imports of miscellaneous manufactures of metal (table *Imports: Manufactures*) and imports of cereals (table *Imports: Cereals*). Both tables contain one record for each trade tie with the code of the exporting country (field *tail*) and the code of the importing country (field *head*). The value of imports (in 1,000 U.S.$) and the share in a country's total imports of this commodity have been registered. These tables are very similar to the arcs list in a Pajek network file. In addition, we created a table of undirected ties (viz., countries that share a border (table *Neighbors*). This table contains a record for each pair of neighboring countries and it is the source of a list of edges in a network data file.

The *Imports: Cereals* table exemplifies a feature of relational database software that is very useful for efficient data entry. Once the table of vertices has been created and filled with data, references to this table can be made from another table. In a table containing lines between vertices, you can look up the (vertex) number of a country directly. In MS Access, for example, the countries can be displayed as a list, from which you can easily pick the right country: start typing the country's name and the software will lead you to the country you are looking for (Figure 138). When you pick a country from this list – press *Enter* when the country is found – the country's (vertex) number is added to the table of ties although its name is displayed. This helps avoiding data entry errors.

Once all data have been entered into the database, Pajek network data files can be created. This boils down to combining the table of the vertices (*Countries*) with one or more tables of ties (e.g., *Imports: Manufactures* and *Neighbors*) in the right layout. In Microsoft Access, the Report utility is most suited for that. If you open the list of reports in the example database, you will see several reports (Figure 139). For exporting a one-mode network, two reports are needed. The first report (*List of vertices*)

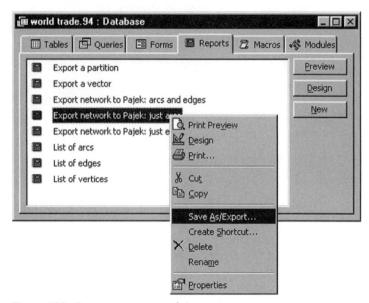

Figure 139. Export a report to plain text.

lists the vertices in the right layout and adds the *Vertices line. The second report (*List of arcs*) contains the formatted list of arcs with the *Arcs line. In the case of an undirected relation, a report is needed starting with *Edges instead of *Arcs (report *List of edges*). The two reports (or three reports in case there are arcs and edges simultaneously) are combined in a master report (*Export network to Pajek: just arcs, Export network to Pajek: just edges,* and *Export network to Pajek: arcs and edges*), which merely concatenates the partial reports.

The master report must be exported to plain text: text without special layout characters. Unfortunately, Microsoft Access is a little uncooperative at this point. It is possible to export the report in plain text format. Right-click the report in the report list (Figure 139) and select *Save As/Export* and subsequently *To an External File or Database* and finally save it with *Text Files* selected as the *Save as type*. Sometimes, however, the saved file has an empty line every four lines, which renders it unreadable to Pajek.

As an alternative, the report can be exported to Microsoft Word (in Rich Text format) with the *Tools>Office Links>Publish It with MS Word* command. Now Access adds page breaks, *which must be deleted* before the file is saved in plain text format. The Rich Text format file is automatically opened in MS Word, where you can delete the page breaks with the command *Replace* (or *Ctrl h*). Enter ^m, which denotes a page break, in the *Find what:* line and replace it with nothing (leave the *Replace with:* line empty). Finally, use the command *File>Save As* and select the *Plain text (*.txt)* type to save the network data file. Give it the .net extension so Pajek can recognize it as a network data file.

Exporting partitions and vectors is less complicated but more sensitive to errors. Partitions and vectors are simply sorted lists of numbers, one number for each vertex on a separate line, preceded by a *Vertices statement. A simple report listing the sorted contents of a field in the table of vertices is all you need to create a partition or vector data file; the reports *Export a partition* and *Export a vector* do this. They can be exported to plain text files in the manner just described. Use the .clu and .vec extensions to enhance recognition by Pajek.

However, the user should be careful. The report can export nonnumeric fields but Pajek cannot handle these. This will be apparent when you try to open a nonnumeric partition or vector in Pajek. There is an even more important limitation. The report lists just the values sorted by vertex number. The value attached to the lowest vertex number is stored in the first line after the *Vertices statement. Reading the partition or vector, Pajek will assume that this value belongs to vertex 1. Therefore, vertex numbers in the database must start with 1 for a partition or vector to match the network. For the same reason, no vertex numbers may be missing in the exported network, so vertex numbers must range from 1 to the number of vertices.

This is required for a partition or vector exported from the database to match a network exported from the same database. Otherwise, the partition or vector will contain fewer vertices than the network, so you cannot combine them in Pajek. If you want to export only some of the vertices in the database, you should either renumber the remaining vertices in the database (in the vertices table as well as in the relations tables!) or export the entire network, partitions, and vectors and remove the unwanted vertices from the network, partitions, and vectors in Pajek (see Chapter 2).

As a final note on exporting vectors (and coordinates in the list of vertices), we want to draw your attention to the language and regional settings of Windows. If decimal places are not separated by a point, Pajek will not be able to read the numbers. You must either adjust your regional settings or replace your local decimal separator by a point by means of a word processor in your data files.

Exporting a *two-mode network* such as corporate interlocks is more complicated. In a relational database, one would probably store the vertices in two tables: one containing the first mode, for instance, the companies (table *Company* in Figure 140), and the second mode, for instance,

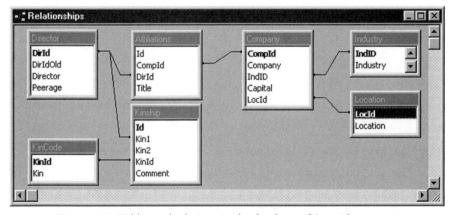

Figure 140. Tables and relations in the database of Scottish companies.

the directors, in another table (table *Director* in Figure 140). Ties connect vertices from one table of vertices to the other (table *Affiliations* in Figure 140). In Pajek, the vertex numbers of the two modes should not overlap. One should number the vertices in the first mode (the firms) from 1 to the number of vertices. The numbering of the other mode (the directors) should start with 1 plus the number of vertices in the first mode. If this precaution is taken (in the example database, queries automatically perform this task), a two-mode network can be exported to Pajek along the lines sketched above, with the additional trick of merging the two tables of vertices into one list.

The example database `Scotland.mdb` contains the data from John Scott's study of interlocking directorates (the example of Chapter 5) and a report for exporting a two-mode network (*Export two-mode network to Pajek*). In this example, special queries ensure that the vertex numbers of directors and companies do not overlap.

In the Pajek Web site, we included an empty MS Access (97) database (`network.mdb`) that you can use as a starting point for your own data collection. The database contains the tables, queries, and reports you need to create Pajek data files for one-mode and two-mode networks. The tables contain a minimum of sample data, which can easily be replaced by your own data. Note that vertex numbers are automatically assigned to vertices in the tables. Do not delete a vertex and its number because that number cannot be used afterwards. Furthermore, do not change the names of the reports, tables, and fields within the tables unless you know very well what you are doing. Renaming may affect the reports and the links between tables. To make the most of the relational database, learn more about the database software or find someone who can advise you.

A1.4   Limitations

Pajek can handle networks up to 9,999,997 vertices. In general, drawings of networks should contain no more than a few thousand vertices because for very large networks the drawing procedure is time consuming and the drawing is visually unattractive. By default, Pajek will not draw networks larger than 5,000 vertices but you can change this limit in the *Options>Read/Write* menu. Available resources on the computer may pose additional limitations.

A1.5   Updates of Pajek

Updates of Pajek can be downloaded from http://vlado.fmf.uni-lj.si/ pub/networks/pajek/default.htm. Due to modifications, newer versions of Pajek may not match the illustrations, command names, and output described in this book exactly.

Appendix 2

Exporting Visualizations

In Chapter 1, several options for exporting graphical output were briefly discussed. We provide more details in this appendix. In Section A2.1, we discuss the graphical formats that Pajek exports to. Next we discuss the options to adjust the layout of the exported image (Section A2.2). *[Draw] Export*

A2.1   Export Formats

Pajek can save a sociogram in six different graphical formats. In most cases, viewers and plug-ins must be installed on your computer before you can display the exported layout. We now discuss each graphic format, how it is exported from Pajek, and how it can be viewed and edited. Note that all references to software and Web sites are made to the year 2004; software updates may have changed and Web sites may have disappeared since then.

A2.1.1   Bitmap

A bitmap exported from Pajek with the *Export>Bitmap* command is merely a screen shot of the Draw screen in its current state, which is saved to a file. Because the bitmap is a very general graphical format, it can be viewed and embedded in most Windows software. A bitmap can be edited in any Windows paint program but editing is cumbersome because you have to edit each pixel (screen point) separately. It is not possible to move entire vertices, lines, or labels. The bitmap format is useful mainly for a quick presentation of a sociogram. For quality images, use Encapsulated PostScript or Scalable Vector Graphics. *Export>Bitmap*

A2.1.2   Encapsulated PostScript

Encapsulated PostScript (and ordinary PostScript) produces two-dimensional vector drawings: each vertex, line, and label is defined as a separate shape with a particular location in the plane. These formats have been developed for quality printing. The drawing or any part of it can be enlarged or reduced without loss of quality. All figures in this book, except for the screenshots, are based on Encapsulated PostScript from

Pajek. Note that partition cluster numbers, which are displayed within vertex labels in the Draw screen, are automatically replaced by numbers inside the vertices in PostScript output (e.g., see Figure 31 in Chapter 3).

Export>EPS/PS   If you export a network layout in Encapsulated PostScript or PostScript formats (the *Export>EPS/PS* command), you can choose among several file types in the *Save As* dialog box. On the one hand, you can choose between Encapsulated PostScript (EPS) and ordinary PostScript (PS). We advise using Encapsulated PostScript always; ordinary PostScript cannot be directly viewed or printed.

On the other hand, you can choose between *What You See Is What You Get* (*WYSIWYG*), *Clip*, and *NoClip*. This choice affects the size and boundary of the exported drawing. In the *WYSIWYG* export, a vertex or label located outside the boundaries of the Draw screen will not be visible in the drawing (although it is defined in the drawing and it will be visible if the bounding box is adjusted) and the drawing may not fit on the standard A4 paper size. The *NoClip* export adjusts the size of the drawing so it can be printed on A4 paper (portrait), and the *Clip* file adjusts the boundaries of the drawing so all vertices and labels are included and there is more or less the same white margin everywhere. We recommend the *Clip* format.

Most Windows applications cannot show Encapsulated PostScript figures, so you have to use a special viewer or translate the drawing into another format. GhostScript and GhostView software is a free viewer for (Encapsulated) PostScript, which can be downloaded from http://www.cs.wisc.edu/~ghost/. Install both programs on your computer and you can view (Encapsulated) PostScript drawings by opening the .eps or .ps file (*File>Open* command) in GhostView. From GhostView, you can print the drawing on any printer and export it in several graphical formats (including Windows MetaFile if you also install pstoedit.exe, which is freely available at http://www.pstoedit.net/). With Acrobat Distiller, which is part of the Adobe Acrobat software package (not free; check http://www.adobe.com/products/acrobat/main.html), you can translate Encapsulated PostScript to a Portable Document Format (PDF), which can be viewed with the free Adobe Acrobat Reader (http://www.adobe.com/ products/acrobat/readstep2.html).

Pajek offers many options for customizing its Encapsulated PostScript export, which we present in Section A2.2. For onscreen editing Encapsulated PostScript drawings, however, you need dedicated drawing software such as CorelDraw. In CorelDraw, you can import Encapsulated PostScript files (*File>Import* command in CorelDraw) and translate it to the vector format of CorelDraw (select the file type "PostScript Interpreted PS,PRN,EPS"). If you ungroup the imported drawing, you can change each element individually. Thus, you can completely customize the sociogram. In Figure 10 in Chapter 2, for instance, we combined the sociogram of world trade in miscellaneous manufactures of metal with a line drawing of the continents (available as outline.wmf). In addition, drawing software such as CorelDraw can export the drawing to a format that can be embedded and viewed in most Windows text processors. We advise using the Windows MetaFile (WMF) format, which is also vector based.

A2.1.3   Scalable Vector Graphics

What PostScript is to printing Scalable Vector Graphics (SVG) is to publishing on the Web. Just as with PostScript, SVG defines each distinct shape and assembles the drawing at the moment it is viewed, so it produces optimal quality in every resolution. In addition, SVG pictures can be changed interactively on the Web. As a consequence, there are several commands for exporting SVG in Pajek's *Export>SVG* submenu, each of which adds a specific type of interaction to the drawing.

Export>SVG

The most basic way of exporting a network as SVG is provided by the *Export>SVG>General* command, which produces an image of the network as it is shown in the Draw screen, without interactivity. In the *Save As* dialog box, enter a filename, which will be used for both the SVG file and the HTML file (Web page) within which the drawing will be displayed. Note that you need both files (in the same directory) to view the drawing. The second SVG export command, *Labels/Arcs/Edges*, exports the drawing with checkboxes, which enable the user to toggle the display of arcs, edges, arc labels, edge labels, and vertex labels.

Export>SVG> General

Export>SVG> Labels/Arcs/ Edges

When the network is drawn with a partition, the *Export>SVG>Partition* submenu contains options for interactively manipulating the classes of the partition. The *Classes* command produces checkboxes with which vertices belonging to a class can be hidden (or displayed), including the lines among them. The lines between different classes can be hidden separately. The *Classes with semi-lines* command produces similar output but lines incident with vertices that are hidden are changed to semi-lines (half lines) and semi-lines are hidden on removal of the vertices with which they are incident. The *Nested Classes* command adds a checkbox for each class in the partition but toggling one checkbox automatically toggles the value of all lower classes. This is very useful for displaying nested classes, such as *m*-slices (Chapter 5) and *k*-cores (Chapter 3). Note that it is possible to display two partitions in the SVG export. If two partitions are selected in the *Partitions* menu of the Main screen, the first partition defines the classes that can be selected by means of the checkboxes, whereas the second partition determines the colors of the vertices in the SVG drawing.

Export>SVG> Partition> Classes

Export>SVG> Partition> Classes with Semi-Lines

Export>SVG> Partition> Nested Classes

If the network contains lines with different values, the SVG export can create checkboxes for showing or hiding lines with particular values. The *Export>SVG>Line Values* submenu contains commands for exporting ordinary classes (*Classes*) and nested classes (*Nested Classes*). Line values must be grouped into classes, so a dialog box appears asking for the number of classes or the class boundaries. In addition, the submenu contains options for the appearance of lines (*Export>SVG>Line Values> Options*), which can receive different colors (*Different Colors* option) or grays (*GrayScale* option), or the line width can be made to represent the class of line values (*Different Widths* option).

Export>SVG> Line Values> Classes

Export>SVG> Line Values> Nested Classes

Finally, it is possible to create a series of SVG images, all linked by previous and next buttons, for a list of networks, partitions, or vectors. First, make sure that the right data objects are selected in the *Options>Previous/Next>Apply to* submenu of the Draw screen. If you have only a sequence of networks to display, the *Network* option should

[Draw]Options> Previous/Next> Apply to

*Export>SVG>
Current and all
Subsequent*
be selected only, but if you have a sequence of networks and a sequence of partitions, both *Network* and *Partition* should be selected. Then select the first network, partition, or vector that you want to export in the drop-down menus of the Main screen, draw the network and, if applicable, partition and vector. Finally, select the *Export>SVG>Current and all Subsequent* option and execute one of the *Export>SVG* commands discussed above.

SVG drawings are viewed in an Internet browser. As mentioned, the SVG drawing is inserted in an HTML page, which is read by a Web browser. Recent browsers such as Microsoft Internet Explorer version 6.0 and higher can display SVG images directly. For older browsers, you need to install a plug in, which can be downloaded from http://www.adobe.com/svg/viewer/install/.

Onscreen editing of SVG images can be done with several software packages, among them Webdraw (http://www.jasc.com/products/webdraw/) and Adobe Illustrator (http://www.adobe.com/products/illustrator/main.html).

A2.1.4   Virtual Reality Modeling Language

*Layout>Energy
>Fruchterman
Reingold>3D*
Virtual Reality Modeling Language (VRML) is a standard language for defining three-dimensional objects that can be published on the Web. In a Web browser, VRML models (e.g., a three-dimensional model of a social network) can be rotated, walked through, and so on. You may optimize the network's layout in three dimensions with the *Layout>Energy>Fruchterman Reingold>3D* command before you export a VRML model from Pajek.

Export>VRML
With the *Export>VRML* command, Pajek exports the network to VRML 1.0. A dialog box prompts for a file name in which to store the model. We advise using the default extension .wrl, which stands for world, so Internet browsers can correctly identify the file type. If the network was drawn with a partition, the spheres in the model, which represent the vertices, have the right colors. Vertex labels will be transformed to anchor names.

For displaying a VRML world in a Web browser, you need a plug in, for instance, Cosmo player (http://www.ca.com/cosmo/home.htm) or Cortona VRML Client (http://www.parallelgraphics.com/products/downloads). Some plug-ins can read only newer VRML models (VRML 2.0 or 97). If so, you need a converter such as the Cortona VRML 1.0 converter or the MS-DOS program VRML1TOVRML2.EXE, which must be run from the MS-DOS prompt with the command VRML1TOVRML2 followed by the names of the VRML 1.0 file and the new VRML 2.0 file separated by spaces. Maybe the original vertex names, which are anchor names in the VRML model, may cause problems; if this happens, open the the VRML file in a plain text editor and adjust or remove the anchor names. Do not forget to save the changed file to plain text.

Some layout properties of VRML models can be set in Pajek (see Section A2.2). If you want to edit a VRML model onscreen, you need special software. Consult http://www.web3d.org/x3d/vrml/tools/authoring/ for VRML design and editing software.

If you want to include an image of a three-dimensional model in a document, it is a good idea to ray-trace it. Ray-tracing is a technique that renders very realistic images from three-dimensional models by calculating (tracing) the trajectory of light from the virtual light sources and the reflection of this light on the surfaces in the model. In Chapter 1 Figure 14 provides an example. POVRay is a good and free software package for ray-tracing (http://www.povray.org/). However, it does not understand the Virtual Reality Modeling language directly, so you must first transform the VRML 2.0 model to the POVRay language, which can be done with the MS-DOS program `vrml2pov.exe`. In the MS-DOS prompt, issue the command `vrml2pov` followed by the names of the VRML 2.0 file and the new POVRay file, separated by spaces. For the POVRay file, use the extension `.pov`. You can open the newly created file in POVRay and render it. The rendered image is automatically saved in the format specified in POVRay's INI file. Enjoy, but realize that it may take quite some time before you master the software and achieve satisfactory results.

A2.1.5 MDL MOL and Kinemages

Molecular structures can be modeled as networks, so the software developed by scientists to visualize molecules can be used for the display of social networks. Pajek can export to two molecule model formats: MDL MOL and Kinemages. MDL MOL models are three-dimensional and they are viewed in a Web browser using a special plug-in (Chime, which can be downloaded from http://www.mdli.com/). This format does not offer real advantages over VRML, so we do not discuss it in detail.

Export>MDL MOLfile

In contrast, the other format – Kinemages – does have special features that need to be mentioned. This format is designed to present sequences of three-dimensional images. In principle, this can also be done in VRML but in Kinemages, it is very easy to add text to each image and to include questions. This software is excellent for teaching purposes and for electronic publishing in the case of undirected networks. For directed or signed networks, Kinemage is less useful because it does not display the direction of arcs or the signs of lines.

Pajek can produce these sequences with the *Export>Kinemages>Current and all Subsequent* command. Just like SVG export, you must select the data objects (network, partition, vector) that you want to export in the *Options>Previous/Next>Apply to* submenu of the Draw screen and you must select the first network (partition, vector) that you want to export in the droplists of the Main screen. With the *Export>Kinemages>Current and all Subsequent* command, Pajek creates one Kinemage file (default extension is `.kin`) containing the series of networks. In the *Save as Type* selection box of the *Save As* dialog box, you can choose whether you want the vertices represented by spheres or by vertex labels in the Kinemage.

Export> Kinemages> Current and all Subsequent

[Draw] Options> Previous/Next> Apply to

You need special software for viewing Kinemages, which is called Mage (http://kinemage.biochem.duke.edu/kinemage/kinemage.php). Open the

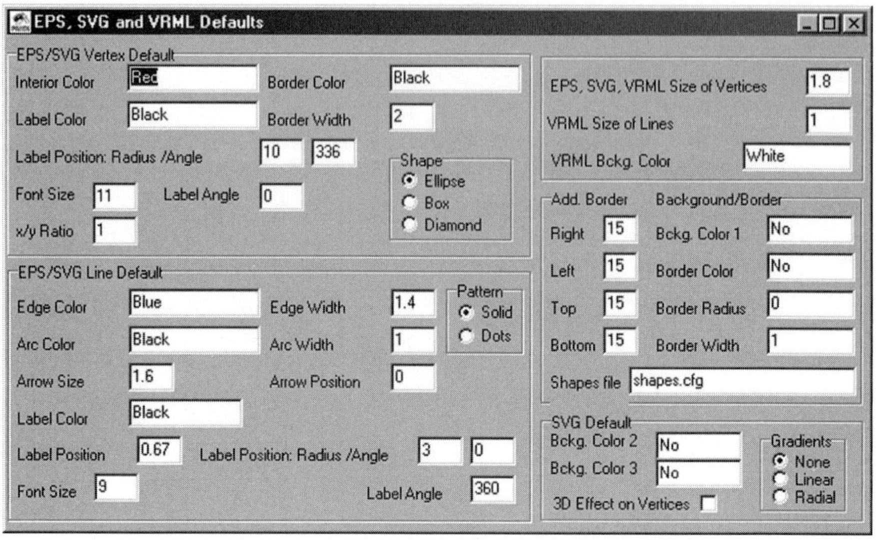

Figure 141. The *Options* screen.

Kinemage created by Pajek in Mage and step through the sequence of images with the *KINEMAGE/Next* (or *Ctrl-n*) command in Mage.

A2.2   Layout Options

[Draw]
Export>Options

PostScript, SVG, and VRML visualizations need additional information about the size, placement, and colors of vertices, lines, labels, and background. This information can be supplied either with the *Options* command in the *Export* menu of the Draw screen or in the network data file. The *Export>Options* (Figure 141) define layout properties of all vertices and lines, whereas the parameters in the network data file define the layout of each individual vertex or line. Layout parameters specified in the network data file override the settings in the *Export>Options dialog screen*. If, for instance, the color of vertices is specified in the network data file, entering a color in the *Options* window has no effect.

The *Export>Options* command opens a window that is divided into five frames, two on the left and three on the right (Figure 141). We discuss each frame separately and, where appropriate, we mention the layout parameter that defines the layout feature in the network data file. Note that you should type the layout parameters at the end of the line defining a vertex, edge, or arc in the network data file and you must separate the parameters and their values by one or more blanks. Consult the document DrawEPS.htm (on the book's Web site) for a description of all layout parameters in the network data file.

[Main] Options>
Ini File>Save
[Main] Options>
Ini File>Load

If you want to save the settings of a particular layout, use the *Options> Ini File>Save* command in the Main screen. This command saves all present settings to a file, which can be loaded (command *Options>Ini File>Load*) to restore the settings.

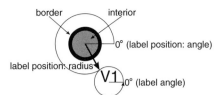

Figure 142. Layout of a vertex and its label.

A2.2.1   Top Frame on the Left – EPS/SVG Vertex Default

This frame defines how vertices are drawn when you export 2D layouts to (Encapsulated) PostScript and Scalable Vector Graphics. Figure 142 shows some important properties of the layout of a vertex and its label.

In the top frame, the color of the interior (*Interior Color*) and border (*Border Color*) of the vertices can be specified. Enter one of the colors that are listed in Table 26 (the colors are shown in the file `Crayola.pdf`, which is included in the documentation accompanying Pajek) and make sure you use upper- and lowercase letters as specified there. The width of the border (*Border Width*; parameter `bw` followed by a number in the network data file) and the shape of the vertex (*Shape*; just type `ellipse`, `box`, `diamond`, `cross`, or `empty` in the network data file – this parameter must precede all other layout parameters except for the vertex's coordinates) can be defined. The user may choose among the predefined shapes ellipse, box, and diamond and he or she may squeeze or stretch the shape horizontally by adjusting the *x/y* ratio (*x/y Ratio*; parameter `x_fact` followed by a number). If this ratio is smaller than 1, the shape of the vertex is squeezed; if it is larger than 1, it is stretched. In Figure 143, the horizontal diameter of the vertex on the left is half the vertical diameter,

[Draw] Export>
Options>
Interior Color

[Draw] Export>
Options>
Border Color

[Draw] Export>
Options>
Border Width

[Draw] Export>
Options>Shape

[Draw] Export>
Options>x/y
ratio

Table 26. *Names of Colors in Pajek*

Apricot	Fuchsia	MidnightBlue	RoyalPurple
Aquamarine	Goldenrod	Mulberry	RubineRed
Bittersweet	Gray	NavyBlue	Salmon
Black	Green	OliveGreen	SeaGreen
Blue	GreenYellow	Orange	Sepia
BlueGreen	JungleGreen	OrangeRed	SkyBlue
BlueViolet	Lavender	Orchid	SpringGreen
BrickRed	LFadedGreen	Peach	Tan
Brown	LightCyan	Periwinkle	TealBlue
BurntOrange	LightGreen	PineGreen	Thistle
CadetBlue	LightMagenta	Pink	Turquoise
Canary	LightOrange	Plum	Violet
CarnationPink	LightPurple	ProcessBlue	VioletRed
Cerulean	LightYellow	Purple	White
CornflowerBlue	LimeGreen	RawSienna	WildStrawberry
Cyan	LSkyBlue	Red	Yellow
Dandelion	Magenta	RedOrange	YellowGreen
DarkOrchid	Mahogany	RedViolet	YellowOrange
Emerald	Maroon	Rhodamine	
ForestGreen	Melon	RoyalBlue	

x/y ratio: 0.5   1.5

Figure 143. The *x/y* ratio of a vertex.

so its *x/y* ratio is 0.5. The horizontal diameter of the other vertex is 50 percent longer than the vertical diameter.

[Draw] Export> Options>Label Color

The color (*Label Color*; parameter lc followed by a color name) and font size (*Font Size*; parameter fos followed by a number) of the label can also be adjusted in this frame. Again, use names of colors as listed in Table 26. In addition, the orientation of the vertex label (*Label Angle*; la followed by a number indicating the degree) can be changed relative to a horizontal line. Zero degrees is usually the best choice because this will display the labels horizontally. Label angles from 360 to 720 degrees position the label relative to the center of the layout, which can be useful when all vertices are drawn in concentric circles.

[Draw] Export> Options>Font Size

[Draw] Export> Options>Label Angle

[Draw] Export> Options>Label Position: Radius/Angle

The most complicated part, however, is the position of the label with respect to the vertex. The position of the label is defined by its distance to the center of the vertex (the radius) and by the angle from the horizontal line starting at this center, ranging from 0 to 360 degrees (*Label Position: Radius/Angle*; parameters lr followed by a number and lphi followed by a degree respectively). If the angle of the label position is zero, the label is resting on this horizontal line at the right of the vertex. If the radius is zero, the label is placed in the center of the vertex. With short labels and large vertices (see Section A2.2.3) or a high *x/y* ratio, the label may fit inside the vertex. To place labels outside but near their vertices, enter a positive number in the *Label Position: Radius* field. It is difficult to give a general rule for a good size of the radius, because it depends on the size of the vertex and the size of the label's type font. Most figures of this book used the sizes shown in Figure 141.

A2.2.2   Bottom Frame on the Left – EPS/SVG Line Default

This frame defines the way the lines are drawn when 2D layouts are exported to (Encapsulated) PostScript and Scalable Vector Graphics. It contains fields defining the appearance of lines and line values or line labels as well as fields that specify the orientation of labels and their location with respect to the lines to which they belong.

[Draw] Export> Options>Edge Color, Arc Color, Label Color, Pattern, Edge Width, Arc Width, Arrow Size, Font Size, Arrow Position

The colors of edges and arcs (*Edge Color* and *Arc Color*; parameter c followed by a color name) and labels (*Label Color*; lc followed by a color name) can be changed by entering names of colors as they appear in Table 26. Note that arcs and edges may receive different colors. You may draw all lines as dotted lines by selecting *Dots* in the *Pattern* field (parameter p followed by Solid or Dots). The width of edges and arcs (*Edge Width* and *Arc Width*; w followed by a number) may also differ; it is good practice to draw edges a bit wider than arcs. The size of the arrowhead (*Arrow Size*; s followed by a number) is specified independently of the arc's width. The size of the labels is defined by their font size (*Fontsize*; fos followed by a number), which should be smaller than the font size of the vertex labels for pleasant results.

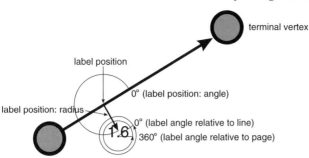

Figure 144. The position and orientation of a line label.

You may decide where to place the arrowhead on the line (*Arrow Position*; ap followed by a number). A number between 0 and 1 is interpreted as a proportion expressing the relative distance from the end to the beginning of the arc; for example, 0 will place the arrowhead at the end of the arc near the terminal vertex and 0.5 will situate the arrowhead in the middle of the arc. A distance larger than 1 is interpreted as an absolute distance from the terminal vertex. This is useful if you want to have all arcs on the same distance from the terminal vertex, regardless of the arc's length. You have to experiment a little to find a nice distance.

The remaining fields concern the orientation and position of the line label (e.g., its value) with respect to the line. Figure 144 illustrates the relevant parameters. First, choose the position on the line (edge or arc) to which the line label is attached (*Label Position*; lp followed by a number). This is similar to the position of the arrowhead: numbers between 0 and 1 are proportions, that is, relative distances from the end to the beginning of the line, and numbers above 1 are absolute distances from the end of the line. In Figure 144, the label position is 0.67, so it is located at two-thirds of the arc, measured from its end. Note that edges do not have a start and an end, so it is most appropriate to position the edge labels halfway.

[Draw] Export>Options>Label Position

Next, the location of the center of the label with respect to the position on the line is defined by two properties that are similar to the location of vertex labels: radius and angle. The radius (*Label Position: Radius*; lr followed by a number) is the distance between the position on the line and the center of the line label that is measured at the specified angle (*Label Position: Angle*; lphi followed by a number of degrees) from the line. In Figure 144, the angle is 270 degrees.

[Draw] Export>Options>Label Position: Radius

[Draw] Export>Options>Label Position: Angle

Finally, the orientation of the line label is defined in the *Label Angle* field (parameter la followed by a number of degrees). An angle smaller than 360 degrees is measured relative to the direction of the line, where zero degrees is parallel to the line. Angles of 360 degrees and more are relative to a horizontal line. For easy reading, an angle of 360 degrees is optimal because it displays line labels horizontally.

[Draw] Export>Options>Label Angle

A2.2.3   Top Frame on the Right

This frame defines additional defaults when we export layouts to Virtual Reality Modeling Language (VRML). The field *EPS, SVG, VRML Size of*

[Draw] Export>Options>EPS,

SVG, VRML
Size of Vertices

[Draw] Export>
Options>
VRML Size of
Lines

[Draw] Export>
Options>VRML
Bckg. Color

Vertices (parameter s_size followed by a number) specifies the default size of vertices when exporting to VRML but also to EPS and SVG. The diameter of lines in VRML can be changed in the *VRML Size of Lines* (no layout parameter for the network data file) field. It is difficult to give general rules about optimal settings for these fields; you have to experiment.

In the *VRML Bckg. Color* field (no layout parameter for the network data file), you can choose a background color for the layout in VRML: just enter one of the color names listed in Table 26.

A2.2.4   Middle Frame on the Right

[Draw] Export>
Options>
Add. Border

This frame defines additional properties of the network layout when we export layouts to Encapsulated PostScript and Scalable Vector Graphic (there are no layout parameters for the network data file). Most fields relate to a border around the layout. With the four fields *Right*, *Left*, *Top*, and *Bottom*, you can add additional space to the right, left, and so on of the picture. This is effective for SVG exports and for EPS exports when the EPS Clip format is selected.

[Draw] Export>
Options>
Border Color

[Draw] Export>
Options>Bckg.
Color

The color of the border (*Border Color*) as well as the background (*Bckg. Color*) can be picked from the color names listed in Table 26. Enter the word *No* in these fields if you do not want a border or background color. The shape of the borderline is characterized by the fields *Border Radius* and *Border Width*. If the radius of the border is zero, the border is a rectangle. Higher values (e.g., 10, 50, or 100) round off the corners. A border width of one unit produces a rather thin borderline and higher values yield fatter borderlines.

[Draw] Export>
Options>
Border Radius

[Draw] Export>
Options>
Border Width

Finally, this window contains a field in which a file can be selected with custom shapes for vertices. The default is the file shapes.cfg. Defining your own custom shapes demands knowledge of the PostScript language.

A2.2.5   Bottom Frame on the Right – SVG Default

[Draw] Export>
Options>Bckg.
Color 2

The last frame contains additional options for exporting Scalable Vector Graphics (again, there are no layout parameters for the network data file).

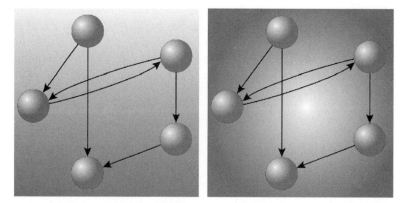

Figure 145. Gradients in SVG export: linear (left) and radial (right).

These layouts can handle gradient colors: an area in which one color gradually blends into another color. You can specify three colors. The first color is the background color defined in the middle frame (see Section A2.2.4). The second color can be selected in the *Bckg. Color 2* field. Use the color names of Table 26 and enter the word *No* if you do not want to use a second color and hence no gradient. If you like, you can select a third color in the *Bckg. Color 3* field. The type of blend can be selected in the *Gradients* field: *Linear* or *Radial* (see Figure 141). In a linear gradient, the original background color is at the top of the area and blends into the second and third colors on its way down. In a radial gradient the middle of the drawing is colored with the original background color. Figure 145 also shows the effects of the *3D Effect on Vertices* option.

[Draw] Export> Options>Bckg. Color 3

[Draw] Export> Options> Gradients

[Draw] Export> Options>3D Effect on Vertices

Appendix 3

Shortcut Key Combinations

The following tables list the shortcut key combinations and the commands they replace. Some shortcuts are accessible from one screen, whereas others are accessible from several screens.

Main Screen

Shortcut	Description and Command
Ctrl-a	Draw the network with all vertices in class 0 of a new empty partition (*Draw>Draw-SelectAll*)
Ctrl-g	Draw the network (*Draw>Draw*)
Ctrl-p	Draw the network and the active partition (*Draw>Draw-Partition*)
Ctrl-q	Draw the network, the active partition, and the active vector (*Draw>Draw-Partition-Vector*)
Ctrl-u	Draw the network and the active vector (*Draw>Draw-Vector*)
Ctrl-s	Repeat session (*File>Repeat session*)
Ctrl-v	Create a new vector holding the values of the active partition (*Partition>Create Vector*)
Ctrl-x	Create a new network with the x coordinates of the vertices from the active vector (*Operations>Vector>Put Coordinate>x*)
Ctrl-y	Create a new network with the y coordinates of the vertices from the active vector (*Operations>Vector>Put Coordinate>y*)
Ctrl-z	Create a new network with the z coordinates of the vertices from the active vector (*Operations>Vector>Put Coordinate>z*)

Hierarchy Edit Screen

Shortcut	Description and Command
Ctrl-t	Change the type of a cluster from unlabeled to Close to Cut to Border in the hierarchy (*Edit>Change Type*)
Ctrl-n	Change the label of a cluster in the hierarchy (*Edit>Change Name*)
Ctrl-s	Toggle the option to show the members of the cluster or all members of the cluster and its subclusters when double-clicking a cluster in the hierarchy (*Edit>Show Subtree*)

Draw Screen

Shortcut	Description and Command
Ctrl-a	Draw the network with all vertices in class 0 of a new empty partition (*[Main] Draw>Draw-SelectAll*)
Ctrl-g	Draw the network (*[Main] Draw>Draw*)
Ctrl-p	Draw the network and the active partition (*[Main] Draw>Draw-Partition*)
Ctrl-q	Draw the network, the active partition, and the active vector (*[Main] Draw>Draw-Partition-Vector*)
Ctrl-u	Draw the network and the active vector (*[Main] Draw>Draw-Vector*)
Ctrl-b	Show the labels of the lines (*Options>Lines>Mark Lines>with Labels*)
Ctrl-o	Do not show the values or labels of the lines (*Options>Lines>Mark Lines>No*)
Ctrl-v	Show the values of the lines (*Options>Lines>Mark Lines>with Values*)
Ctrl-l	Show the labels of the vertices (*Options>Mark Vertices Using>Labels*)
Ctrl-n	Show the numbers of the vertices (*Options>Mark Vertices Using>Numbers*)
Ctrl-d	Do not show labels or numbers of the vertices (*Options>Mark Vertices Using>No*)
Ctrl-r	Toggle real sizes of vertices (*Options>Mark Vertices Using>Real sizes On/Off*)
S	Spin around the normal in one direction
s	Spin around the normal in the opposite direction
X	Spin around the x axis, the bottom approaching the viewer
x	Spin around the x axis, the top approaching the viewer
Y	Spin around the y axis, the left approaching the viewer
y	Spin around the y axis, the right approaching the viewer
Z	Spin around the z axis clockwise
z	Spin around the z axis counterclockwise

Glossary

The book's important structural concepts are listed and explained below in alphabetical order. Numbers refer to the sections presenting the concepts.

Concept	Description	Section
Actor	Actor refers to a person, organization, or nation that is involved in a social relation. Hence, an actor is a vertex in a social network.	1.3
Acyclic network	An acyclic network does not contain cycles.	10.4
Adjacency matrix	An adjacency matrix is a square matrix with one row and one column for each vertex in a network. The content of a cell in the matrix indicates the presence and possibly the sign or value of a tie from the vertex represented by the row to the vertex represented by the column.	12.2
Adjacent	Two vertices are adjacent if they are connected by a line.	3.3
Adoption category	Adoption categories classify people according to their adoption time relative to all other adopters.	8.3
Adoption rate	The adoption rate is the number or percentage of new adopters at a particular moment.	8.2
Aggregate constraint	The aggregate constraint on a vertex is the sum of the dyadic constraint on all of its ties.	7.4
Arc	An arc is a directed line. Formally, an arc is an ordered pair of vertices.	1.3.1
Articulation point	See: Cut-vertex	7.3
Asymmetric dyad	An asymmetric dyad is a pair of vertices connected by unilateral arc(s).	10.3
Attribute	An attribute is a characteristic of a vertex measured independently of the network.	2.3
Balance model	The balance model applies to an unsigned directed network if it consists of two cliques that are not interrelated.	10.3
Balanced (semi-)cycle	In a signed graph, a (semi-)cycle is balanced if it does not contain an uneven number of negative arcs.	4.2
Balanced signed graph	A signed graph is balanced if all of its (semi-)cycles are balanced. A signed graph is balanced if it can be partitioned into two clusters such that all positive ties	4.2

(*continued*)

(continued)

Concept	Description	Section
	are contained within the clusters and all negative ties are situated between the clusters.	
Betweenness centrality	The betweenness centrality of a vertex is the proportion of all geodesics between pairs of other vertices that include this vertex.	6.4
Betweenness centralization	Betweenness centralization is the variation in the betweenness centrality of vertices divided by the maximum variation in betweenness centrality scores possible in a network of the same size.	6.4
Bi-component	A bi-component is a component of a minimum size of 3 that does not contain a cut-vertex.	7.3
Bipartite network	See: Two-mode network	5.3
Block	A block contains the cells of an adjacency matrix that belong to the cross section of one or two classes.	12.4
Blockmodel	A blockmodel assigns the vertices of a network to classes and it specifies the permitted type(s) of relation within and between classes.	12.4.1
Blockmodeling	The technique to obtain a blockmodel is called blockmodeling.	12.4.2
Blood marriage	A blood marriage is the marriage of people with a close common ancestor.	11.4
Bridge	A bridge is a line whose removal increases the number of components in the network.	7.3
Brokerage role	A brokerage role of a vertex is a particular pattern of ties and group affiliations.	7.5
Cell	A cell of a matrix is the intersection of a row and a column.	12.2
Clique	A clique is a maximal complete subnetwork containing three vertices or more.	3.6
Closeness centrality	The closeness centrality of a vertex is the number of other vertices divided by the sum of all distances between the vertex and all others.	6.3
Closeness centralization	Closeness centralization is the variation in the closeness centrality of vertices divided by the maximum variation in closeness centrality scores possible in a network of the same size.	6.3
Clusterability model	The clusterability model applies to an unsigned directed network if it consists of two or more cliques that are not interrelated.	10.3
Clusterable (semi-)cycle	A cycle or semicycle is clusterable if it does not contain exactly one negative arc.	4.2
Clusterable signed graph	A signed graph is clusterable if it can be partitioned into clusters such that all positive ties are contained within clusters and all negative ties are situated between clusters.	4.2
Complete network	A complete network is a network with maximum density: all possible lines occur.	3.3
Component	A (weak) component is a maximal (weakly) connected subnetwork.	3.4
Contextual view	In a contextual view of a network, vertices in all but one class are shrunk.	2.4.3
Coordinator role	A vertex is a coordinator if it is situated on a path between two vertices within its own class (group) that are not directly connected.	7.5

Concept	Description	Section
Critical mass	The critical mass of a diffusion process is the minimum number of adopters needed to sustain a diffusion process.	8.4
Cut-vertex	A cut-vertex is a vertex whose deletion increases the number of components in the network.	7.3
Cycle	A cycle is a closed path.	4.2
Degree	The degree of a vertex is the number of lines incident with it.	3.3
Degree centrality	The degree centrality of a vertex is its degree.	6.3
Degree centralization	Degree centralization of a network is the variation in the degrees of vertices divided by the maximum degree variation that is possible in a network of the same size.	6.3
Delete a vertex	Deleting a vertex from a network means that the vertex and all lines incident with this vertex are removed from the network.	7.3
Dendrogram	A dendrogram is a chart visualizing the results of hierarchical clustering.	12.3
Density	Density is the number of lines in a simple network, expressed as a proportion of the maximum possible number of lines.	3.3
Diffusion curve	A diffusion curve displays the prevalence of an innovation in the course of time.	8.2
Digraph	A digraph or directed graph is a graph containing one or more arcs.	1.3.1
Dimension of a partition	The number of entries (vertices) of a partition.	4.4
Distance	The distance from vertex u to vertex v is the length of the geodesic from u to v.	6.3
Domain	In a directed network, the (input, output) domain of a vertex is the number or percentage of all other vertices that are connected by a path to this vertex.	9.5
Dyad	A dyad is a pair of vertices and the lines between them.	10.3
Dyadic constraint	The dyadic constraint on vertex u exercised by a tie between vertices u and v is the extent to which u has more and stronger ties with neighbors that are strongly connected with vertex v.	7.4
Edge	An edge is an undirected line. Formally, an edge is an unordered pair of vertices.	1.3.1
Ego-centered approach	An ego-centered approach to a network considers the structural characteristics of individual vertices.	6.1
Egocentric density	Egocentric density is the density of the ego-network without ego.	7.4
Ego-network	The ego-network of a vertex contains this vertex, its neighbors, and all lines among the selected vertices.	7.4
Endogamy	Endogamy or intermarriage means that families are linked by several kinship ties.	11.4
Equivalent (class, position)	Actors with similar patterns of ties are said to be relationally equivalent, to constitute an equivalence class, or to occupy equivalent positions in the network.	12.3
Event	An event is a happening, context, or organization where actors may gather.	5.3

(*continued*)

Concept	Description	Section
Exposure	The exposure of a vertex in a network at a particular moment is the proportion of its neighbors that have adopted before that moment.	8.3
Extract a subnetwork	To extract a subnetwork from a network, select a subset of its vertices and all lines that are incident only with the selected vertices.	2.4.1
Family of child or orientation	A person's family of child or orientation (FAMC) is the family in which this person is a child.	11.3
Family of spouse or procreation	A person's family of spouse or procreation (FAMS) is the family in which this person is a parent.	11.3
Forest	A forest is a graph consisting of two or more distinct (unconnected) trees.	11.4
Gatekeeper	A vertex is a gatekeeper if it is situated on a path from a vertex of another class (group) toward a vertex of its own class, provided that these vertices are not directly connected.	7.5
Genealogical generation	A genealogical generation is a set of people connected to a (close) common ancestor at the same remove.	11.3
Generalized blockmodeling	In generalized blockmodeling, the permitted block types are specified for each individual block.	12.4.3
Generation jump	In a genealogy, a generation jump occurs when people marry who are connected to a common ancestor at different removes.	11.3
Geodesic	A geodesic is the shortest path between two vertices.	6.3
Global view	A global view is a sociogram of a network in which all classes are shrunk.	2.4.2
Graph	A graph is a set of vertices and a set of lines between pairs of vertices.	1.3.1
Hierarchical clustering	Hierarchical clustering is a statistical technique for subdividing units into increasingly more homogeneous subsets.	12.3
Hierarchical clusters model	The hierarchical clusters model applies to an unsigned directed network if it consists of connected clusters such that clusters within ranks are not related and clusters between ranks are related by null dyads or asymmetric dyads pointing toward the higher rank with the additional provision that a cluster contains no cycles of asymmetric dyads.	10.3
Hierarchy	A hierarchy is a data object for classifying vertices if a vertex may belong to several classes. It is especially suited for a hierarchical clustering of vertices, where units are subdivided into more and more homogeneous subsets.	3.6
Homophily	Homophily is the phenomenon that similar people interact a lot, at least more often than with dissimilar people.	3.1
Image matrix	An image matrix is a simplification of an adjacency matrix by shrinking each block to one new cell indicating the block type.	12.4.1
Immediacy index	The immediacy index is the average number of citations of the articles in a journal during the year of its publication.	11.6

Concept	Description	Section
Impact factor	The impact factor of a journal is the average number of citations to articles in this journal.	11.6
Incidence matrix	An incidence matrix is a rectangular matrix with one row for each vertex from one mode (subset) and one column for each vertex from the other mode (subset) in a two-mode network. The content of a cell in the matrix indicates the presence and possibly the sign or value of a tie from the vertex represented by the row to the vertex represented by the column.	12.2
Incident	A line is defined by its two endpoints, which are the two vertices that are incident with the line.	1.3.1
Indegree	The indegree of a vertex is the number of arcs it receives.	3.3
Induced subnetwork	A subset of vertices from a network and all lines that are incident only with these vertices is called an induced subnetwork.	2.4.1
Isomorphic	Two networks are isomorphic, that is, they have the same structure, if a permutation of the vertices in one network produces the other network.	12.2
Itinerant broker	A vertex is an itinerant broker if it is situated on a path between two vertices from the same class to which the brokering vertex does not belong, that are not connected directly.	7.5
k-Connected component	A k-connected component is a maximal subnetwork in which each pair of vertices is connected by at least k distinct (noncrossing) semipaths or paths.	3.4
k-Core	A k-core is a maximal subnetwork in which each vertex has at least degree k within the subnetwork.	3.5
Liaison	A vertex is a liaison if it is situated on a path between two vertices in different classes (groups), which are different from its own class that are not connected directly.	7.5
Line	A line is a tie between two vertices in a network: either an arc or an edge.	1.3.1
Local view	A sociogram of an induced subnetwork offers a local view.	2.4.1
Loop	A loop is a line that connects a vertex to itself.	1.3.1
Main path	In an acyclic network, a main path is a path from a source vertex to a sink vertex with the highest traversal weights on its arcs.	11.6
Main path component	In an acyclic network, a main path component is a component in the network after removal of all arcs with traversal weights below a particular value (usually the lowest traversal weight on the network's main paths).	11.6
Matrix	A matrix is a two-way table containing rows and columns.	12.2
m-Slice	An m-slice is a maximal subnetwork containing the lines with a multiplicity equal to or greater than m and the vertices incident with these lines.	5.4
Multiple lines	If a particular arc or edge, that is, a particular ordered or unordered pair of vertices, occurs more than once, there are multiple lines.	1.3.1

(continued)

Concept	Description	Section
Multiplicity	Line multiplicity is the number of times a specific line (ordered or unordered pair of vertices) occurs in a network.	5.3
Neighbor	A vertex that is adjacent to another vertex is its neighbor.	3.3
Nested	Subnetworks are said to be nested if one subnetwork is a subset from the other.	3.5
Network	A network consists of a graph and additional information on the vertices or the lines of the graph.	1.3.1
Nonblood relinking	Nonblood relinking refers to multiple marriages between families where no couple has a close common ancestor.	11.4
Null dyad	A null dyad is a pair of vertices that are not connected by lines.	10.3
One-mode network	In a one-mode network, each vertex can be related to each other vertex.	5.3
Optimization technique	An analytic technique searching for the best solution according to a criterion function by repetition is called an optimization technique.	4.4
Ore graph	The Ore graph is a sociogram of kinship ties in which men are represented by triangles, women by ellipses, marriages by (double) lines, and parent–child ties by arcs pointing from parent to child.	11.3
Outdegree	The outdegree of a vertex is the number of arcs it sends.	3.3
Partial order	In a partial order, some but not all pairs of units (e.g., vertices) are ordered.	10.5
Partition	A partition of a network is a classification or clustering of the vertices in the network such that each vertex is assigned to exactly one class or cluster.	2.3
Path	A path is a walk in which no vertex in between the first and last vertex of the walk occurs more than once.	3.4
Pedigree	The pedigree of a person is the set of his or her ancestors.	11.3
Permutation	A permutation of a network is a renumbering of its vertices.	12.2
P-graph	The P-graph or parentage graph is a genealogical network, in which couples and unmarried individuals are the vertices and arcs, representing individuals, point from children to parents.	11.4
Popularity	The popularity or indegree of a vertex is the number of arcs it receives in a directed network.	9.3
Position	A position is a particular pattern of ties.	12.3
Prevalence	The prevalence of an innovation is the cumulative percentage of adopters at a particular time.	8.2
Proportional strength	The proportional strength of a tie with respect to all ties of a person is the value of the line(s) representing a tie, divided by the sum of the values of all lines incident with a person.	7.4
Proximity prestige	The proximity prestige of a vertex is the proportion of all vertices (except itself) in its input domain divided by the mean distance from all vertices in its input domain.	9.6
Ranked clusters model	The ranked clusters model applies to an unsigned directed network if it consists of cliques and ranks such that cliques within ranks are not related and	10.3

Concept	Description	Section
	cliques between ranks are related by asymmetric dyads pointing toward the higher rank.	
Rate of participation	In a two-mode network, the degree of a vertex is called the rate of participation of an actor if the vertex refers to an actor.	5.3
Reachable	We say that a vertex is reachable from another vertex if there is a path from the latter to the former.	6.3
Regular block	A regular block is a block containing at least one arc in each row and in each column.	12.4.3
Regular equivalence	Vertices that are regular equivalent do not have to be connected to the same vertices, but they have to be connected to vertices in the same classes.	12.4.3
Relinking index	The relinking index measures the amount of relinking in a P-graph.	11.4
Representative	A vertex is a representative if it is situated on a path from a vertex of its own class (group) toward a vertex of another class, provided that these vertices are not directly connected.	7.5
Restricted domain	The restricted (input, output) domain of a vertex in a directed network is the number or percentage of all other vertices that are connected by a path of a selected maximum length to or from this vertex.	9.5
Secondary structural hole	In the ego-network of a vertex, a secondary structural hole exists if there is a vertex outside the ego-network that is at least as central as a vertex in the ego-network but not directly linked to this vertex. In this case, ego can replace the tie with the neighbor by a tie to the vertex outside the ego-network.	7.5
Semicycle	A semicycle is a closed semipath.	4.2
Semipath	A semipath is a semiwalk in which no vertex in between the first and last vertex of the semiwalk occurs more than once.	3.4
Semiwalk	A semiwalk from vertex u to vertex v is a sequence of lines such that the end vertex of one line is the starting vertex of the next line and the sequence starts at vertex u and ends at vertex v.	3.4
Shrink a network	To shrink a network, replace a subset (class) of its vertices by one new vertex which is incident to all lines that were incident with the vertices of the subset in the original network.	2.4.2
Signed graph	A signed graph is a graph in which each line carries either a positive or a negative sign.	4.2
Simple graph	A simple undirected graph contains neither multiple edges nor loops. A simple directed graph does not contain multiple arcs.	1.3.1
Sink vertex	In an acyclic network, a sink vertex is a vertex with a zero outdegree.	11.6
Size of an event	In a two-mode network, the degree of a vertex is known as the size of an event if the vertex refers to an event.	5.3
Social capital	The number and intensity of a person's social ties is called his or her social capital or sociability.	6.3
Social contagion	Social contagion is the diffusion of behavior or information via social ties.	8.2
Social generation	A social generation is the set of people who are born in the same period: a birth cohort.	11.3

(*continued*)

(continued)

Concept	Description	Section
Sociocentered approach	A sociocentered approach to a network considers the structural characteristics of the entire network.	6.1
Source vertex	In an acyclic network, a source vertex is a vertex with zero indegree.	11.6
Star-network	A star-network is a network in which one vertex is connected to all other vertices but these vertices are not connected among themselves.	6.3
Strong component	A strong component is a maximal strongly connected subnetwork.	3.4
Strongly connected	A network is strongly connected if each pair of vertices is connected by a path.	3.4
Structural equivalence	Two vertices are structural equivalent if they have identical ties with themselves, each other, and all other vertices.	12.3
Structural hole	There is a structural hole in the ego-network of a vertex if two of its neighbors are not directly connected.	7.4
Structural property	A structural property is a characteristic (value) of a vertex that is a result of network analysis.	2.3
Structural relinking	Structural relinking occurs when families intermarry more than once in the course of time.	11.4
Symmetric-acyclic model	The symmetric-acyclic model applies to a directed network if it consists of clusters of vertices that are linked by symmetric ties directly or indirectly and if the ties among the clusters produce an acyclic network (when the clusters are shrunk).	10.5
Symmetrize	To symmetrize a directed network is to replace unilateral and bidirectional arcs by edges.	3.3
Threshold	The threshold of a vertex is its exposure at the time of adoption. It is equal to the proportion of its neighbors that have adopted earlier than this vertex.	8.3
Threshold category	A threshold category is a set of vertices with similar thresholds.	8.3
Threshold lag	A threshold lag is a period in which an actor does not adopt although he or she is exposed at the level at which he or she will adopt later.	8.4
Transitive triad	In a transitive triad, each path of length two is closed by an arc from the starting vertex to the end vertex of the path.	10.3
Transitivity model	The transitivity model applies to an unsigned directed network if it consists of cliques such that cliques within ranks are not related and cliques between ranks are related by null dyads or asymmetric dyads pointing toward the higher rank.	10.3
Transposed network	A transposed network is a network in which the direction of all arcs is reversed.	9.3
Traversal weight	The traversal weight of an arc or vertex is the proportion of all paths between source and sink vertices that contain this arc or vertex.	11.6
Tree	A tree is a connected graph that contains no semicycles.	11.4
Triad	A triad is a (sub-)network consisting of three vertices.	3.6
Triad census	The triad census of a directed network is the frequency distribution of the sixteen types of triads in this network.	10.3

Concept	Description	Section
Two-mode network	In a two-mode network, vertices are divided into two sets and vertices can be related only to vertices in the other set.	5.3
Undirected graph	An undirected graph contains no arcs: all of its lines are edges.	1.3.1
Valued network	A valued network is a network in which lines have (variable) values.	5.3
Vector	A vector is a data object assigning a numerical value to each vertex in a network.	2.5
Vertex (vertices)	A vertex (singular of vertices) is the smallest unit in a network	1.3.1
Walk	A walk is a semiwalk with the additional condition that none of its lines is an arc of which the end vertex is the arc's tail. One might say that you always follow the direction of arcs in a walk.	3.4
Weakly connected	A network is weakly connected if each pair of vertices is connected by a semipath.	3.4

Index of Pajek Commands

The index is arranged by the screen from which commands are available: the Draw screen, Editing Network screen, Hierarchy screen, Main screen, and Report screen. Commands are listed alphabetically within each screen and subcommands are nested within commands. If a subcommand or option is not listed, inspect the higher level (sub)command.

Report Screen

Subject Index